TH
OF HOUSTON

The First National Women's Conference

An Official Report to the President,
the Congress and the People of the United States
March, 1978

National Commission on the
Observance of International Women's Year
Washington, D.C.

"I'm so glad you are giving the gift of *The Spirit of Houston* to the future" - Gloria Steinem

Special thanks to Gloria Steinem and to "Baby" E.R.A. McCarthey

Published by Natzweiler Press, PO Box 215, Newport, VT 05855 USA

ISBN: 978-0-9884358-6-5   **ISBN for ebook: 978-0-9884358-5-8**

Contact dmh@dianamarahenry.com

for bulk orders, special reprints for your organization,
photograph licensing, exhibits & speaking engagements.

Photographs on front and back covers, half title and copyright pages, Gloria Steinem essay, four pages following page 301, and as listed at the end of the table of contents: Copyright © Diana Mara Henry/dianamarahenry.com

Special thanks to Melba Tolliver   Special thanks to Vinie Burrows

"Thank you for holding this precious gift for so long, so patiently."
- Melba Tolliver, journalist.

An Introductory Statement
by Gloria Steinem

If this book survives to be read by our relatives of the distant future, it will have two virtues. (1)

First, it will be one of the few accounts of history made and recorded from the bottom up. We have only to think of our school texts that concentrated on the uppermost few – royal marriages, official treaties, presidential candidates, foreign policy debates – to understand how rarely we heard of what most people were actually doing. Even those records were often filtered by distant historians, with the result that ideas and movements among ordinary people. Whose massive pressures may have been the genesis of actions at the top, had to reach the stage of violent revolution before we learned of them at all.

This volume is one of the exceptions. It is a documentation of history being made from the bottom up, by populist process, and described here for posterity, by those who were there and made it happen.

Second, *The Spirit of Houston* may be something even more rare: a published record of the political agenda of women as a group. Certainly, its scope goes beyond the usual bow toward women who married or gave birth to important men, or who excel in male spheres of interest as exceptions. To complete the agenda that is documented here, women had first to conceive a series of open "town meetings' in each state and territory of the United States (many were to involve 20,000 to 20,000 women, and to be the biggest political meetings ever held in their states, plus a national, delegated conference to follow. They had to press Congress for legislation and public funds to finance the meetings – and that was just the beginning. They then built bridges among economic, racial, ethnic, religious and interest groups in order to achieve a representative planning body for each of the fifty-six meetings, and evolved a debate and balloting procedure that would allow the participants to vote on all the basic issues, to recommend other issues for national consideration, and to elect the proportionate number of delegates allotted to each area's population.

It was as if women had recreated for themselves a temporary version of the national political structure that had substantially excluded them for 200 years – with little money or conventional experience. And with no promise of personal reward or political jobs at the end. Equally important, they accepted a commitment to democratic inclusiveness that the original ideas of the country did not address. True, the American definition of democracy has broadened, since our founders created a constitution for a limited constituency of white, property-owning males, but the state meetings that led up to Houston were generally more representative by race, age, economic status, ethnicity and religion than the official legislature making decisions in those states. And the Houston Conference was more representative by those measures than either the House of Representatives or the Senate and more democratic in its procedures – from allowing floor debates, amendments and substitute motions to encourage voting by individual conscience rather than by geographical blocs or for political reward – than the political conventions that were its closest model.

This long and complex process was often frustrating and never perfect, but it surprised many Americans, including some of the women who worked hardest to make it happen, by far surpassing the standards set by comparable Establishment events. It raised hopes for a new openness and inclusiveness in national political events to come.

"Houston was a kind of Constitutional Convention for American Women," explained one European observer. "They ratified the existing Constitution by demanding full inclusion in it, and then outlined the legislative changes that must take place if female citizens are to fully enjoy those rights for the first time."

This mammoth project begins to sound unprecedented – and there are many factual ways in which that is true. But comparable events have happened in the past. Women have taken action against the political system of male dominance for as many centuries as it has existed, and some of those actions have been at least as impressive in their own contexts, and more courageous. If we are to preserve the events recorded in this book, we should be aware that similar changeful, challenging, women-run events have been unrecorded, suppressed, or even been ridiculed in the past.

As a student reading American history in the schools of the 1950s, I read that white and black women had been "given' the vote in 1920 – an unexplained 50 years after black men had achieved that right. I learned nothing about the more than 100 years of struggle by nationwide networks of women who organized and lectured around the country at a time when they were not supposed to speak in public, who lobbied their all-male legislatures, demonstrated in the streets, went on hunger strikes and went to jail; who publicly burned the speeches of President Wilson in order to protest their government's insistence that it was fighting "for democracy" in World War I- when half of American citizens had no political rights at all. In short, I did not learn that several generations of my foremothers had nearly brought the country to its knees in order to win a separate legal identity, including the right to vote, for women as a group.

At least the right to vote was cited in history books, however, as one that American women had not always enjoyed. Other parts of that legal identity- the goal of the long, first wave of feminism – were not mentioned. How many of us were taught what it meant, for instance, for women to struggle against their status of the human property of husbands and fathers? It was a condition of chattel so clear that the first seventeenth-century American slave-holders adopted it, as Gunnar Myrdal had pointed out, as the "nearest and most natural analogy" for the legal status of slaves. As young students, how many of us understood that the rights of an adult female American to own property, to sue in court or to sign a will, to keep a salary she owned instead of turning it over to a husband or father who "owned" her; to go to school, to have legal custody of her own children, to leave her husband's home without danger of being forcibly or legally returned; to escape a husband's right to physical discipline; to challenge the social prison of being a lifelong minor if she remained unmarried or a legal non-person if she did marry – how many of us were instructed that all of these rights had been won through generations of effort by an independent women's movement?

When we studied American progress toward religious freedom, did we read about the many nineteenth-century feminists who challenged the patriarchal structure of the church; who dared question such scriptural rhetoric as the injunction of the Apostle Paul to "Wives, submit yourselves to your husbands, as unto the Lord"? Were we given a book call *Women's Bible*, a scholarly and very courageous revision of the scriptures undertaken by Elizabeth Cady Stanton?

If we read about religious and political persecution in America, did we learn that the frenzy of the New England witch trials, tortures and burnings were usually the persecutions of independent or knowledgeable women, of midwives who performed abortions, and taught contraception, of woman who challenged the masculine power structure in various ways?

When we heard about courageous people who harbored runaway slave, did they include women like Susan B. Anthony who helped no only black claves, but runaway wives and children escaping the brutality of white men who "owned" them?

Of course, to record the fact that blacks and women were both legally chattel, or that the mythology of "natural" inferiority was (and sometimes still is) used to turn both into a source of cheap labor, is not to be confused with equating these two groups. Black women and men suffered more awful restrictions on their freedom, a more overt cruelty and violence, and their lives were put a greater risk. Angelina Grimke, one of the white Southern feminists who worked again both race and sex slavery, always pointed out that "We have not felt the Slave-holder's last…we have not had our hands manacled." (2) White women were sometimes injured or killed in "justified" domestic beatings, or sold as indentured workers as a punishment for poverty or for breaking the law. Hard work combined with the years of coerced childbearing designed to populate this new land may have made white women's life expectancy as low as half that of white males. (The average frontier family seems to have been a two-mother family: when a woman died after multiple childbirths, her husband married again to have another worker and more children. Early American graveyards full of young women who died in childbirth testify both to the desperation with which many women sought out midwives for contraception or abortion, and to the motive for punishing such practice as immoral, dangerous; perhaps even the work of witches) Nonetheless, white women were far less likely than black slaves to risk or lose their lives, and particularly less so than black women who were used as breeders of more slaves as well as workers. In contrast, the more typical white female punishment was the loss of her identity, or to have her spirit broken. As Angelina Grimke explained, "I rejoice exceedingly that our resolution should combine us with the Negro. I feel that we have been with him; that the iron has entered our souls …our hearts have been crushed. (3)

But why did so many history books assume that women and blacks could have no issues in common; so much so that they failed to report coalitions of the past? Historians seem to pay little attention to movements among the powerless, Or perhaps the intimate challenge presented by a majority coalition of women of all races and minority men was (and still is) too threatening to the profound politics of a caste system based on sax and race.

Certainly, the lessons of history were not ignored because they were not explicit. Much of the long struggle against black slavery and for women's rights had been spent as a functioning, conscious coalition. (*"Resolved*, There never can be a true peace in this Republic until the civil and political rights of all citizens of African descent and all women are practically established. (4)"That statement was made at a New York Convention in 1863.) Like most early feminists, Elizabeth Cady Stanton believed that sex and race prejudice had to be fought together; that both were "produced by the same cause, and manifested very much in the same way. The Negro's skin and the women's sex are both [used as] prima facie evidence that they were intended to be in subjection to the white Saxon man." (4) Frederick Douglass, the fugitive slave who became an important national leader of the movement to abolish slavery, vowed in his autobiography that, "When the true history of the antislavery cause will be written, women will occupy a large space in its pages, for the cause of the slave has been peculiarly women's cause."(5) And there were many more such conscious lessons and statements.

If more of us had learned the parallels and origins of the abolitionist and suffragist movements, there might have been less surprise when a new movement called Women's Liberation grew from the politicization of white and black women in the civil rights movement of the 1960s. If we had been taught that women's connections to other powerless groups were logical, that women lacked power as a caste and that we might be understandably relieved when men rejected domination and violence as proofs of manhood, certainly I and many other women of my generation would have wasted less time being mystified by our frequent, odd and unexplained sense of identification with all the "wrong" groups – the black movement, migrant workers, or with our male contemporaries defying the "masculine" role by refusing to fight in Vietnam.

As it was, however, suffragists were often portrayed as boring, ludicrous blue-stockings, certainly no heroines you would need in modern America where we were "the most privileged women in the world." We were further discouraged from exploring our strengths by accusations of penis-envy, the dominating-mother syndrome, careerism, black matriarchy, and other punishable offenses. Men emerged from World War II, Freudian analysis and locker rooms with vague threats that they could replace uppity women with more subservient ones – an Asian or European war bride instead of a "spoiled" American a "feminine" white woman, to replace a "black matriarch" or just someone younger as "the other woman."

There were many painful years of reinventing the wheel before we re-learned organically what our foremothers had discovered and could have been taught to us: that a false mythology – limited ability, childlike natures, special job skills (always the poorly paid ones), greater emotionalism and more sexual natures, less respect for members of our own group, chronic lateness and irresponsibility, and happiness withing our "natural" place – was being used to keep all women and minority men in the role of cheap labor and support system.

"The parallel between women and Negroes is the deepest truth of American life, for together they form the unpaid or underpaid labor on which America runs." (2) That was Gunnar Myrdal writing in 1944 in a rather obscure appendix to his landmark study on racism, An American Dilemma. Even in the 60's when I discovered those words – and wished devoutly that I had read them years earlier – I still did not know that Susan B. Anthony had put the issue even more succinctly almost a century before Myrdal. "Woman," she said, "has been the great unpaid laborer of the world." (4)

The current movements toward racial justice and feminism have had some success in pressuring for courses in women's history, black history, the study of Hispanic Americans, American Indians, and many others (perhaps all better collectively referred to as "remedial history") but these subjects still tend to be special studies taken only by the interested. They are rarely an integrated, inescapable part of the American history texts read by all students.

And if the recent past of our own country is still incomplete for many of us, how much less do we learn about other countries and more distant pasts?

What do we know about the African warrior queens of Dahomey, for instance, who led armies against colonial invaders? Or the merchant women of West Africa who dominate the consumer markets of their countries? If we know little about the relationships of our own New England witch hunts to patriarchal politics, how much less do we know about the more than eight million women who were burned at the stake in medieval Europe, perhaps in an effort to wipe out remains od prehistoric, woman-goddess religions? If the exceptional American women who were explorers, outlaws, doctors, pirates, soldiers, and inventors are only just being rediscovered, what about those American Indian nations that honored women in authority more than "advanced "cultures that were to follow?

How are we to interpret the discovery that many of the "pagan idols," "false gods" and "pagan temples" so despised by the Judeo-Christian teachings and the Bible in particular were representations of a female power: a god with breasts? How will our vision of pre-history change now that archeologists have discovered that some skeletons- assumed to be male because of their large-boned strength, or because they were buried with weapons and scholarly scrolls – are really female? (In America, the archeological find described as the Minnesota Man has recently been designated the Minnesota Woman. In Europe, some "warrior-skeletons have turned out to be female.) Now that we are beginning to rediscover the interdependency of sexual and racial caste systems in our own history, and in our own lives, will political science courses begin to explain that a power structure dependent on race or class "purity" – whether it is women and blacks in the American South and South Africa, or women and Jews in Nazi Germany _ will also restrict the freedom of women because our bodies are the means of production, the necessary perpetuators of race and class lines?

The revelatory, mind-expanding era is worldwide; the international movements against caste- against all systems that dictate power and lifetime roles bases on sex or race- are the most profound and vital movements of this century. They are changing our hopes for the futures and our assumptions about the past.

Sometimes those revelations can be angering. It seems that our ancestors knew much that we have had to re-learn with such pain.

In the National Plan of Action adopted at Houston, there are many echoes of the first wave of feminism. The high incidence of battered women and the reluctance of t police to interfere are shocking facts that struck many Americans as new discoveries. Knowing more about the history of a husband's legal right to "own" and discipline a spouse could have helped to uncover those facts sooner. A wife's loss of her own name, legal residence, credit rating and many other rights might have seemed les "natural" and inevitable if we had known that our marriage laws were still rooted in the same English common law precedent ("husband and wife are one person in law …that of the husband") (7) that nineteenth-century feminists had struggled so ((hard to escape. We would have been better prepared for arguments that the Equal Rights Amendment would "destroy the family" or force women to become "like men" if we had known that the same accusations, almost word for word, were leveled against the suffrage movement.) Our own foremothers were called "unsexed women," "entirely devoid of personal attraction," who had been "disappointed in their endeavors to appropriate breeches.") (8) Even the charge that the era would be contrary to states' rights and constitute a "federal power grab" is a repeat of the argument that a citizen's right to vote should be left entirely up to the states; a problem that caused suffragists to proceed state by state, and to delay focusing on the Nineteenth Amendment for many years.

In a way, the unity represented by the minority women's resolution – perhaps the single greatest accomplishment of the Houston Conference – was also the greatest example of the high price of lost history. After all, black women had been the flesh-and-blood links between abolition and suffrage; yet hey had suffered double discrimination and invisibility, even at the time. ("There is a great stir about colored men getting their rights," explained Sojourner Truth, the great black feminist and anti-slavery leader, "but not a word about colored women.") (9) Then American leaders destroyed the great caste systems of sex and race by offering the vote and a limited acceptance to black men, but refusing the majority and intimate challenge presented by females as a group. Black women were forced to painfully and artificially slice up their identities by choosing to support their brothers at their own expense, or, like Sojourner Truth, to advocate "keeping the thing going…" because if we wait till it is still, it will take a great while to get things going again." (9) Once it was clear that black men were going to get the vote first, Black women were further isolated by some white suffragists who, embittered by the desertion of white and black male allies, used the racist argument that the white female "educated" vote was necessary to outweigh the black male "uneducated: vote. Divisions deepened Sojourner Truth's argument that it would "take a great while to get things going again" if the two great parallel causes were divided turned out to be true. It was a half century later, and many years after her death, before women of all races won the issue.

When the first, reformist prelude to feminism started up again in the early and mid '60s, it was largely a protest of the middle-class, white housewives, against the "feminine mystique" that kept them trapped in the suburbs. For black women who often had no choice but to be in the labor force, that was a lifestyle that some envied and few could afford. Only after the civil rights movement and feminism's real emergence again in the later '60s – after the analysis of women as a caste, not just as an integrationist few - did the organic ties between the movements against racial and sexual caste begin to grow again. In spite of great racial divisions in the country, and in spite of an economic and social structure that exploits racial tensions among women, the Women's Movement is now the most integrated and populist force for change in the country.

Houston was the first public landmark in a long, suspicion-filled journey across racial barriers. At last, there were enough minority women (more than a third of all delegates) to have a strong voice – not only black women, but Hispanic women as the second largest American minority, Asian American women, American Indian women and many more. But how much less perilous this journey would have been if we had known about those bridges of the past; if we had not had to build new coalitions through what seemed a wilderness.

Houston was part of a second wave, a continuation – but it also provided historical lessons of its own.

Reproductive freedom finally joined such accepted rights as freedom of speech or assembly. Some women came to the conclusion out of a simple, personal concern for health, or an understanding that, if they did not control their bodies from the skin in, they could never control their lives from the skin out. Others felt that women's role as the most basic means of production would remain the source of their second-class status as long as outside forces were allowed to either restrict or compel that production. For both reasons, the feminist-invented phrase of "reproductive freedom" was chosen over "population control." The first signifies an individual's basic right to decide to have or not have children, but the second legitimizes some external force or power over women's lives. This affirmation of reproductive freedom as a basic human right was a long way from the burning of healers, midwives and witches, but there is still a long way to go before the stated goal of reproductive freedom becomes a reality in women's lives.

"Sexual preference," the second issue of sexuality, included the issue of lesbianism. Ironically, the effort to frighten women off was exactly what caused many to vote for civil rights for lesbians, even though they might not have supported their issue before. Until the label of "lesbian" no longer holds the threat of lost jobs, child custody or a place to live – until women can no longer be punished for their private sexual choices – all women will continue to be threatened into conformity by the potential danger of being called "lesbian." Furthermore, it is the patriarchal societies that wish to control women's bodies as a means of producing children that also try to control and condemn any sexual forms that cannot end in conception. Whether it's male homosexuality, lesbianism, contraception or any heterosexual forms of expression that cannot lead to conception. It is the same political motive that tries to restrict them all.

The politics of sexuality and reproduction had been the most difficult for the first wave of feminists s to discuss publicly, much less to change. But these issues of such importance to women's lives and survival were brought out into the open in Houston, and recognized as fundamental to women's self—determination.

Houston also symbolized an end to much or the Left (and who mistrusted efforts "inside the system") and those reformers and or older, more conservative women (who mistrusted efforts to work "outside the system.) If one person made that bonding possible, it was probably Bella Abzug, a main author of the idea for the Conference, and the presiding officer of its Commissioners. As one of the few American political leaders to rise through social movements, not through political party structures, she had gained trust and colleagues on both sides; with the more radical feminists because of her devotion to issues, and with more conservative women because she had served in Congress and gained Government support for the Conference. Houston was the result of hard work by thousands of women, but Bella Abzug may be the one person without whom there would have been no such event.

In fact, one of the most moving and impressive experiences of Houston was its blending of tactics and styles. Prefeminist, either/or, polarized thinking seemed to give way to an understanding that victory was more likely if we surrounded a goal from all sides.

For myself, Houston and all the events surrounding it has become a personal landmark in history; the sort of event one measures all other dates in life as being "before" or "after."

I had mistrusted it as an idea. (What sort of conference could be supported by the Government without betraying women's real issues and needs?) And I had feared it as an approaching trial. "Might not the anti-woman, right-wing minority turn it into a public battleground?) Though I finally came to work very hard in its preparation, I would have given almost anything to be able to avoid the possible conflict, to stop worrying, to stay home, to delay this event that I cared about too much

I thought my fears were rational, but in retrospect, I realize they were not.

Yes, I had learned, finally, that individual women could be competent, courageous and loyal to each other, in spite of growing up without the sight of women being honored in authority, and without a knowledge of women's hidden history, I had learned from my sisters in this second wave of feminism. But I still did not know that women as a group could be competent, courageous and loyal to each other; that we could conduct large, complex events and honor each other's diversity; that we could literally make a history that was our own.

But we can. Houston taught me that. And I hope this lesson will not be lost, but carried into the future.

- Gloria Steinem

 This essay was originally written for *What Women Want*, Simon and Schuster, 1978.
[2] Gunnar Myrdal. *An American Dilemma*. New York: Harper and Brothers, 1944, p.1073
[3] Grimke, in Elizabeth Cady Stanton et al., *The History of Woman Suffrage*, Vol. II. Rochester, Charles Mann, 1899.
[4] Stanton, op.cit.
5 *Life and Times of Frederick Douglass, written by himself*. 1892) NY, Collier, 1962 p.469
[6] Myrdal, *op.cit*. p. 1077
[7] Blackstone, *Commentaries*
[8] *New York Herald*, September 7, 1853
[9] Sojourner Truth, in Stanton, *op. cit.*, Vol 8, p.193

National Advisory Committee for Women

United States Department of Labor
200 Constitution Avenue, NW
Washington, DC 20210

August 7, 1978

Room C5321
(202) 523-6707

CO-CHAIRS:
Bella S. Abzug
Carmen Delgado Votaw

HONORARY CHAIR:
Judy Carter

MEMBERS:
Owanah Anderson
Unita Blackwell
Erma Bombeck
Cecilia Preciado Burciaga
Marjorie Bell Chambers
Sey Chassler
Mary Crisp
Miriam I. Cruz
Laura de Herrera
Piilani C. Desha
Donna E. de Varona
Gretta Dewald
Judith Heumann
Koryne Horbal
Mildred M. Jeffrey
Jeffalyn Johnson
Lane Kirkland
Odessa Komer
Florine Koole
Elizabeth Koontz
Esther Landa
Brownie Ledbetter
Mary Helen Madden
Billie Nave Masters
Joyce Miller
Nancy Neuman
Jean O'Leary
Brenda Parker
Claire Randall
Carolyn Reed
Ann Richards
Richard Rossie
Jill Ruckelshaus
Eleanor Smeal
Tin Myaing Thein
Marlo Thomas
Maxine Waters
Addie Wyatt

Dear Friend:

We are pleased to send you a printed copy of The Spirit of Houston, the official report of the National Commission on the Observance of International Women's Year.

To bring you up to date on what has happened since the National Women's Conference met in Houston November 18-21, 1977, here is a rundown on some highlights:

The National IWY Commission presented an advance text of the official report to President Carter and Congressional leaders in a ceremony at the White House on March 22, 1978.

The National IWY Commission, whose mandate under Public Law 94-167 expired March 31, 1978, has been replaced by the National Advisory Committee for Women under an Executive Order issued by the President on June 20, 1978. The NACW is holding its first official meeting in August.

As mandated by PL 94-167, the President sent a message to Congress at the end of July presenting his legislative recommendations based on sections of the 26-plank National Plan of Action adopted by the Houston Conference. The NACW will comment after it studies the recommendations.

A 470-member Continuing Committee, a grass roots, non-governmental group, was appointed by the National IWY

Commission, selected primarily from among the Houston delegates. The Committee held its first meeting on March 22, 1978 and met again on June 9 in Washington, where it also participated in the National ERA March the following day. The Committee elected officers, including Co-chair Minette Doderer, the Senate, State House, Des Moines, Iowa 50319 and Co-chair Anne B. Turpeau, 1901 19th Street, N.W., Washington, D.C. 20009

On a grass roots level, the "spirit of Houston" is alive and flourishing in the states. Houston delegates are organizing local and state coalitions of women, campaigning for ERA ratification and other planks in the National Plan of Action, lobbying for Federal and state legislation, meeting with their governors and legislators, and holding public meetings to report on Houston.

For example: In Kentucky, more than two dozen groups formed the Kentucky Women's Agenda Coalition and were successful in getting a displaced homemakers bill enacted. They also organized a dinner to honor women legislators, including Lt. Governor Thelma Stovall, who vetoed the legislature's rescission of the ERA last spring when the Governor was out of the state. ...Regional meetings were held in Indiana, Pennsylvania, New Hampshire and other states...Louisiana women organized three statewide conferences--on Native American Women, Battered Women, and Women and the Law.... Minnesota women put togeter an educational presentation on Houston for the campuses and church groups.... In the District of Columbia, Houston delegates were successful in getting local officials to announce they would not pay for travel expenses of District employees attending conventions in states that have not ratified ERA....Guam women founded a women's center....In California, Assemblywoman Maxine Waters made an analysis of existing and pending state legislation in comparison with National Plan of Action recommendations.

Much more is going on. Please let us hear from you about what is happening in your community and state on issues of interest to women.

The National Advisory Committee for Women will monitor the Federal and state governments for implementation of the National Plan, and will function as a strong advocate of equal rights and opportunities for women.

Sincerely,

Bella S. Abzug
Co-Chair

Carmen Delgado Votaw
Co-Chair

NATIONAL COMMISSION ON THE OBSERVANCE OF INTERNATIONAL WOMEN'S YEAR

Presiding Officer:

Bella S. Abzug, New York, New York

Commissioners:

Ruth J. Abram, New York, New York
Maya Angelou, Sonoma, California
Elizabeth Athanasakos, Fort Lauderdale, Florida
Betty Blanton, Nashville, Tennessee
Cecilia Preciado-Burciago, Palo Alto, California
Liz Carpenter, Austin, Texas
John Mack Carter, New York, New York
Sey Chassler, New York, New York
Ruth C. Clusen, Green Bay, Wisconsin
Audrey Rowe Colom, Washington, D.C.
Jane Culbreth, Leeds, Alabama
Harry T. Edwards, Ann Arbor, Michigan
Rita Elway, Seattle, Washington
Beverly Everett, New Sharon, Iowa
Betty Ford, Palm Springs, California
Bernice S. Frieder, Lakewood, Ohio
Martha W. Griffiths, Romeo, Michigan
Dorothy Haener, Detroit, Michigan
Rhea Mojica Hammer, Chicago, Illinois
LaDonna Harris, Albuquerque, New Mexico
Lenore Hershey, New York, New York
Koryne Horbal, Minneapolis, Minnesota
Mildred M. Jeffrey, Detroit, Michigan
Jeffalyn Johnson, Arlington, Virginia
Coretta Scott King, Atlanta, Georgia
Mary Anne Krupsak, Canajoharie, New York
Margaret Mealey, Washington, D.C.

Jean O'Leary, New York, New York
Mildred Emory Persinger, Dobbs Ferry, New York
Connie Plunkett, Carrollton, Georgia
Ersa Poston, Washington, D.C.
Claire Randall, New York, New York
Alice S. Rossi, Amherst, Massachusetts
Gloria Scott, Houston, Texas
Eleanor Smeal, Pittsburgh, Pennsylvania
Jean Stapleton, Los Angeles, California
Gloria Steinem, New York, New York
Ethel Taylor, Bala-Cynwyd, Pennsylvania
Carmen Delgado Votaw, Bethesda, Maryland
Gerridee Wheeler, Bismarck, North Dakota
Addie Wyatt, Chicago, Illinois

Commissioners Appointed as Members of Congress:

Senator Birch Bayh, Indiana
Senator Charles Percy, Illinois
Representative Margaret Heckler, Wellesley, Massachusetts
Representative Elizabeth Holtzman, New York, New York

Honorary Commissioner:

Rosalynn Carter

Executive Director:

Dr. Kathryn Clarenbach

CREDITS

Chief Writer: Caroline Bird.

Chief Editor/Writer: Mim Kelber.

Chief Photographers: Pat Field, Diana Mara Henry (photos © copyrighted, 1978).

Editor/Writer: Helene Mandelbaum.

Writing and Editing: Adele Blang, Kathy Bonk, Kay Clarenbach, Linda Dorian, Catherine East, Judy Frie, Marjorie Godfrey, Fran Henry, Maxine Hitchcock, Pat Hyatt, Anne Kasper, Dorothy Lasday, Shelah Leader, Tom Mahoney, Lee Novick, Susan Rubin, Sheryl Swed.

Production Assistants: Ann R. English, Vanna Shields, Agnes Sutphin, Sheryl Swed.

Layout: Irene Bebber.

Cover photo of torch runners Sylvia Ortiz, Peggy Kokernot and Michele Cearcy by *Diana Mara Henry*.

Special thanks to Pat Field for this reprint edition from Diana Mara Henry

Torch relay, Houston Day-by-Day and other photos by Pat Field. White House, Houston Day-by-Day, Seneca Falls South and other photos by Diana Mara Henry.

The sections on the State meetings, Houston Day-by-Day and other material were written by Caroline Bird.

The Introduction and Declaration of American Women were written by Mim Kelber.

The International Perspectives section was written by Maxine Hitchcock and Commissioner Mildred Persinger.

The report on the torch relay was written by Tom Mahoney.

We wish to acknowledge the special assistance of the following in researching and writing the background essay on the Minority Women's plank: Commissioners Cecilia Preciado-Burciago, Rita Elway, LaDonna Harris, Gloria Scott, Gloria Steinem, and Carmen Delgado Votaw; and Dorothe Dow, Billie Nave Masters, Gracia Molina Pick, Sandy Sewell, Dr. Elizabeth Stone, Sheryl Swed, Tin Myaing Thien, Mariko Tse.

Commission Editorial Committee: Liz Carpenter, Sey Chassler, Beverly Everett, Dorothy Haener, Gloria Steinem, Carmen Delgado Votaw.

Additional photos: Adela Alonso, Nancy Battaglia, Jessica Z. Brown, Helen Bremberg, Eunice Burns, Teresina B. Guerra Clawson, Marcia Fram, Charley Kubricht, Bettye Lane, Evelyn Light (Academy Press), Anne Marvin, Suzanne Paul, Janice Rubin, Debbe Sharpe, Betsy Siegel, Totsie, Anne Walter, Gannett-Rochester Newspapers; Women's Bureau, U.S. Dept. of Labor; Dick Swartz, Administrator of Children, Youth and Family, U.S. Dept. of Health, Education and Welfare; Genesco Migrant Center.

TABLE OF CONTENTS

PHOTO CREDITS
© Diana Mara Henry 1978

Pages 6, 7, 12, 14, 18, 21, 32, 78, 90, 108, 118 (top right, bottom left), 119, 121 (top and center), 123 (bottom right), 124 (except center left), 125 (bottom), 126 (left and center), 127, 132, 134, 136, 137 (top and center), 138 (center and right), 139, 140 (top left and bottom), 141 (center and right), 142, 143, 145, 147 (top left), 148 (top and right), 149 (top), 150 (left), 151 (bottom right and left), 152, 153 (top left and right), 155 (left), 161, 163 (bottom), 165 (right), 166 (bottom), 168 (top), 176, 181 (top right and left), 182 (left top and bottom), 183, 195, 206, 245 (Betty Ford), 247 (Coretta Scott King).

NATIONAL COMMISSION
ON THE OBSERVANCE OF
INTERNATIONAL WOMEN'S YEAR

U.S. Department of State
Washington, D.C. 20520
202-632-6888

March 22, 1978

The President
The White House
Washington, D.C. 20500

Dear President Carter:

In behalf of the National Commission on the Observance of
International Women's Year, I am pleased to transmit to you
our official report on the National Women's Conference and
the work of the Commission.

We are proud of what we have done and mindful of what still
must be done.

We know that you share our determination to promote equal
rights, equal opportunities and equal responsibilities for
women, and we look forward to continuing to work with you for
the achievement of our goal.

With deep appreciation for your understanding and your
cooperation,

                          Sincerely yours,

                          Bella S. Abzug
                          Presiding Officer

Members of National Commission at White House ceremony (left to right): Jean O'Leary, Beverly Everett, Eleanor Smeal, Carmen Delgado Votaw, Ethel Taylor, Bernice Frieder, Mildred Persinger (rear), Bella Abzug, Audrey Rowe (rear), Gloria Steinem, Margaret Mealey, Jeffalyn Johnson, Addie Wyatt, Jane Culbreth, Mary Anne Krupsak, Connie Plunkett, Mildred Jeffrey, Claire Randall, Liz Carpenter.

House Speaker Thomas "Tip" O'Neill and Richard Moe, Chief of Staff to Vice President Mondale, are presented with copy of Official Report at ceremony in the Blue Room of the White House.

President Carter receives advance text of Official Report from Presiding Officer Bella Abzug at ceremony in the East Room on March 22, 1978 attended by several hundred women from all parts of the nation. Looking on are First Lady Rosalynn Carter and Presidential Assistant Midge Costanza (left), Secretary of Commerce Juanita Kreps and Secretary of Transportation Brock Adams (right) and members of National Commission.

At the ceremony, President Carter announced he was appointing a National Advisory Committee for Women to replace the National Commission, whose legislative mandate expired March 31, 1978. He also announced creation of an Inter-Departmental Task Force on Women.

On June 20, the President appointed a 40-member National Advisory Committee for Women, with Bella Abzug and Carmen Delgado Votaw as co-chairs. Judy Carter is honorary chair. The committee is housed in Room C5321, U.S. Department of Labor, 200 Constitution Avenue, N.W., Washington, D.C., 20210.

INTRODUCTION

There was never anything like it.

For the 20,000 women, men, and children who were there, for the millions of Americans who read about it, listened on the radio, or watched on television, the National Women's Conference, held in Houston, Texas from November 18 to 21, 1977, was a unique experience.

It was a first in so many ways.

It was the first time the Congress and the President had authorized, sponsored, and financed a national gathering of women to talk about and act upon issues of concern to women.

It was the first time women had come together as elected representatives from every State and Territory in the Nation to voice their needs and hopes for the future.

It was the first time women of so many different income groups, ages, lifestyles, and ethnic, racial, and religious groups; from so many cities, towns, suburbs, rural areas, farms, and islands had been able to gather in one place. Indeed, for many women it was the first time they had ever been to a national meeting.

Mothers, daughters, and grandmothers. Single, married, divorced, or widowed women. Homemakers. Working women. Students. The President's wife and two former First Ladies. Members of Congress. Public officials. Leaders of the Democratic and Republican national committees. Representatives from every major women's organization in the country. Disabled women. White, black, Hispanic, American Indian, Eskimo, and Asian American women. Women of fame and women who lead ordinary lives. They were all there, together.

How they got there and what they did is told in detail in this official report to the President, to the Congress, and to the people of the United States.

BACKGROUND

It was a conference more than two years in the planning. Its immediate impetus was International Women's Year, proclaimed for 1975 by the United Nations against a background of rising demands for equal rights and responsibilities among women the world over. In an historic sense, its antecedent was the first Women's Rights Convention attended in Seneca Falls, New York, July 19-20, 1848, by 300 people, mostly women, who were summoned to discuss "the social, civil, and religious condition and rights of women."

American participation in International Women's Year began with a proclamation issued by President Nixon on January 30, 1974 calling upon the Congress and the people of the United States, interested groups, Federal, State, and local officials, and others to observe IWY with practical and constructive measures for the advancement of women in this Nation.

On January 9, 1975, President Ford initiated IWY observances by issuing Executive Order No. 11832, which created the National Commission on the Observance of International Women's Year "to promote equality between men and women."

The President appointed 35 women and men to the National Commission, designated Jill Ruckelshaus as Presiding Officer, and directed it to deal "with those inequities that still linger as barriers to the full participation of women in our Nation's life."

Americans, he said, "must also support and strengthen the laws that prohibit discrimination based on sex."

The National Commission conducted a year-long series of events in connection with International Women's Year. It also established 13 committees to investigate particular aspects of discrimination against women.

Acting under a Presidential extension, the committees held hearings, interviewed experts on women's issues, conducted research and surveys, and produced 115 specific recommendations for remedial action that were incorporated by the National Commission into its formal report to the President in 1976.

That report, "... *To Form a More Perfect Union ... Justice for American Women*," a comprehensive and well-researched 382-page study of the status of women 200 years after the birth of our Nation, is a companion document to *The Spirit of Houston*.

President Ford also created an Interdepartmental Task Force for IWY consisting of at least two representatives, a woman and a man, from each Federal department and agency. They were assigned to examine their agencies' programs in terms of actual and potential impact on women. Forty-eight agencies complied, with reports that ranged from a single-page letter disclaiming responsibility to several that were 70 to 80 pages long and described serious plans for involving women and women's programs in their work.

The momentum of International Women's Year continued into the American bicentennial year of celebration and self-appraisal. Women leaders in this country saw a need to build upon the United Nations' IWY conference, held in Mexico City in June 1975, the world's first large-scale, official international meeting devoted primarily to women's concerns. The U.N. conference, including the U.S. delegation, had unanimously voted approval of a World Plan of Action to improve the conditions of women and had proclaimed 1975 to 1985 as the United Nations Decade for Women.

The Mexico City conference had generated some widely reported political disputes and confrontations among the various national delegations, many of them led by men who were there to present the official viewpoints of their governments. But for the thousands of women who attended the U.N. conference or the non-Governmental IWY Tribune meeting in another part of Mexico City, simply the coming together of so many women from so many different nations was a profoundly moving and consciousness-raising experience. The discovery of common feelings and problems of discrimination among women, who are a majority of the world's population, and the knowledge that the state of womanhood transcends geographic barriers inspired in many the belief that women could begin to take control of their own lives and, in the process, work for a better world with more humanist values.

In Congress, Representative Bella Abzug of New York, who had introduced a bill early in 1975 proposing that a national women's conference be held as part of the Bicentennial celebration, scheduled a hearing on the legislation after she returned from Mexico City. Representative Patsy Mink, who had also attended the U.N. Conference, introduced a similar bill. Other women Members of the House (there were none in the Senate) united to work with them for adoption of the legislation.

After hearings before Representative Abzug's House Government Operations Subcommittee and floor debate, Public Law 94-167 was passed by the House on December 10, 1975; by the Senate on December 23; and signed by President Ford the following day. The appropriation was made in June, 1976. (President Carter expanded the National Commission to 42 members in an Executive Order issued March 28, 1977, and designated Bella Abzug as Presiding Officer.)

PUBLIC LAW 94-167

The new law stated that "International Women's Year, and its World Plan of Action, have focused attention on the problems of women throughout the world," and said that the Bicentennial was a "particularly appropriate time" to evaluate the discrimination that American women face because of their sex.

It directed the National Commission to convene a National Women's Conference, to be preceded by State or regional meetings.

The Conference, it said, shall—

"recognize the contributions of women to the development of our country;

"assess the progress that has been made to date by both the private and public sectors in promoting equality between men and women in all aspects of life in the United States;

"assess the role of women in economic, social, cultural and political development;

"assess the participation of women in efforts aimed at the development of friendly relations and cooperation among nations and to the strengthening of world peace;

"identify the barriers that prevent women from participating fully and equally in all aspects of national life, and develop recommendations for means by which such barriers can be removed;

"establish a timetable for the achievement of the objectives set forth in such recommendations; and

"establish a committee of the Conference which will take steps to provide for the convening of the second National Women's Conference … to evaluate the steps taken to improve the status of American women."

Congress appropriated $5 million for the law, which amounted to less than a nickel for each female in the country. Along with Federal funding, perhaps the most significant section of the law was its requirement that the Conference include representatives of a variety of groups that "work to advance the rights of women" and place "special emphasis on the representation of low-income women, members of diverse racial, ethnic, and religious groups, and women of all ages."

This insistence on democratic diversity proved to be the key to the success of the Houston meeting, with its unprecedented cross-section of women.

The National Commission insured the grass roots quality of its project by allocating more than half of its $5 million appropriation to State coordinating committees to hold public meetings in the 50 States and Territories. Scholarships and free or low-cost transportation and lodgings were made available in most States to women who would not otherwise have been able to attend. Nineteen percent of the States' grant funds were spent for transportation and subsistence for participants. Some States provided day care facilities to encourage women with young children to come, and special arrangements were made for disabled women. Outreach committees used TV, radio, and advertising to interest the general public. As a result of these efforts, an estimated 150,000 women and men came to the meetings and elected delegates to the national conference.

Similar arrangements were made to enable women of all ages and racial, ethnic, and income groups to attend the Houston meeting. In addition to the half-million dollars spent on the Houston meeting itself, a comparable amount was spent by the States from their grant money for the travel, hotel, and food expenses of those elected delegates who could not afford to attend the national conference on their own.

When the meeting officially opened in Houston on November 19, 1977 (registration began the preceding day), present were 1,403 delegates, 370 delegates-at-large, and 186 alternates, including a sprinkling of male delegates, plus thousands of invited guests, observers, and members of the general public who watched the plenary sessions from the sidelines and participated in dozens of other associated events scheduled by the Commission.

NATIONAL PLAN OF ACTION

The main work of the delegates was to vote on a proposed National Plan of Action, a 26-plank program that was itself the product of a lengthy democratic process that had taken almost a year.

The Commission had suggested that each State and Territorial meeting consider a so-called core agenda of recommendations on major issues affecting women, winnowed down from the 115 recommendations in "... To Form a More Perfect Union ..." A majority of the State meetings, though they were not required to do so, had approved these 14 resolutions after debating, amending, or expanding them. In addition, the meetings had approved more than 4,000 other recommendations on a variety of subjects.

The substance of any recommendations that had the approval of 12 or more State or Territorial meetings was included in the proposed National Plan, as were additional recommendations from the Commission. Most of the 26 planks were compilations of recommendations that had emerged from this procedure. Only one of the 26 planks was unchanged. Approved by 41 State meetings, it stated simply: "The Equal Rights Amendment should be ratified."

All 26 planks in the National Plan of Action were open to debate on the floor at the Houston meeting. Seventeen were adopted by large majorities; one, on equal credit, was unanimously approved. Three amended resolutions and four substitute resolutions were also overwhelmingly passed. One was rejected.

With only 20 percent of the delegates opposing some or most of the planks, there emerged from Houston a consensus on what American women need and want to achieve equal rights, equal status, and equal responsibilities with men.

At the heart of the consensus was the belief that final ratification of the Equal Rights Amendment is needed, as one speaker said, "to put women in the Constitution" and to establish a framework of justice for their efforts to remove remaining barriers to equality.

Their other demands (the National Plan is reprinted in full in the first section of this report) ran the gamut of issues that touch women's lives: equal opportunities for women in the arts and humanities, in the media, in elective and appointive office, in credit and insurance, in business and education, in formulating foreign policy; extension of social security benefits to homemakers and programs to provide counseling and other services for displaced homemakers; assistance to battered women, disabled women, minority women, older women, rural women, and women in prison; concern for women's health needs and the right to choose abortion, with Federal and State Medicaid benefits for those who cannot afford it; pregnancy disability benefits for employed women; civil rights for lesbians; protection against rape and child abuse; comprehensive child care facilities; welfare reform, educational and job programs for poor women; an end to all discrimination in employment and an opening up of new job opportunities for women.

IMPACT OF THE PLAN

The recommendations ranged from the enactment of new laws and the amendment and enforcement of existing laws to more sweeping demands for full employment, a national health security system, and peace and disarmament, policies that would obviously benefit all Americans—men, women, and children alike.

Some of the women's demands can be met by the present session of Congress, by Executive order, by action in the States and in the private sector, or by a determination of those in power to insure more effective enforcement of programs that have been allowed to languish or be circumvented.

More long-range demands, such as those for a full employment economy, a national health system, and an end to the arms race, imply a fundamental reshaping of our present society that would require mass movements of men and women working together to seek to accomplish them.

No attempt was made to apply a price tag to the National Plan of Action, nor is it possible to estimate what it would cost if each recommendation were to become a reality. Some, indeed, would not cost anything. There is no additional expenditure involved in giving women an equal chance with men to receive an arts grant, or in voting more women into office, or in making a woman a department head, or in appointing women to the U.S. Su-

preme Court, or in portraying women more realistically in the media and in textbooks. Some proposals clearly would cost more money. Equal pay for equal work and for work of "equal value" would cost employers more, as would ending double discrimination against minority women. That, in fact, is why there has been such resistance to paying women what they deserve. Child care facilities, education and job training programs, health insurance, and other social programs would require Federal spending. Whether or not in the long run these would involve spending *more* money or only a reordering of present priorities for spending depends on decisions about the kind of society we wish to live in. A full employment society, for example, that would make jobs available as a fundamental human right to all who seek work will

undoubtedly require outlays of mone initially, but the return in human pr ductivity and dignity is incalculabl Finally, one plank in the National Pla calls for spending *less* money. It pr poses cutting the military budget ar converting excessive weapons manu facturing capacity "to production fo meeting human needs."

Throughout history, women hav been underestimated, undervalue underpromoted, and underpaid. W do not ask the price of justice. W should not ask the price of equality.

The "rainbow of women" who cam to Houston came with a belief in ou democratic system and a hope tha justice and equality for women wi become engrained in that system They look to the President, to the Con gress, to their allies, and to them selves for the achievement of the hopes.

NATIONAL PLAN OF ACTION

Adopted at National Women's Conference
November 18 to 21, 1977
Houston, Texas

Note: Delegates from Puerto Rico, the Virgin
Islands, Guam, American Samoa, the Trust
Territories and the District of Columbia as well
as delegates from 50 States participated in the
National Women's Conference and
formulation of the National Plan of Action. All
recommendations adopted by the National
Women's Conference and the National
Commission on the Observance of IWY apply
to Territories as well as to States, wherever
they are relevant.

13

DECLARATION OF AMERICAN WOMEN 1977

We are here to move history forward.

We are women from every State and Territory in the Nation.

We are women of different ages, beliefs and lifestyles.

We are women of many economic, social, political, racial, ethnic, cultural, educational and religious backgrounds.

We are married, single, widowed and divorced.

We are mothers and daughters.

We are sisters.

We speak in varied accents and languages but we share the common language and experience of American women who throughout our Nation's life have been denied the opportunities, rights, privileges and responsibilities accorded to men.

For the first time in the more than 200 years of our democracy, we are gathered in a National Women's Conference, charged under Federal law to assess the status of women in our country, to measure the progress we have made, to identify the barriers that prevent us from participating fully and equally in all aspects of national life, and to make recommendations to the President and to the Congress for means by which such barriers can be removed.

We recognize the positive changes that have occurred in the lives of women since the founding of our nation. In more than a century of struggle from Seneca Falls 1848 to Houston 1977, we have progressed from being non-persons and slaves whose work and achievements were unrecognized, whose needs were ignored, and whose rights were suppressed to being citizens with freedoms and aspirations of which our ancestors could only dream.

We can vote and own property. We work in the home, in our communities and in every occupation. We are 40 percent of the labor force. We are in the arts, sciences, professions and politics. We raise children, govern States, head businesses and institutions, climb mountains, explore the ocean depths and reach toward the moon.

Our lives no longer end with the child-bearing years. Our lifespan has increased to more than 75 years. We have become a majority of the population, 51.3 percent, and by the 21st century, we shall be an even larger majority.

But despite some gains made in the past 200 years, our dream of equality is still withheld from us and millions of women still face a daily reality of discrimination, limited opportunities and economic hardship.

Man-made barriers, laws, social customs and prejudices continue to keep a majority of women in an inferior position without full control of our lives and bodies.

From infancy throughout life, in personal and public relationships, in the family, in the schools, in every occupation and profession, too often we find our individuality, our capabilities, our earning powers diminished by discriminatory practices and outmoded ideas of what a woman is, what a woman can do, and what a woman must be.

Increasingly, we are victims of crimes of violence in a culture that degrades us as sex objects and promotes pornography for profit.

We are poorer than men. And those of us who are minority women—blacks, Hispanic Americans, Native Americans, and Asian Americans—must overcome the double burden of discrimination based on race and sex.

We lack effective political and economic power. We have only minor and insignificant roles in making, interpreting and enforcing our laws, in running our political parties, businesses, unions, schools and institutions, in directing the media, in governing our country, in deciding issues of war or peace.

We do not seek special privileges, but we demand as a human right a full voice and role for women in determining the destiny of our world, our nation, our families and our individual lives.

We seek these rights for all women, whether or not they choose as individuals to use them.

We are part of a worldwide movement of women who believe that only by bringing women into full partnership with men and respecting our rights as half the human race can we hope to achieve a world in which the whole human race—men, women and children—can live in peace and security.

Based on the views of women who have met in every State and Territory in the past year, the National Plan of Action is presented to the President and the Congress as our recommendations for implementing Public Law 94-167.

We are entitled to and expect serious attention to our proposals.

We demand immediate and continuing action on our National Plan by Federal, State, public, and private institutions so that by 1985, the end of the International Decade for Women proclaimed by the United Nations, everything possible under the law will have been done to provide American women with full equality.

The rest will be up to the hearts, minds and moral consciences of men and women and what they do to make our society truly democratic and open to all.

We pledge ourselves with all the strength of our dedication to this struggle "to form a more perfect Union."

ARTS AND HUMANITIES

The President should take steps to require that women:

☐ Are assured equal opportunities for appointment to managerial and upper level posts in Federally funded cultural institutions, such as libraries, museums, universities, and public radio and TV;

☐ Are more equitably represented on grant-awarding boards, commissions, and panels;

☐ Benefit more fairly from Government grants, whether as individual grant applicants or as members of cultural institutions receiving Federal or State funding.

Judging agencies and review boards should use blind judging for musicians, including singers, in appraising them for employment, awards, and fellowships as well as for all articles and papers being considered for publication or delivery and for all exhibits and grant applications, wherever possible.

Background:
"One becomes a genius, and the feminine situation has, up to the present, rendered the becoming practically impossible."

For more than two centuries, American women have built a climate for the arts in this country. They are the major appreciators and consumers of all the arts and humanities. They lead the way in going to plays, concerts, and dance recitals, reading serious literature, attending lectures, visiting art shows and museums, and seeing to it that talented youngsters take lessons in music and art. Without their volunteer services, thousands of art museums would close. According to *Museums, U.S.A.*, a study made by Louis Harris, 57 percent of all museum staff workers are volunteers, virtually all of them women.

Women are more than passive appreciators. The Women's Caucus for Art reports that 75 percent of all art students are women; they also outnumber men in schools of acting and in creative writing courses.

Yet in spite of their deep involvement in the arts, women are conspicuously absent from the ranks of artists who have won recognition and acclaim.

Women created only 10 percent of the masterpieces shown in the New York Metropolitan Museum of Art;

nine percent of those in the New York Museum of Modern Art; and only six percent of those in the Corcoran Gallery in Washington, reported *Time* magazine. Women composers of classical fame are rare, and women conductors are even rarer. And though women do better in literature, they account for only 21 percent of the listings in the 1977 Directory of Poets and Writers.

For centuries, answers to the question of why there have not been more great women artists and composers have implied that women are genetically incapable of creativity in the arts. This view defeats a woman before she begins. But feminists are challenging this argument, and in the new climate of encouragement of women's rights, many talented women are coming to the fore in the arts and humanities.

"One is not born a genius," wrote Simone de Beauvoir, author of *The Second Sex*. "One *becomes* a genius, and the feminine situation has, up to the present, rendered the becoming practically impossible."

The fault, says Dr. Linda Nochlin, professor of art history at Vassar College, lies not "in our stars, our hormones, our menstrual cycles, or our empty internal spaces, but in our institutions and our education—educa-

tion understood to include everything that happens to us from the moment we enter, head first, into this world of meaningful symbols, signs and signals."

Centuries of repression The discrimination is rooted in history. Most women artists before the 19th century were either daughters or wives of artists and were trained by their male relatives. Unlike the men, however, they were not allowed formal academic training or the study of anatomy; therefore, they usually had to limit themselves to the arts of portraiture and still life. Some worked anonymously.

Even under these unfavorable conditions, some women artists succeeded. The works of Italian artist Artemisia Gentileschi, the best known woman painter of the 17th century; Rosa Bonheur, Kathe Kollwitz, Marie Laurencin, Mary Cassatt, and contemporary American artists Georgia O'Keefe, Lee Krasner, Loren MacIver, and Alice Neel are among the 83 women artists from 12 countries whose works are being shown in an unprecedented historical exhibit, "Women Artists: 1550-1950," which is acquainting the public with the achievements of famous and not-so-famous women artists. Typically, this exhibit, seen by capacity crowds and widely acclaimed by critics, was turned down by every major museum in the midwest and east coast when its touring schedule was first planned.

There is ample evidence that our institutions of support, as well as education, in the arts continue to discriminate against women, denying them the opportunities they need to nurture their talents. Continuing attitudes that women are second-rate artists also inhibit women into suppressing their gifts. All too often a woman artist will give up her own creative work for a routine job that will support her husband or lover in the development of his creative talent because both accept his as intrinsically superior. Pat Mainardi, writing in the

The Dove Fountain, a bronze sculpture more than six feet long, four feet high and 20 inches wide, was created by sculptor Jimilu Mason of Alexandria, Virginia in honor of the National Women's Conference in Houston.

The fountain is an abstract of the International Women's Year bird symbol designed to embrace the theme of the United Nations Decade for Women: Peace, Equality and Development.

The sculptor explains: "The clear stream of water symbolizes the continuity and power of the ocean with its never-ending capacity to produce life and to effect dramatic changes on whatever it touches. This is woman.

"Yet, water possesses the gentle capacity for cleansing, refreshment and healing. This, too, is woman. The water is an integral part of the bronze, actually completing the flowing form of the dove.

"The reflected light surface of the bronze symbolizes the richness of the limitless potential released in women who discover their creative centers and become themselves reflectors of the changing patterns of opportunity for women."

newsletter, *Womanart*, recalls that during the 1960's, a fellow art student suggested that the tuition fees of women should be used to provide scholarships for deserving men.

In the colleges Discrimination against women on college faculties is devastating for women artists because teaching is the most reliable and often the only way for a composer, a poet, a playwright, or an artist to earn a living. But the universal pattern is that women are the students and men are the teachers. According to a study made for the National Commission on the Observance of International Women's Year, women hold half the graduate degrees in art history but only a quarter of the faculty positions in that discipline. The disproportion is about the same in music and is much worse in English. Women are 70 percent of the undergraduates majoring in English but are only seven percent of the English professors.

Like women workers in general, women in the arts and humanities are clustered in the lower paying, least desirable jobs. In university departments of English, foreign language, history, art, music, and philosophy, they are concentrated in lower ranking, untenured posts.

Librarians are generally poorly paid, and most are women. The proportion of male librarians increased, however, during the 1960's when Federal funding created well-paid administrative posts. In the Federal system, women hold only 13 percent of the library positions at the highest grade level, while 50 percent of the lowest rated library workers are women.

It is the same story in Federally funded museums: although most museum workers are women, nearly 80 percent of the senior positions are held by men.

The performing arts Women have the same problems of inadequate access and pay in the performing arts. According to a report of the American Symphony Orchestra League, women comprised only one-fourth of the players in orchestras with budgets of more than $1 million during the 1974-75 season. The percentage of women was smaller in the more prestigious orchestras and larger in orchestras with low budgets. Only four percent of the managers of major symphonies were women, though they did better in metropolitan and community orchestras where pay has always been lower. For large orchestras and small, the rule held true: the more money a job pays, the less likely it is to go to a woman.

The theater is no exception. Although women do relatively better in drama because female characters are needed, there have always been more roles for men than for women. According to a Screen Actors Guild study, the ratio in television is 70 to 30, with male characters outnumbering females by two to one in children's programs.

In architecture, a profession with very few women, women have customarily been excluded from access to training and experience. A 1975 Task Force on Women in Architecture found that it was hard for women students to obtain the internships and apprenticeships essential to career advancement. In addition, women were regarded as specially fitted to design residences and kitchens, work generally less well paid and prestigious than the design of larger structures. The Task Force found that male architects averaged 61 percent more pay than females in the profession.

Blind judging Experiments in blind judging have demonstrated that the wide discrimination against women in the arts has nothing to do with their ability. A study published in the February 1976 issue of *Visual Dialog* showed that between 1960 and 1972, women painters and sculptors did better in shows in which their names were concealed than in shows that disclosed their names and sex.

Women scholars are handicapped in getting promotions on college faculties because they publish, on the average, fewer scholarly papers. Recent studies suggest that this poorer record is not due to lack of industry or ability. After two years of blind review of papers submitted for publication by women teachers of classical languages, the proportion of papers accepted from women tripled.

Women musicians have also benefited from blind auditions—one-third of all major orchestras now do preliminary auditions with applicants performing behind a screen.

The Endowments Creative art everywhere depends on subsidy from private or public patrons. Key sources of funds are the National Endowment for the Arts and the National Endowment for the Humanities, which support symphonies, dance and theatre companies, and museums and also make grants to individual artists and scholars. Both endowments enlist the help of eminent artists and scholars in awarding grants.

The National Endowment for the Arts was formerly headed by Nancy Hanks and is now chaired by Livingston L. Biddle, Jr. Only 25 percent of its grant advisory panels in 1977 were women. During its first 10 years of existence, however, the Arts Endowment awarded 33 percent of its grants to women, though only 31 percent of applicants were women. In 1976, 17 percent of the grant advisory panels of the Endowment for the Humanities were women. This agency, now headed by Joseph Duffy, has increased the proportion of women on its grant advisory bodies, as has the Arts Endowment.

The Federal Government itself become a large art consumer. In 1 the Carter Administration invited artists to create a print series, with sales proceeds going to the De cratic Party and to the artists. Non the 10 invited was a woman. Wor in the Arts, an organization create fight just this kind of discriminat began an investigation and was that Georgia O'Keefe and Lo Nevelson had been invited to par pate, but neither could acc Women in the Arts identified m other women artists who w qualify. The ensuing dialogue led White House meeting. Subseque Presidential Assistant Marg "Midge" Costanza wrote to Mich Straight at the National Endowm for the Arts, urging him to look into situation of women artists and to itiate remedial procedures to women more equitable represe tion" on the panels of the Endowm

Women artists coalesce
Women in the Arts also investiga the program of the General Servi Administration, which buys art Federal buildings. Much to surprise even of those running program, it was discovered women were receiving only 10 cent of all GSA commissions.

A nationwide effort to achieve ognition for women in art is being i ated by the newly formed Coalitio Women's Arts Organizations, wl held its first full meeting in Jan 1978. The Coalition is calling equal opportunity and equal re sentation for women in all arts grams and institutions, on decis making bodies, and in grants awards. The Coalition is also seel greater recognition of the arts school curricula and special fun for women's arts projects, all as of the struggle to eliminate the criminatory practices that womer tists face, practices that relate n their talent, training, or effort bu their sex.

BATTERED WOMEN

The President and Congress should declare the elimination of violence in the home to be a national goal. To help achieve this, Congress should establish a national clearinghouse for information and technical and financial assistance to locally controlled public and private nonprofit organizations providing emergency shelter and other support services for battered women and their children. The clearinghouse should also conduct a continuing mass media campaign to educate the public about the problem of violence and the available remedies and resources.

Local and State governments, law enforcement agencies, and social welfare agencies should provide training programs on the problem of wife battering, crisis intervention techniques, and the need for prompt and effective enforcement of laws that protect the rights of battered women.

State legislatures should enact laws to expand legal protection and provide funds for shelters for battered women and their children; remove interspousal tort immunity in order to permit assaulted spouses to sue their assailants for civil damages; and provide full legal services for victims of abuse.

Programs for battered women should be sensitive to the bilingual and multicultural needs of ethnic and minority women.

Background:
"Wife abuse is chronic and widespread at all economic and social levels."

Wife beating is a nationwide social problem. While nobody knows exactly how many American wives are physically assaulted by their husbands, the National Institute of Mental Health believes that at least 7.5 million couples go through a "violent episode."

A random sample of official reports indicates that wife abuse is chronic and widespread at all economic and social levels. In New York State, 14,167 abuse complaints were handled in Family Court in 1972; 23,136 complaints in 1975. Boston, Massachusetts police responded to 11,081 family disturbance calls in 1974. And Boston City Hospital records show that 70 percent of the assault victims received in its emergency rooms are women who have been attacked in their homes, usually by a husband or lover. In Kansas City, Missouri family assault calls comprised 46,137 or 82 percent of all disturbance calls in 1972. In Oakland, California the police responded to 16,000 family disturbance calls during a six-month period in 1970.

Physical abuse of wives is not merely an urban phenomenon. In one rural area, researchers found that police calls for "family fights" were exceeded only by calls relating to automobile accidents. In a rural Michigan county, 42.7 percent of all 1974 assault complaints were cases of wife assault. Another study of 40 known violent families and 40 neighboring families revealed that even among the supposedly nonviolent families, more than a third had experienced at least one incident of spousal assault.

Wife beating affects women of all ages, classes, and races. Police in Fairfax, Virginia, one of the wealthiest counties in the United States, reported receiving 4,073 family disturbance calls in 1974. Another study found that the number of wife abuse cases reported in the white upper-middle class community of Norwalk, Connecticut was approximately the same as that reported in a West Harlem black working-class neighborhood of the same size.

These findings come from a number of sociological, police, and legal studies. Many of them are summarized in Del Martin's book, *Battered Wives*, published by Glide Press, and "The Assaulted Wife: Catch 22 Revisited," written by S. Eisenberg and P. Michlow for the *Women's Right's Law Reporter*, vol. 3.

Acceptance of wife abuse Many Americans consider spousal violence an acceptable form of behavior. A survey conducted by the Harris Poll in 1968 for the National Commission on the Causes and Prevention of Violence found that one in four men (and fewer than one in seven women) approved of slapping a spouse under some circumstances.

The FBI estimates that 25 percent of all murders in the United States occur within the family and that of these, one-half are husband-wife killings. The Kansas city police found women to be the most frequent homicide victims. However, women who kill are seven times more likely to be motivated by self-defense than men. Even where wife abuse does not result in the death of one of the spouses, the effect on other members of the family is likely to be severe and to perpetuate the problem. One observer believes that at least 10 percent of children who witness parental violence become adult batterers themselves. In a study prepared by students at Western Michigan University School of Social Work, it was found that of assaulters whose family history was known, over one-half had witnessed parents involved in assaultive situations and two-fifths had been abused themselves.

Police response The reaction of police personnel often frustrates and undermines the battered woman's attempts to get protection and help. The training manuals used by most local police forces follow the old advice (since revised) of the International Association of Police Chiefs to avoid arrest, restore the peace, and leave.

The police do not make the safety of the victim their prime concern, and she frequently is in mortal danger. The Kansas City Police Department found that police had been called at least once before the actual murder took place in 85 percent of domestic homicide cases; and in 50 percent of the cases, the police had been called five times, reports Susan Jackson in an unpublished work, "In Search of Equal Protection for Battered Wives."

A woman who has been beaten may tell the police that she wishes to make a citizen's arrest, but most people are not aware of this right, and the police rarely tell victims about it.

In New York City, 59 abused women resorted to a class action suit against New York City policemen and family court personnel for unlawfully denying them assistance after they reported beatings.

Legal obstacles   The law itself contributes to the problem. Under English common law, which is the basis for much American law, a man had the right to "correct his wife for her misbehavior." In nearly 23 States, one spouse may not sue another, and this prevents a woman from bringing a civil suit against a husband who injures her. In many other States, limitations on the right to sue make it an ineffective and uncertain remedy. A recent court decision in Pennsylvania held that a woman who had been beaten by her husband could not sue him for the medical expenses required to treat her injuries. In New York a husband charged with a family offense is entitled to a court-appointed lawyer, while his wife is not so entitled and must act as her own prosecuting attorney. Only one State in the country allows a wife to charge her husband with rape if he forces sexual intercourse. In New Hampshire the penalties for wife beating or simple assault range from a verbal warning to a small fine. In some States, the husband will not be arrested unless the type of battering is severe enough to charge the husband with a felony. District attorneys rarely prosecute those who assault their spouse. And many women do not prosecute for fear of reprisal.

The economic bind   It is not easy for a battered woman to extricate herself from the marriage. If she should divorce, she is unlikely to be awarded alimony or child support. And even when she does receive such support, studies show that a large majority of all husbands will default in their payments. If she works, her average earnings are much less than those of a man.

Emergency help   The number of existing emergency shelters is grossly inadequate to provide physical protection for women in immediate danger. A television program on ABC, aired in November 1977, reported that there were only 30 shelters in the 50 States.

Leaving her home to go to a shelter is the only recourse for a woman in danger in most States. But in Massachusetts, she may get an order to have her husband vacate the premises if she is instituting action for divorce or separate maintenance. Violation of the court order is considered trespass and is enforced by the police. The order is in effect for 90 days, and it can be renewed. (Massachusetts General Law, chapter 28k, sec. 34b, 1970, amended 1975.)

The essential features of such an injunction are that it can be obtained, if necessary, very quickly and that it has strong enforcement provisions.

Pending legislation   Several bills have been introduced in Congress by Representatives Barbara Mikulski, Lindy Boggs, and Newton Steers, Jr., that call for establishing a grant program to support community groups that would provide direct assistance to battered spouses and support research on domestic violence. Hearings on the legislation were scheduled for March 1978.

BUSINESS

The President should issue an Executive order establishing as national policy:

☐ The full integration of women entrepreneurs in Government-wide, business-related, and procurement activities, including a directive to all Government agencies to assess the impact of these activities on women business owners.

☐ The development of outreach and action programs to bring about the full integration of women entrepreneurs into business-related Government activities and procurement.

☐ The development of evaluation and monitoring programs to assess progress periodically and to develop new programs.

The President should amend Executive Order 11625 of October 13, 1971 to add women to its coverage and to programs administered by the Office of Minority Business Enterprise.

The President should direct the Small Business Administration (SBA) to add women to the definition of socially or economically disadvantaged groups as published in the *Code of Federal Regulations* and take all steps necessary to include women in all the services and activities of the SBA. These steps should include community education projects to encourage women to participate in SBA programs, particularly minority women, including blacks, Hispanic Americans, Asian Americans, and Native Americans.

The President should direct all contracting agencies to increase the percentage of the annual dollar amount of procurement contracts awarded to women-owned businesses and to maintain records by sex and race or ethnicity for monitoring and evaluation.

The President should direct the General Services Administration to amend, so as to include women, the Federal Procurement Regulations requiring that all firms holding Government contracts exceeding $5,000 insure that "minority business enterprises have the maximum practicable opportunity to participate in the performance of Government contracts."

The President should direct the Department of Labor, Office of Federal Contract Compliance Programs, to assure that compliance officers monitor the awards of subcontracts in order to assure that women-owned businesses are equitably treated.

Background:

"Women-owned businesses and minority-owned businesses together received less than 1 percent of the more than $130 billion in contracts awarded by the Federal Government."

Businesswomen are very poorly represented in the American economy. In 1972, the only year for which figures were available, women owned 4.6 percent of all American businesses, accounting for only 0.3 percent of all business receipts.

Very little has been done to increase these numbers. National programs for assistance to business owners do not make any special provision for women entrepreneurs, and many women do not qualify for help under minority programs. Nor do women get their share of Federal contracts. In 1975, women-owned businesses and minority-owned businesses together received less than one percent of the more than $130 billion in contracts awarded by the Federal Government.

Most businesses owned by women are smaller and less profitable than those owned by men—retail stores, coffee shops, personal services. Of the 402,025 women-owned businesses surveyed in the 1972 study, 98 percent were owned by one woman; 13 percent had no paid employees; and only 27 percent had more than five employees. The average annual income of women-owned businesses without employees was $10,000.

Small Business Administration

A major source of financial and technical assistance to small businesses is the Small Business Administration. The agency does not have a separate program for women, and as a result, they receive only a small share of its attention and assistance. In 1976, the SBA gave 11 percent of its business loans (and only eight percent of its total loan dollars) to under 3,000 women-owned businesses. This amounted to .75 percent of all women-owned businesses. More than three-quarters of the aid went to the retail and service firms that have been traditional business outlets for women.

Women as a group are not presumed disadvantaged in business and are not defined as eligible for participation in the section 8(a) program of the SBA that arranges subcontracts for small business concerns "which are owned and controlled by socially or economically disadvantaged persons." Women who are not members of recognized minority groups have had a difficult time being accepted as "socially disadvantaged."

Women as a group were not included as a "minority" when the Office of Minority Business Enterprise was created in 1971. As a result, they are excluded from an avenue of financial and technical aid that would allow them to participate more fully in the small business sector of the Nation's economy.

Charting the need In September 1977, the Department of Commerce announced the formation of an Interagency Task Force on Women Business Owners, charged by President Carter with identifying obstacles, including Federal practices, that discourage women from entering business. The Task Force, which was preparing to make its report at this writing, includes representatives of Federal departments and agencies with special interest in business and procurement issues. Anne Wexler, Deputy Under Secretary of Commerce for Regional Affairs, chairs this Task Force, which was assigned to identify and assess the adequacy of current data; propose methods of collecting additional information; identify discriminatory practices and/or conditions; assess current Federal discriminatory programs and practices; and propose changes in Federal laws, regulations, and practices, including the impact, if any, on the Federal budget.

Legislation A bill to establish an Associate Administrator for Women's Business Enterprise (S. 1526) was introduced by Senators Dewey Bartlett (R., Okla.) and Jacob Javits (R., N.Y.), with full support of the National Association of Women Business Owners. The head of SBA, A. Vernon Weaver, has publicly stated opposition to this bill. Rather than create a separate program for women, he favors integrating women's needs into all aspects of SBA programs. The bill passed the Senate in August 1977 and was referred to a subcommittee of the House Committee on Small Business.

Current action The Agency for International Development (AID) is seeking to provide more contracts to firms owned by minorities and women. AID has also expressed a desire to include more women-owned firms as contractors and/or grantees.

CHILD ABUSE

The President and Congress should provide continued funding and support for the prevention and treatment of abused children and their parents under the Child Abuse Prevention and Treatment Act of 1974.

States should set up child abuse prevention, reporting, counseling, and intervention programs or strengthen such programs as they already have. Child abuse is defined, for this purpose, as pornographic exploitation of children, sexual abuse, battering, and neglect.

Programs should:

☐ Provide protective services on a 24-hour basis;

☐ Counsel both victim and abuser;

☐ Create public awareness in schools and in communities by teaching how to identify and prevent the problems;

☐ Encourage complete reporting and accurate data collection; and

☐ Provide for prompt, sensitive attention by police, courts, and social services.

Background:
"...at least 2,000 die every year of abuse or neglect."

Violence against children is widespread and underreported. The National Center on Child Abuse and Neglect estimates that between 100,-000 and 200,000 youngsters are regularly assaulted by their parents with cords, sticks, fists, hot irons, cigarettes, and booted feet. Nearly the same number are sexually molested, and as many as 700,000 may be denied food, clothing, or shelter. The Center estimates that at least 2,000 die every year of abuse or neglect. Most physical battering is directed against children less than four years old.

No one will know exactly how many children are affected until central registries are set up to count cases on the basis of uniform standards, but the figures that do exist are startling, and there is evidence that the number of children in danger is increasing. More than 5,000 New York City children, for example, were abused during 1976, and 83 died from abuse by their parents, according to *The New York Times* (July 11, 1977). This was 18 percent higher than in 1975 and 55 percent higher than in 1974.

The risk for girls Children of both sexes are abused, but the crime has special impact on females. Girls are more apt to be sexually abused than boys and are more likely to be exploited through pornography.

Incest may be more widespread than anyone expects. Nearly half of the runaway girls studied by Odyssey Institute in New York had been sexually attacked by relatives in their homes, leading to an estimate by Judianne Densen-Gerber, a psychiatrist, that one out of every 20 females in the country has been the victim of incestuous attack.

Nor are children safe from pornographic exploitation for profit with the cooperation of their parents. In 1971 Nassau County, N.Y. District Attorney William Cahn uncovered a quarter-million-dollar, four-state business using children from 3 ½ to 14 years of age as sex models undergoing such acts as rape, sodomy and incest before the cameras. Parents knowingly brought their children from as far away as Florida to be paid for "performing," Shirley Camper Soman reported in her book, *Let's Stop Destroying Our Children.*

Since neglected and battered children are apt to grow up to be child abusers, there is a danger that female children may transmit abuse to the next generation when they become mothers themselves. Mothers who abuse children outnumber fathers 48 percent to 40 percent, primarily because mothers bear the burden of child rearing. And the wife of a man who abuses his children may find herself abused as well.

Early intervention According to Carol Parry, assistant commissioner in charge of New York City's Special Services for Children, early intervention is the key to winning the battle against child abuse and neglect. Unless intervention occurs, more than half of the children abused today will be abused again later.

Although every State has had some form of child abuse law at least since 1965, many communities have no facilities or services for 24-hour protection. In some States protection does not cover adolescents up to age 18, and not all States have set up machinery to collect and channel reports of neglected and abused children.

Schools have been successfully enlisted in pilot projects. Teachers, nurses, principals, and counselors in the public schools of Montgomery County, Maryland have been taught to detect child abuse from the appearance and behavior of the child. Between 1974 and 1975 reports of suspected abuse or neglect doubled in the county, and confirmed cases of physical abuse quadrupled. Abusive adults were referred for counseling and were encouraged to join self-help parent groups.

Community services have been set up, and many more are needed. Under a grant from the National Center on Child Abuse and Neglect, Children's Bureau, U.S. Department of Health, Education and Welfare, a Center for Comprehensive Emergency Services to Children was established in Nashville, Tennessee. After one year the number of abused children reported in Nashville increased 264 percent, but at the same time the number of abused children who had to be placed in institutions declined dramatically. The Nashville Center has prepared a guide that tells how to set up intake, outreach, and follow-up services, neighborhood crisis centers, emergency shelters for families and adolescents, and how to recruit and train emergency caretakers, homemakers, and foster family homes.

Current legislation A bill providing $50 million for carrying out the Child Abuse Prevention and Treatment Act during 1978 and 1979 has passed the House and Senate and is awaiting conference action as of this writing. Half of the funds have been earmarked for demonstration projects and research into the causes and treatment of child abuse; 20 percent is for grants to States to develop and carry out child abuse and neglect prevention and treatment programs. The bill also authorizes $2 million for each of fiscal years 1978 and 1979 for programs and projects designed to prevent, identify, and treat sexual abuse of children.

The legislation defines "sexual abuse" as the obscene or pornographic photographing, filming, or depiction of children for commercial purposes, or rape, molestation, incest, prostitution, and other forms of sexual exploitation under circumstances which harm or threaten the child's health or welfare.

CHILD CARE

The Federal Government should assume a major role in directing and providing comprehensive, voluntary, flexible-hour, bias-free, non-sexist, quality child care and developmental programs, including child care facilities for Federal employees, and should request and support adequate legislation and funding for these programs.

Federally funded child care and developmental programs should have low-cost, ability-to-pay fee schedules that make these services accessible to all who need them, regardless of income, and should provide for parent participation in their operation.

Legislation should make special provision for child care facilities for rural and migrant worker families.

Labor and management should be encouraged to negotiate child care programs in their collective bargaining agreements.

Education for parenthood programs should be improved and expanded by local and State school boards, with technical assistance and experimental programs provided by the Federal Government.

City, county, and/or State networks should be established to provide parents with hotline consumer information on child care, referrals, and follow-up evaluations of all listed caregivers.

Background:
"More than two of every five mothers of preschoolers are at work or looking for work."

Nearly half of all the children in the country—more than 28 million under 18—had mothers working outside the home in 1976. More than six million of these children were younger than six years old. At least 4½ million had mothers who were single, separated, divorced, or widowed heads of families, according to U.S. Department of Labor statistics.

For millions of working parents, for mothers who are in school or in job-training programs, for women who are ill and unable to care for their young children on a round-the-clock basis, access to child care facilities is of prime importance. The crucial issue for them is not whether there should be child care but how to achieve good quality child care at prices that parents can afford to pay.

Working mothers Today, more mothers than ever before are working, and their numbers increase every year. The majority of American mothers now enter the labor force when their children are of school age. More than two out of every five mothers of pre-schoolers are at work or looking for work.

Most mothers work outside the home because they need the money. A large number of American families need two incomes to get along. In more than nine million families with two working parents, the husband earns less than $10,000 a year, and half of these families would fall below the poverty level without a second income.

A woman who is the sole support of her children has an even greater burden. If she earns the national median income for women of $130 a week before taxes, or $6,770 annually, she will find many child care services priced beyond her reach.

Who provides child care? For most working parents, child care is makeshift, informal, unavailable, or prohibitively expensive. Many children are cared for at home by a relative, neighbor, or nonrelated babysitter. Husbands and wives frequently work different shifts so that they can share child care responsibility, with

the result that they have little time to spend together. One-fourth of all children of working parents, including some four million children under 14, were grouped in the category "arrangements unknown," according to Joseph H. Reid, executive director of the Child Welfare League, in testimony before a joint congressional hearing in 1975. Among this group were almost two million 7-to-13 year-old "latch-key children" who cared for themselves until a parent came home from work.

The most accessible type of care outside the home is family day care provided in private homes where women take in groups of children. Only 10 percent of such homes are licensed. Although many provide a satisfactory level of care in a personal setting, they are unregulated, and many caregivers have no formal training.

Nursery schools serve a small but growing number of children, though usually only for part of the day. (Of the pre-schoolers enrolled 11 years ago, 18 percent had working mothers. That percent doubled by 1976.) There are also parent cooperatives in which fathers and mothers share duties as caregivers for a specified number of hours, but this involvement is impractical when both parents work during the day.

About 18,000 day care centers provide care for only about two percent of the children of working mothers. Yet mothers surveyed in 1971 by the National Council of Jewish Women preferred this type of care to any other because of the stable environment and the learning opportunities for their children.

Indeed, more mothers *not* in the labor force are also recognizing the value of a part-time educational setting away from a child's home. Twenty-nine percent of the 3-and 4-year-olds in private nursery schools in 1976 had mothers working only at home, compared with only 12 percent in 1967.

Although there are some nonprofit child care centers supported by charitable organizations or by public funds (care for 250,000 children is

27

currently subsidized to some extent), most are private, proprietary businesses. Because their fees are high and are based on potential profit, it is unusual for private centers or franchised chains to provide service in poor communities, where the need is great, or to attract well-trained caregivers by offering competitive salaries and benefits.

Child care at the parents' workplace received a great deal of publicity in the late 1960's, but such programs are very few and far between. A small number of plants provide such facilities. Another small group of employers assists working parents by keeping registries of available services, granting vouchers to purchase day care, or by contracting with existing day care centers to hold spaces for children of employees.

A few Federal agencies in the Washington, D.C. area have been providing on-site day care facilities for employees and others at moderate cost, but in March 1978, the Office of Management and Budget was planning to eliminate them. Only after protests from federally employed women, the National Commission, and other groups were hearings scheduled by the OMB to allow public discussion of the proposed change.

Migrant working families and other agricultural workers have a special need for child care facilities because of their particular working and living conditions, with both fathers and mothers working in the fields under isolated circumstances and with no access to the kind of arrangements that parents in towns and cities can improvise.

Labor unions have shown only a minimal interest in adding child care to their health and welfare packages. (A few exceptions include the Amalgamated Clothing Workers; the Seafarers International Union in Ponce, Puerto Rico; and the Amalgamated Meat Cutters and Butcher Workmen in Cleveland, Ohio.) The most obvious reason has been the absence of women in union leadership.

The quality of child care The working parent's search for convenient, affordable, dependable, quality child care is often lonely, desperate, and conducted under pressure of a deadline. Even where there are central registries of child care providers, evaluations of the services they offer are not commonly available. The Day Care and Child Development Council of Tompkins County in New York State, which operates a successful referral service, emphasizes the necessity of carefully checking caregivers before they are put on a list.

In this country, the Government supports child care chiefly as a tool to move poor mothers off public assistance and into low-paying jobs. Women in welfare programs, such as Aid to Families with Dependent Children, feel they should have the right to stay home with their young children if they so choose. But they also need access to free or low cost child care centers when they are able to work or wish to return to school or enter job training programs that would enable them to become self-supporting.

The Federal policy of limiting child care services to low-income women ignores the needs of lower-middle-class and middle-class working women who are frequently placed in a bind: their incomes are above the poverty level but not high enough to pay for private care, even if it should be available. Women in this situation often find themselves forced to give up their jobs to stay home with their children, and their only source of income then becomes welfare assistance. To break this chain, women seek comprehensive, federally-funded child care facilities with moderate sliding fee schedules based on ability to pay.

In other societies, day care is seen not only as an essential service to parents but as a positive, healthy, emotional, and intellectual experience for the child. In contrast with other industrialized nations, the United States has a poor record in providing child care services.

Education for parenthood Caregivers, as well as parents, would benefit from increased attention to teaching parenting skills. Our society has always expected future parents to learn how to be good parents from their own family experiences, yet in 1970 one out of every five persons between the ages of 14 and 17 did not live in a home where both parents were present. In addition, the average family is now smaller, so fewer young people learn how to raise children by watching their own parents or caring for younger brothers and sisters.

Child-rearing skills can be taught. The Office of Education and the Office of Child Development in the Department of Health, Education and Welfare, supported by the National Institute of Mental Health, have funded a program called Exploring Childhood that is given in junior and senior high schools. Programs to teach baby care and child development have also been developed by Girl Scouts, Boy Scouts, 4-H Clubs, and other organizations concerned with the welfare of children.

Legislative update Legislation supporting a Federal child care program has been at a standstill since former President Nixon vetoed the Child and Family Services Act of 1971. A revised bill, the Child and Family Services Act of 1975, received no action in the last Congress. This comprehensive legislation would provide for strictly voluntary and direct parental participation in operating child and family services in communities; support for establishing and maintaining part-day or full-day care in the home or in other child care facilities; after school programs and information and referral services; pre-

natal care; programs to meet the special needs of minorities, Indians, migrants, and bilingual children; and food nutrition services.

Meanwhile, Congress did pass the Child Day Care Services Act (PL 94-401), which authorized an additional $240 million in Title 20 Social Service funds to help day care centers meet their health and safety codes already in effect and to upgrade the quality of their programs.

However, new Federal standards for staffing (postponed until October 1977 by this act) have again been delayed. At this writing, a report was to be made to Congress in April 1978 on the appropriateness of the Federal Government setting any standards for child care. A series of State workshops seeking public interaction will then be scheduled throughout autumn 1978, and new or revised standards will be developed based on this local input. Any new Federal standards would therefore not be expected before spring 1979.

Some parents who must pay for private day care are now receiving a small tax break. The Tax Reform Act of 1976 provides up to $800 in tax credits to cover child care, care for incapacitated adults, and house care expenses for working parents, regardless of their income level. Divorced parents who receive child support are now eligible, and a couple is eligible even if one spouse works only part time or goes to school. And families that pay relatives for child care are now eligible, as long as that relative is not a legal dependent.

But when family income, even with two parents working, still falls near the poverty level, the current tax credit provides almost no relief at all. Such low income families are also not eligible for public child care funds under Title 20, a support system that gives priority to welfare clients. Legislation to assist the working family that "falls through the cracks" was being drafted by the Senate Child and Human Development Subcommittee for introduction in late spring 1978. The bill is expected to focus on local community control in a variety of settings, including family group homes.

CREDIT

The Federal Equal Credit Opportunity Act of 1974 should be vigorously, efficiently and expeditiously enforced by all the Federal agencies with enforcement responsibility.

The Federal Reserve Board should conduct a nationwide educational campaign to inform women of their rights under the law.

Background:
"A widow with an income of $25,000 a year...was refused an American Express card."

It has always been more difficult for women to obtain credit, mortgages, and loans than for similarly situated men. The Federal Equal Credit Opportunity Act, passed in 1974, made it unlawful for anyone to be denied credit on the basis of sex or marital status. The Act was amended in 1976 to prohibit discrimination on the basis of race, color, religion, age, national origin, the receipt of public assistance, or previous exercise of right under consumer protection legislation. But the law has not been enforced vigorously enough to eliminate credit discrimination against women. Too many women are still denied credit when they want to buy a car or a home, start a business, or finance an education.

Why the law was passed Public hearings held by the National Commission on Consumer Finance in 1972 found that women were routinely discriminated against. It was hard for a single woman to obtain credit; married women could not get any credit in their own names. Creditors were unwilling to count the wife's income when a married couple applied for a loan or mortgage. And when a woman was divorced or widowed, she had a particularly difficult time reestablishing credit for herself.

Provisions of the law The Federal Equal Credit Opportunity Act makes such discrimination illegal. The most important provisions are:
1. A woman may not be refused credit because she is a woman.
2. She may not be refused credit because she is single, married, separated, divorced, or widowed.
3. Creditors may not ask about her childbearing or birth control plans and cannot refuse to count her income because she is of childbearing age.
4. Alimony, child support, and part-time earnings may not be discounted as income.
5. A woman will be able to keep her own credit accounts and her own credit history if her marital status changes.
6. A homemaker will be able to build her own credit record because new accounts must be carried in the names of both husband and wife if both use the account.
7. If she is denied credit, she can find out why.

Enforcement The Act can be enforced in two ways: by private litigation or by actions brought by the 12 Federal agencies charged with overseeing compliance in the institutions that they regulate or monitor.

Many women's groups, consumer advocates, and civil rights organizations believe the compliance agencies, with the exception of the Federal Trade Commission, are not doing an effective job. Enforcement problems have been cited by attorneys in the Federal Reserve Board's Equal Credit Division.

Some of the specific charges:
1. Although the Equal Opportunity Credit Act has been in effect for more than two years, enforcement procedures are still being written. Only recently have agencies begun training their examiners and revising their handbooks to include credit discrimination.
2. No effective punitive action is mandated for creditors found to be violating the law. Linda Cohen, NOW Credit Task Force Coordinator, characterizes a recently proposed enforcement policy as "a slap on the wrist." There is no threat of significant financial penalty for violators, no suggestion that persons who have been discriminated against be advised of their right to sue, and no mention of how long and how badly an institution may violate the law before serious action will be taken.
3. Some enforcement agencies have a conflict of interest. If an agency advises a consumer that she has the right to sue, this may be harmful to the institution that the agency is charged with regulating.
4. No cease and desist orders have been issued by the regulatory agencies. Other than in the Federal Trade Commission, the only lawsuits filed have been initiated by individuals.

5. Discrimination continues. Since the law went into effect, the following cases have been documented in newspaper stories and by the National Credit Union Association:

A well-paid professional woman was told by her credit union that only a portion of her salary could be counted in a loan application because she is of childbearing age.

A Washington woman with no outstanding debts and a good credit rating was turned down in her request to buy furniture on an installment plan because part of her income is from child support.

A widow with an income of $25,000 a year from Social Security and her husband's estate was refused an American Express card because she didn't have a job.

A black woman was refused a mortgage because her home had no basement. She sued when she discovered the lender had made loans on other homes without basements.

A Texas woman earning nearly $10,000 in a management job was refused a $500 loan because she wouldn't ask her unemployed new husband to co-sign the note. Before her marriage she had repaid three separate bank loans of $1,000 each.

A divorced college professor, owner of a house and two cars and a substantial bank account, was denied a department store credit card in her own name but permitted to continue to use an old card in her former husband's name.

Learning credit rights   The speed with which ECOA becomes a practical reality will also depend on the rapidity with which American women learn their credit rights.

"Very few women have heard of ECOA," notes Linda Cohen. "They sit in credit offices and don't even know they're being discriminated against. If they knew their rights, they'd say 'treat me fairly or else,' And they would not be discriminated against."

Eileen Shanahan, a former *New York Times* economics reporter, had to quote from stories she herself had written about the law in order to get a department store credit card in her own name. "If I had trouble, the *ordinary* woman who wasn't as positive about the law would have lost the argument," she says.

Establishing credit history   One valuable provision of the law is apparently being largely ignored. The nonwage-earning homemaker who shares her husband's accounts—by using the charge card to make a purchase, or by writing the checks to pay the bill—may now have the identical credit history in her name as well as his. This is automatic on new accounts but must be requested for established accounts.

Between June 1 and October 1, financial institutions sent out 310,000,-000 information notices with a form to be returned if a woman wanted the account to be listed in her name as well as her husband's. A spot survey conducted by the Commercial Credit Corporation found a response rate of only nine percent. Yet this provision is potentially vital to all women. Census Bureau studies show that 85 percent of American women will be on their own at some time during their lives. The Federal Government must spearhead an educational campaign to teach all women that their financial survival may depend on their ability to use their credit rights.

DISABLED WOMEN

The President, Congress, and State and local governments should rigorously enforce all current legislation that affects the lives of disabled women.

The President, Congress, and the administration should expeditiously implement the recommendations of the White House Conference on Handicapped Individuals and develop comprehensive programs for that purpose.

Disabled women should have access to education, training, and employment based on their needs and interests rather than on the preconceived notions of others.

The Federal Government should enact legislation which will provide higher income levels so that disabled women can afford to live independently and at a decent standard of living. The disabled woman must have the right to determine for herself whether she will live in or out of an institutional setting. Funds and services should be available to make independent living a reality.

Congress should appropriate sufficient funds to insure the development of service programs controlled by disabled people.

Disabled women should have the right to have and keep their children and have equal rights to adoption and foster care.

Congress should mandate health training and research programs focused on the health needs of the disabled.

Information developed by disabled women should be disseminated to medical professionals and women so that all women can make decisions about children based on knowledge rather than on fear.

National health care legislation must provide for the unique requirements of disabled women without reference to income.

Congress should enact legislation to remove all work disincentives for all disabled individuals who wish to have paid employment.

The President and Congress should work closely with disabled individuals in the development of the welfare reform act and all other legislation concerning disabled persons.

Medicaid and Medicare should cover all the medical services and supplies that are needed by disabled women.

The President and Congress should encourage all States to utilize Title 20 funds for the provision of attendant care and other such services for disabled women.

The President and Congress should enact legislation to include disabled women under the 1964 Civil Rights Act and afford them judicial remedy.

The President and Congress and International Women's Year must recognize the additional discrimination disabled women face when they are members of racial, ethnic, and sexual minority groups, and appropriate steps must be taken to protect their rights.

In the passage of the National Plan of Action, the word "woman" should be defined as including all women with disabilities. The term "bilingual" should be defined as including sign language and interpreters for the deaf. The term "barriers" against women and "access" should be defined as including architectural barriers and communications barriers.

Congress and the President should support U.S. participation in and funding for the International Year of the Handicapped as proclaimed by the United Nations for 1981.

Background:
"...many disabled women are being deprived of their rights, and society is being deprived of their talents and abilities."

As many as 20 million women may suffer the double discrimination of sex plus disability. Employers, landlords, credit institutions, and schools exclude them from a participation of which they are capable. Laws enacted to prohibit discrimination and to require special physical facilities have not been enforced, and there are no provisions for the special problems of disabled women. This includes the right to bear children. Too many doctors assume that a disabled woman is incapable of bearing, rearing, or adopting a child. Because they are denied access to education, training, and employment, many disabled women are being deprived of their rights, and society is being deprived of their talents and abilities.

The numbers   Statistics on handicapped persons are hard to obtain. Only since 1970 has the census asked about handicaps, and then only in a five percent sampling. Based on that sample, it was estimated that one out of 11 adults was disabled, or about five million women. When statistics have been gathered, sex is often not indicated. Section 504 of the Vocational Rehabilitation Act of 1973 defines the handicapped person as one who has a mental or physical impairment or who is regarded as having such an impairment.

Recent Laws   Within recent years, several laws have been enacted that guarantee basic rights to handicapped individuals. The passage of the Vocational Rehabilitation Act with its civil rights Section 504, the Revenue Sharing Act of 1972, the Education for All Handicapped Children Act of 1975, the Urban Mass Transit Act of 1970 as amended, and the earlier Architectural Barriers Act (1968) should have enabled the handicapped to enter the mainstream of American life.

No enforcement   But enforcement has been poor because most of the programs had no compliance system built into them. During oversight hearings last year before the Subcommittee on the Handicapped, extensive testimony was given that there are no efficient procedures for handling complaints, and that complaints are dealt with very slowly, if at all. Since then, Secretary of Health, Education and Welfare Joseph A. Califano, Jr. signed the regulations for Section 504 of the Rehabilitation Act on April 28, 1977.

Enforcement has also been poor for the Architectural Barriers Act, which mandates that all Federal buildings and all buildings built using Federal funds after 1968 must have access for handicapped persons. The compliance board for this act is composed of the very agencies the act is supposed to regulate, such as the Department of Transportation (DOT).

Public transportation   One of the most important issues for disabled persons is access to public transportation. Twelve consumer organizations have filed suit against DOT for failing to require low-floor, wide-door ramped buses for subsidized public transport (Transbus Case). Because of this suit and others filed throughout the country, Transportation Secretary Brock Adams in April, 1977 mandated that all transit operators have to buy accessible buses after September 1979.

But even the current regulations are inadequate. As it now stands, in subways, for example, the station facility must be accessible, the elevator to the subway car must be accessible, but there is no requirement for access to the subway car.

Education   In 1971 the Pennsylvania Association of Retarded Children challenged the State's policy of excluding retarded and disabled children from school, and for the first time a court ruled that the State had to provide an education for all children. This and other court cases led to the Education for All Handicapped Children Act of 1975. But enforcement on the local level is not easy, and it is not unusual for the parent of a disabled child to have to take the local school board to court. Across the country, many thousands of children get less than their constitutional right, educationally, and some get virtually no education.

Employment and vocational training   Disabled women suffer the double discrimination of often being trained for less skilled jobs because they are female. Disabled women are much less likely to have paid employment than men. In *Jobs for the Disabled* (1977), Levitan and Taggart found that 60 percent of disabled men have paid employment, compared with 29 percent of disabled women. These figures are based on 1972 social security statistics.

Under the new HEW regulation, employers will no longer be allowed to give preemployment physical examinations. Employment cannot be denied for physical reasons unless the disability is job-related. Fringe benefits can no longer be modified or withdrawn unless there is an actuarial basis for doing so.

Health care   Under the new guidelines, doctors with Medicaid or Medicare patients, and those who have offices in a clinic or hospital built with Federal funds, must have an accessible office.

The Disabled Women's Caucus has asked that Medicare and Medicaid coverage be extended to cover interpreters and attendants necessary for health care. The Caucus also notes that birth control clinics do not have information in braille or on tapes. Doctors have ignored a disabled woman's right to bear or not bear children. A disabled woman who receives any kind of financial aid is often urged to give up her child, and some States have laws which do not allow disabled persons to adopt, even though disabled women may be capable mothers.

EDUCATION

The President should direct the vigorous and expeditious enforcement of all laws prohibiting discrimination at all levels of education and oppose any amendments or revisions that would weaken these laws and regulations.

Enforcement should apply to elementary, primary, secondary, postsecondary, graduate, vocational and technical schools, including sports and other programs, and granting of scholarships and fellowships.

Federal surveys of elementary and secondary schools should gather data needed to indicate compliance with Federal antidiscrimination laws, and these data should be collected by sex as well as race or ethnicity. The Civil Rights Commission should conduct a study to evaluate the enforcement of laws prohibiting sex discrimination in physical education and athletics and to consider the usefulness and feasibility of per capita expenditure in physical education and athletics as a measure of equal opportunity.

Leadership programs for working women in postsecondary schools should be upgraded and expanded, and private foundations are urged to give special attention to research on women in unions.

Bilingual vocational training, educational and cultural programs should be extended and significantly expanded, with particular attention to the needs of Hispanic Americans, Native Americans, Asian Americans, and other minority women.

State school systems should move against sex and race stereotyping through appropriate action, including:

☐ Review of books and curriculum.

☐ The integration into the curriculum of programs of study that restore to women their history and their achievements and give them the knowledge and methods to reinterpret their life experiences.

☐ Pre-service and in-service training of teachers and administrators.

☐ Nonsexist and nonracist counseling at every level of education, with encouragement of women to increase their range of options and choices to include both nontraditional and traditional occupations and to increase understanding of women's rights and status in various occupations.

mained in charge, as they had always been, despite the rising number of women going into higher education.

According to the *Digest of Educational Statistics,* women were 45 percent of college undergraduates in fall 1975 and 46 percent of graduate students. In 1976, women accounted for 52 percent of college students age 14 to 34.

The effects of an educational system that discriminates against women have not only damaged those who have pursued teaching as a profession but have also been devastating for many women. An educational system run by men has denied women the opportunity to develop their talents and abilities. In textbooks, classrooms, and gymnasiums, women have been taught to undervalue themselves. At every level, they have been offered more limited options than men; they have been denied the training that would enable them to enter higher paying, more rewarding fields of work.

This discrimination continues, even though it is now illegal under Title 9 of the Education Amendments Act of 1972. Despite affirmative action programs, recent statistics show only slight progress for women in some areas. Women who work in education continue to lag behind men in pay and promotions. Women as students are still being prevented from making full use of their capabilities.

Salaries and promotions The top positions in most schools are held by men, even when the faculty is predominantly female.

The National Institute of Education reported that in 1975, 63 percent of elementary and secondary teachers were women. Yet women were principals in less than two percent of the high schools and in only 18 percent of the primary schools. Out of 16,000 school districts in the country, only 75 were administered by women. These figures represent a serious setback for women. In 1928, only eight years after women won the right to vote, 55 percent of primary school principals were women.

Background:
"In classrooms, textbooks, and gymnasiums, women have been taught to undervalue themselves."

Women have always played a major role in the education of the young as part of their childrearing responsibilities. When an expanding and industrializing nation needed to educate large numbers of its children during the 19th century, Catharine Beecher proclaimed in lectures, pamphlets, and books that women are ideally suited to the task. It was part of her lifelong campaign to "professionalize" the work that women had been doing

at home, and its effects are still being felt to this day. Women became teachers in overwhelming numbers, but because it was "women's work," especially in the lower grades, the pay remained low well into this century.

Then education became big business, supported by Government money, and the better paying, policy-making jobs went to men, even in the elementary schools that women had been running by themselves. In the colleges and universities, men re-

The figures in higher education are not any better. The salaries of male professors averaged $3,000 more than female professors' in 1975-76, and the gap was greater than a year earlier. Between 1974 and 1975, the percentage of women declined in the highest ranks of professor and associate professor. And, according to the American Association of University Professors, the number of women faculty actually fell from 22.5 percent in 1974-75 to 21.7 percent in 1975-76.

Limited options With so few women in leadership positions, it is not surprising that women students are often inadequately prepared for the world of work. During their lifetime, according to the U.S. Bureau of Labor Statistics, 90 percent of the girls and young women now in school will work outside their homes.

Vocational education does not prepare them for gainful employment. In 1976, 38.7 percent of the girls enrolled in vocational programs were studying homemaking skills and not skills related to earning wages, according to Department of Health, Education and Welfare statistics. Of the rest, 27.4 percent were being taught office skills, such as typing and filing, which would prepare them only for work in the low-paid female ghetto. Only 4.9 percent of the female vocational students were in trade and industrial programs that lead to higher paying jobs, compared with about 60 percent of the male vocational students.

Women have been discouraged from learning the skills that would prepare them for highly paid technical work. According to recent surveys by the Endicott Report and the College Placement Council, future employment prospects are brightest in many of the fields that use quantitative skills—fields such as engineering, accounting, banking, and insurance.

Women have been conditioned to believe that they do not have the skills for these jobs. A study by the National Assessment of Educational Progress found that boys and girls perform almost equally on mathematics and verbal tests as late as nine years old. As they grow older, however, girls' verbal scores rise and their math scores decline in comparison to boys' scores. A study of college students entering the University of California at Berkeley in 1973 showed that only eight percent of the women had four years of high school mathematics, compared with 57 percent of the entering men. This meant that 92 percent of incoming women students could major in only five out of the 20 available fields. (The figures were quoted in testimony before the congressional hearings on equal opportunity in education.)

It is not surprising, then, that women are underrepresented in technical and scientific fields. According to the 1975 Endicott Report, five to six percent of scientists and engineers, less than 10 percent of medical doctors, and less than one percent of mathematicians and physicists are women. Although almost as many women as men are now in graduate school, the percentage of scientific doctoral degrees awarded to women today is essentially the same as it was in the 1920's, according to the American Association for the Advancement of Science. Women earn 45 percent of all bachelor degrees and 44 percent of master degrees, but in mostly "female" fields.

In 1975, some law schools were still admitting fewer than 20 percent women students, and in 1976-77, women were only 25 percent of the entering classes in medical schools.

Textbooks The message of many textbooks and storybooks is that girls and women take second place to men and that they must accept certain roles. Women appear in only 31 percent of all textbook illustrations, according to a 1974 report for the National Foundation for the Improvement of Education. Men occupy at least 150 roles in texts, while most women occupy traditional female-roles like housewife, teacher, and secretary. In primary school materials, boys are pictured as active; girls as passive. Boys are shown outdoors; girls indoors. Boys perform adventurous and skillful tasks; girls groom themselves and tend to their homes. Girls are affectionate and nurture dolls and pets; boys are brave and fierce. These stereotypes are limiting to girls and boys equally.

Stereotyping does not stop in the elementary schools. A study completed in 1974 by a Citizens Advisory on Sex Inequality in Lexington, Massachusetts found that in a widely used algebra text for grades 8 through 10, boys are shown working, earning high grades, painting, pushing mowers; girls are shown spending money and dieting. In high school civics books studied by Jennifer MacLeod and Sandy Silverman, there are 1,104 listings for men; 33 for women.

Women are invisible in history books, according to Janice Law Trecker, whose study was published by the National Council for Social Studies. She found that topics uniquely concerned with women, such as women's suffrage, are given short shrift. Birth control is usually omitted entirely. One text devotes five pages to the story of the six-shooter; five lines to the life of a frontier woman.

Counseling reinforces the images about a "woman's place." In a 1975 study for HEW, Janice Bick cites scores in one of the most popular aptitude tests:

"Many young women do not appear to have strong vocational interests and they may score high in certain 'premarital' occupations; elementary-school teacher, office worker, stenographer-secretary."

Too many guidance counselors do not take a young woman's career aspirations seriously and try to steer her into low-paying, conventional career choices.

One well-qualified high school senior wrote to HEW that she was discouraged by her counselor from pursuing a career as a veterinarian. "She said," wrote the student, "that at our age it's the maternal instinct, and after a few years of college, we outgrow it."

Women in sports Title 9 regulations specifically call for equal athletic opportunities for girls and women—and athletics is the single largest category of complaints filed by students under Title 9, reports NOW's project PEER, which monitored HEW enforcement.

Desegregation of school sports has received so much publicity and controversy that it seems as if the battle is won. Far from it. Although girls' participation in varsity high school athletic programs shot up 560 percent between 1971 and 1976, boys still take part in team sports more than twice as often as girls, and not one State offers girls as many varsity teams as boys.

Colleges may be even further behind. In a 1974 study of intercollegiate athletics, it was estimated that the average budget of women's athletic departments was only two percent of the budgets for men's athletics.

In 1976, a high school student in Mannington, West Virginia was told by her principal to "watch the boys" if she liked sports.

Enforcing Title 9 Although Title 9 has been law since 1972, little has been done to enforce it. Nearly 900 complaints of discrimination on elementary and secondary levels were made to HEW, but only 179 of those were investigated and resolved, reported the Project on Equal Education Rights (PEER), which conducted a year-long study for NOW (National Organization for Women) Legal Defense and Education Fund.

Under its enforcement powers, HEW has done little else but work on these few complaints, PEER charged, and worked on them very slowly. It has not taken the necessary steps to inform the public—parents and students—what their rights are under Title 9. It contacted all schools initially to tell them about the law, but it has not published its rulings. "Other government agencies have long recognized that most rulings have universal regulation," notes PEER's report. "Solve the problem of the tennis coach in Tallahassee and you have resolved matters in Terre Haute, Fall River and Dubuque. If the word reaches them."

HEW has responsibility under the law to initiate checks in all schools to make sure that opportunities are available equally to girls and boys, women and men. HEW completed checks in only 12 of the country's 17,000 school districts, PEER reports. It has not issued clear and consistent rulings on a number of issues that have been brought to the department; it has changed rulings when they became controversial, and for 10 months, between August 1976 and June 1977, there was a virtual moratorium—HEW stopped making decisions on Title 9 almost completely. The moratorium has been lifted, and some of this backlog has been cleared up, but in October 1977, the agency released its enforcement plan for the following year and promised to investigate only 21 (seven percent) of the complaints the office expects to receive during the year.

"Hundreds of people have written HEW for help under Title 9," says Holly Knox, director of PEER. "They couldn't get into classes or couldn't get jobs; they were denied equal pay or the chance to play sports solely because of their sex. HEW turned its back on most of them. Citizens who had every right to expect government help were either ignored or offered relief when it no longer mattered." HEW has claimed that limited resources in the Office of Civil Rights restrict the priority enforcement of Title 9, yet the PEER report shows that an average of just six complaints a year was given to each investigator assigned to cases involving the public schools.

In four years, PEER reports, with nearly 900 complaints, over 100 staff people in 10 regional offices devoted at least part-time to Title 9, and a small army of staff in Washington, very little has been accomplished. The following are the only accomplishments documented in the Government's own files:

Out of 16,000 school districts:

☐ Only 18 agreed to change their employment practices to treat both sexes fairly;

☐ Twenty-one agreed to upgrade sports programs for girls;

☐ Seventy-seven districts agreed to open up single-sex courses to both sexes;

☐ Twenty agreed to change sex-biased student rules; and

☐ Twenty-one institutions agreed to miscellaneous other changes.

Until fairly recently one subject was totally missing from curricula—the female experience. A new organization, the National Women's Studies Association (NWSA), has been formed to give women's studies some national direction and coordination. But its efforts are just beginning. "Compared with the number of colleges and universities in the country, the number of women's studies programs that are recognized and budgeted is small," said Blanche Hersh, coordinator of women's studies at Northeastern Illinois University in Chicago.

"Research on women is missing in the disciplines; and because the systematic scholarly study of women has not been fostered, there is no accurate presentation of the female experience," said Catherine Stimpson, a Barnard College professor who edits *Signs*, a scholarly journal in the field of women's studies.

"History has overlooked half of the human existence," noted Patricia Palmier, Ph.D. candidate at Harvard.

Pending legislation The new Vocational Education bill pending before Congress in early 1978 extends and revises previous legislation, mandating criteria for distributing vocational education funds within the States. Each State must allocate $50,000 of its Federal allotment for these purposes and must develop curricula and guidance programs reflecting women's changing roles.

The Career Implementation Act (S1328) would assure equal access to career education programs. The proposed Labor-HEW Appropriations Act (HR7555) carries an amendment that would ban timetables, ratios, and quotas for achieving equity in education. This would reduce effective enforcement of Federal regulations. Action has been postponed until later in 1978. The late Senator Humphrey proposed a bill (S255) that would establish a separate Department of Education. Another bill (HR7) would provide career education in elementary and secondary schools, but there is no indication that it attempts to eliminate sex stereotyping or discrimination.

ELECTIVE AND APPOINTIVE OFFICE

The President, Governors, political parties, women's organizations and foundations should join in an effort to increase the number of women in office, including judgeships and policy-making positions, and women should seek elective and appointive office in larger numbers than at present on the Federal, State and local level.

The President and, where applicable, Governors should significantly increase the numbers of women appointed as judges, particularly to appellate courts and supreme courts.

Governors should set as a goal for 1980 a significant increase and, by 1985, equal membership of men and women serving on all State boards and commissions. Concerted efforts should be directed toward appointing women to the majority of State boards and commissions which have no women members.

Political parties should encourage and recruit women to run for office and adopt written plans to assure equal representation of women in all party activities, from the precinct to the national level, with special emphasis on equal representation on the delegations to all party conventions.

The national parties should create affirmative action offices for women. Women's caucuses and other women's organizations within the party should participate in the selection of its personnel and in the design of its program, which should include greatly improved financial assistance for female delegates and candidates.

Background:

"Counting historically, the figures are astounding. Since the beginning of the Republic, there have been 1,726 Senators; of them, 11 have been women. Of a total 9,591 members of the House, only 87 have been women. It defies reason to believe that imbalances of this magnitude are not reflected in the outcome of the legislative process."

Women have been excluded from political power since the establishment of our Nation as the world's first constitutional democracy more than 200 years ago. The white male founders of a Nation born in a revolution based on the concept of representative government denied representation to women along with slaves, Indians, and criminals.

When women's rights advocates gathered for their first public meeting in Seneca Falls, New York in 1848, they focused on women's lack of political power as the source of their inability to change their lives or the laws that made them chattels of men. Paraphrasing the Declaration of Independence, they wrote a Declaration of Sentiments, which said, as one of many pointed indictments of male rule, "Having deprived her of this first right of a citizen, the elective franchise, thereby leaving her without representation in the halls of legislation, he (man) has oppressed her on all sides."

During much of the remaining century and until August 26, 1920, when the 19th amendment granting women suffrage at last became part of the Constitution, hundreds of thousands of women and their male sympathizers engaged in struggles for "this first right of a citizen." Even as they demanded the right to vote, a few hardy women anticipated the next step by running for office, including the Presidency. Their attempts met with ridicule.

Montana, one of several States that granted women the franchise before 1920, had the distinction of electing the first woman to Congress in 1917. Republican Jeanette Rankin added another distinction to her uniqueness—the first vote she cast in the House of Representatives opposed American entry into World War I.

The struggle for suffrage   In order to win the right to vote, women had to develop and master techniques that became standard fare in future political campaigns: they gathered petitions, rang doorbells, set up card files of voters and legislators, organized at the precinct level, lobbied, demonstrated, and held mammoth parades. During World War I, under the leadership of militant suffragist Alice Paul, some women used more radical techniques, such as chaining themselves to the fence outside the White House and going on hunger strikes in jail.

Looking back on the eventually successful struggle, suffrage leader Carrie Chapman Catt reported:

"To get the word 'male' in effect out of the Constitution cost the women of the country 52 years of pauseless campaign. ... During that time they were forced to conduct 56 campaigns of referenda to male voters; 480 campaigns to get Legislatures to submit suffrage amendments to voters; 47 campaigns to get State constitutional conventions to write woman suffrage into State constitutions; 277 campaigns to get State party conventions to include woman suffrage planks; 30 campaigns to get Presidential party conventions to adopt woman suffrage planks in party platforms; and 19 campaigns with 19 successive Congresses."

Once suffrage was achieved, the vast political experience amassed by women was not used to gain elective or appointive office for themselves in any significant numbers. Carrie Chapman Catt favored working within the existing political parties to achieve feminist goals; other suffrage leaders advocated organizing a separate women's political party or maintaining themselves as a special interest group. The die was cast when the newly formed League of Women Voters decided, after much debate, to concentrate on mobilizing public opinion behind reform programs and educating women in the tasks of citizenship on a nonpartisan basis.

Suffrage leaders went their separate ways, working hard and effectively for a variety of causes—peace and disarmament, abolition of child labor and sweat shops, consumer safeguards, social welfare laws, and protective legislation for women.

Within five years after ratification of the 19th amendment, the women's movement, which once had an estimated two million supporters, was down to a relatively small core of activists. Women did not vote in as large numbers as had been hoped, and they tended to follow male voting patterns. Women used their votes to elect men, but in fact, they had little choice, as few women had the resources to run for public office.

Lacking an independent power base, women became dependent on male party officials for concessions. The political power structure, including both elective and appointive office, remained virtually an all-male preserve, whereas women were consigned to the drudgery of inner party chores, the "housework" of politics.

Women in Congress The "astounding" figures at the beginning of this essay (quoted from an article by Ken Bode in *The New Republic,* March 4, 1978) illuminate the massive, persistent, and deliberate exclusion of women from the government of this Nation, in which they are a majority of the population.

Today, of the 100 members of the U.S. Senate, frequently described as "the most exclusive men's club in the world," only one is a woman—Muriel Humphrey, appointed recently as a temporary replacement for her deceased husband. Of the 435 members of the House of Representatives, only 18 are women.

It is a reflection on the process rather than on the women, many of whom have proved to be able legislators, that widowhood became the surest route to Congress. Of the total 99 women who have served in Congress since the beginning of this republic (Bode's count did not include Mrs. Humphrey), more than one-third (38) were appointed because they were widows of Members. The eight women appointed to the Senate served for only fractions of a term—months or weeks. The first woman to serve in the Senate was there for only one day. She was Rebecca Felton, an 87-year-old suffragist from Georgia, appointed in 1922 as a token fill-in until the regularly elected male Senator arrived.

Nine years passed before the second woman member appeared in the Senate—this time a widow appointee from Arkansas, Hattie Caraway.

Senator Caraway and Margaret Chase Smith of Maine, who was named to a House seat left vacant by her husband and then made it on her own to the Senate, have been the only women to serve in the Senate for more than one term.

In Congress, the highest number of women ever to be there at the same time was in the 1961-62 session when 20 women served.

Other 'astounding' figures The first woman appointed to the Cabinet was Frances Perkins, who was Secretary of Labor throughout the Roosevelt administration from 1933 to 1945. In the Eisenhower administration, Oveta Culp Hobby headed the Department of Health, Education and Welfare from 1953 to 1955. Carla Hills was Secretary of Housing and Urban Development in the Ford administration. President Carter is the first President to have two women in his cabinet: Secretary of Commerce Juanita Kreps and Secretary of Housing and Urban Development Patricia Harris. Thus, the total of women Cabinet officials throughout American history is five.

There has never been a woman President. There has never been a woman on the U.S. Supreme Court; and until the election in their own right of Connecticut Governor Ella Grasso in 1974 and Washington Governor Dixie Lee Ray in 1976, there had been only three women governors: Nellie Ross of Wyoming, who took over for her deceased spouse; "Ma" Ferguson of Texas; and Lurleen Wallace of Alabama, both of whom stood in for their husbands.

Only with the formation of the multipartisan National Women's Political Caucus in 1971, and subsequently with the Women's Education for Delegate Selection Fund, the Women's Education Fund, and the Women's Campaign Fund did women begin organizing on a nationwide scale to encourage and support women for elective and appointive office and to demand equal representation of women in the structures of the Democratic and Republican parties.

The efforts of these and other groups have helped to produce a significant increase in the number of women in office in recent years, particularly at the local level, but the overall picture remains predominantly male.

Figures supplied by the National Women's Political Caucus, the Women's Education Fund, the Center for the American Women and Politics at Eagleton Institute, Rutgers University, a major research facility, and the Congressional Clearing House on Women's Rights show the following:

In 1976-77, women held about eight percent of more than 10,000 public offices, including Members of Congress, State executives and cabinet officers, State legislators, county commissioners, mayors, and local council members. This compares with five percent in 1974-75. Of 41 elected lieutenant governors, only three are women.

Although there are 735 women mayors, only four are in major cities: San Antonio, Phoenix, Oklahoma City, and San Jose, California. A woman, Carol Bellamy, was recently elected president of the New York City Council, next in line to the mayor.

Women constitute 9.3 percent of State legislators. Of 1,981 State senators, 99 are women; of 5,581 State assembly members, 601 are women. Six States have no women in their senates, and 17 have only one.

In mid-1977, women were only 1.8 percent of State appellate and trial court judges: 110 women out of 5,940.

Women are making a little more progress on school boards, the elective office closest to home and easiest to attain. A survey by the National School Boards Association in 1976 found that nearly 20 percent of those serving were women, up from 11 percent in 1974. But one out of five remains a very small number, particularly since it is women who do most of the work in parents' associations and are most involved in the education of children.

Women hold only 15 percent of the appointed positions on State boards and commissions, and more than half of these bodies have no women at all.

Carter administration record

Women appointed to the Carter administration have been of extraordinarily high caliber, and in the Departments headed by Juanita Kreps and Patricia Harris, almost half the appointments have been women. Eleanor Holmes Norton, head of the Equal Employment Opportunity Commission, has also appointed equal numbers of women.

But on the whole, women remain notably underrepresented in Government policymaking positions. According to the Congressional Clearing House on Women's Rights, women hold only 16 percent of the top jobs in the administration, but the percentage also includes women appointed to nonsalaried commission posts. At the end of February 1978, of the so-called "plum" jobs in the administration, men held 466; women, 60.

President Carter has named six women to ambassadorships, the same number appointed by President Ford.

The judiciary Only 12 women have ever served in the Federal courts. No woman has been on the U.S. Supreme Court. Two have served on the U.S. Court of Appeals. The other 10 were in the U.S. District Court, Court of Claims, Court of Customs and Patent Application, and Customs Court. Judges are appointed to these courts for life. (There are other Federal judgeships in which the appointees serve for a term of years, such as the D.C. Superior Court, the D.C. Court of Appeals, the U.S. Tax Court, etc.)

At present, only six women are among the 492 lifetime Federal judges; there are currently 33 vacancies. There is one woman on the U.S. Court of Appeals and five in the U.S. District Courts. Of the 525 authorized Federal judgeships, only 1.1 percent are held by women.

Only one of the 35 Carter nominations to the Federal judiciary is a woman, and none of his 10 appointments to the U.S. Court of Appeals is a woman.

Last year, President Carter established a Circuit Judge Nominating Commission, consisting of panels of citizens to review applications for U.S. Courts of Appeals judgeships and, on the basis of merit, select five names to be sent to the White House from which the President would select his nominee. Of the 10 panels set up so far, their membership having been selected by administration officials, none is chaired by a woman.

An omnibus judgeship bill pending in Congress at this writing would increase the number of Federal judges by 140-to-150. Whether this will enlarge the opportunities for women or decrease the already miniscule percentage of women in the judiciary remains to be seen.

Public opinion The absence of significant numbers of women in public office can no longer be attributed to their unavailability or to public prejudice. A Gallup poll in September 1975 reported that 71 percent of Americans feel that the country would be governed as well *or better* with more women in public office, and 73 percent said they would vote for a qualified woman for President. Eighty percent said they would vote for a woman for Congress or for governor or mayor.

The use of the word "qualified" illustrates the double standard that still prevails for women in politics. Ruth Mandel, director of the Center for American Women and Politics, which has analyzed the background and records of elected women officials, said recently: "I never met a woman in office who didn't feel she had to be more effective, more successful, more dedicated, more responsible, more moral, more everything, in order to be taken seriously." At the same time, qualities of strength and leadership admired in male politicians are often viewed negatively, and described as overly aggressive when they appear in women political leaders.

Women seeking political office are handicapped by lack of money and support from party officials and the political "establishment." Few hold top positions in the business community or in organized labor, traditional sources of campaign funds. "There are 'old boy' networks," according to Pam Fleischaker of the Women's Campaign Fund. "What we need are some 'old girl' networks." Women State legislators who answered a Democratic National Committee questionnaire testified that they have a harder time raising money for their campaigns than men do. Americans for Democratic Action has estimated that it costs an incumbent Member of Congress close to $1 million to defend his seat. The candidate challenging him has to spend more, and when women run, they are usually the challengers.

Writing in *Politicks* March 14, 1978, political analyst Alan Baron noted: "Most women nominees run in districts their parties feel are almost impossible to win. So these women have virtually no chance; if the districts looked good, of course, prominent male politicians would be running."

The National Women's Political Caucus (NWPC) and other women's groups maintain that support for women candidates will increase when women gain more power within the political parties. A major focus of the NWPC, the Women's Education Fund, and other groups has been to obtain affirmative action programs to guarantee equal representation of women in all levels of the political parties and at their nominating conventions.

As a result of their efforts, the number of women delegates to the 1972 Democratic convention increased to 40 percent compared with 13 percent four years earlier, and to 30 percent in the Republican Party, up from 17 percent in 1968. In 1976, 31.4 percent of Republican delegates were women, but at the Democratic convention the number of women delegates declined to 34 percent because of a relaxation of affirmative action rules.

A women's caucus at the 1976 Democratic convention compromised on its demand for equal representation of women in future conventions in exchange for a commitment from Presidential nominee Jimmy Carter to give women significantly larger roles in the Government and the judiciary and within the Democratic Party.

Although a woman is co-chair of the Republican National Committee and women are organized into a caucus in the Democratic National Committee, neither party has yet made a major commitment to the election or appointment of more women to national office by seeking out potential women candidates, encouraging them to run, or by providing financial, political, or logistical support.

Can women make a difference?

There have not been enough women in high political office to determine whether their presence in large numbers would affect national or local policies. However, one can assume that there would be a positive effect on society. During the height of the Vietnam war, an analysis showed that the majority of women Members of Congress, Democrats and Republicans, opposed the war. A study by Shelah Leader, Ph.D., who taught political science at Cornell University, also found that women legislators tend to vote somewhat differently from men legislators. Women legislators in both parties, she reported, are more apt than men of their party to vote for laws that help women, particularly the Equal Rights Amendment, and for measures promoting maternal and child health. Another study showed that Congresswomen as a group were more responsive to the needs of senior citizens.

In *The New Republic* article quoted earlier (March 4, 1978), in which he said that the lack of women in Congress must surely affect the legislative process, Ken Bode noted: "Last fall, for example, when the Congress was deadlocked over the Hyde amendment on Federal payments for abortions and the budgets of two of the largest agencies of government were held hostage in the process, all 27 members of the conference committee debating the question of abortion, arguably of some concern to women, were male." He concluded: "No society that so systematically excludes half its members from the governing process can be called democratic."

Although the public climate has become more favorable to women in politics and government and women have made some gains, the fact remains that more than 200 years after the birth of our Nation, women hold only a shred of political power.

EMPLOYMENT

The President and Congress should support a policy of full employment so that all women who are able and willing to work may do so.

The President should direct the vigorous and expeditious enforcement of all laws, executive orders and regulations prohibiting discrimination in employment, including discrimination in apprenticeship and construction.

The Equal Employment Opportunity Commission should receive the necessary funding and staff to process complaints and to carry out its duties speedily and effectively.

All enforcement agencies should follow the guidelines of the EEOC, which should be expanded to cover discrimination in job evaluation systems. These systems should be examined with the aim of eliminating biases that attach a low wage rate to "traditional" women's jobs. Federal legislation to provide equal pay for work of equal value should be enacted.

Congress should repeal the last sentence of Sec. 703(h) of Title 7, Civil Rights Act (1964) which limits enforcement of that law by incorporating the more restrictive standards of the Equal Pay Act.

As the largest single employer of women in the Nation, the President should require all Federal agencies to establish goals and timetables which require equitable representation of women at all management levels, and appropriate sanctions should be levied against heads of agencies that fail to demonstrate a "good faith" effort in achieving these goals and timetables.

The Civil Service Commission should require all Federal agencies to establish developmental and other programs in consonance with upward mobility and merit promotion principles to facilitate the movement of women from clerical to technical and professional series, and make all Federal women employees in Grades (GS) 11 through 15 eligible for managerial positions.

Agencies and organizations responsible for apprenticeship programs should be required to establish affirmative action goals and timetables for women of all racial and ethnic origins to enter into "non-traditional" training programs.

Federal laws prohibiting discrimination in employment should be extended to include the legislative branch of the Federal Government.

In addition to the Federal Government, State and local governments, public and private institutions, business, industry and unions should be encouraged to develop training programs for the employment and promotion of women in policy-level positions and professional, managerial and technical jobs.

Special attention should be given to the employment needs of minority women, especially blacks, Hispanics, Asian Americans and Native Americans, including their placement in managerial, professional, technical and white collar jobs. English-language training and employment programs should be developed to meet the needs of working women whose primary language is not English.

The Congress should amend the Veteran Preference Act of 1944 (58 Stat. 387, Chapter 287, Title 5, US Code) so that veterans preference is used on a one-time-only basis for initial employment and within a three-year period after discharge from military service, except for disabled veterans. It should modify the "rule of three" so that equally or better qualified nonveterans should not be unduly discriminated against in hiring.

Title 7 of the 1954 Civil Rights Act should be amended to prohibit discrimination on the basis of pregnancy, childbirth or related medical conditions.

The President should take into account in appointments to the National Labor Relations Board and in seeking amendments to the National Labor Relations Act of 1936 the obstacles confronting women who seek to organize in traditionally nonunionized employment sections.

Unions and management should review the impact on women of all their practices and correct injustices to women.

Enforcement of the Fair Labor Standards Act and the Social Security Act as they apply to household workers and enforcement of the minimum wage should be improved.

Federal and State governments should promote Flexitime jobs, and pro-rated benefits should be provided for part-time workers.

All statistics collected by the Federal Government should be gathered and analyzed so that information concerning the impact of Federal programs on women and the participation of women in the administration of Federal programs can be assessed.

Background:
"The trend toward women working outside the home began building in the 50's and exploding in the 70's. For the last couple of years, American women have been pouring into the nation's offices, stores and factories...."

Women have always worked. No economy has ever been able to sustain itself on the work of men alone, and the United States is no exception. We began as a nation of farmers, skilled crafts and trades people, with men and women working to produce the goods and services needed to survive. Women wove cloth, made garments, candles and furniture, butchered and preserved food and often labored side by side with their husbands in the fields and in trade, while also bearing the responsibility for rearing children and keeping house. Women slaves worked as field hands and servants.

As the Industrial Revolution offered more free men a chance to work for wages outside home and farm, most women remained at home with the children and tasks that had not been industrialized. They were, of course, unpaid, and no monetary value has ever been attached to their indispensable labor in the home and family. But even in Colonial times, some women worked for money. The Declaration of Independence, for instance, was printed by Mary Goddard, a woman who ran a printing business in Baltimore.

Later, a rising proportion of women followed traditional women's work out of the home and into schools, hospitals, textile mills and clothing factories, canneries, retail stores and eventually into the clerical or "housekeeping" work of offices.

According to the U.S. Department of Labor Women's Bureau *Handbook on Women Workers*, "One of the most spectacular changes in the American economy in the past quarter century has been the dramatic increase in the number and proportion of women who work for pay outside the home. Over the last 25 years the number of women in the labor force more than doubled. ..."

By September 1977, 48.9 percent of women over age 16 were in the labor market, swelling their ranks to 40.5 million against 57.2 million men in the work force. They were 41 percent of the labor force.

"The trend toward women working outside the home began building in the 50's and exploding in the 70's," *The New York Times* reported November 19, 1977. "For the last couple of years, American women have been pouring into the nation's offices, stores and factories at rates surpassing all projections made by the Department of Labor."

The Women's Bureau handbook pointed to a number of factors contributing to the growth of women in the labor force: "... the trend toward smaller numbers of children in families and a change in the pattern of spacing children; the large increase in the number of families headed by women; and the increase in the life expectancy of women. Other major factors are the rapid growth of white collar jobs in which women are primarily employed and the increase in part-time employment opportunities." It also noted the particularly large increase in labor force participation by young married women with small children and the changing attitude toward careers for women outside the home.

The New York Times analysis cited inflationary pressures, "which gave rise to the two-paycheck family" and other economic, demographic, technological and social forces: "Women are marrying later, having fewer children, divorcing more often, living decades beyond the lifespans of their grandmothers. Hence, their work-life profiles are beginning to look more and more like those of men."

Accompanying the increase of women in the labor force has been their movement, albeit in very small numbers, into nontraditional jobs; they are going into the skilled trades, into bus and truck driving, into telephone repair work, into police and fire departments, into engineering, accounting, insurance and management, into the law and medicine.

But despite these breakthroughs and despite some highly publicized token "firsts" for women in traditionally male occupations, a majority of women workers remain clustered in retail, service, clerical and other low paying jobs, and even when they do the same work as men, they are often paid less. Women's average earnings continue to be much lower than those of men. In 1976, women who worked year round earned, on average, 60 percent of what male workers earned. This income gap has remained relatively unchanged for the past 20 years, according to the Labor Department. Industry saves billions of dollars each year by underpaying women.

For women who work, equality of the pay envelope and equality of job opportunities are still a long way off.

Full employment Unemployment has been higher for women than for men in 29 of the past 30 years. In 1977, three and a quarter million women were unemployed, or 8.2 percent, compared with 6.2 percent of men.

In November 1977, President Carter endorsed a modified version of the Humphrey-Hawkins full employment bill. In its original form, the bill would have provided jobs for all who are willing and able to work, using a combination of public and private sector employment programs. The modified bill, which was being debated in the House in March 1978, called for reducing unemployment to four percent by 1983, without creating new federally-funded jobs. It would, however, establish "as a national goal the fulfillment of the right of all Americans able, willing and seeking work to full opportunities for useful paid employment at fair rates of compensation."

Full employment is important to millions of women who must work for a living, to millions more caught up in the poverty-welfare cycle, to millions of others who would enter the labor market if jobs were available.

Like minority workers, women are often the last hired and the first fired, and in periods of recession they are especially vulnerable to loss of jobs. During times of mass unemployment, women are forced to compete with men for the same jobs, and this has resulted at times in a backlash against the women's movement, against affirmative action programs and against other efforts by women to remedy economic inequities.

Despite the huge numbers of women who must support themselves and their families, women are still too often seen as working for "pin money" and they are expected to "go back home" when jobs are scarce. A national policy committed in word and deed to full employment is essential to women and men alike.

Laws Banning job discrimination

Whether unemployment is high or low, most women are shortchanged in the job market. They are denied better paying jobs. They are denied so-called "male" jobs such as construction, which carry higher pay. They are denied promotions available to men. And in spite of laws to the contrary, they are still denied equal pay. Only a very few women have been able to force their employers to comply with laws prohibiting discrimination in employment.

Women have been discouraged from bringing charges of discrimination by cumbersome procedures, delays because of big backlogs of unsettled cases, fear of reprisal from their employers, costs of litigation, and court decisions that have supported flagrantly discriminatory practices of employers.

In testimony before the House Subcommittee on Employment Opportunities in October 1977, Assistant Secretary of Labor Donald Elisburg admitted that the system for monitoring affirmative action programs required of all Federal contractors "has quite simply not responded to the Department's policies and intentions." In August 1977, a Navy contractor lost all of its Federal contracts because of failure to develop an acceptable affirmative action program, but it was only the 13th contractor to be dropped since the program was created in 1965.

EEOC reorganization   In June, 1977, the Equal Employment Opportunity Commission was coping with a backlog of 130,000 complaints under Title 7 of the Civil Rights Act of 1964.

In February 1978, President Carter sent to Congress a sweeping plan to reorganize Federal enforcement of laws prohibiting employment discrimination, to cope with the backlog, and to keep up with new cases of discrimination. In addition to speedier processing of individual charges of discrimination, EEOC will undertake reviews of patterns and practices of employment that systematically keep women down. The plan consolidates within EEOC civil rights functions now dispersed in many Government agencies, providing a single civil rights agency for the Federal Government.

Pay discrimination is illegal under both the Equal Pay Act of 1963, which is part of the Fair Labor Standards Act enforced by the Department of Labor, and under Title 7 of the Civil Rights Act of 1964, enforced by the EEOC. The reorganization plan transfers to the EEOC responsibility for enforcing both laws.

Title 7 is the broader statute. It prohibits discrimination in hiring, promotion, assignment, and all other

terms and conditions of employment, including compensation of every kind. The Equal Pay Act is limited to discrimination in compensation, and it defines discrimination rather narrowly. It specifically permits differences in pay between men and women for work of "equal skill, effort, and responsibility" if they arise under a bona fide seniority plan. EEOC would be more free to attack discrimination in pay if it were not required to follow the restrictive definition of discrimination set forth in the Equal Pay Act.

With the reorganization, EEOC expects to investigate facts in discrimination charges by face to face conferences within 30 days after the filing of a complaint. A separate staff will be assigned to handle backlog cases. In seeking a budget supplement to implement the new procedures, EEOC Commissioner Eleanor Holmes Norton said she hoped "to eliminate the backlog in two years." The reorganization plan was to go into effect automatically within 60 days of its submission by the President unless rejected by either house of Congress.

Government as employer As the largest single employer of women, the Federal Government should be a model, setting high standards for private employers to match. It has declared itself in favor of equal opportunity and merit promotion for its own employees for a century. Yet affirmative action guidelines of the U.S. Civil Service Commission are weaker than those imposed, at least in theory, on Federal contractors. Civil Service guidelines do not, for instance, require Federal agencies to assess disparities in their employment profiles, or to develop annual goals for eliminating them.

Apprenticeships Women have traditionally been excluded from apprenticeship programs that lead to high paying skilled work. Those few admitted have had to deal with harassment from male coworkers. Labor Department figures for 1976 show that of 11 million skilled blue collar workers, only 545,038 were women. In that same year, the percentage of women carpenters, electricians, painters, plumbers, machinists, mechanics and stationary engineers ranged from less than one percent to about three percent of the totals.

The Department of Labor has announced it will soon issue final regulations requiring contractors on Federal construction jobs to employ women at least 3.1 percent of the total hours after one year, 5 percent after two years, and 6.9 percent after three years—very modest goals indeed.

Congress as employer Congress exempted itself as an employer from the equal employment opportunity laws, and its own staff practices fall far short of compliance. In July 1977, the House Commission on Administrative Review found that male administrative assistants averaged $39,000 a year while women administrative assistants averaged $17,000. The Commission suggested setting up a grievance panel with power to recommend but not enforce changes.

More recently, the Senate passed a bill prohibiting discrimination on the basis of sex, and the Senate Governmental Affairs Committee has developed guidelines for enforcement.

Fully Employed Women Continue To Earn Less Than Fully Employed Men of Either White or Minority* Races

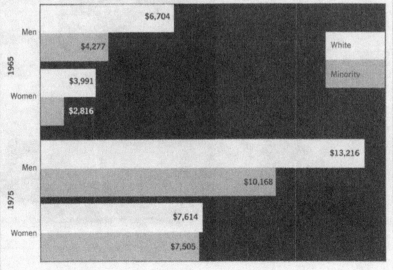

1965

Men — White $6,704 / Minority $4,277

Women — White $3,991 / Minority $2,816

1975

Men — White $13,216 / Minority $10,168

Women — White $7,614 / Minority $7,505

*Includes all races other than white.

Source: Prepared by the Women's Bureau, Employment Standards Administration, U.S. Department of Labor, from data published by the Bureau of the Census, U.S. Department of Commerce.

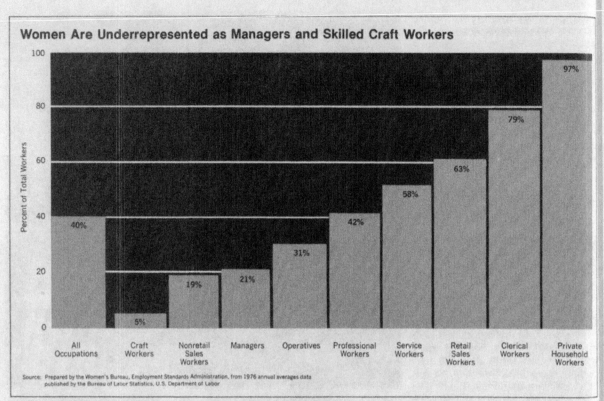

Women Are Underrepresented as Managers and Skilled Craft Workers

Percent of Total Workers

All Occupations	40%
Craft Workers	5%
Nonretail Sales Workers	19%
Managers	21%
Operatives	31%
Professional Workers	42%
Service Workers	58%
Retail Sales Workers	63%
Clerical Workers	79%
Private Household Workers	97%

Source: Prepared by the Women's Bureau, Employment Standards Administration, from 1976 annual averages data published by the Bureau of Labor Statistics, U.S. Department of Labor

In the House, an agreement was reached between management and employees to end discrimination. However, a report that suggested guidelines for resolution of grievances and called for enforcement of the agreement to eliminate discrimination was defeated in the first session of the 95th Congress; it was to be brought up again in 1978.

Minority women Minority women, who experience the double discrimination of race and sex, are more apt to be in the labor force than white women, but they are almost twice as likely to be unemployed and to suffer more job loss when the economy is depressed.

Unemployment rates in 1977 averaged 14 percent for black women aged 16 and over, compared with 8.2 percent for all women in this age range, according to the Department of Labor report entitled *Employment and Earnings*. Another Department of Labor publication reports that the unemployment rate for Hispanic women aged 20 and over in 1977 averaged 10.1 percent, also considerably higher than the seven percent rate for all women in this age range.

Minority women tend to work in the lower paid occupations because they have not had access to the training that would give them needed skills for higher paying white collar and professional jobs. The March 1977 figures for Hispanic women, for example, indicate that only 8.2 percent of Hispanic women were in professional and technical occupations compared with 15.5 percent of all women. More than one-fourth of all Hispanic women were factory and transport workers, compared with 15.4 percent of all women in March 1977.

Minority working women are also more apt to have small children, and to be the sole support of those children, making it imperative for them to have secure, well paying jobs, and access to child care services. (For more details, see background report on Minority Women plank.)

Veterans' preference   By law, women have had severely limited access to service in the armed forces, and consequently, the provisions of the Veteran Preference Act make it harder for them to gain entry into better paying government jobs. They also are threatened with losing their jobs when veterans are protected during a cutback. Because of preferential treatment accorded them, veterans (98 percent of whom are male) are twice as likely to be employed by the Federal Government. Because of preference, veterans who constitute 20 percent of those eligible for managerial Federal posts accounted for

34 percent of those selected in 1974, compared with 41 percent of eligible women, of whom only 27 percent were selected.

President Carter's plan to reorganize the Civil Service Commission proposes to limit somewhat the preferential treatment accorded veterans, but women would continue to be at a considerable disadvantage in competing for Federal employment opportunities.

Pregnancy discrimination   Congress is currently considering legislation that would make it illegal to exclude pregnancy from disability benefits for working women. The bill (S. 995) has passed the Senate; the House version (H.R. 6075) was reported out of the House committee on Education and Labor in March 1978, but an anti-abortion amendment was

added to the bill, making it objectionable to most of its supporters.

Unions   Women in clerical, operative, and service jobs who belong to unions earn a fifth to a fourth more money than non-union workers in their fields, according to an article by Virginia A. Bercquist in *The Monthly Labor Review*, October 1974, but the proportion is dropping because more women are going into unorganized, white collar jobs. These women would profit if they were organized in unions.

Congress is considering labor reform legislation that will make it easier for unions to organize and recruit new members. S. 1883 increases the penalties for employers who violate workers' rights to organize, and speeds up handling of unfair labor practices and union election cases. It assesses double back pay

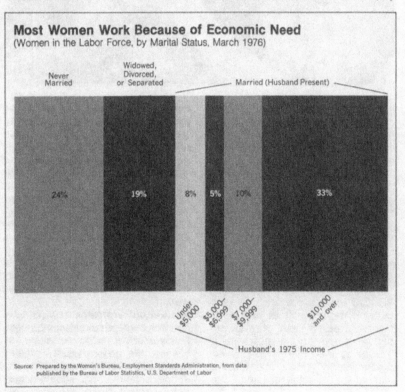

Most Women Work Because of Economic Need
(Women in the Labor Force, by Marital Status, March 1976)

Source: Prepared by the Women's Bureau, Employment Standards Administration, from data published by the Bureau of Labor Statistics, U.S. Department of Labor

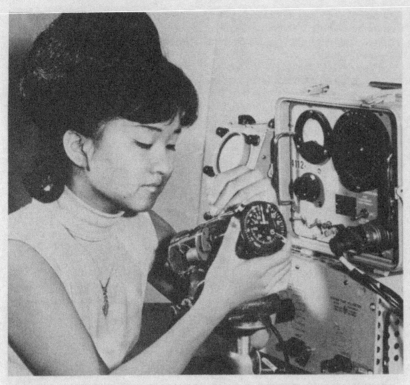

for illegal discharge compensation and provides remedies for refusal to bargain, mandatory election time limits, and cancellation of Government contracts with firms such as J.P. Stevens that violate the labor law.

Women are underrepresented in union leadership. Although women make up 21.3 percent of overall union membership, membership reports of the unions show that women held only seven percent of union governing board posts in 1974, and these are primarily in lesser posts. No woman has ever served on the policy-making AFL-CIO executive council. The federation's departments as well as its standing committees, trades departments and regional offices are all headed by men. Even in unions with predominantly female membership, such as the International Ladies Gar-

ment Workers Union, no women are in the top leadership. Perhaps the best record on women is held by the unaffiliated United Auto Workers, which has a Women's Department, has women filling about 14 percent of its top local union offices, and has helped support the Coalition of Labor Union Women.

More women in top union posts would result in more active organizing drives that would benefit men as well as women, more union support for equal employment opportunity and more attention to the needs of women workers.

Household workers   All but two percent of the several million household workers in the United States are women, the great majority of them members of minority groups. They are at the bottom of the income totem pole, without fringe benefits, promotions or vacations. Many are not getting the social security coverage required by law, or the legal minimum wage to which they have been entitled since May 1974.

Flexitime   Many women accept lower wages, limited opportunity, and few fringe benefits in order to work part-time or at hours compatible with their home responsibilities.

New York State, pleased by successful experiments, has authorized each State agency to set up alternative work schedules. These include flexitime, under which an employee has leeway of arrival and departure time providing she puts in the required number of hours; compressed work weeks, in which a full week's work is done in four long days, leaving a long weekend; and permanent part-time jobs, convenient for mothers and older workers.

Current Federal policy permits Federal agencies to develop flexitime policies within the limits of existing law, which requires an eight-hour day and 40-hour workweek.

Legislation pending before Congress would set up a three-year test program to experiment with all forms of alternative work schedules. Under the proposed bill (H.R. 7814) each agency could create such experiments if it so desired. The Civil Service Commission would monitor these test results and report back to the President and Congress. The House Committee on Post Office and Civil Service has reported the bill out and a similar bill, (S. 517) has been introduced into the Senate, but no action has been taken.

Data on women   Federal agencies are not now required to assess the impact of their programs on women or to publish information on how many women participate in policy-making decisions. Without such statistics, the progress of women cannot be charted, and finally assessed.

EQUAL RIGHTS AMENDMENT

The Equal Rights Amendment should be ratified.

Background:

"Women have waited more than 200 years for the equality promised by the Declaration of Independence to all men."

Women will not have equality in the United States unless it is guaranteed by the Constitution. In 1978, more than 200 years after the founding of this Nation, American women, 51.3 percent of the population, still are not the equals of men before the law. The rights they have are unclear and incomplete and are at the mercy of conflicting State laws and inconsistent court decisions. There is no clear standard to guide legislators in writing laws about women or to guide judges in interpreting them.

The Equal Rights Amendment has been ratified by 35 States, in which three-fourths of the U.S. population live. Approval by only three more States is needed to make the ERA part of the Constitution. Under the preamble to the amendment approved by Congress, ratification must be completed by March 22, 1979, unless Congress votes to extend that date.

Although a majority of Americans favor equal rights for women, ratification in the remaining States has been blocked by a well-organized, well-financed minority that relies on many of the same false arguments that were used to prevent women from getting the vote, namely, that ERA would destroy the family and morality. In some States, ratification has been held up by the negative votes of as few as two or three male legislators.

The Equal Rights Amendment itself is short and simple:

"Section I: Equality of rights under the law shall not be denied or abridged by the United States or by any State on account of sex.

"Section 2: The Congress shall have the power to enforce, by appropriate legislation, the provisions of this article.

"Section 3: This amendment shall take effect two years after the date of ratification."

Why an amendment is needed

The Declaration of Independence, signed in 1776, stated that "all men are created equal" and that governments derive their powers "from the consent of the governed." Women were not included in either concept. The original American Constitution of 1787 was founded on English common law, which did not recognize women as citizens or as individuals with legal rights. A woman was expected to obey her husband or nearest male kin, and if she was married, her person and her property were owned by her husband. The power of the ballot was denied to her by the States, which also denied it to Indians, slaves, the mentally unfit, and criminals.

It has been argued that the ERA is not necessary because the 14th amendment, passed after the Civil War, guarantees that no State shall deny to "any person within its jurisdiction the equal protection of the laws."

Early court decisions made clear, however, that women were not necessarily persons under the 14th amendment. In a famous lower court ruling in 1872, the judge in the trial of Susan B. Anthony, who was charged with committing a Federal offense because she voted in the 1872 Presidential election, stated flatly: "I have decided as a question of law ... that under the 14th amendment, which Miss Anthony claims protects her, she was not protected in a right to vote." The

judge prevented Anthony from appealing to the U.S. Supreme Court, but in the same year the high court approved an Illinois law prohibiting women from being licensed to practice law. *Bradwell* v. *State*, 83 U.S. 916, Wall. 130 (1872).

Since then, the Supreme Court has struck down some gender discrimination laws but has allowed others to stand, and no majority opinion has articulated sex as a "suspect" classification, like race, under the 14th amendment. See also *Goesart* v. *Cleary*, 335 U.S. 464 (1948) and *Hoyt* v. *Florida*, 368 U.S. 57 (1961). Indeed, the first time sex classifications were struck down by the Supreme Court was as recently as 1971. *Reed* v. *Reed*, 404 U.S. 71 (1971).

If the courts had interpreted sex classifications by the same strict scrutiny standard as race classifications under the 14th amendment, the need for a constitutional amendment would have been less compelling. When the court does consider a particular basis of classification—such as race—to be suspect, it triggers a "compelling State interest" standard of judicial review which, as a practical matter, the State can rarely, if ever, satisfy. Thus, under constitutional challenges, race-based classifications are often struck down as unconstitutional.

Just as women were not included under the 14th amendment, they were also omitted from the 15th amendment, which enfranchised former slaves, but males only. This exclusion from coverage resulted in a century-long struggle that ended with approval of the 19th amendment guaranteeing women the right to vote.

Aside from the fact that women have been subjected to varying, inconsistent, and often unfavorable decisions under the 14th amendment, the Equal Rights Amendment is a more immediate and effective remedy to sex discrimination in Federal and State laws than a case-by-case interpretation under the 14th

MOST OF THE U.S. IS FOR THE ERA

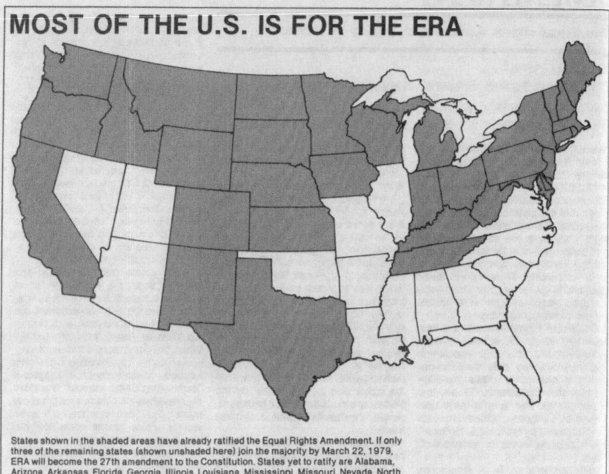

States shown in the shaded areas have already ratified the Equal Rights Amendment. If only three of the remaining states (shown unshaded here) join the majority by March 22, 1979, ERA will become the 27th amendment to the Constitution. States yet to ratify are Alabama, Arizona, Arkansas, Florida, Georgia, Illinois, Louisiana, Mississippi, Missouri, Nevada, North Carolina, Oklahoma, South Carolina, Utah, Virginia.

amendment could ever be. The critical distinction is that under the ERA, sex is a prohibited classification, not a classification that is subject to some level of judicial review and that, therefore, may or may not be sustained.

What the ERA will do   In interpreting the ERA, the courts can be expected to rely on the legislative history as expressed in the majority report of the Senate Judiciary Committee and in the congressional debates on passage of the amendment. That the courts will interpret the ERA responsibly and with an understanding of the underlying legislative intent is evident from the existing decisions interpreting equal rights amendments in those 16 States which have such amendments in their constitutions.

Based on this record, it is fair to say that:

ERA will enshrine in the Constitution the value judgment that sex discrimination is wrong.

ERA will require the Federal Government and each State to review and revise all laws and official practices to eliminate discrimination based on sex.

ERA will insure that governments do not enact future laws that discriminate on the basis of sex. Many State and Federal laws have been revised and new laws enacted to eliminate sex discrimination as a result of the debates on ERA. But these laws could be changed by new Congresses and new State legislatures, and failure to ratify the ERA may result in some losses of recent gains. A constitutional amendment provides a permanent basis for progress.

50

ERA will be the basis for recognition of the principle (ignored in most family law) that the homemaker's role in marriage has economic value and that marriage is a full partnership. Under Pennsylvania's ERA, for example, the State supreme court ruled in 1975 that non-monetary contributions to a marriage, such as household work and child care, must be considered when a couple's household goods are divided as a result of divorce.

ERA will insure equality of opportunity in public schools, state colleges and universities, employment training programs of Federal, State, or local governments, and in governmental recreation programs.

ERA will insure equal opportunity, privileges, and benefits in all aspects of Government employment.

ERA will insure that families of women workers receive the same benefits as families of men workers under the social security law, Government pension plans, and workers' compensation laws.

ERA will insure that married women can engage in business freely and dispose of separate or community property on the same basis as married men.

ERA will give the same rights to a woman as to a man in marital law and allow a married woman to maintain a separate domicile for voting purposes, for passports, for car registration, etc. (A husband may be in the military service and maintain his legal domicile "back home," but his wife may want to vote for the local school board where the kids go to school, for example.)

What ERA will not do   *ERA will NOT* change or weaken family structure. Courts do not interfere in the private relationship of an ongoing marriage, and ERA will strengthen families by implicitly giving value to each spouse's contribution to and support of the other.

ERA will NOT require the States to permit homosexual marriage. The amendment is concerned with discrimination based on gender and has nothing to do with sexual behavior or with relationships between people of the same sex. After the State of Washington had passed an Equal Rights Amendment to its own constitution, the State supreme court held that a State law prohibiting homosexual marriage was not invalidated.

ERA will NOT have any impact on abortion laws. The U.S. Supreme Court decisions on abortion were made under present constitutional provisions addressed to privacy issues and based on the 1st, 9th, and 14th amendments.

ERA will NOT require co-ed bathrooms. The legislative history to which the courts would refer makes it clear that "the amendment would not require that dormitories or bathrooms be shared by men and women." Sexual equality will not be obtained at the expense of the constitutionally guaranteed right to privacy.

ERA will NOT require that there be as many women as men in combat roles in the military service, but it will give women equal access to the skills, training, education, and other benefits that military services provide. There is no draft now, but if a national emergency requires one in the future or if it is reinstated for any reason, women would be subject to the draft just as men would be, under a system that would undoubtedly provide for exemptions for specific categories, e.g., parents of dependent children, persons with physical, mental, or emotional illness, conscientious objectors, and others.

The military services would have the same right to assign women as they have to assign men, but this does not mean that women would be automatically assigned to combat, unless they volunteered for such duties. As a matter of fact, in modern warfare a very small percentage of men in the armed services actually serve in combat, and the decision as to who is best equipped for combat is up to the commanders. Meanwhile, to deny women the opportunity to freely enter the military services today is to deny them an equal expression of patriotism as well as career, educational, and job opportunities.

ERA will NOT be a "gigantic power grab by the Federal bureaucracy" to take over jurisdiction that now belongs to the States, as is frequently charged. Once ERA is ratified, States and the Federal Government have two years within which to bring their laws into conformity. If this is not done, the courts may declare invalid or extend to both sexes State or Federal laws or practices that are contrary to the ERA. The State will still be able to enact a new law or regulation that is in conformity. The first 10 amendments to the Constitution—the Bill of Rights—guarantee that the States will not pass laws infringing on freedom of speech, freedom of religion, freedom of the press, freedom from unreasonable search and seizure, the right to trial by jury, etc. None of these amendments denies States the right to enact laws

in these areas, but they do not have the right to enact laws that violate these constitutional guarantees. Adoption of ERA will guarantee that neither the States nor the Federal Government will pass laws or engage in official practices that discriminate because of gender.

ERA opponents cite, as the basis for some of their claims about the effects of the amendment, testimony by Professors of Law Paul Freund and Philip Kurland and interpretations of former Senator Sam Ervin. However, they fail to quote these law professors on the importance of legislative history in interpreting the ERA. Both Freund and Kurland testified in Congress before the committee reports on ERA were issued and before the debates in the House and Senate that established the legislative history of the ERA and the intent of Congress in approving the amendment.

Senator Ervin based his interpretation on his belief that the language of the amendment is so clear that the courts will have no choice but to interpret it his way and that, therefore, they will not look to legislative history. However, all the other members of the Senate Judiciary Committee and large majorities of both the House and Senate interpreted the language differently from Senator Ervin.

Where it stands now The Equal Rights Amendment, the 27th amendment, was passed by a vote of 354 to 23 in the U.S. House of Representatives on October 12, 1971. The U.S. Senate approved it March 22, 1972 by a vote of 84 to 8 after decisively rejecting, one by one, nine different proposals to alter and defeat it. It will become part of the U.S. Constitution when three-fourths of the States (38) have ratified it, and it will go into effect two years after the ratification date.

As of March 1978, ERA has been ratified by 35 States: Alaska, California, Colorado, Connecticut, Delaware, Hawaii, Idaho, Indiana, Iowa, Kansas, Kentucky, Maine, Maryland, Massachusetts, Michigan, Minnesota, Montana, Nebraska, New Hampshire, New Jersey, New Mexico, New York,

North Dakota, Ohio, Oregon, Pennsylvania, Rhode Island, South Dakota, Tennessee, Texas, Vermont, Washington, West Virginia, Wisconsin, and Wyoming.

Three States—Idaho, Nebraska, and Tennessee—later voted to rescind ratification, a move of doubtful legality. An opinion issued by Assistant Attorney General John Harmon declares the States do not have the power under the Constitution to rescind. Congressional precedents and the 14th and 15th amendments provide the underpinning for this view.

Fifteen States have not ratified: Alabama, Arizona, Arkansas, Florida, Georgia, Illinois, Louisiana, Mississippi, Missouri, Nevada, North Carolina, Oklahoma, South Carolina, Utah, and Virginia.

Who supports ERA ERA has been endorsed by the last six Presidents of the United States, passed by the Congress, ratified by 35 States, approved by the Democratic and Republican national committees, and supported by more than 200 organizations, including: American Association of University Women; American Baptist Women; American Bar Association; the AFL-CIO and 26 affiliated unions; American Home Economics Association; American Jewish Congress; American Veterans Committee; B'nai B'rith Women; Board of Church and Society, United Methodist Church; Catholic Women for the ERA; Child Welfare League of America; Christian Church (Disciples of Christ); Coalition of Labor Union Women; Common Cause; General Federation of Women's Clubs; Girl Scouts of the U.S.A.; League of Women Voters; Lutheran Church; NAACP; National Catholic Coalition for the ERA; National Coalition of American Nuns; National Council of Churches (of Christ); National Council of Jewish Women; National Council of Negro Women; National Federation of Business and Professional Women's

Clubs; National Organization for Women; National Secretaries Association; National Woman's Party; National Women's Political Caucus; United Auto Workers; United Presbyterian Church, U.S.A.; and Young Women's Christian Association.

The outlook Under a seven-year limitation set by Congress, ERA must be ratified by March 22, 1979. If it is not ratified by then, the amendment would have to be reintroduced in Congress and go through the entire ratification process again. However, in the opinion of the Department of Justice, Congress may vote to change the date by which ratification must be completed. A bill has been introduced by Congresswoman Elizabeth Holtzman to extend that deadline to 1986.

ERAmerica, a coalition of major organizations set up to fight for ratification, NOW, the League of Women Voters, the American Association of University Women, the Business and Professional Women, other groups, and an overwhelming majority of the delegates to the National Women's Conference are making final ratification of ERA a priority.

The ratification battle has narrowed down to a few States where some legislators, despite public commitments to support ERA, have succumbed to last-minute political pressures and voted against it. Pro-ERA forces are conducting national education campaigns on the issue and are lobbying, fundraising, and organizing support and campaigning for defeat of anti-ERA legislators. More than 80 major national organizations are boycotting nonratified States and are cancelling meetings that were scheduled to be held there. An important factor in the National Commission's decision to hold its National Women's Conference in Houston was that Texas has ratified the ERA.

Women have waited more than 200 years for the equality promised by the Declaration of Independence to all men. Two years after the United States of America celebrated its Bicentennial, it is time to extend democracy to all American citizens and to put women into the Constitution at last.

HEALTH

Federal legislation should establish a national health security program. Present Federal employees' health insurance policies and any future national health security program should cover women as individuals.

Health insurance benefits should include:

☐ Preventive health services.

☐ Comprehensive family planning services.

☐ Reproductive health care.

☐ General medical care.

☐ Home and health support services.

☐ Comprehensive mental health services.

States should license and recognize qualified midwives and nurse practitioners as independent health specialists, and State and Federal laws should require health insurance providers to directly reimburse these health specialists.

States should enact a patient's bill of rights which includes enforceable provisions for informed consent and access to and patient ownership of medical records.

Federal legislation should be enacted to expand the authority of the Food and Drug Administration to:

☐ Require testing of all drugs, devices, and cosmetics by independent sources other than the manufacturers.

☐ Extend test periods, beyond the present grossly inadequate one year or 18 months.

☐ Have immediate recall of hazardous, unsafe, or ineffective drugs, devices, and cosmetics.

☐ Require a patient information package insert with every drug and device marketed. This insert should include warnings about possible risks.

☐ Require by law the reporting of significant adverse reactions noted by physicians or by the manufacturers of drugs, devices, and cosmetics.

Congress should appropriate funds for increased research on safe, alternative forms of contraception, particularly male contraception. Research to identify the risks of present forms of contraception and estrogen-based drugs should be given higher priority. Outreach programs should be established by the Department of Health, Education and Welfare to identify and provide services for victims of hazardous drug therapy.

The Department of Health, Education and Welfare should provide additional funds for alcohol and drug abuse research and treatment centers designed to meet the special needs of women.

Federal and State governments should encourage fair representation of women on all Federal, State, and private health policy and planning bodies.

Congress should appropriate funds to establish and support a network of community-based health facilities to offer low cost, reproductive health services.

The President should appoint a special commission to conduct a national investigation of conditions in nursing homes and mental institutions and propose standards of care.

Congress should appropriate funds to encourage more women to enter the health professions, and Congress should allocate funds only to those health professions schools whose curricula are clearly nonsexist.

The Secretary of Health, Education and Welfare should undertake a special investigation of the increase in surgical procedures such as hysterectomy, Ceasarean section, mastectomy, and forced sterilization.

Background:
"Women have begun to rebel against male-dominated health care."

Through most of human history, women have been the healers. They watch the health of their families, and paid or unpaid, they still do most of the work of caring for the sick, the disabled, and the elderly. But policy on professional medical care, drugs, research, hospitals, and environmental hazards is controlled by men who are frequently unsympathetic if not actually ignorant of the special health needs of women.

One example of this unresponsiveness is the danger to women exposed to chemicals used in kitchens, offices, factories, and bathrooms, as well as in cosmetics and hair dyes. According to the Massachusetts Coalition for Safety and Health, substances that can harm reproductive organs or fetuses include trichloroethylene, used by typists in white-out correction fluid, and the radiation from microwave ovens used by homemakers and flight attendants.

Mental health services are another area of neglect. According to Phyllis Chesler, author of Women and Madness, these are used twice as often by women as men but are still not available to many women who need help. Health education is needed to slow the rapid rise of smoking among teenage girls, as documented by the American Cancer Society. Family planning services are also needed, particularly for teenagers, among whom an "epidemic" of pregnancy is occurring. Research is needed to find safer contraceptives. And there are many other health needs of women that are not being met.

Women require more health care than men. They bear the children. On average, they live longer than men and are more likely to acquire the age-connected chronic diseases that require many health care visits.

In the past few years, women have begun to rebel against male-dominated health care. Health was the third most popular issue at the IWY State meetings held prior to the Houston Conference. More than 400 resolutions were passed recommending changes in health care policy and priorities.

Health insurance Many existing health insurance plans on which any future national health program might be based cover married women as dependents of men rather than as individuals in their own right. A woman who is divorced or widowed may lose her health coverage. A single woman may be denied pregnancy benefits. A man does not lose out on health insurance because he chooses to remain single, or because his marriage is disrupted by death or divorce. And family-based health insurance is expensive. According to the Committee on National Health Insurance, administration of the Canadian national health plan is cheaper in part because everyone is covered as an individual.

Women often get shortchanged in health insurance policies coverage of their unique health needs.

In their 1977 report published by the Women's Equity Action League, "Sex Discrimination in Insurance," Naomi Naierman, Ruth Brannon, and Beverly Wall found that a majority of new health plans do not cover maternity, whereas those that do charge prohibitively expensive rates for the restricted benefits offered.

They also reported that working women are seldom covered for loss of income due to disabilities or pregnancy. Many policies still exclude all conditions related to the female reproductive system. The general ex-

clusion of preventive health care deprives women of insurance coverage for breast and uterine cancer screening and family planning services, while the general exclusion of mental health services bears more heavily on women than on men because women are more apt to use them.

Finally, health insurance policies make little or no provision for the care of a chronically ill patient at home, where most of them are kept. Without any money for even occasional help, that care can become an intolerable human burden for the family, and that burden almost invariably falls on a wife or mother.

Many national health programs intended to remedy these and other defects of the medical care system have been proposed in Congress, but the most comprehensive are the Kennedy-Corman Health Security Act (H.R. 22 and S. 3), which has been introduced for eight consecutive years, and the Health Services Act (H.R. 6894), introduced by Congressman Ron Dellums (D., Calif.).

Midwives and nurse practitioners Few American babies are born naturally. Drugs, a dramatically rising proportion of Caesarean births—Medical World News says they doubled between 1970 and 1976—and the routine use of fetal monitoring of the infant during labor have made the normal event of childbirth into a medical procedure that often appears to be designed more for the convenience of hospitals and doctors than for the mother. "Is it beneficial to the woman and her newborn to have her lie flat on her back during labor and delivery," asks Dr. Hania W. Ris of the University of Wisconsin, "or does it only provide comfort for the obstetrician?"

Male medical control of childbirth has not necessarily made it safer. According to Doris Haire, president of the American Foundation for Maternal and Child Health, mothers and babies are more apt to live and babies are less apt to be damaged in countries such as Sweden and France where more parents choose to have their children born at home under the care of a trained midwife. Ann H. Sablosky, a social worker on the board of the National Women's Health Network, studied the record of midwifery in the United States and concluded that midwives could make the majority of uncomplicated births cheaper and more natural without sacrificing safety.

Nurse practitioners, nurse and lay midwives, and physician assistants are new categories of health workers dominated by women. Nurse practitioners are registered nurses qualified by extra training to practice nursing independently of the supervision of a physician. Yet under Medicare rules requiring the approval of a doctor, these independent practitioners cannot be reimbursed for their fees.

Patient's Bill of Rights The doctor's word is law, but women are beginning to question some of the heroic remedies practiced on their bodies, and consumer health advocates share their doubts. In 1977 Undersecretary Hale Champion of the Department of Health, Education and Welfare testified that American surgeons were making work for themselves by prescribing needless operations. Evidence is accumulating that many mutilating mastectomies might not have been necessary and, according to Peg Beals, past president, International Childbirth Association of Ann Arbor, and a nurse herself, some doctors prefer Caesareans because they save time and produce larger fees.

In December 1977 HEW Secretary Joseph A. Califano, Jr. admitted that Federal officials had not been "nearly meticulous enough" in preventing over-zealous doctors, social workers, and prison officials from forcing women to be sterilized.

In her article, "Forced Sterilization," in the February 1976 issue of *Sister Courage,* Dr. Judith Herman estimated that 20 percent of married black women have been sterilized, compared with seven percent of married white women. The Committee to End Sterilization Abuse, an organization based in New York City, contends that more than a third of the women of childbearing age in Puerto Rico have been sterilized. According to *The New York Times* of May 24, 1977, Dr. Donnie Uri estimates that one out of every four American Indian women has been sterilized, in many cases without realizing what was being done.

In 1978 HEW was adopting new, stricter standards for sterilization operations funded by the Federal Government. The new rules require the written consent of the patient in her primary language, a 30-day waiting period, with certain exemptions, and a statement from the doctor that he/she has informed the patient of the risks and benefits of the operation and the fact that her welfare or Medicaid benefits will not be cut off should she refuse. The Federal Government will no longer fund hysterectomies performed solely for contraception.

Experimentation on women without their consent has also been documented. According to an article in the June 15, 1973 issue of *Medical World News,* for instance, a San Antonio, Texas physician gave placebos instead of contraceptive pills to 75 Chicana women who had come to the clinic for help in preventing pregnancies. Eleven unplanned pregnancies resulted from this "experiment." A Senate Health and Scientific Research subcommittee heard testimony March 7, 1978 from Food and Drug Administration Commissioner Donald Kennedy that physicians hired by drug companies have made misrepresentations to women

in labor to win their "informed consent" for use of experimental drugs on their newborn babies.

Women are especially disadvantaged by the reluctance of doctors and hospitals to let patients see their own medical records. According to a compilation made for the Health Law Project of Philadelphia in 1976 by Carole F. Soskin, little more than a dozen States require doctors and hospitals to make any disclosure of their medical records to a patient. None gives the patient unconditional access, much less ownership.

A Colorado statute, one of the most favorable, makes all records available for the patient to inspect except those referring to a psychological problem. Outright ownership is the only practical way for a woman to be able to take her medical records with her when she moves to a new community or travels.

Safety Women take two-thirds of all drugs prescribed by physicians, according to a study reported by Janet Holloway to the American Public Health Association Women's Caucus in 1976. Not only do millions of women take contraceptive pills every day, but women live longer and doctors are much more apt to prescribe "mood" drugs for them. According to Holloway, women take 72 percent of the antidepressants, 76 percent of the analgesics, and most of the tranquilizers. The cosmetics they use may be an additional risk to their health.

Under existing food and drug laws, powerful new compounds whose long-term effects are unknown are tested on the public at large. According to the Women's Health Concerns Committee, valium is the most frequently prescribed drug in the United States, yet it is only 10 years old. Its effects over a long period of time have not yet been determined. The Committee also points out that there is no serious testing of the vaginal douches many women use, and that regulation of the Intra-Uterine Device (IUD) for contraception leaves much to be desired. Federal control over the IUD was not established until 1976, and then only over new devices to be marketed in the future, leaving unregulated the IUD's that four to six million women were already using.

The contraceptive pill has been shown to cause blood clots, stroke, heart attack, high blood pressure, urinary tract infections, gall bladder disease, and deaths in some of the presumably healthy 10 million women who take it every day. An article by Jerry Weaver in the March-April 1976 issue of *Women and Health* cites detailed evidence of the serious and sometimes fatal side effects of the pill for certain groups of women.

The National Women's Health Network reports that estrogen hormone supplements, prescribed in hard-sell advertising campaigns to make women "forever feminine," have been proven neither safe nor effective in relieving menstrual and menopausal symptoms. The drugs have been linked with cancer of the breast and uterus. DES (diethylstilbestrol), widely prescribed to prevent miscarriages, has been shown to produce a number of cases of vaginal cancer in the young daughters of women who received this therapy. Only since 1978, after a sharply contested lawsuit by consumer advocates, have pharmaceutical manufacturers been required to provide labeling information on the risks and benefits of estrogen drugs.

In March 1978 the Senate subcommittee mentioned earlier was hearing testimony on legislation supported by the Carter administration to strengthen Federal control over the testing of new drugs, to monitor adverse effects of drugs already on the market, and to make it easier to withdraw those which prove dangerous.

In spite of the proven hazards of the contraceptive pill and the IUD, only two percent of the money spent on research by the National Institutes of Health has been earmarked for research on human reproduction in recent years.

Alcoholism and women   Alcohol is a problem for almost as many women as for men, according to the National Council on Alcoholism. Among heavy drinkers, females are twice as likely as males to develop cirrhosis of the liver, and gynecological problems and miscarriages may also be associated with alcoholism. Authorities disregard women alcoholics and shame keeps them from asking for help.

Margaret Rudolph, director of the National Association of Halfway Houses, reports that only 30 of the 600 centers for helping alcoholics serve women exclusively. The Women's Health Network says that less than three percent of the treatment grants by the National Institute on Alcohol Abuse and Alcoholism are for women's programs.

Mental institutions   More women than men are subject to the inhuman conditions prevailing in many mental institutions and nursing homes for the elderly. In *Women and Madness,* Phyllis Chessler reported that many women are involuntarily committed to mental institutions where they are physically abused, medically neglected, and forced to work as cooks and cleaners. Because of their greater longevity, women are a majority of the occupants in nursing homes and homes for the elderly. The poor level of care in many of these institutions has been repeatedly exposed by congressional and other investigations.

Reproductive health   The rise in teenage pregnancies, documented in the background on the Reproductive Freedom plank, is due at least in part to the difficulty teenagers have in obtaining reliable, low-cost, confidential reproductive health services. When legal abortions are not available or are too expensive, women are forced to rely on dangerous, illegal methods of ending their pregnancies.

In October 1977, a Mexican American woman died in a hospital in McAllen, Texas from complications caused by a cheap abortion in a nearby town, just after the U.S. Supreme Court ruled that States did not have to fund abortions under Medicaid. "The Government cannot stop abortions," *The New York Times* commented. "It can only stop paying for them."

Women's health centers   In many communities, women themselves have had to provide birth control and abortion information and services that doctors and hospitals have been reluctant to offer. Since the U.S. Supreme Court decision of 1973 upholding the right to abortion, the number of women's health centers has increased to more than 400, according to Carol Downer of the Los Angeles Feminist Women's Health Center. Where State law permits, at least 50 of these centers perform out-patient abortions at one third the cost of the procedure in hospitals. The low-cost, supportive educational services and nonjudgmental atmosphere of these women-run facilities make them especially helpful to teenage women.

Medical policy   Many observers agree with Dr. Vicente Navarro of Johns Hopkins University that the health care of women will not improve until more women are involved in making medical policies. According to an estimate made by the Women's Work Project, published in the May-June 1976 issue of *Women and Health,* 80 percent of the health workers in the United States are women, but 90 percent of the physicians and administrators who make health policy are men. The Association of American Medical Colleges reports that an alltime high of 25 percent of the entering medical school classes in the fall of 1977 were women. But, according to Mary Roth Walsh, author of *Doctors Wanted: No Women Need Apply,* the number of women in influential medical positions remains unchanged.

HOMEMAKERS

The Federal Government and State legislatures should base their laws relating to marital property, inheritance, and domestic relations on the principle that marriage is a partnership in which the contribution of each spouse is of equal importance and value.

The President and Congress should support a practical plan for covering homemakers in their own right under social security and facilitate its enactment.

Alimony, child support, and property arrangements at divorce should be such that minor children's needs are first to be met and spouses share the economic dislocation of divorce. As a minimum, every State should enact the economic provisions of the Uniform Marriage and Divorce Act proposed by the Commissioners on Uniform State Laws and endorsed by the American Bar Association. Loss of pension rights because of divorce should be considered in property divisions. More effective methods for collection of support should be adopted.

The Bureau of the Census should collect data on the economic arrangements at divorce and their enforcement, with a large enough sample to analyze the data by State.

The Federal and State governments should help homemakers displaced by widowhood, divorce, or desertion to become self-sufficient members of society through programs providing training and placement and counseling on business opportunities, advice on financial management, and legal advice.

Background:
"...legal realities of a marriage contract degrade and demean the wife's role."

The low value that our society places on the homemaker's role is reflected in support laws, property laws, divorce laws, and inheritance laws. If our children, sons as well as daughters, cannot expect that work in the home will be recognized as of equal value and as deserving equal dignity with work done outside the home, the institution of the family and society itself will suffer.

When a man and a woman enter into a marriage, they often believe that they are entering a cooperative partnership, but the legal realities of a marriage contract degrade and demean the wife's role.

Wife as chattel The low value placed on the wifely role has its roots in English common law. In his 1765 Commentaries on the Laws of England, William Blackstone wrote that "a wife is a superior servant to her husband ... only chattel with no personality, no property and no legally recognized feelings or rights." Property laws, inheritance laws, and domestic relations laws in the United States grew out of the same principles.

While many changes have been made as a result of the women's movements in the 19th and 20th centuries, many discriminatory laws remain. For example:

In 1977 in Georgia, the house occupied by a family, if titled in the husband's name, belongs only to him, even if the wife is the wage earner and makes all payments. In 1977 in Arkansas, a husband can dispose of all property, even jointly owned, without his wife's consent. In Maine joint business profits belong solely to the husband. In 43 of the 50 states a woman cannot charge her husband with rape even though they are living apart and he forces her to have sexual relations with him.

Homemakers' lack of security
The full-time homemaker who works at home—unpaid—to attend to the family's day-to-day maintenance has no economic security. She receives no pay. She has no health or disability insurance in her own right. She has no retirement plan and receives no social security payments in her own right. If she "loses her job" through widowhood or divorce, she is ineligible for unemployment insurance.

The assumption is that her husband will support her, but the courts have been unwilling to interfere with the "sanctity" of the marital relationship, and in most States there is no way to enforce support unless she files for divorce or separation. When living under the same roof, the husband may give his wife as little as he wishes to run the home regardless of his income. He may be required to pay any bills she incurs, but merchants will be quick to deny credit to a wife if they believe they may have to sue her husband in order to collect.

Not only does the law assume a wife's work is not worth much, but it also assumes that the money belongs to the man who earned it even though the woman may have managed and saved it.

A homemaker does not legally have an equal share of the couple's economic assets except in eight community property states: Arizona, California, Idaho, Louisiana, Nevada, New Mexico, Texas, and Washington. Even then the wife may not have real control. In Louisiana the husband has total control and charge of all community property, including the wife's earnings.

Homemakers and social security
Homemakers who have not worked in employment covered by social security have no protection in their own right. Divorced women married less than 10 years (20 years for benefits prior to January 1979) cannot collect social security benefits based on their husband's earnings. (The Bureau of the Census reports

that 25 percent of divorces occur after 15 years of marriage.) If a divorced man remarries, his second wife is eligible for benefits after one year. If he dies, his second wife may become entitled to benefits if she had been married to him for nine months.

Alimony and child support The best evidence of the worth ascribed to the homemaker in the law can be found in property settlements at divorce, the awarding of alimony, or maintenance and child support. With the Bureau of the Census now reporting one divorce for every two marriages, divorce has become a major source of economic hardship for women.

The National IWY Commission's Committee on the Homemaker found many divorced wives and their children living on welfare, even when the husband was under a court order to support them. The women and children were living on an average of $218 a month, while the men were living on close to $800 a month. (The National Commission has published reports on the legal status of homemakers in each State.)

The RAND Corporation surveyed one-parent households in California and found that three out of five were on welfare, and almost all were headed by women.

There are not enough data available on economic arrangements at divorce to analyze them on a State-by-State basis, but all available evidence indicates that alimony is granted in only a very small percentage of cases; that fathers by and large are contributing less than half to the support of children in divided families; and that enforcement of alimony and child support awards is very inadequate.

Child support is actually awarded in only 44 percent of all divorces, and one study found that after three years, only 19 percent of divorced fathers were paying any support at all. Most

court-ordered support payments fall below welfare in amount, according to an Alabama report. Judges have almost total discretion in making awards. In only a few States, such as Alaska, New Mexico and Washington, is there a recommended schedule of payments based on the net salary of the parent paying support.

Alimony is awarded in only 14 percent of all divorces, and no more than seven percent of divorced men actually make such payments. The courts in many States, including Pennsylvania, Indiana, and Texas, are not empowered to award any continuing alimony. No alimony at all is awarded in 90 percent of Iowa divorces. In Washington, D.C., South Carolina, Virginia, and Louisiana, wives found "at fault" in divorces may receive no alimony although men "at fault" are not penalized by having to make larger payments.

When it comes to dividing up the assets of a marriage at the time of divorce, most States do not require the courts to take into consideration the value of work in the home. The exceptions are: Colorado, Delaware, Indiana, Maine, Missouri, Montana, Nebraska, and Ohio. In Kentucky a homemaker's services must be considered, but even here they are downgraded. The general rule of thumb is that the wife receives approximately one-third of the jointly held property if she has been a homemaker and up to a maximum of one-half if she has been a wage earner.

Until recently, Pennsylvania State law did not require that a homemaker's contributions be considered when dividing up the household goods of a marriage, but the Pennsylvania Supreme Court determined that under the State's Equal Rights Amendment, a woman's work in the home must be considered as much of a contribution to the marriage as a man's job and that she is entitled to an equal share of the household goods.

Economic provisions of Uniform Marriage and Divorce Act: Many of the economic inequities that erode the lives of dependent spouses and children would be corrected if each State were to enact the economic pro-

visions of the Uniform Marriage and Divorce Act.

Some of the more important provisions of the act are:

1. The contribution of the spouse as homemaker must be considered when dividing property.

2. The courts are authorized to order child support from either or both parties and must consider five relevant factors, including the standard of living the child would have enjoyed had the marriage not been dissolved.

3. Procedures would be established for payment of support or maintenance orders through a court officer and for enforcement by the appropriate prosecuting attorney.

4. The courts may order the person obligated to pay support or maintenance to assign part of his or her earnings or trust income to the person entitled to receive payments.

5. A decree ordering maintenance or support could be modified only as to installments accruing subsequent to the motion for modification and only upon a showing of changed circumstances so substantial and continuing as to make the terms unconscionable.

Some needed reform is not included in UMDA: It does not have a section requiring disclosure of assets. It does recommend that in community property States the family home or right to live therein be awarded to the spouse having custody of any children; however, this recommendation is not included for common-law (non-community property) States, an omission that may be of great importance in families where the only property owned is the home.

Wisconsin has enacted a new divorce law that may be one of the best in the nation. Some features are improvements on UMDA. Copies may be obtained from the Wisconsin Commission on the Status of Women, 30 West Mifflin Street, Madison, Wis. 53703.

Legislation Displaced Home-makers: Legislation providing 50 centers for counseling, training, and placement of displaced homemakers was introduced by Representative Yvonne Burke (D-California) and Senator Birch Bayh (D-Indiana). House and Senate hearings have been held. The bill, which has 100 cosponsors, is expected to be included in the Comprehensive Employment and Training Act (CETA), to be renewed in 1978.

Social Security coverage for home-makers: Representative Donald M. Fraser (D-Minnesota) introduced legislation in the 94th Congress to bring homemakers into the Social Security system. More recently, Representative Martha Keys (D-Kansas) has cosponsored the Fraser bill, which was reintroduced in the 95th Congress. The bill, which has 60 cosponsors, would amend the Social Security Act to establish individual records for both partners in a marriage. Both husband and wife would be credited with the family income on social security records, and those records would stay with each throughout life. The effect would be to give divorced women a social security record. The bill would also provide disability coverage for both spouses and would lower the age at which the surviving spouse could collect benefits to age 50, which is the time most widowed women with children lose benefits because their children have come of age. Hearings were held in July 1977, and further hearings were expected to be held in July 1978.

INSURANCE

State legislatures and State insurance commissioners should adopt the Model Regulation to Eliminate Unfair Sex Discrimination of the National Association of Insurance Commissioners. The regulation should be amended and adopted to include prohibition of the following practices:

☐ Denying coverage for pregnancy and pregnancy-related expenses for all comprehensive medical/hospital care.

☐ Denying group disability coverage for normal pregnancy and complications of pregnancy.

☐ Denying health insurance coverage to newborns from birth.

☐ Requiring dependents who convert from spouses' contracts to their own to pay increased premiums for the same coverage or be forced to insure for lower coverage.

☐ Denying coverage to women with children born out of wedlock and denying eligibility of benefits to such children.

☐ Using sex-based actuarial mortality tables in rate and benefit computation.

Background: "Women cannot buy certain kinds of insurance."

A thorough investigation of sex discrimination in insurance convinced former Pennsylvania Insurance Commissioner Herbert S. Denenberg that "discrimination against women is built right into the insurance system." The charge is amply documented by the report of the Michigan Insurance Department's Women's Task Force as well as in similar reports published by other States. A particularly pervasive discrimination is the exclusion of coverage for pregnancy and related expenses in health and disability insurance, whether purchased individually or through employers.

Women cannot buy certain kinds of insurance, a number of experts testified before the Joint Congressional Committee on Economic Discrimination Against Women. Working women may not be able to get noncancellable policies, lifetime benefits, riders offering future coverage on favorable terms, or even as much dollar protection against loss of income through disability as males, even when their earnings are the same. They may not be able to get disability insurance at all for a number of reasons: if they work in certain occupational categories for which coverage is available for men; if they cannot demonstrate a well-established pattern of full-time employment; if they earn their money at home; or if they are homemakers.

Disability payments for pregnancy When disability policies are available to women, they generally do not regard pregnancy as a disability. The policies do not cover loss of income due to childbirth, abortion, or miscarriage and they may require waiting periods before coverage is effective or impose other limitations on the coverage of disabilities caused by "diseases of the female genital organs." Disabilities resulting from disorders of female reproductive organs may not be covered at all, though disorders of male reproductive organs are generally covered.

Health insurance policies often exclude maternity expenses or severely limit the benefit both in amount and eligibility. Sterilization operations may be covered for males but not for females. "All female reproductive organs" may be excluded on the basis of a woman's medical history. And, as in disability policies, health policies may deny favorable riders to women.

The rationale used by the insurance companies to exclude pregnancy from disability benefits is that pregnancy is a choice for which the woman is solely responsible and for which she must suffer the disabilities. But Barbara Shack, assistant director of the New York Civil Liberties Union, pointed out to the Joint Congressional Committee that since "women serve the biological function of continuing the species, society should share the disabilities and costs instead of penalizing her for her necessary physiological role."

Pregnancy benefits: current status Lack of maternity coverage means that American women and their families must pay most of the cost of pregnancy, childbirth, and the medical care of their newborn babies. On December 7, 1976, in *General Electric v. Gilbert*, the U.S. Supreme Court ruled that Title 7 of the Civil Rights Act of 1964 did not require companies to treat pregnancy benefits on the same basis as other temporary disabilities.

Outraged women immediately pressed for a law prohibiting discrimination on the basis of pregnancy. The Senate bill was passed on September 16, 1977, and a House bill, to which an anti-abortion rider was attached, was approved in committee in March 1978. The American Council of Life Insurance objects that the additional cost of providing pregnancy benefits could cost business $1.7 billion in 1978, but AFL-CIO studies put it at only $130 million.

Insurance based on marital status Insurance also discriminates against women on the basis of marital status. Inequities of many kinds arise when women are covered as dependents of men rather than as individuals in their own right. Health insurance plans may cover the wives but not the husbands of employees. They may enroll men but not married women as individuals. Female employees may receive smaller maternity benefits than the wife of a male employee, and they may get none at all if they are single. When a woman is divorced and covered under a group health plan by her husband's employer, she may have to pay sharply increased premiums in order to continue her protection on an individual basis. Similar discrimination exists in auto insurance, where the common practice of insuring the husband for the family car results in much higher premiums for the divorced female when she seeks coverage in her own name.

Life insurance coverage for a married woman may depend on the amount of her husband's coverage and may require that the husband's policy be larger. Group plans often treat widowers less favorably than widows. A wife covered under a company pension plan may be left without protection after divorce, and she may be left entirely without income if her husband dies before retirement age.

Finally, car and homeowner's insurance discriminates against the rising proportion of women who are single, divorced, or living alone. In New York State, for instance, an 18-year-old woman pays less car insurance if she is married than if she is single. According to Catherine Timlin, who conducted a study of insurance for the Los Angeles chapter of the National Organization for Women, "carriers say there is no one to take out the trash or clear the brush if a woman is living alone, so there is a fire hazard."

Higher costs for women Insurance costs women more than men. In disability protection, the amount of coverage can be less for a woman, waiting periods longer, and premiums higher for the same benefits available to men. If disability protection is available to a homemaker, she may have to pay more for it than if she had been employed outside the home.

In health insurance, women are frequently charged higher rates for individual policies even when maternity benefits are excluded. Premiums for group health insurance may rise with the proportion of women in the group.

Barbara Shack, in her testimony, blamed these high costs on the prevailing attitude in the insurance industry that "women are only temporary members of the work force, dependent on a male primary wage earner, burdened with home responsibilities that cause her to feign sickness so she can collect insurance benefits, or poised to have a litter and retire as the happy homemaker, duping her employer and the insurance companies out of benefits intended for regular members of the work force." As she and every other expert before the committee pointed out, this attitude deprives many millions of women and their families of economic security that is available to men.

Sex-based rate tables The heart of discrimination against women is the maintenance of separate rate tables based on the difference in risk between the sexes. Former Congresswoman Martha Griffiths, who chaired the congressional hearings on discrimination in insurance, noted that women generally are considered high risks by insurance companies. "The people in this category, whom the insurance companies usually refer to as clunkers, include all women along with residents of poor neighborhoods, reckless drivers, and those who work in hazardous occupations."

Testifying at that same hearing, Pennsylvania Commissioner Denenberg said that the time has come to drop classifications by sex. He pointed out that the companies used to have a separate classification for blacks, but that is now "unacceptable from a public policy standpoint. Like classifications based on color, sex classifications have also become suspect. ... With changes in the economic position of women, the once homogeneous classification of women has become less meaningful."

The insurance companies may soon have no choice. Courts are beginning to demand the pooling of these risks as other differences among individuals are pooled. In *Marie Manhart et al v. City of Los Angeles Department of Water and Power*, the Court of Appeals upheld an injunction against "requiring individual female employees to make larger contributions than individual male employees to the Department of Water and Power employee retirement plan."

Model regulations and their drawbacks Some States are moving against insurance inequities. About a fourth have endorsed the reforms of the Model Regulation to Eliminate Unfair Sex Discrimination adopted by the National Association of Insurance Commissioners in 1975, but according to Naomi Naierman, author of *Discrimination in Insurance*, loopholes in the NAIC prohibitions make it easy for companies to get around them. She points out, for instance, that a company may comply by making health insurance for pregnancy available only at prohibitively high cost or in limited quantity.

At best, the NAIC Model Regulations do not touch coverage for maternity and equality of benefits for men and women, principles mandated by regulations of the Equal Employment Opportunity Commission.

Under the Model Regulation, the following practices are prohibited:

1. Denying coverage to females gainfully employed at home, employed part time, or employed by relatives when coverage is offered to males similarly employed.

2. Denying policy riders to females when the riders are available to males.

3. Denying maternity benefits to an insured or prospective insured individual purchasing an individual contract when comparable family coverage contracts offer maternity benefits.

4. Denying, under group contracts, dependent coverage to husbands of female employees when dependent coverage is available to wives of male employees.

5. Denying disability income contracts to employed women when coverage is offered to men similarly employed.

6. Treating complications of pregnancy differently from any other illness or sickness under the contract.

7. Restricting, reducing, modifying, or excluding benefits relating to coverage involving the genital organs of only one sex.

8. Offering more restrictive benefit periods and more restrictive definitions of disability income contract.

9. Establishing different conditions by sex under which the policyholder may exercise benefit options contained in the contract.

10. Limiting the amount of coverage an insured or prospective insured person may purchase based on marital status unless such limitation is for the purpose of defining persons eligible for dependent benefits.

INTERNATIONAL AFFAIRS

WOMEN AND FOREIGN POLICY

The President and the executive agencies of the Government dealing with foreign affairs (Departments of State and Defense, USIA, AID, and others) should see to it that many more women, of all racial and ethnic backgrounds, participate in the formulation and execution of all aspects of United States foreign policy. Efforts should be intensified to appoint more women as Ambassadors and to all U.S. delegations to international conferences and missions to the United Nations. Women in citizen voluntary organizations concerned with international affairs should be consulted more in the formulation of policy and procedures.

The foreign affairs agencies should increase with all possible speed the number of women at all grade levels within the agencies, and a special assistant to the Secretary of State should be appointed to coordinate a program to increase women's participation in foreign policy and to assume responsibility for U.S. participation in and the funding of the U.N. Decade for Women. All concerned agencies of the executive branch should strive to appoint women on an equal basis with men to represent the U.S. on all executive boards and governing bodies of international organizations and on the U.N. functional commissions. A permanent committee composed of Government officials and private members, the majority of them women, should be appointed to advise the State Department on the selection of women candidates for positions on U.S. delega'tions, on governing bodies of international agencies, and in the U.N. system.

U.N. COMMISSION ON THE STATUS OF WOMEN

The U.S. Government should work actively for the retention and adequate funding of the U.N. Commission on the Status of Women, and it should recommend that the commission meet annually rather than biennially.

WOMEN IN DEVELOPMENT

The U.S. Agency for International Development and similar assistance agencies should give high priority to the implementation of existing U.S. legislation and policies designed to promote the integration of women into the development plans for their respective countries. They should also continue to study the impact on women in the developing world of U.S. Government aid and commercial development programs over which government has any regulatory powers. These agencies should actively promote the involvement of these women in determining their own needs and priorities in programs intended for their benefit.

HUMAN RIGHTS TREATIES AND INTERNATIONAL CONVENTIONS ON WOMEN

In pressing for respect for human rights, the President and the Congress should note the special situation of women victims of oppression, political imprisonment, and torture. They should also intensify efforts for ratification and compliance with international human rights treaties and conventions to which the United States is signatory, specifically including those on women's rights.

PEACE AND DISARMAMENT

The President and the Congress should intensify efforts to:

☐ Build, in cooperation with other nations, an international framework within which serious disarmament negotiations can occur.

☐ Reduce military spending and foreign military sales; convert excessive weapons manufacturing capacity to production for meeting human needs.

☐ Support peace education in schools and advanced study in the fields of conflict resolution and peace keeping.

To this end the United States should take the lead in urging all nuclear powers to start phasing out their nuclear arsenals rather than escalating weapons development and deployment and should develop initiatives to advance the cause of world peace.

INTERNATIONAL EDUCATION AND COMMUNICATION

Government agencies, media, schools, and citizen organizations should be encouraged to promote programs of international education and communication emphasizing women's present and potential contribution—particularly in developing countries—to economic and social well-being. Improved methods should be devised for collection and dissemination of this needed information in order to make adequate data available to policy makers and the public.

INTERNATIONAL WOMEN'S DECADE

The U.S. should give vigorous support to the goals of the U.N. Decade for Women, Equality, Development, and Peace in the General Assembly and in other international meetings; should give financial support to Decade activities; and should participate fully in the 1980 mid-Decade World Conference to review progress toward targets set in the World Plan of Action adopted unanimously by the World Conference of International Women's Year, 1975.

Background:
"Women's voices are seldom heard in government on the global issues."

Women and Foreign Policy "Mr. Carter spent his second full day on the job in the company of the *men* who will be involved in the shaping of his foreign policy and defense postures." *The New York Times* of January 23, 1977 did not, of course, italicize *men* when it printed that sentence. The exclusion of women from almost every aspect of foreign policy is simply taken for granted.

This unfair exclusion is against the stated policies of the U.S. Government and the U.N. World Plan of Action unanimously adopted by the International Women's Year Conference in Mexico City.

Foreign Service Agencies. Women are grossly underrepresented at mid- and upper-level positions in the three major foreign affairs agencies, the State Department, the United States Information Agency, and the Agency for International Development (AID). For instance, in the State Department as a whole (including both civil service posts at home and Foreign Service posts abroad), only 4.3 percent of senior level and 15.1 percent of mid-level positions are held by women.

There is evidence that the State Department is just beginning to utilize the talents of its women. The Office of Equal Opportunity found that women lagged three to five years behind male colleagues in getting promotions and that women were clustered in support services rather than in policymaking. Discouraged by this lag, women were leaving the Foreign Service at middle levels, taking their valuable talents with them.

Delegations. Although the percentage of women on U.S. international delegations has doubled since 1975, the base year for the 1976 IWY Commission recommendation for an increase, it was still only 10 percent in September 1977. Since few women are in the technical and policymaking posts from which international delegations are chosen, efforts to appoint them have been sporadic and unsystematic.

Early in 1978 the Secretary of State directed that women and minorities should always be on the lists from which recommendations for delegations are made. One source for these names is the advisory and coordinating groups that meet under U.S. Government auspices to plan for U.S. participation in international conferences. Another source is the rosters requested earlier by the IWY Commission from Government agencies which suggest qualified delegates in their areas.

Women's Groups. Women's voices are seldom heard in Government on the global issues of food, energy, population, disarmament, and environment, which directly affect their lives. Nongovernmental women's organizations are deeply concerned with and knowledgeable on many international issues and could make important contributions to policy formation.

U.N. Commission on the Status of Women An all-male United Nations group of 26 experts charged with restructuring the U.N.'s economic and social development work recommended abolishing all of the functional commissions, including the Commission on the Status of Women.

This commission, which should be retained, has brought improvements in the status of women and focused international attention on the contributions of women in development. Its work has resulted in many significant documents on international policy, including the Convention on Political Rights of Women (1952), the Convention on the Nationality of Mar-

ried Women (1957), the Convention on Consent to Marriage, Minimum Age for Marriage, and Registration of Marriages (1962), the Convention for Suppression of Traffic in Persons and of the Exploitation of the Prostitution of Others (1950), and the Convention on the Recovery Abroad of Maintenance (1956).

Very few women have represented the United States on the governing boards of U.N. organizations and specialized agencies.

Women employees at the U.N. have noted a sharp contrast between the organization's professed goals of equality for women and its practices, both in its international programs and in its discriminatory employment and promotion patterns within the Secretariat and U.N. agencies.

Women in Development The work of women is essential to every society even though it is largely unpaid and uncounted in the gross national product. Women bear and rear the children who are the world's basic resource for economic growth, and they have the critical responsibility for managing population growth in a world of diminishing resources and increasing poverty.

According to the U.N. Economic and Social Council, Third World women living in predominantly rural societies have added burdens. These women produce 40 to 80 percent of the food and carry, in addition, major responsibility for family nutrition, health care, water supply and sanitation, and the education of the young. Although this contribution is central to any development, it has been largely ignored by their own governments as well as in programs of assistance set up by the United States Agency for International Development and similar organizations.

New techniques and training programs have been introduced to increase male employment and productivity. In agriculture, new methods, machinery, marketing programs, and farm credit are made available to men who either supplant women in their traditional jobs, lowering women's status and depriving them of small incomes from occasional food surpluses, or turn to cash-cropping for export, thus increasing the work women must do to provide subsistence food.

New factories lure men to city jobs, leaving women behind as the heads and usually as sole support of their families. In fact, almost 30 percent of rural families in the Third World are now headed by women. Young women frequently migrate to enter the urban labor force as menials or prostitutes or, if they work in factories, they tend to be exploited by the policies and operations of multinational corporations.

These poor, neglected women are caught in a depressing downward spiral. Because they must work harder for less money, they have even less time for what little education is available to them. UNESCO has reported that the illiteracy rate among women of the world has actually grown in the last 15 years from 58 to 62 percent.

U.S. Action. The United States has recognized the importance of women in developing nations. Recent amendments to foreign assistance legislation known as the "Percy Amendments" require U.S. assistance programs to consider their impact on the women of the countries affected, include women as beneficiaries and participants, and refrain from any program that would affect women adversely.

AID plans for implementing this policy call for clear statements about the involvement of women in every program and preference for projects that use women in technical and managerial positions.

Human Rights Treaties and Conventions In spite of the preamble to the U.N. charter, many of its articles, and multinational treaties supporting basic human rights and freedoms, gross violations of the human rights of women continue to occur throughout the world. These include physical and sexual abuse, imprisonment, and torture for political reasons.

A majority of the following International Conventions on Women have not been ratified by the United States:

I. United Nations Conventions:

A. Convention on the Nationality of Married Women (1957). U.S. action: none.

B. Convention on Consent to Marriage, Minimum Age for Marriage, and Registration of Marriage (1962). U.S. action: signed but never submitted to the Senate.

C. ILO Discrimination (Employment and Occupation) Convention (1958). U.S. action: none.

D. ILO Convention on Equal Remuneration (1951). U.S. action: none.

E. Convention on the Suppression of the Traffic in Persons and of the Exploitation or the Prostitution of Others (1951). U.S. action: none.

F. UNESCO Convention Against Discrimination In Education (1962). U.S. action: none.

G. Convention on the Elimination of All Forms of Racial Discrimination (1965). U.S. action: none.

H. Convention on the Recovery Abroad of Maintenance (1957). U.S. action: none.

I. U.N. Convention on the Political Rights of Women (1952). U.S. action: ratified January 22, 1976 by the Senate; went into force for the United States on July 7, 1976.

J. Supplementary Convention on the Abolition of Slavery, the Slave Trade, and Institutions and Practices Similar to Slavery (1956). U.S. action: ratified December 6, 1967.

II. Organization of American States (OAS) Conventions:

A. Inter-American Convention on the Granting of Political Rights to Women (1948). U.S. action: ratified January 22, 1976; went into force for the United States on July 7, 1976.

B. Civil Rights of Women (1948). U.S. action: none.

C. Nationality of Women (1933). U.S. action: ratified with reservations June 30, 1934.

(Dates in parentheses are dates of adoption by U.N./OAS)

Peace and Disarmament World military expenditures approached $370 billion in 1977, according to Ruth Sivard, *World Military and Social Expenditures,* 1977 (W.M.S.E. Publications, Box 1003, Leesburg, Virginia 22075.) She calculates that this amounts to $370 a *minute* since the birth of Christ.

Military spending on this scale is unprecedented in a time of comparative peace. At the present rate, the average U.S. citizen can expect to work three or four years of his or her life to pay for the arms race, in addition to the huge indirect costs of diverting resources to nonproductive uses.

It is obvious that a great many human needs could be provided for with the money now spent on the military. Sivard has calculated, for instance, that the world spends 60 times as much on equipping each soldier as on educating each child, and six times as much on military research as it spends for energy research. The world carries more insurance against the potential of war than against the actual, immediate problems of crime, illness, hunger, and poverty.

Developing Nations. Developing nations account for about one-fifth of the world expenditure on arms and spend as much on their military programs as they do on education and health care combined. Much of this money is spent in the United States. According to the U.S. Arms Control and Disarmament Agency, the United States sold $29 billion worth of arms to developing nations between 1966 and 1975.

President Carter has announced his intention of reducing our arms sales abroad, but a backlog of orders, a burgeoning arms industry, and political decisions work to accelerate the arms race in developing countries.

Nuclear Stockpile. The United States and the Soviet Union, the world's two nuclear giants, have a nuclear force capable of destroying the other several times over. The United States alone has a nuclear arms stockpile equivalent to 615,000 times the force of the atomic bomb dropped on Hiroshima in World War II.

Five countries are known to have nuclear weapons, and 30 others may soon be able to make nuclear weapons by using plutonium from nuclear reactors and widely available technology.

Disarmament and Women. The momentum of the arms race propels us toward the catastrophe of nuclear war. As a leader in that race, the United States must work with the Soviet Union and other nuclear powers to build a peaceful world. We must move with all possible speed to distinguish what we can do by ourselves, what we must do in partnership with the Soviet Union, and what measures must await the concurrence of other countries.

Women have a financial as well as a human interest in detente. Disarmament could release funds for programs affecting their welfare which now are stalled for lack of money: quality education, child care, national health, subsidized housing, and help for women returning to the work force.

Women are often frustrated in their attempts to make the world safer and more peaceful partly because they are not consulted when foreign policy decisions are made. But as private citizens and members of voluntary organizations they can raise their voices, do their homework, argue the case against massive armament, and support disarmament initiatives.

International Education and Communication In spite of a great deal of demographic, economic, and social data, information explaining the actual situation of women around the world is not readily available.

Americans get little news about events outside their own country. Newspaper coverage of international events, for instance, averages a half column of newsprint a day. Only three percent of undergraduate college students take courses dealing with international affairs, and according to a survey by the American Association of Colleges of Teacher Education, only five percent of teachers are exposed to international perspectives in preparing for certification.

This information gap makes it difficult for American women to understand the impact of development programs on women in developing countries, or even how to find out more about women in other cultures, let alone what they can do about it. There is, however, an available remedy.

Almost every American woman belongs to at least one voluntary organization—a PTA, a church group, a political party, a labor union, a civic organization, or a professional association. Most of these are also affiliated with a national parent group whose membership may run into hundreds of thousands or millions. The voice of that united membership can definitely be heard by governments.

A worldwide communications network of women's organizations could help to foster increased international understanding of women's lives and concerns and establish a roster of resource women throughout the world.

International Women's Decade The United Nations Decade for Women, 1975-1985, is an outgrowth of the World Conference of the International Women's Year held by the United Nations in Mexico City in 1975. The World Plan of Action, adopted unanimously at that conference and later by the U.N. General Assembly, targeted such areas as education, employment, and health for special

attention at a Mid-Decade Conference scheduled for 1980 in Iran.

In preparation, a system of progress reporting has been set up to guide governments and intergovernmental bodies. Within the U.N. system, agencies are directed to assess the impact of their programs on women. A new agency, the International Research and Training Institute for the Advancement of Women, has been proposed to provide data and training. The United States is among the countries that have contributed to the Institute, but it awaits $3 million in pledges before it can begin operation.

Encouraged by women's voluntary organizations, the U.S. Congress has made a pledge to the Voluntary Fund for the Decade. The Fund goes primarily to support projects undertaken by women themselves in the regions, but requests for its use have lagged because they come through governments, and governments have not paid much attention to women's projects.

Since the U.N. Decade for Women comes from a U.S. initiative at the United Nations and bears the unanimous endorsement of all governments, the United States is obligated to support the Decade and urge other members to do the same.

MEDIA

The media should employ women in all job categories and especially in policy-making positions. They should adopt and distribute the IWY media guidelines throughout their respective industries. They should make affirmative efforts to expand the portrayal of women to include a variety of roles and to represent accurately the numbers and lifestyles of women in society. Training opportunities should be expanded so that more women can move into all jobs in the communications industries, particularly into technical jobs.

Appropriate Federal and State agencies, including the Federal Communications Commission, U.S. Commission on Civil Rights, Department of Health, Education, and Welfare, Department of Justice, and State civil rights commissions should vigorously enforce laws which prohibit employment discrimination against women working in the mass media. These agencies should continue studying the impact of the mass media on sex discrimination and sex-role stereotyping in American society.

Special consideration should be given to media which are publicly funded or established through acts of Congress. Particularly, public broadcasting should assume a special responsibility to integrate women in employment and programing.

Women's groups and advocacy groups should continue to develop programs to monitor the mass media and take appropriate action to improve the image and employment of women in the communications industries. They should join the campaign to de-emphasize the exploitation of female bodies and the use of violence against women in the mass media.

Women and minorities have traditionally faced financial problems in their attempts to establish power bases within the broadcast industry. During the late 1930's and 1940's when the Federal Communications Commission was distributing broadcast licenses, lack of money kept both these groups from applying for ownership of radio or TV stations.

Throughout the 1950's, women's roles on television were limited to the zany and incompetent, as in "I Love Lucy," and to the second fiddle homemaker-mother, as in "Father Knows Best."

The new wave of feminism in the United States sparked a keen interest in the impact of the media on the role of women in society. Women's groups monitor television, broadcasting and the press, and special publications report on how women are faring in these media. During the early 1970's, women's organizations staged an 11-hour sit-in at the offices of the male editor of the *Ladies' Home Journal* (winning the right to write and edit one issue of the magazine); picketed newspapers and companies using sexist advertising campaigns; and filed complaints challenging the licenses of TV and radio stations accused of discrimination in hiring of women.

In 1975, the Corporation for Public Broadcasting (CPB) released a comprehensive analysis of the poor record in hiring and in the portrayal of women within the public broadcasting system. More recently, the U.S. Civil Rights Commission published a damning report entitled, "Window Dressing on the Set: Women and Minorities in Television."

The study concluded: "Television drama does not reflect the sexual and racial/ethnic make-up of the United States. White males are overrepresented; female characters are underrepresented; and minority women are nearly invisible."

The IWY Commission in its 1976 report to President Ford made specific recommendations for improving hiring practices and portrayal of women, incorporating them in 10 Media Guidelines that are reprinted here.

Background:
"The reality of the lives most women lead does not come through on the screen or in the press."

So powerful are the nation's mass media that their perceptions of women's roles in American society are often taken as gospel by an image-conscious public, regardless of accuracy or taste.

On any given day, one can see a film, watch a television program or read a magazine article in which women are exploited as sexual toys or objects of violence, depicted as childlike or neurotic, shown as ignorant and in need of male guidance. Even in what is presumed to be woman's own domain—the home—TV commercials show women being instructed by authoritative-sounding men in how to launder clothes, wax floors or make coffee.

Although the media's treatment and employment of women have improved in response to organized pressures, the prevailing reality of the lives most women lead does not come through on the screen or in the press. By and large, what women perceive themselves to be and how the public is conditioned to perceive them are two different things.

Women make coffee, not policy

The most telling reason for this disparity is a statistic: though women hold 25 to 35 percent of jobs in the media, only about five percent are in policy-making positions.

The mass media have historically been male-dominated, particularly in positions of power. Suffrage leader Susan B. Anthony noted in 1900: "As long as newspapers and magazines are controlled by men, every woman upon them must write articles which are reflections of men's ideas. As long as that continues, women's ideas and deepest convictions will never get before the public."

Pending solutions President Carter recently sent to Congress a proposal to reorganize the public broadcasting system in the United States. The bill includes anti-discriminatory provisions comparable to Title 6 and Title 7 of the Civil Rights Act and Title 9 of the Education Amendments of 1972. House and Senate Communications subcommittees in March 1978 were considering the President's proposal, together with a report on job discrimination in public broadcasting by a task force composed of representatives from the Justice Department, HEW, FCC and EEOC.

More sweeping legislative proposals have been developed by the Office of Communication of the United Church of Christ, which call for reforming the Communications Act of 1934. The Office notes that this 44-year-old law no longer is attuned to the problems of the fast-developing broadcasting and telecommunications industries.

Non-traditional jobs About 20 percent (2400) of the jobs in the broadcast industry are held by technicians, sound experts and other technical specialists. Women occupy only about six percent of these positions. Similarly, in the film industry, women hold about three percent of technical positions. These jobs are generally well paid and union organized, and provide good benefits for employees.

Many technicians at TV and radio stations have held their positions since the stations were established in the 1940's and 1950's. Although turnover is generally low, many television technicians are reaching retirement age. This should open more opportunities for women. Broadcast technicians are no longer required to fit the stereotype of the tall, strong, husky male since television equipment is lighter and less bulky than film cameras used in the past.

Jobs in media technical fields provide viable alternatives to the clerical or service positions in the media where women tend to be segregated, receiving low pay and accorded low status.

Top Federal positions The President appoints most of the top Federal media policymakers. Women serve as commissioners on the FCC and Federal Trade Commission, as well as on the Board of Directors of the Corporation for Public Broadcasting. However, female participation on boards and commissions has been limited to 10 to 15 percent. The same minimal representation is found in figures on women serving on the boards of directors of major corporations that own the commercial media.

Organizations including the Screen Actors Guild, the National Women's Political Caucus and the National Organization for Women have been working actively for the appointment of more women to Federal agencies that monitor the media.

Among these agencies are the National Endowment for the Arts; the National Endowment for the Humanities;

the recently reorganized Council on Arts and Humanities; the Office of Telecommunications Policy (being transferred from the White House to the Department of Commerce); and the contract compliance offices of the General Services Administration and the Department of Labor.

Other agencies that deal with the media are the Office of Education, the National Institute of Education and the National Institutes of Health and Mental Health, all of HEW; the EEOC; Department of Justice; and Civil Rights Commission.

The State Department will soon select delegates to attend the World Administrative Radio Conference in 1979 in Geneva, Switzerland. Other international agencies dealing with education have targeted women and the mass media as a key issue during the United Nations Decade for Women.

Long-range goals The impact of the American mass media increases with advancements in new technologies. Entire cities are wired for cable television, satellites connect countries and continents, and video tape recorders can be purchased for home and personal use. As these technologies advance, it is important for women to continue to push for full integration at all levels of the privately and publicly owned mass media and to improve the image of women.

10 Media Guidelines

1. The media should establish as an ultimate goal the employment of women in policymaking positions in proportion to their participation in the labor force. The media should make special efforts to employ women who are knowledgeable about and sensitive to women's changing roles.

2. Women in media should be employed at all job levels—and, in accordance with the law, should be paid equally for work of equal value and be given equal opportunity for training and promotion.

3. The present definition of news should be expanded to include more coverage of women's activities, locally, nationally, and internationally. In addition, general news stories should be reported to show their effect on women. For example, the impact of foreign aid on women in recipient countries is often overlooked, as is the effect of public transportation on women's mobility, safety, and ability to take jobs.

4. The media should make special, sustained efforts to seek out news of women. Women now figure in less than 10 percent of the stories currently defined as news.

5. Placement of news should be decided by subject matter, not by sex. The practice of segregating material thought to be of interest only to women into certain sections of a newspaper or broadcast implies that news of women is not real news. However, it is important to recognize and offset an alarming trend wherein such news, when no longer segregated, is not covered at all. Wherever news of women is placed, it should be treated with the same dignity, scope, and accuracy as is news of men. Women's activities should not be located in the last 30-60 seconds of a broadcast or used as fillers in certain sections or back pages of a newspaper or magazine.

6. Women's bodies should not be used in an exploitive way to add irrelevant sexual interest in any medium. This includes news and feature coverage by both the press and television, movie and movie promotion, "skin" magazines, and advertising messages of all sorts. The public violation of a woman's physical privacy tends to violate the individual integrity of all women.

7. The presentation of personal details when irrelevant to a story—sex, sexual preference, age, marital status, physical appearance, dress, religious or political orientation—should be eliminated for both women and men.

8. It is to be hoped that one day all titles will be unnecessary. But in the meantime, a person's right to determine her (or his) own title should be respected without slurs or innuendoes. If men are called Doctor or Reverend, the same titles should be used for women. And a woman should be able to choose Ms., Miss, or Mrs.

9. Gender designations are a rapidly changing area of the language, and a decision to use or not to use a specific word should be subject to periodic review. Terms incorporating gender reference should be avoided. Use firefighter instead of fireman, business executive instead of businessman, letter carrier instead of mailman. In addition, women from at least the age of 16, should be called women, not girls. And at no time should a female be referred to as "broad," "chick," or the like.

10. Women's activities and organizations should be treated with the same respect accorded men's activities and organizations. The women's movement should be reported as seriously as any other civil rights movement; it should not be made fun of, ridiculed, or belittled. Just as the terms "black libbers" or "Palestine libbers" are not used, the term "women's libbers" should not be used. Just as jokes at the expense of blacks are no longer made, jokes should not be made at women's expense. The news of women should not be sensationalized. Too often news media have reported conflict among women and ignored unity. Coverage of women's conferences is often limited solely to so-called "splits" or fights. These same disputes at conferences attended by men would be considered serious policy debates.

MINORITY WOMEN

Minority women share with all women the experience of sexism as a barrier to their full rights of citizenship. Every recommendation of this National Plan of Action shall be understood as applying equally and fully to minority women.

But institutionalized bias based on race, language, culture, and/or ethnic origin or governance of territories or localities has led to the additional oppression and exclusion of minority women and to the conditions of poverty from which they disproportionately suffer.

Therefore, every level of Government action should recognize and remedy this double discrimination and ensure the right of each individual to self-determination.

Legislation, the enforcement of existing laws, and all levels of Government action should be directed especially toward problem areas such as involuntary sterilization; monolingual education and services; high infant and maternal mortality rates; bias toward minority women's children; confinement to low level jobs; confinement to poor, ghettoized housing; culturally biased educational, psychological, and employment testing (for instance, civil service); failure to enforce affirmative action and special admission programs; combined sex and race bias in insurance; and failure to gather statistical data based on both sex and race so that the needs and conditions of minority women may be accurately understood.

Minority women also suffer from Government failure to recognize and remedy problems of our racial and cultural groups. For instance:

AMERICAN INDIAN AND ALASKAN NATIVE WOMEN:

American Indian/Alaskan Native women have a relationship to Earth Mother and the Great Spirit as well as a heritage based on the sovereignty of Indian peoples. The Federal Government should guarantee tribal rights, tribal sovereignty; honor existing treaties and congressional acts; protect hunting, fishing, and whaling rights; protect trust status; and permanently remove the threat of termination.

Congress should extend the Indian Education Act of 1972; maintain base funding of education instead of replacing it with supplemental funding; provide adequate care through the Indian Health Service; forbid the systematic removal of children from their families and communities; and assure full participation in all Federally funded programs.

ASIAN/PACIFIC AMERICAN WOMEN:

Asian/Pacific American women are wrongly thought to be part of a "model minority" with few problems. This obscures our vulnerability due to language and culture barriers, sweatshop work conditions with high health hazards, the particular problems of wives of U.S. servicemen, lack of access to accreditation and licensing because of immigrant status, and to many Federally funded services.

BLACK WOMEN:

The President and Congress should provide for full quality education, including special admission programs, and for the full implementation and enforcement at all levels of education.

The President and Congress should immediately address the crisis of unemployment which impacts the black community and results in black teenage women having the highest rate of unemployment.

The Congress should establish a national program for the placement of "children in need of parents," preferably in a family environment, where the status of said children is affected by reason of racial or ethnic origin.

The President and Congress should assure Federally assisted housing to meet the critical need of black women, especially of low and moderate income; should direct the vigorous enforcement of all fair housing laws; and provide the allocation of resources necessary to accomplish this housing goal.

The President, Congress, and all Federal agencies should utilize fully in all deliberations and planning processes the Black Women's Plan of Action, which clearly reflects and delineates other major concerns of black women.

HISPANIC WOMEN

Deportation of mothers of American-born children must be stopped and legislation enacted for parents to remain with their children; citizenship provisions should be facilitated.

Legislation should be enacted to provide migrant farm working women with the Federal minimum wage rate, collective bargaining rights, adequate housing, and bilingual-bicultural social services delivery.

Classification of existing Hispanic American media as "foreign press" must be stopped to ensure equal access to major national events.

Additionally, the Federal Communications Commission must provide equal opportunity to Hispanic people for acquisition of media facilities (radio and television), and for training and hiring in order to provide Spanish-language programing to this major group.

Puerto Rican women emphasize that they are citizens of the United States and wish to be recognized and treated as equals.

Background:
"The combined effect of race, sex and economic class can produce extreme hardship..."

Minority* women have contributed immeasurably to the cultural life and economic strength of the United States. Moreover, their increased experience in recognizing and combatting discrimination, plus their greater need to seek employment outside the home, have often put them in the leadership of the struggle for equality for all women. Nonetheless, minority women have been ignored, stereotyped, or treated as invisible by media and historical accounts of the American women's movement. Their economic position places them in the lower socioeconomic stratum, in a high concentration disproportionate to their numbers in the population. Thus, the combined effect of race, sex, and economic class can produce extreme hardship in the lives of these American women.

Even obtaining accurate data about minority women's lives and needs becomes an object lesson in the multiple discrimination minority women face in a white male-dominated society. The U.S. Bureau of the Census has often been shown to undercount minorities and has assembled advisory groups from those communities to help devise more accurate statistics in the future. Yet the current figures are still the basis of formulating social policy, as well as the comparisons offered below. In addition, Hispanic groups are frequently reported as part of the white population, thus skewing both white and minority data, and statistical information is rarely broken out by race or ethnic subgroup plus sex. (See background on Statistics Plank.) The available

information does give some idea of the special problems of the approximately 19 percent of all female Americans who are members of races recorded as other than white (including black, American Indian, Japanese, Chinese, Filipina, Korean, Hawaiian, Eskimo, Aleut and others), as well as Hispanic women (including Mexican American, Puerto Rican, Cuban and other Spanish origins.)

For these approximately 15 million minority women and girls, all the resolutions in this National Plan of Action have special significance. They often reflect needs that are even greater than those of white women. Some selected information in the areas of health, reproductive freedom, education, and employment is cited here:

Health. In 1975, the life expectancy for minority women was 72.3 years, compared with 77.2 years for white women. Maternal mortality was 29.0 per 100,000 minority women, as opposed to 9.1 per 100,000 white women. The infant mortality rate among minorities was 24.2 per 1,000 live non-white births as compared with 16.1 per 1,000 in the population at large. Poor nutrition is more likely to be a problem for the minority woman, as well as for the children she bears. She is less likely to see a doctor or dentist or to be covered by health insurance and is less likely to have access to a hospital or clinic within practical distance of her home. This lack of access to good or adequate health care is a function of economic status. It represents a clear example of the interaction of income with race and sex.

Reproductive Freedom. Minority women are less likely to have access to information, health care, and family planning techniques that make reproductive freedom a reality. Because of the disproportionate presence of mi-

nority women among poorer groups dependent on Federally funded health care, the recent restrictions on Medicaid funding for abortion are especially likely to increase the incidence among them of death and injury from illegal or self-induced abortions, as well as the incidence of unwanted births.

Restrictions on abortion also increase the potential of coerced sterilization through "bargaining": that is, allowing a woman to have an abortion only if she also agrees to be sterilized. Because of patterns and biases in the medical and birth control fields, as well as greater dependency on publicly supported teaching hospitals, minority women are more likely to be the subject of experimental medical techniques and drugs and more likely to undergo sterilization (both hysterectomies and tubal ligations) without informed consent.

Employment. The double discrimination against minority women ranks them below minority men and white men in earning power, as U.S. Bureau of Labor Statistics data show. In 1975, for instance, the average minority female worker earned 26 percent less than the average minority male; and 43 percent less than the average white male. These figures become more meaningful when it is realized that minority women account for 28 percent of the 7.5 million families headed by women.

In addition, unemployment rates for minority women in general persist at considerably higher levels than those for white women and minority and white men. For example, their unemployment rate was 13.3 percent in 1977 compared with the 7.8 percent rate of their white counterparts. This disparity is most pronounced among teenage women. The unemployment rate for female minority teenagers, for instance, was 39.0 percent in 1976.

---

*Members of the Minority Caucus in Houston agreed that "minority" was a more popularly understood term—and more accurate in the United States context—than "Third World" or others.

The rate was 35.4 percent for minority teenage males; 16.4 percent for white teenage females; and 17.3 percent for white teenage males.

In March 1977, only 45 percent of employed minority women were in white collar jobs, compared with 66 percent of employed white women. About 23 percent of employed white women were working in the generally higher-paying, professional-technical, and managerial positions, compared with 18 percent of minority women. Sixteen percent of employed minority women were in the lower paying operative occupations (e.g., assemblers, inspectors, semiskilled factory workers) compared with 10 percent of white women.

Median income for all white families in the United States was about $15,620 in 1976. The median for minority families was $9,817. For families headed by women, however, median income was $8,226 for whites and $5,140 for minorities. In general, minority women tend to be a necessary support of larger households, and/or to be married to men with lower incomes, thus producing a greater pressure on their earnings.

One-third of all families headed by women are below the poverty level. Proportionately twice as many families headed by black and Hispanic women live below the poverty level as families headed by white women.

Education. Minority women as a group still receive somewhat less formal education than white women. White women aged 25 and older had completed 12.4 years (median) of school in March 1977, for instance, compared with 11.7 years for minority women in the same age group. In March 1977, 64 percent of minority women workers had graduated from high school, including 12 percent who had completed four or more years of college. The comparable figures for white women workers were 77 percent and 15 percent, respectively. The important fact is, however, that minority women with high school or higher education levels still receive lower salaries than comparably edu-

cated white women and lower salaries than minority and white men with much less education.

These limited examples are only indications of a profound problem. Specific factors combine to have greater and different impact on various groups of minority women. The following sections address special problems and social patterns in the major groupings of minority women.

American Indian and Alaskan Native Women. The American Indian/Alaskan Native population is the smallest minority group in the U.S.; about one million, or less than one percent of the total population. Many of its members assert, however, that it is also the most undercounted. About half of this population lives on tribal reservations or in Alaskan villages. These are the poorest of all the minority groups. On reservations, where the unemployment rate is over 60 percent, many families have no recordable income at all, and average annual family income is between $300 and $500. These families also are in effect the wards of the Federal Government, with the Bureau of Indian Affairs in the Department of the Interior controlling the water, mineral rights, and other governance of their land, as well as the administration of their schools. The U.S. Public Health Service is frequently their only medical resource.

There are 789 different tribal entities within the U.S. Traditions and beliefs vary greatly: in some tribes, for instance, women play a much more powerful role than they do in the dominant American culture; in others, a lesser role. Women's identification with their tribal nations is often strong. The 1970 census figures indicate that for half of all Indian women, a tribal language is primary, with English as a second language.

Nonetheless, American Indian/Alaskan Native women share many overall, cross-tribal concepts: a fundamental identification with the land, for instance, and a view of the individual as an integral part of the community and of an interrelated system of nature that is a circle, a whole.

Due to health and social problems, Indian men are outnumbered by women 97 to 110. According to a 1969 U.S. Department of Labor report, more than 36 percent of all Indian women had no incomes. Of the remainder, 86 percent received less than $5,000 a year and half received less than $1,697. Among those in the labor force, only two percent have administrative or managerial positions. In 1970, their unemployment rate was 10.2 percent: double the rate for all women. They also average 10.5 years of education, as opposed to 12.1 years for all women, and only 34.6 percent complete high school. In reservation families, the children may be removed by Government authority to be raised in outside schools, families, or institutions, sometimes without the informed consent of relatives. According to testimony given at a hearing held by the Department of Health, Education and Welfare in January, 1978, Indian women are more likely to be sterilized than other women including other minority women.

In addition to problems experienced as women, American Indian/Alaskan Natives share their group's special concerns: the deprivation of hunting, fishing, and whaling rights, for instance, that may diminish or eliminate the group's chief food supply and a center of its traditional economy, and the appropriation of traditional lands.

In spite of many handicaps, including their severe, sexist stereotyping in American films and popular culture, American Indian/Alaskan Native women may have leadership positions and experience in decision-making as a result of more egalitarian tribal customs. A national communications network is being developed among them as a result of their participation in the Houston Conference.

Asian/Pacific American Women. This group is highly diversified, including women of Chinese, Japanese, Philippine, Korean, Vietnamese, Indian, Indonesian, Thai, and Malaysian origin, as well as Pacific Americans such as Samoans, Guamanians, and Native Hawaiians. Because more detailed information and statistics have been kept about the Chinese, Japanese, and Filipino populations, these three groups are often inaccurately used to represent all Asian Americans.

In addition, official statistics on Pacific Americans are sketchy and often more than eight years old. Taken together, according to Bureau of the Census figures, these groups number about one percent of the U.S. population. Their percentage of the total American female population cannot be calculated according to the usual ratios, however, because of certain anomalies in immigration patterns. The Exclusionary Immigration Act of 1924, for instance, ruled that Chinese males could not bring in "alien" wives, thus insuring an unequal sex ratio that still continues. Filipino workers brought into the United States, frequently as migrant farm workers, suffered a similar restriction. Anti-miscegnation laws also kept many immigrants from marrying white American women, thus limiting the community and distorting family patterns. The Filipino community is still predominantly male. But among Korean, Vietnamese, and Japanese groups, large numbers of women arriving as brides of U.S. servicemen have made recent immigration predominantly female. About half of all Asian American women now in the U.S. are foreign-born.

In addition, there has been a history of legislation restricting the immigration and/or citizenship of persons of "Asiatic" origins. Detention camps established during World War II also had a destructive impact on the welfare of many Japanese families, often depriving them of livelihood and land.

Manipulations of female-male ratios and family patterns have created special tensions for many Asian/Pacific American women. Most dramatic is the plight of so-called "war brides," more than 300,000 of whom arrived from Asian countries immediately following World War II and whose influx continues. In 1973 alone, more than 7,000 transracially married Asian women, many of them Vietnamese, entered the United States. Regional studies indicate that such women often suffer from problems of language and cultural barriers, isolation even from other members of their communities in the United States, and, perhaps disproportionately, from abandonment and wife-battering. One study of Fort Lewis, a military reservation near Tacoma, Washington, for instance, indicates that between 200 and 500 Asian-born wives live in the area, as well as between 1,500 and 2,000 deserted or divorced wives of military men. When these women leave their husbands, are divorced or abandoned, they often experience even more economic, linguistic, racial, and cultural problems on their own behalf than they did as Asian-born wives.

Many Asian/Pacific Americans experience tensions between the attitude toward them as women inside and outside their communities. The habit of valuing a daughter less than a son is often stronger within the traditional Chinese community, for instance. On the other hand, some experience a higher status, whether because of the greater educational attainment among Filipinas, on average, than among their counterpart men (due largely to the recent influx of Filipina health professionals), or because of the greater status afforded to women by many native Hawaiian and other Pacific American groups.

About 50 percent of Asian American women are in the labor force. Levels of unemployment are slightly lower, and educational levels slightly higher, among Chinese American and Japanese American women than among white women. In many Asian American communities, there is also a strong tradition of order, self-governance, and business enterprise. Facts such as these have led to the frequent view of Asian/Pacific Americans as a "model minority" with few problems. In popular culture, Asian American women have been stereotyped as subservient to men or as "dragon ladies." This has served both to conceal and perpetuate such realities as the confinement of many Asian American women to a garment industry with sweatshop conditions (San Francisco's Chinatown has the highest tuberculosis rate in the country, for instance); their disproportionate employment in clerical, health and service professions, in spite of high educational attainment; their median income (in 1969) of only $2,931; and the isolation produced by language, culture, race, and the lack of political power.

Black Women. (Also see the Black Women's Action Plan, in the appendix of this report. The Action Plan was the consensus of the several Black Caucuses that met before and during the Houston Conference, and provides additional background research.) According to the Bureau of the Census, there were nearly nine million black women in the U.S. in 1977. Black women have been diligent in their quest for self-determination and equal opportunity, working towards destruction of vestiges of race, sex, and social-economic class discrimination. Their political experience has often put them at the forefront of the many struggles for individual justice.

In 1977, the median income of black women was approximately $6,000 less than that of white men. Proportionately more black women are employed than white women in low-paying, low-status jobs and remain unemployed at a rate double that of white women and more than double that of white men. Unemployment remains especially high among teenage black women. Large numbers are high school dropouts, unskilled and untrained. If present trends continue, many of these young women will become heads of households facing the problems of raising families and working at low-paying jobs or not working at all.

A 1974-75 National Urban League report indicates that one of every four black women is unable to find work. Among black families headed by females, 43 percent are below the poverty level but do not receive any support from welfare programs. They rely primarily on earnings from low-paying jobs rather than public assistance. Many families headed by black women are forced to utilize public assistance as a way to supplement income from very low-paying jobs. The median income of families headed by black females in 1977 was $5,069.

Negative conditions continue to affect black women in many areas of their lives—health, housing, lack of access to credit, education—and in the care of their families and children. Roughly 6.4 percent of all black women held college degrees, according to the 1977 Census. The impact of those degrees is not felt in economic gain. They still receive lower incomes, sometimes less than those earned by white males who have not completed

high school. For example, in 1975 a white male high school graduate earned $10,726 as opposed to $8,960 for a black woman with four or more years of college.

However, education still remains one of the principal methods of increasing economic choices and social mobility among blacks. Affirmative action and equal opportunity requirements relating to females are complicated by the variable of race, often causing black females to be counted twice in fulfilling affirmative action goals, while in actuality they receive only partial benefits. Public higher education for young black females is imperative because in most cases their families cannot afford private education. If this avenue of public education is blocked, the impact will be great on both black women and black families.

Poor health, substandard housing, and inadequate child care impact severely on black women who are poor. Discrimination and lack of enforcement of fair housing laws continue to deny black women and their families access to decent housing, a necessity for sound family development.

Black women recognize the gains they have made but are very much aware that they must obtain many more even to "catch up" to where white women have started from. Alliances are being formed with minority women of other groups and the larger society of women in general to advance their goals.

Hispanic Women. According to the Bureau of the Census, in March 1977 there were 5.7 million women of Spanish origin in the United States. These include persons of Mexican, Puerto Rican, and Cuban origin, as well as Central or South American, and other Spanish-speaking areas.

Hispanic women are younger than those in the overall population. In 1976, for instance, their median age was 22.2, as compared with 29.9 for non-Hispanic women. This fact increases their need for reproductive health services, as well as for educational facilities and child care. Female-headed Hispanic families tend

to be larger than those headed by non-Hispanic women. Family size combines with a higher rate of unemployment, a lower educational level, and lower incomes to trap more Hispanic women into the cycle of poverty and the self-fulfilling prophecy of failure. In 1977, for instance, 37 percent of Hispanic women over 25 had completed high school, compared with 64.4 percent for other women.

Often restricted by language as well as by cultural, racial, and economic bias, Hispanic women are even more likely to be concentrated at the low end of the job ladder than are non-Hispanic women. Of all women employed fulltime by the Federal Government in white collar positions, only 2.2 percent are Hispanic.

Within this Hispanic population, the three largest groups are those of Mexican American, Puerto Rican and Cuban origin.

Mexican American Women. Even when taken separately from other Hispanics, Mexican Americans constitute the second largest minority group in the United States. Though they are often stereotyped as migrant workers—and they do constitute the largest proportion of migrants in general, as well as of female migrants—44.4 percent live in central cities.

Chicanas complete an average of 10 years of school, about two years less than do women in the population at large. In 1976, about 71 percent of Chicanas earned less than $5,000 a year. Low-paying, low-skilled jobs contribute to their low annual income: at $2,925, it is the lowest among all women of Hispanic origin. They are also the largest single ethnic group among household workers. Eighteen percent have completed less than five years of school; only 24 percent have completed high school; and, of those 25 years old or more, only 3.2 percent are college graduates.

In March 1976, 17.2 percent of all Mexican American families were headed by women. Of those female household heads who worked at any time during 1975, 60.3 percent had earnings below the poverty level.

Because they have often entered the United States at the Mexican border—and may be assumed to have done so illegally, whether or not this is actually the case—Chicanas are often the subjects of checking, questioning, and threatened or actual deportation by the United States Immigration and Naturalization Service. Though reliable deportation statistics are not available, there are documented incidents of Chicanas who could not provide "adequate" proof of citizenship or immigrant status, and were speedily deported, leaving their American-born children behind.

Puerto Rican Women. The 1977 Census shows 1.7 million Puerto Ricans in the United States. Of these, 934,000 are female. Puerto Rican women complete an average of 10.1 years of school; 24 percent attain a high school education; and only two percent are college graduates.

As with other Spanish-speaking women, Puerto Rican women are often disadvantaged by lack of bilingual services and programs. This has a direct effect on their educational attainment and employment opportunities.

Nearly half of Puerto Rican women participating in the labor force are operatives and service workers. Of those Puerto Rican women with incomes, 66 percent earn less than $5,000. Data indicate that in 1976, 38 percent of Puerto Rican families in the United States were headed by women, a percentage substantially above the national average of 13.3 percent.

Cuban American Women. The Cuban origin population is estimated to be around one million. In educational attainment they stand somewhat higher than other groups of Hispanic women. However, bilingual and bicultural education and services are a priority for them. Adjustment of legal status and slow procedures in immigration matters continue to be obstacles to their full integration into employment and political life.

OFFENDERS

States should review and reform their sentencing laws and their practices to eliminate discrimination that affects the treatment of women in penal facilities. Particular attention should be paid to the needs of poor and minority women.

States should reform their practices, where needed, to provide legal counseling and referral services, improved health services emphasizing dignity in treatment for women in institutions, and protection of women prisoners from sexual abuse by male and female inmates and correctional personnel.

Corrections boards must provide improved educational and vocational training in a nonstereotyped range of skills that pay enough for an ex-offender to support her family.

Law enforcement agencies, courts, and correctional programs must give special attention to the needs of children with mothers under arrest, on trial, or in prison.

States must increase efforts to divert women offenders to community-based treatment facilities such as residential and nonresidential halfway houses, work release centers, or group homes as close to the offender's family as possible.

Disparities in the treatment of male and female juvenile offenders must be eliminated; status offenses must be removed from jurisdiction of juvenile courts; and States are urged to establish more youth bureaus, crisis centers, and diversion agencies and receive female juveniles detained for promiscuous conduct, for running away, or because of family or school problems.

Background:
"Only one out of 10 violent crimes is committed by a woman."

Women make up a relatively small proportion of the prison population, and until recently little data had been collected or any effort made to understand their special problems. Studies have shown that they are treated differently and frequently fare worse than men in statutes, in courts, and in correctional institutions.

Who they are According to the U.S. Justice Department's Law Enforcement Assistance Administration, most incarcerated women are under 30, and 50 percent are black. Most are mothers, though only 10 percent had been living with husbands before they went to prison. The majority are less educated than women as a group, and most of them want to work when they are released.

Uniform Crime Reports of the FBI indicate that most women are arrested for crimes against property such as larceny, forgery, embezzlement, and fraud. Only one out of 10 violent crimes is committed by a woman.

Discrimination in sentencing
Some States have laws that permit indeterminate sentences for women, and this leads to longer sentences for women than for men convicted of the same crime. The traditional theory has been that women are more responsive to rehabilitation and therefore should be incarcerated for longer periods. Since 1970, some State laws allowing longer sentences for women have been found in violation of the 14th amendment and the equal protection clause.

Institutions for women After sentencing, a woman will probably be sent farther from her home than a male offender. Because of the relatively small number of female offenders (5,600 women out of 196,000 inmates in State and Federal prisons in December 1970), there are fewer institutions for them (four Federal institutions for women, 23 for men; 40 State prisons for women and 250 for men). With smaller and fewer facilities, there is less opportunity to provide specialized quarters. The result is that hard core repeaters, juveniles, and first offenders are sometimes placed together.

Women's prisons are less likely to have full-time medical staffs or adequate hospital facilities. General support services—counseling, library, religious, and recreational—may not exist at all. In those institutions in which men and women are housed in separate sections, women often do not have access to the programs and services that are available to the men.

Job training Women in prison have fewer opportunities for rehabilitation and vocational training than do men. In a 1976 study of some 6,200 women offenders by the Female Offender Resource Center of Washington, D.C., 84 percent said that their greatest problem was a lack of job skills. Lack of education was the second most important problem.

There are an average of 10 vocational training programs in men's prisons as opposed to an average of less than three programs in women's institutions, a Yale Law Review survey found in 1973. The men's programs are usually in financially rewarding fields such as plumbing and electronics, while women's prisons offer training in only low paid skills such as housekeeping, cosmetology, nursing aid, and clerical work.

Mothers and children Between 70 and 80 percent of the women in prison are mothers, and approximately half of these are the sole support of their children. There are very few programs geared to their special needs. They may face such problems as loss of contact with their children after arrest, possible loss of custody, possible placement of children in foster homes, or referral to adoption agencies.

Alternatives to prison Half-way houses and other programs in which a woman can be rehabilitated close to home have been tried successfully in some cases. In Pennsylvania, community-based programs have been organized to provide women offenders with housing, legal counsel, child care, employment, job training, education, and individual counseling. Several programs in California have demonstrated that correction within the community is more effective in reducing the number returning to crime then severe forms of punishment.

Work-release (under which a sentenced prisoner is confined only at night or on weekends and is permitted to work) is not used as extensively for female offenders as for men. In a 1974 *Southern California Law Review* study, women in California prisons were found to be excluded from work-release programs for "economic reasons." The rationale offered by prison officials is that since there are fewer women offenders than men, it is not economical to spend limited program funds on them; women don't need jobs to support themselves or dependents; it is more expensive to provide separate housing for women.

Juveniles At every point in the juvenile justice system young women are treated differently and usually more harshly than young men. There appears to be greater willingness to institutionalize girls for far less serious offenses than those for which boys are committed. More young girls are in custody for what are called status offenses—acts not considered criminal if committed by an adult—such as promiscuity, running away, truancy, unruly behavior. According to a study by the National Assessment of Juvenile Corrections Project, 75 percent of the girls in juvenile correctional facilities were status offenders, as compared with 25 percent of boys in juvenile correctional facilities. The rest were declared delinquent (behavior considered criminal if committed by an adult). Because of the vagueness of the wording of many status offender laws, girls are too frequently locked up "for their own safety and well-being" or to protect their "morals."

Once institutionalized, girls have less recreation, less vocational training, and less quality care in counseling than boys, and like their older sisters, they remain in custody longer.

OLDER WOMEN

The Federal and State governments, public and private women's organizations, and social welfare groups should support efforts to provide social and health services that will enable the older woman to live with dignity and security. These services should include but not be limited to:

☐ Innovative housing which creates as nearly as possible an environment that affords security and comfort.

☐ Home health and social services, including visiting nurse services, homemaker services, meals-on-wheels, and other protective services, that will offer older women alternatives to institutional care, keeping them in familiar surroundings as long as possible.

☐ Preventive as well as remedial health care services.

☐ Public transportation in both urban and rural areas for otherwise housebound women.

☐ Continuing education in order to insure that the older woman will be an informed and intelligent user of the power which will be hers by virtue of the increase of her numbers.

☐ Immediate inclusion of geriatric education in the curriculum and training of all medical personnel in order that the elderly will receive optimum medical attention. This applies particularly to nursing home staff.

☐ Bilingual and bicultural programs, including health services, recreation, and other programs, to support elderly women of limited English-speaking ability.

☐ Elimination of present inequities in social security benefits.

☐ Recognition of the economic value of homemaking in social security benefits.

☐ Passage of the Displaced Homemakers bill.

☐ Expansion of coverage for medical and health care costs.

☐ Inclusion of older women as active participants in all kinds of policymaking positions at every level of government.

☐ The image of the older woman is changing, and there should be wide publicity focused on this. The effective use of the media is essential to furnishing information to the older woman so as to insure her informed participation in the decisionmaking process which continuously affects the quality of her life and the life of her community.

☐ Mandatory retirement should be phased out.

Background:
"Most older persons need only a little help—assistance in personal shopping or someone to prepare an occasional hot meal—and these small needs are sometimes the hardest to meet."

Poverty, isolation, and inadequate medical care deprive many older women of a productive and secure old age. The number of people facing this deprivation is increasing. More Americans live longer, and women outlive men by a widening margin. A woman's life expectancy is 76 years compared to 68 for men. On average, women live eight years longer than men.

Living alone in poverty After a lifetime of caring for men and children, women are left the poorest of the elderly, according to U.S. Bureau of Labor Statistics data. In 1976 women over 65 had the lowest median income of any age or sex group: $2,800, about half the income of men their age. Black women are poorer than the average—nearly half the black women over 65 were living below the poverty level.

Most women outlive their spouses. On average, a woman can expect to live the last 11 years of her life as a widow, (most men are married when they die)—and she will be worse off financially than when her husband was alive. The stereotype of the "rich widow" is a myth that occurs more often in operettas and fiction than in real life.

Women mentioned loneliness twice as often as men when a 1976 Harris poll asked about the worst aspects of growing older. Wherever they live, in cities or country, elderly women depend on public transportation. When it doesn't exist, or is too expensive, they are isolated in their homes. Most women over 65 do not have regular access to a car, reports the Bureau of the Census.

Older women living alone in big cities are often afraid to go out of their homes. According to a University of California study, one-third of the females robbed on our city streets are women over 65. They are six times as likely to become victims of crime as the rest of the population. Four out of five of these crimes against elderly women occur near their homes, frequently because it is known that they receive retirement checks in the mail.

Housing designed for the lifestyle and incomes of older people would permit them to live together in a more secure and supportive environment where needed services would be readily available.

Home care services Because women are more likely to live to an older age when disability is frequent, nearly three-fourths of the elderly living in institutions are women. According to Representative Claude Pepper of Florida, chair of the House Select Committee on Aging, 40 percent of the elderly who enter nursing homes are not sick; they simply cannot feed themselves adequately.

In a plea for a national policy toward the aged that will keep them out of institutions as long as possible, Dr. James H. Sammons, executive vice president of the American Medical Association, said. "Most older persons need only a *little* help—assistance in personal shopping or someone to prepare an occasional hot meal—and these small needs are sometimes the hardest to meet."

Nearly a fourth of the elderly now living in nursing homes could live on their own with proper services, estimate the National Retired Teachers Association and the American Association of Retired Persons, but nursing, home health care, homemaking, meals-on-wheels, transportation, escort, recreation, legal, and counseling services are available only sporadically. A few programs are funded through the Older Americans Act and Title 20 of the Social Security Act, but these funds do not begin to meet the need. Less than one percent of Medicare funds was spent for home health services in 1975.

Medicare inadequacies Medicare insurance for the elderly costs them more and covers less of their medical costs than it did when the system was enacted in 1965. Inflation and the rising number of eligible participants have reduced the benefits available. In fiscal 1976, for instance, Medicare covered only 43 percent of the total health care costs of the elderly.

Though Medicare provides hospital insurance, it does not automatically take care of doctor's bills. That option must be chosen and paid for. People with low incomes are technically eligible for Medicaid, but to receive such total care the patient often has to be institutionalized.

Medicare offers no coverage at all for many of the services older people must have: annual health examinations; eyeglasses, required by more than 90 percent of the elderly; dental care, which half have neglected for five years; hearing aids, used by a fifth of the elderly and needed by half; prescription drugs, on which the elderly spend an average of $100 per year.

Productive years Concern for their health needs sometimes obscures the fact that a majority of older people want to and can be productive contributing citizens. An American Medical Association survey found that 82 percent of people over 65 have no limitations on their mobility. The Gray Panthers, an activist group advocating better conditions for the elderly, has campaigned against media stereotyping which portrays them as "stubborn, rigid, inflexible, forgetful, and confused." Mobilized by their organizations, however, older people can be a potent political force, reported *The New York Times* in an article on October 10, 1977. Their basic demands are to remain as independent as possible and to have a voice in making decisions that affect them.

Mandatory retirement Many older people want to work as long as they are able. Eight percent of women over 65 are gainfully employed, and according to a recent Harris poll, 30 percent would like to work.

Unfortunately, an elderly man is more acceptable to employers. In the preretirement decade, ages 55 to 64, unemployment is more than double for women; after age 65, the disparity increases.

Some are forced from their jobs by mandatory retirement rules in government, business, and educational institutions. For several years a number of organizations have joined the elderly in lobbying for a change in these rules that are thought to affect about 41 percent of the 21 million workers who are covered by pension plans.

A Congressional Committee on the Aging heard testimony that compared older workers favorably with younger colleagues in dependability, judgment, work quality and volume, human relations, and absenteeism and noted that older workers have fewer on-the-job accidents.

"Chronological age alone is a poor indicator of ability to perform a job," concluded the report of the House Committee on Education and Labor. By October 1977 both the Senate and the House had passed a bill adding five years to the statutory ban on age-based discrimination in the workplace, including involuntary retirement. When and if the bill becomes law, it will postpone for five years the age at which most Americans (with the exception of some teachers and highly paid executives) can be retired against their will.

Many older people who are not working have gone back to school. They are a growing number on every educational campus, and many more would be attending classes if they could afford tuition and had transportation available to them.

RAPE

Federal, State, and local governments should revise their criminal codes and case law dealing with rape and related offenses to:

☐ Provide for graduated degrees of the crime with graduated penalties depending on the amount of force or coercion occurring with the activity.

☐ Apply to assault by or upon both sexes, including spouses as victims.

☐ Include all types of sexual assault against adults, including oral and anal contact and use of objects.

☐ Enlarge beyond traditional common law concepts the circumstances under which the act will be considered to have occurred without the victim's consent.

☐ Specify that the past sexual conduct of the victim cannot be introduced into evidence.

☐ Require no more corroborative evidence than is required in the prosecution of any other type of violent assault.

☐ Prohibit the Hale instruction where it has been required by law or is customary.

Local task forces to review and reform rape law and practices of police, prosecutors, and medical personnel should be established where they do not now exist. Such task forces should also mobilize public support for change. Rape crisis centers should be established (with Federal and State funding) for the support of victims, and the confidentiality of their records should be assured. Bilingual and bicultural information resources should be made available where necessary.

Federal and State funds should be appropriated for educational programs in the public school system and in the community, including rape prevention and self-defense programs.

The National Center for the Prevention and Control of Rape within the National Institute of Mental Health should be given permanent funding for operational costs, for staff positions, research and demonstration programs, and for a clearinghouse on sexual assault information and educational material with regard to prevention, treatment of victims, and rehabilitation of offenders. In addition, rape centers should be consulted by NIMH in the setting of priorities and allocation of funds. The National Center should be continued in order to insure community involvement, and the composition of the committee should be reviewed to assure minority representation and a majority of women.

State legislatures should expand existing victim compensation for the cost of medical, surgical, and hospital expenses; evidentiary examinations; counseling; emergency funds for housing, etc.; and compensation for pregnancy and pain and suffering.

Background:
"Rape leaves its victims with psychological damage far greater than that inflicted by virtually any other violent crime."

A crime of violence directed primarily at women, rape is the fastest growing crime in the United States. Because of the nature of the crime, its victims face humiliation and embarrassment compounded by the insensitive treatment they receive from police and the courts.

The number of reported rapes increased 48 percent in the United States between 1970 and 1975, according to FBI statistics. In 1975 alone there were 56,000 reported rapes, or one every nine minutes. The rise in number of cases may partly be due to better police reporting and the increasing willingness of victims to go to the police, but rape is still one of the most underreported crimes. Two studies in the Washington, D.C. area estimate that the number of rapes may range from three and a half to nine times those actually reported. (The studies were conducted by the Metropolitan Washington Council of Governments and the District of Columbia City Council.)

Convictions are low   The rate of conviction for those accused of rape is low. No arrest is made in 49 percent of all reported cases. The FBI's Uniform Crime Reports for 1975 indicate that only 58 percent of those arrested were actually prosecuted. And of these, almost one-half were acquitted or charges were dismissed. The rate of conviction is lower than in other crimes for a number of reasons: victims are reluctant and even afraid to testify; the evidence required by many State laws may be impossible to produce; and medical and legal authorities have traditionally viewed rape victims with suspicion and hostility.

Some sexual assaults are not even considered rape under the common law definition, which is the basis for most statutory and case law. According to this definition, rape is the unlawful carnal knowledge (penetration, however slight) of the victim by the alleged assailant without the victim's consent. Other forms of sexual assault, such as oral and anal contact and use of objects, are not included in this traditional definition. Under common law, sexual intercourse by a man with his wife against her will can never constitute rape, leaving many women without legal protection against a violent husband.

The myths about rape   Rape is not a crime of sexual passion; it is a crime of violence. In most cases (85.1 percent, according to Menachim Amir, author of *Patterns in Forcible Rape*, published by the University of Chicago), force is used: choking, beating, roughness, or use of a weapon. Amir also reports that 71 percent of rapes are planned—the place arranged, enticement used, or the victim deliberately sought.

Rape victims do not come from any specific age or socioeconomic groups. Women of all ages, races and economic background get raped. Rape Awareness, a Miami group, reported that victims range from two months to 85 years of age.

Contrary to common myth, rape victims do not secretly enjoy or invite the violation. Rape leaves its victims with psychological damage far greater than that inflicted by virtually any other violent crime. In a study on *Rape and Its Victims,* the Department of Justice described it as "one of the most brutal of all crimes. Rape victims need sustain no physical injury to suffer severe and long-lasting pain; few crimes are better calculated to leave their victims with lasting psychic wounds."

Some of these wounds were reported by Andra Media and Kathleen Thompson in their book *Against Rape,* published by Farrar, Straus and Giroux in 1974. After being raped, women said:

They were afraid of men;
Their sex lives had suffered;
They felt less independent or were afraid of being on their own;
They felt worthless and had lost their self-respect.

Rape "altered" their lives in a major way, reported 89 percent of the victims interviewed for a study by the Queens Bench Foundation, an organization of women attorneys and judges.

Another myth without any basis in fact is that rape victims accuse men they know as a form of revenge. In New York City, the police statistics for one year showed that only 3.4 percent of rape complaints were unfounded—a rate comparable to that of other crimes. And of these unfounded reports, only 0.4 percent were believed to be motivated by "revenge." Most adult victims are raped by strangers, according to a study in the District of Columbia, published in *Sexual Behavior,* December 1968. Children, on the other hand, are more likely to be attacked by someone they know.

The victim and the law   The rape victim usually faces skepticism, contempt, embarrassing questioning, and generally callous treatment by police officers, hospitals, and criminal prosecutors at a time when she is most in need of consideration and support. The ordeal may increase the trauma she has already suffered, and it makes future victims reluctant to cooperate even with those authorities who seem zealous in pursuing rapists.

She also faces obstacles in State laws about evidence that are "based on a deeply suspicious view of both the nature of woman and sexual intercourse," according to the authors of *Sex Discrimination and the Law,* published by Little, Brown and Company in 1975.

Rape is the only crime in which the victim has to prove that she did not consent and did not want, even subconsciously, to be raped. Her past sexual history can be introduced to show consent or undermine her credibility, but the past behavior of the defendant, even if criminal, is often not considered relevant.

Many State codes have definitions of consent that place untenable burdens upon the victim. Accused rapists have been acquitted because the victim did not resist enough. A woman has to prove that she resisted even when resistance had been clearly impossible—when the assailant had a weapon, for example. In New York the burden of proof on a victim is now just somewhat lighter—the statute was amended to require that a woman resist as much as is realistically possible, given the circumstances of the attack.

Corroboration While most States do not require corroborative testimony to bring a case to trial, such evidence is usually needed to get a conviction. Criminals who intimidate their victims with weapons or threats of harm generally do not leave evidence behind, and such evidence is not required for many other substantive crimes. It places the testimony of a sex victim on the same footing as the word of a small child, whose testimony alone does not ordinarily suffice to establish a crime.

The Hale instruction   Judges are required by law in some States, and by tradition in others, to instruct the jury that "rape is an accusation easily to be made and hard to be proved, and harder to be defended by the party accused, though ever so innocent." These words of caution, known as the Hale instruction, date back to the 17th century jurist Lord Chief Justice Matthew Hale. They only enforce the suspicion that constantly haunts a rape victim and make it even more likely that the criminal will go unconvicted.

Legislation   The National Center for the Prevention and Control of Rape was created in 1976 (Public Law 94-63) as a result of legislation introduced by Senator Charles Mathias of Maryland. It had an initial appropriation of $3 million in 1976 and $5 million in 1977. It has a professional and support staff of six people and is under the auspices of the National Institute of Mental Health, U.S. Department of Health, Education and Welfare.

The Center's responsibility is to develop, implement, and evaluate promising models of health and related services for rape victims, their families, and for offenders. It encourages research into the legal, social, and medical aspects of rape, and through its research and demonstration program is developing public information and training materials aimed at preventing and treating problems associated with rape.

As of March 1978, legislation was expected to be introduced by Senator Mathias authorizing the Center to enter into contracts with States, local government agencies, and nonprofit organizations, including local rape crisis centers, to develop and establish training programs and other direct services (including counseling techniques for both the victim and the offender), for paraprofessional, professional, and volunteer personnel in law, social services, mental health, and other related services that deal with rape problems.

REPRODUCTIVE FREEDOM

We support the U.S. Supreme Court decisions which guarantee reproductive freedom to women.

We urge all branches of Federal, State, and local governments to give the highest priority to complying with these Supreme Court decisions and to making available all methods of family planning to women unable to take advantage of private facilities.

We oppose the exclusion of abortion or childbirth and pregnancy-related care from Federal, State, or local funding of medical services or from privately financed medical services.

We urge organizations concerned with improving the status of women to monitor how Government complies with these principles.

We oppose involuntary sterilization and urge strict compliance by all doctors and medical and family planning facilities with the Department of Health, Education and Welfare's minimum April 1974 regulations requiring that consent to sterilization be truly voluntary, informed, and competent. Spousal consent should not be a requirement upon which sterilization procedures are contingent. If the patient does not speak English, appropriate staff must be found to explain the procedures and HEW regulations in the primary language of the patient.

Particular attention should be paid at all levels of Government to providing confidential family-planning services for teenagers, education in responsible sexuality, and reform of laws discriminating against unwed parents and their children.

Programs in sex education should be provided in all schools, including elementary schools.

Federal, State, and local governing bodies should take whatever steps are necessary to remove existing barriers to family planning services for all teenagers who request them.

Each school system should assist teenage parents with programs, including child care arrangements, that will encourage them to remain in school, provide educational and vocational training leading to economic independence, and teach prenatal health and parenting skills.

human right to have readily available the means of controlling reproduction. As the World Plan of Action adopted in Mexico City acknowledged, the "exercise of this right is basic to the attainment of any real equality between the sexes."

The Supreme Court decision In its historic (*Rowe v. Wade*) decision of January 22, 1973 affirming the right of a woman to choose abortion, the U.S. Supreme Court held that the constitutional right of privacy "is broad enough to encompass a woman's decision whether or not to terminate her pregnancy."

The decision, written by Justice Harry Blackmun and concurred in by six other justices, cited the hardships a State could impose upon a pregnant woman by denying her this choice:

"Specific and direct harm medically diagnosable even in early pregnancy may be involved. Maternity, or additional offspring, may force upon the woman a distressful life and future. Psychological harm may be imminent. Mental and physical health may be taxed by child care. There is also the distress, for all concerned, associated with the unwanted child, and there is the problem of bringing a child into a family already unable, psychologically and otherwise, to care for it. In other cases ... the additional difficulties and continuing stigma of unwed motherhood may be involved. All these are factors the woman and her responsible physician will consider in consultation."

While holding that the right of personal privacy includes the abortion decision, the Supreme Court decision also ruled that "this right is not unqualified and must be considered against important State interests in regulation."

Accordingly, the court held that for the first three months of pregnancy, the abortion decision must be left to the woman and her physician. In the next stage, approximately the second trimester, the State "in promoting its interest in the health of the mother, may, if it chooses, regulate the abortion procedure in ways that are reasonably related to maternal health." It is not until the stage of

Background:

"Each year, before the Supreme Court decision was handed down, physicians had to treat about 350,000 women suffering from complications arising from illegal abortions. Each year, some women died..."

Decisions relating to childbearing are rightfully the responsibility of the individual woman.

It is the woman's body that carries and nurtures the embryo and fetus. It is the woman who experiences the physical and psychological changes of pregnancy. It is the woman who has the discomforts and sometimes the medical complications that may accompany childbearing. It is the woman who feels the pain of childbirth. It is the woman who may suffer postpartum depression. And it is the woman who bears the major responsibility of caring for and raising the child and who often must leave school or her work to do so.

Every woman, regardless of her age, economic condition, race or ethnic origin, education, marital status, rural or metropolitan residence, is entitled as a fundamental

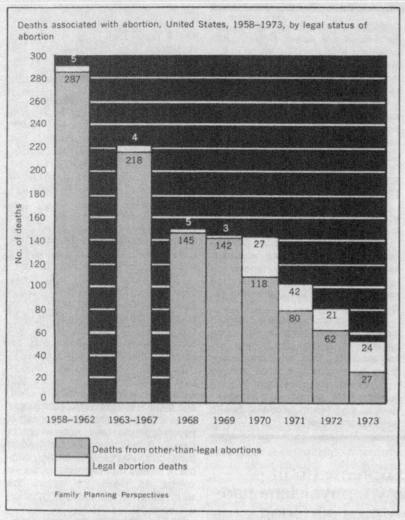

Deaths associated with abortion, United States, 1958–1973, by legal status of abortion

No. of deaths

Year		
1958–1962	5 / 287	
1963–1967	4 / 218	
1968	5 / 145	
1969	3 / 142	
1970	27 / 118	
1971	42 / 80	
1972	21 / 62	
1973	24 / 27	

Deaths from other-than-legal abortions

Legal abortion deaths

Family Planning Perspectives

viability, usually defined as the time when the fetus can sustain life outside the womb of the mother, the court said, that "the State in promoting its interest in the potentiality of human life may, if it chooses, regulate, and even proscribe abortion, except where it is necessary, in appropriate medical judgment, for the preservation of the life or health of the mother."

Before the Supreme Court issued its decision, most States had anti-abortion laws dating back to the 19th century. Protection of the woman's health was the major concern behind enactment of these laws because, before aseptic surgical techniques were developed, abortions were extremely dangerous and sometimes fatal, even when performed by physicians. Today, however, with a variety of techniques available and with abortions more available to women in the early stages of pregnancy, abortion is safer than childbirth.

Throughout the period when State antiabortion laws were in effect, an estimated one million American women were having abortions each year. About 10,000 of these women, usually white, middle-class, or rich women, succeeded in having abortions performed legally in hospitals. The great majority had to resort to bootleg abortionists. Prohibition of abortion was no more effective than the constitutional prohibition of liquor. In fact, illegal abortions were so common and profitable that they were said to be the third largest source of criminal revenue, following only narcotics and gambling. (D. Lowe, *Abortion and the Law*, cited in *The Rights of Americans*, edited by Norman Dorsen.)

Maternal deaths Each year, before the Supreme Court decision was handed down, physicians had to treat about 350,000 women suffering from complications arising from illegal abortions. Each year some women died as a result of those complications. In 1972, according to the Abortion Surveillance Report of the Government Center for Disease Control in Atlanta, when an estimated 550,000 legal abortions were performed, 88 abortion-related deaths were reported. Of these, about 63 were associated with illegal abortions. In 1975, when just under 900,000 legal abortions were performed, related deaths were down to 44.

As abortions have become more readily available, the trend is toward earlier, and therefore, safer abortions. In 1975, approximately 87.9 percent of all legal abortions were performed at 12 weeks or less, when the medical risk is slighter than in continuing pregnancy.

"Elimination of dangerous illegal abortions removed the main single cause of maternal deaths," the Planned Parenthood Federation of America reported in 1973. Effective use of contraception was another factor in reducing maternal mortality rates, it said, citing evidence that contraceptive practices improved markedly, "perhaps related to the contraceptive counseling provided in facilities performing abortions."

The report cited data from New York State, where, following State legalization of abortion, there was a marked decrease in the maternal death rate and a steep decline in numbers of women who were hospitalized or died because of botched abortions. It also reported a 54 percent decline in the number of newborn infants left for placement or simply abandoned.

Planned Parenthood noted that "about seven in 10 of the legal abortions of New York residents would have taken place anyway—most of them illegally—in the absence of the new law. In other words, the primary impact of legalizing abortion is to make safer, less expensive and more open a procedure which would have taken place anyway."

Constitutional amendment

Some abortion opponents favor so-called "right to life" amendments to the Constitution that would define the unborn as a "person," either "from the moment of conception" or at every stage of its biological development.

The Supreme Court held, however, that a fetus is not a person. "We need not resolve the difficult question of when life begins," its decision said. "When those trained in the respective disciplines of medicine, philosophy and theology are unable to arrive at any consensus, the judiciary, at this point in the development of man's knowledge, is not in a position to speculate as to the answer."

Medicine does not define when the "moment of conception" occurs. Is it when the egg is fertilized, or some five to eight days later when the process of implantation occurs? The state of pregnancy itself cannot be determined with certainty until some three weeks after implantation.

Philosophers and theologians hold a variety of views on when human life begins, with some contending that it is the undefined "moment of conception," others holding that it is when the fetus is viable, and still others supporting the view that it begins with live birth.

Lawyers have pointed out that conferring personhood on the unborn would create legal chaos. A memorandum prepared by Planned Parenthood attorney Harriet Pilpel noted: "Presumably the state could enjoin a safety regimen on every woman from the moment she conceived (assuming anyone could figure out what that moment was) and hold her accountable criminally and civilly for any injury the fetus suffered." In criminal law, she said, an individual committing a lesser crime that incidentally resulted in the miscarriage of a woman might be held guilty of murder; in general tort law, if a pregnant woman were in an accident, someone acting on behalf of the fetus might sue for negligence. As legal persons, unborn fetuses might inherit property, even if never born alive, or they might be counted as dependents for income tax purposes. All Americans could cite their gestation period to claim that they have instantly aged by seven to nine months, which would affect everything from birth certificates to death certificates, voting age, retirement, pension systems, insurance policies, etc.

Attorneys cite the potentially mischievous consequences of the ambiguously worded "right to life" amendments as evidence that the moral and religious concerns of people who oppose abortion are not subjects that can be appropriately dealt with in legal terms, particularly in a society with constitutional guarantees of separation of church and state.

Ban on Medicaid

Despite the constitutional guarantee of the right to abortion, in recent years antiabortion forces have been increasingly successful in restricting access to abortion through congressional, State and local actions. Some hospitals refuse to perform abortions and many women do not have access to abortion services in their local areas. In 1977 the Supreme Court ruled that States may decide not to fund abortions. Congress and a number of State legislatures have passed laws to prevent use of Medicaid funds for abortion, even though these funds are available for the full scope of medical services, including childbirth. A House committee recently attached an antiabortion rider to a pregnancy disability bill, and similar riders were being proposed for other legislation.

The result of these restrictive actions is that Medicaid recipients must either accept compulsory pregnancy and motherhood; face the dangers of cheap, amateurish or self-induced abortion; or worry about increased danger to their health caused by the delay while they try to raise the money for an abortion. The Government Center for Disease Control has reported the death of one woman who could not get a Medicaid-funded abortion, and other deaths have been reported among women who have resorted to back alley abortionists.

Women most severely affected by these restrictions are members of minority races, since they are disproportionately represented among the poor who rely on Medicaid for their health care.

(For comments on sterilization, see HEALTH plank background.)

Support for birth control

Most women prefer not to rely on abortion as a method of reproductive control, but they insist that it must be available to them as a choice. The most effective way to reduce the number of abortions is to provide safe, failproof contraception and to make sure that it is available to all fertile women and men.

The health consequences of unwanted and mistimed childbearing have been amply demonstrated. They are especially serious for teenagers and the poor, for whom pregnancy is inherently more risky. Babies born to women in these high-risk categories are less likely to survive and are more likely to have birth defects, mental retardation, and other long-term handicapping conditions.

The health and social benefits of family planning are well documented. Research indicates that the timing and spacing of births and the number of children born into a family are probably the most influential determinants of maternal, infant, and even long-term family health.

Yet only two percent of the money spent on research by the National Institutes of Health is earmarked for research in human reproduction and development of new techniques for fertility reproduction.

Teenagers and pregnancy Sexual activity is beginning at an increasingly early age. Teenagers account for almost half of the out-of-wedlock births in the United States. Their birth rate is higher in the United States than in 18 other countries; they have higher rates of death during childbirth; and their babies have a higher death rate during the first year of life. (Many of these statistics come from a 1976 study, *11 Million Teenagers, What Can Be Done About the Epidemic of Adolescent Pregnancies in the United States*, the Alan Guttmacher Institute.)

Most teenagers do not use birth control, and several studies note that those who visit birth control clinics have usually been active for at least a year. Two doctors from Johns Hopkins University, John F. Kanter

and Melvin Zelnick, in a study of teenage pregnancies reported a "pattern of having sex, becoming pregnant, and then going on to use birth control."

Ideally, education about reproduction and responsible sexuality should be provided at home by caring parents. Yet most young people do not receive adequate information. Dr. Robert C. Sorenson, author of *Adolescent Sexuality in Contemporary America,* interviewed more than 400 teenagers in 1973. Sixty-eight percent of the girls and 80 percent of the boys said their parents did not tell them about birth control. The Draper World Population Fund Report says that most sexually experienced teenagers who have not used contraceptives have a confused idea about the risks of pregnancy. Nearly 40 percent of those studied believed that pregnancy could not occur because they were too young or had infrequent intercourse.

Despite the acute need to create opportunities for teenagers to discuss their concerns and anxiety about sexuality and the need for increased knowledge about reproduction, contraception, and health hazards, only six States and the District of Columbia require the teaching of family life and sex education in the schools. In many areas, lack of parental consent and other barriers stand in the way of teenagers who want contraceptive information and services.

Teenage mothers Pregnancy is the most common reason for teenage girls to drop out of school. Without a high school education and some kind of skill, the teenage mother will be unable to support her child, and she may be its sole support. One-third of all babies born to teenagers are born out of wedlock, and teenage parents who are married have a higher divorce rate than older parents.

Until very recently most programs for pregnant adolescents and teenage mothers were designed to supply emergency aid for prenatal and early postpartum care, but once a girl became a mother, she was left to her own resources. Centers that offer comprehensive programs on a continuing basis can "reverse the terrible statistics of teenage pregnancy," according to Eunice Kennedy Shriver, reporting on such a center in Baltimore. The young mothers were given practical vocational training. Counselors helped them care for their babies and build solid family relationships with their own parents, and with the young fathers when that was possible. Two years later, less than one percent of the girls enrolled in the program had become pregnant again compared with the average of 20 percent repeat pregnancies for teenage mothers in general.

The right to choose Public opinion polls show majority support among both American men and women for the right to choose abortion. Women who assert their right to control their own bodies oppose compulsory abortion, compulsory pregnancy, or compulsory sterilization. In a secular democracy founded on concepts of individual rights and diversity of viewpoints, the right of American women to reproductive freedom must be fully protected.

RURAL WOMEN

The President and Congress should establish a Federal rural education policy designed to meet the special problems of isolation, poverty, and underemployment that characterize much of rural America. Such a policy must be consciously planned to overcome the inequality of opportunities available to rural women and girls.

The Office of Management and Budget should set and enforce a policy that data collected on beneficiaries of all Federal programs shall be reported by sex, by minority status, and by urban/rural or metropolitan/nonmetropolitan areas, based on a standard definition.

Data on employment of women and public programs on behalf of working women should include in their definitions farm wives and widows who perform the many tasks essential to the farm operation.

A farm wife should have the same ownership rights as her spouse under State inheritance and Federal estate laws. Tax law should recognize that the labor of a farm wife gives her an equitable interest in the property.

The President should appoint a joint committee from the Departments of Labor, Agriculture, and Justice to investigate the Louisiana sugar plantations system's violations of human rights, especially of women. This commission should also investigate conditions of other seasonal and migratory workers in all States and Territories of the United States.

All programs developed on behalf of rural women should be certain to include migrant, black, Native American, Alaskan, Asian, and Hispanic women and all isolated minorities, and affirmative action programs should be extended to include all disenfranchised groups.

Background:
"Because they are isolated, and live in sparsely settled areas, it is much more difficult...to provide services they desperately need."

Nearly a third of the people in this Nation live in what are considered rural areas; of these, 34 million are women and girls. While all of them are certainly not poor, rural residents account for 40 to 50 percent of the Americans in poverty. In general, rural residents have a higher incidence of social problems and receive a lower per capita share of the Federal dollars designed to meet those problems than the rest of the population.

The special needs of rural women have been ignored by the Federal Government, concluded the National Advisory Council on Women's Educational Programs, after a year-long study and consultations in Madison, Wisconsin; Stockton, California; Santa Fe, New Mexico; and Boone, North Carolina.

Efforts to improve the quality of rural life do not necessarily benefit men and women equally, nor can it be assumed that efforts to improve the status of women benefit rural as well as urban women.

Statistics on rural women Statistics that include specific categories for rural women are virtually nonexistent. No breakdowns into urban/nonurban classifications were made in nearly 100 statistical tables that appeared in the "Statistical Portrait of Women in the United States" published by the Census Bureau in April 1976. Federally supported programs that operate in rural areas, such as Cooperative Extension Services, are not required to report the extent to which women are involved or benefit.

Farm women Those rural women who are farmers receive little economic or legal recognition for the extensive work they do. The 1976 Federal inheritance tax reform increased the exemption allowed to a surviving spouse, but otherwise the wife's labor on the farm does not legally earn her as much right as her husband to the capital they have accumulated together. The burden is particularly heavy for family farmers whose property evaluations are high, when the cash available to pay taxes is ordinarily low.

Women as well as men consider farm work their careers, and farm women at the Houston Conference specifically urged that references to women in business include them. Many women are farm managers, and 25 percent of all college majors currently in agriculture are women.

Services for rural women The needs of rural women—farm and nonfarm, and migrant workers, Indians on reservations, and Alaskans are not substantively different from the needs of urban and suburban women. But because they are isolated and live in sparsely settled areas, it is much more difficult, and more costly to provide services they desperately need and for which many of these women are least able to pay.

Among the most critical needs, identified by rural women themselves, are education and training, job oppor-

to train teachers locally have become State colleges and universities. Teachers are less likely to come from—or return to—their own communities, and other functions formerly served by rural schools have disappeared completely. Many State education departments no longer have experts in rural education, and teacher training programs in human relations that are supposed to make teachers sensitive to race, class, and sex-stereotyping usually ignore or are inadequate for the needs of rural women.

Rural to urban New problems arise when rural people must quickly adopt "urban" lifestyles. This can happen when a rural area develops quickly, with destruction to the environment and to personal lives, caused by what may look to outsiders like progress—mechanization of mines, development of mills and factories, etc.

Suddenly, there may be a mix of people with very high incomes (and no experience in budgeting) living in close proximity to those who remain poor. In a "boom" town, there will be virtually no services—and a very high rate of personal and social problems.

tunities and placement, health education and health care, child care, early childhood education and special education, opportunities for personal growth and recognition, political participation, and understanding and achieving legal rights.

In some areas, services that once existed have disappeared in the name of progress. Local hospital and health services have consolidated to save money, leaving isolated communities completely unserved and many without doctors. Women suggest training rural women as paramedics to serve their own communities.

One-room schools have been absorbed by regional districts, and the old county "normal" schools that used

Relocation of migrant workers is also becoming more prevalent, especially in the Midwest, on the West Coast, and along the Eastern seaboard. Many of these people are Spanish-speaking, and their needs in all areas must be met in ways that recognize language barriers and varying cultural patterns.

Migrant workers In calling for an investigation of violations of human rights of Louisiana sugar plantation workers, particularly women, delegate Lorna Bourg of Louisiana said that the workers' mail is opened, their pay poor, and their health needs neglected. She said 60 percent of all adults living on the plantations have serious medical problems, and only a small percentage of the children are in good health.

SEXUAL PREFERENCE

Congress, State, and local legislatures should enact legislation to eliminate discrimination on the basis of sexual and affectional preference in areas including, but not limited to, employment, housing, public accommodations, credit, public facilities, government funding, and the military.

State legislatures should reform their penal codes or repeal State laws that restrict private sexual behavior between consenting adults.

State legislatures should enact legislation that would prohibit consideration of sexual or affectional orientation as a factor in any judicial determination of child custody or visitation rights. Rather, child custody cases should be evaluated solely on the merits of which party is the better parent, without regard to that person's sexual and affectional orientation.

Background:
"Homosexuals are entitled to the same civil rights as are other American citizens. There is no evidence that they harm others or society at large to any greater degree than do heterosexuals."

Despite increasing public understanding that sexual preference is a private matter of choice protected by the Constitution, homosexuals face widespread discrimination in every area of their lives.

As women, lesbians encounter double discrimination; their employment and earning opportunities are already limited because of their sex; their lifestyle challenges stereotypes of a woman's role; and their right to raise their children, if they have any, is threatened in the courts where judges may declare them "unfit" mothers. As Americans, they find their civil rights in jeopardy, and they are subject to potential harassment through selective enforcement of criminal laws.

There are no reliable figures on the number of homosexuals and lesbians in the population, because only recently have large members felt that it was safe to stop concealing their sexual preference. However, according to a March 18, 1977 letter from Paul H. Gebhard of the Kinsey Institute for Sex Research to the National Gay Task Force, the Institute's studies indicate that one out of five American women has had some form of overt lesbian experience after puberty. Gebhard estimated that 13.95 percent of males and 4.25 percent of

females, or a combined average of 9.13 percent of the total population, have had extensive homosexual experience. His conclusion: "... a significant percentage of the American population is predominantly homosexual in its sexual and affectional preference."

Lesbians point out that they are often the focus of attempts to "keep women in their place." A woman who does not choose to play a traditional or male-centered secondary role may find herself labeled too strong, too aggressive, too masculine, and finally, a lesbian. The fear of the effects of that label may limit the non-lesbian woman in the expression of her individuality. Only when the word "lesbian" has lost its power to intimidate and oppress will women feel free to be strong and independent human beings.

The changing view of lesbian and homosexual lifestyles has been influenced by positive statements issued by authorities on human be-

havior. In December 1973 the American Psychiatric Association ruled that homosexuality (in its generic sense) should no longer be listed as a "mental disorder," and said: "Homosexuals are entitled to the same civil rights as are other American citizens. There is no evidence that they harm others or society at large to any greater degree than do heterosexuals."

This position was endorsed a year later by the American Psychological Association, which said: "Homosexuality per se implies no impairment in judgment, stability, or general social or vocational capabilities."

Employment The most overt kind of job discrimination encountered is the refusal of the employer to hire or retain a lesbian or homosexual employee. A number of large employers, including AT&T, IBM, CBS, McDonald's, Honeywell, Procter & Gamble, and others have publicly stated their opposition to discrimination on the basis of sexual preference. Many other organizations and companies have no such policies, and discrimination is still prevalent in employment. The U.S. Civil Rights Commission has acknowledged jurisdiction "under the equal administration of justice" and is including homosexuals in studies such as police brutality, but it thus far refuses to recognize discrimination against gay people as an appropriate subject for its investigations and recommendations in employment, housing and public accommodations. The same is true of many of the various agencies, commissions, and boards established around the country at the State and local levels to oversee extension of full civil rights to minorities that are discriminated against.

Lesbians seeking Government employment that requires security clearance also encounter obstacles. They must be approved by either the State or Defense Departments, and in the past these departments have routinely denied clearance to known homosexuals or lesbians, using the rationale that they are vulnerable to blackmail. However, an openly gay

person is no more vulnerable to blackmail than anyone else. In 1976 the Defense Department effectively revised its automatic practice of denying security clearance to open gays, and since that time there have been almost no denials of security clearance to avowed homosexuals or lesbians.

In the armed services, however, those discovered to be gay are invariably discharged, frequently with a "less than honorable" label that can be a barrier to employment or promotion for the rest of the person's life.

The schools The most insidious form of employment discrimination is that based on false assumptions. There is considerable resistance to hiring acknowledged lesbians or homosexuals for jobs such as teaching or counseling that involve close contact with young people on the grounds that they might influence their students' sexual behavior. But according to the American Psychiatric Association, "there is no evidence that homosexuals molest children to any greater extent than do heterosexuals," or that they are "dedi-

cated to proselytizing persons of any age group."

Those in a position to know, the National Education Association and the American Federation of Teachers, have issued statements deploring discrimination against lesbian and homosexual teachers.

Housing Single lesbians living alone are discriminated against along with other singles. Lesbians living together face even more difficult problems, especially if they wish to rent or purchase a house. In an area zoned for family use, two women (or two men) may not be considered a family.

Credit A lesbian woman trying to obtain credit has two strikes against her: as a woman, her income is considered less secure than that of a man; as a lesbian, she may be considered less stable. A heterosexual married couple may co-sign loans, but a lesbian couple often may not, even if both partners are employed and have good individual credit ratings.

Child custody Many lesbians and homosexuals either first realize or come to accept their sexual orientation after they are already married, and sometimes after they have had children. Lesbian mothers may lose their children when they divorce, though specialists in child development do not support the view of some judges that lesbians are "unfit" mothers.

Dr. Benjamin Spock does not believe that parental visitation rights and child custody should be decided on the basis of a parent's sexual orientation. "I know of no evidence," he says, "that homosexual parents are more apt to raise homosexual children. Most homosexuals are the children of conventionally heterosexual parents."

Dr. Judd Marmor of the University of Southern California, a nationally known psychiatrist, says he knows of "no evidence that predominantly heterosexual parents are more loving, supportive, or stable in their parental roles than homosexual women and men."

Lesbians and the law Under the Constitution, it is not possible for any State or for Congress to make it illegal to be a lesbian or homosexual. However, in March 1976 the U.S. Supreme Court, in a widely criticized decision, affirmed the right of States to prohibit certain sexual acts between persons of the same sex.

In its decision, the Supreme Court upheld the constitutionality of a Virginia statute, nearly 200 years old, prohibiting a variety of sexual acts, including some kinds of heterosexual activity. The issue in dispute, however, affected only homosexual relations between consenting adults in private.

The Supreme Court decision did not say that States must retain or pass anti-sodomy laws, and in fact, some States repealed their sodomy laws after the decision. By May 1977, California, Colorado, Connecticut, Delaware, Hawaii, Illinois, Indiana, Iowa, Maine, New Hampshire, New Mexico, North Dakota, Ohio, Oregon,

South Dakota, Washington, West Virginia, and Wyoming had decriminalized sexual activities between consenting adults in private. Thirty-two States still have laws on the books that restrict private sexual behavior between consulting adults, laws that affect both heterosexuals and homosexuals but are selectively enforced against the latter.

Laws protecting the civil rights of lesbians and homosexuals have been passed in about 40 cities and municipalities around the country. They range from small college towns like Chapel Hill, North Carolina and Youngstown, Ohio to major cities like Detroit, Washington, D.C., Minneapolis, and Boston. The newly elected mayor of New York, Edward Koch, issued an executive order banning discrimination against gays in city employment, including the police and fire departments.

At the Federal Government level, several bills have been introduced, with 39 co-sponsors, amending the Civil Rights Act of 1964 to prohibit discrimination in employment, housing, public accommodations, and other areas on the basis of affectional or sexual preference. They are pending before the House Civil and Constitutional Rights Subcommittee, Representative Don Edwards, chair, but no hearings have been scheduled or projected.

Support for gay rights Among the organizations that have supported civil rights for lesbians and homosexuals, in addition to the National Gay Task Force, are the American Bar Association, American Psychiatric Association, American Medical Association, American Federation of Teachers, National Education Association, American Civil Liberties Union, Civil Service Commission, National Council of the Churches of Christ, National Federation of Priests Councils, American Jewish Committee (New York Chapter), Episcopal Church, Lutheran Church of America, National Association of Mental Health, National Organization for Women, National Women's Political Caucus, and Young Women's Christian Association.

STATISTICS

The Office of Management and Budget should require all departments and agencies to collect, tabulate, and analyze data relating to persons on the basis of sex in order to assess the impact of their programs on women.

The U.S. Bureau of the Census should aggressively pursue its efforts to reduce the undercounts of minority Americans, including blacks, Hispanic Americans, Asian Americans, and American Indians. The Department of Health, Education and Welfare should continue its efforts to implement the usage of special group identifiers in all vital statistics recordkeeping. These statistics should be recorded and reported by sex and subgroup.

Background:
"Undercounts of minorities deprive them of Federal funds designed especially to help the disadvantaged."

Federal statistics of all kinds have not identified women and minorities well enough to show exactly how they are disadvantaged. And when they are counted, the count is frequently inaccurate or absorbed into data that report on such ambiguous units as "households" or families.

Head of household One of the longstanding problems for women has been the concept of "head of household." In the Bureau of Census statistics, the husband was always considered the "head" no matter how much the wife earned. And the average family was described as consisting of a breadwinning father, homemaking mother, and two school-age children, even though, according to the Bureau's own figures, only a small percentage of all families have been at this lifestage in recent years—six percent in 1976, for example.

Many of these defects are being remedied. The 1980 census will drop the word "head," and the U.S. Bureau of Labor Statistics has already begun to analyze data on individual persons in the family and their relationship to other family members. This will make it possible to compare the unemployment rate of wives with employed husbands with the rate for wives whose husbands are also unemployed.

Once statistics begin to accumulate on this basis, those who make policy will have to recognize that social and family programs must be addressed to women in a great variety of family situations: single parents, childless women, women living alone or with unrelated persons, and others.
Employment statistics When employment figures are not collected by sex, it is difficult to assess the progress or lack of progress women are making in specific areas. This is particularly true in agencies. In the civil service, for example, reports of the number of persons promoted from one grade to the next do not identify them by sex—virtually eliminating an easy way to find out how many women are gaining access to the higher level grades from which they have been almost entirely excluded.

Statistical breakdowns by sex are necessary in many other areas. Inequities cannot be corrected unless accurate counts are kept.
Minority undercounts Members of minority groups are often left out of statistics entirely. They are undercounted as individuals and in their communities, making it more difficult to assess—and meet—their needs.

The Bureau of the Census estimates that 2.5 percent of the population, or 5.3 million people, were not counted in the 1970 census. They believe that 7.7 percent of all blacks were left out, compared with only 1.9 percent of whites.

They have not been able to identify the undercount as accurately for other minorities. Hispanics, Asian Americans, Pacific Islanders, and Native Americans have frequently been placed in the "other" category in statistical counts, which can obscure the specific needs of these large ethnic groups.

With the help of citizens advisory councils representing the Hispanic, Asian, and Pacific Island communities, the National Center for Health Statistics is asking States to add special identifiers to birth and death certificates. More than a dozen States with high minority populations have already agreed to provide more information, but it will be a time-consuming process to calculate the undercounting by comparing birth, death, and immigration records with the decennial counts.

Undercounts of communities in which minorities are concentrated deprive them of Federal funds designed especially to help the most disadvantaged. These communities are underrepresented politically and are short-changed in all programs for which Federal and State money is allocated on the basis of population, such as women's programs, health care facilities, vocational education, bilingual education, veterans' education, public works, and community development projects for bringing housing up to standard.

Action to eliminate some of these problems in data-gathering and analysis is the responsibility of both the Director of the Office of Management and Budget and the Secretary of Commerce. The OMB director provides departments and agencies with the instructions for submission of all types of data essential to the review of budgetary and legislative proposals, management and reduction of paperwork. In the fall of 1977, the responsibility for establishing policies and standards for Federal statistics was transferred from the OMB head to the Secretary of Commerce. Coordination between these two officials is necessary to get more accurate and detailed data that will be used to assess the impact of programs on women.

WOMEN, WELFARE, AND POVERTY

The Federal and State governments should assume a role in focusing on welfare and poverty as major women's issues. All welfare reform proposals should be examined specifically for their impact on women. Inequality of opportunity for women must be recognized as a primary factor contributing to the growth of welfare rolls.

Women in poverty, whether young or old, want to be part of the mainstream of American life.

Poverty is a major barrier to equality for women. Millions of women who depend on income transfer programs or low-paying jobs for their basic life support may be subject to the multiple oppression of sexism, racism, and poverty—and they are often old or disabled.

Many other women, because of discriminatory employment practices, social security laws, differential education of men and women, and lack of adequate child care, are just one step away from poverty. Consequently, the elimination of poverty must be a priority of all those working for equal rights for women.

Along with major improvements in the welfare system, elimination of poverty for women must include improvements in social security and retirement systems, universal minimum wage, nontraditional job opportunities, quality child care, comprehensive health insurance, and comprehensive legal services. A concerted effort must be made to educate the public about the realities of welfare, the plight of the blind, the aged, the disabled, and single-parent families and other low-income women.

We support increased Federal funding for income transfer programs (e.g., Social Security, SSI, and AFDC). Congress should approve a Federal floor under payments to provide an adequate standard of living based on each State's cost of living for all those in need. And, just as with other workers, homemakers receiving income transfer payments should be afforded the dignity of having that payment called a wage, not welfare.

We oppose the Carter administration proposal for welfare reform (H.R. 9030), which among other things eliminates food stamps, threatens to eliminate CETA training and CETA jobs paying more than minimum wage, and does not guarantee adequate day care. We oppose proposals for "workfare" where welfare mothers would be forced to "work off" their grants, which is work without wage, without fringe benefits or bargaining rights, and without dignity. H.R. 9030 further requires those individuals and families without income to wait weeks, possibly months, before even the inadequate grant is available.

We strongly support a welfare reform program developed from ongoing consultation with persons who will be impacted. This program should: 1) be consistent with the National Academy of Science recommendation that no individual or family living standard should be lower than half the median family income level for substantial periods (after taxes) and that this income should not fall below the Government-defined poverty level of family income even for shorter periods; (2) help sustain the family unit; and (3) insure that women on welfare and other low-income women who choose to work not be forced into jobs paying less than the prevailing wage.

In order to improve the status of women, the following actions should be taken:

a. To insure that welfare and other poor are not discriminated against as an economic class, affirmative action guidelines should be drawn up to provide that all employers who are recipients of Federal and/or State contract monies be required to show that they are hiring recipients.

b. There should be targeting of funds by local CETA advisory boards for the placement and training of women in nontraditional higher paying jobs, consistent with the original mandate.

c. The Department of Labor should make a study of jobs and wages based on a standard of comparable worth and speedily move the implementation of that study in all Governmental positions.

d. Unions should devote additional energy to the organization of women to upgrade pay and working conditions for women in traditional employment.

Quality child care should be a mandated Title 20 service available to all families on an ability-to-pay basis through training, education, job search, and employment.

Congress should encourage education of women by insuring that Federal and other education grants do not reduce an individual's or family's eligibility for public assistance in AFDC or in any other program.

Comprehensive support services and social services must be provided and adequately funded.

Background:
"Substandard income traps a woman and her family in a poverty cycle...that as a general rule causes great physical, psychological, and many times moral damage not only to the woman but also to her children."

Millions of American women live in poverty and either receive assistance or need it. They need direct income assistance so they can meet their day-to-day requirements for food, shelter, and clothing. They need back-up assistance in the form of child care, educational opportunities, job counseling, and training and employment programs to make it possible for them to become self-supporting at better than mere subsistence levels.

The largest number of poor women are the three million women caring for eight million children who make up 90 percent of all families receiving help under the Aid to Families with Dependent Children (AFDC) program. Another large group are the elderly, blind, or disabled women who receive help under the Supplemental Security Income (SSI) program. Many other women under age 65 and not caring for children receive aid under State General Assistance programs and/or receive food stamps.

Untold numbers of other poor women receive no help. They don't fit into any of the above categories, and very few States provide any comprehensive general assistance programs to reach those left out of Federal programs.

Poverty among American women is a shifting condition. Although the majority of poor women are white, the condition of minority women is deteriorating. In its study, *The State of Black America 1978,* the National Urban League reported: "The number of poor families headed by black women increased sharply from 1.0 to 1.1 million between 1975 and 1976, raising the proportion of families headed by black women that were poor from 50 to 52 percent. But the number and proportion of poor families headed by white women fell sharply over the same period."

Rising unemployment among black women was seen by the National Urban League as directly related to the increasing number of poor black women. "While almost three-fourths (71 percent) of the black families headed by unemployed women were poor in 1976, only one-fourth (26 percent) of the black families headed by employed women were poor," it said.

The human side   In the national debate over welfare reform, it is important to remember that the lives, hopes, and well-being of millions of women and their children are at stake. The human side of what happens to women in AFDC programs was described at the Department of Health, Education and Welfare hearings March 10, 1977 by Lupe Anguiano, head of the National Women's Political Caucus Welfare Task Force, who lived in San Antonio, Texas housing projects with families headed by women on AFDC.

"I found that substandard income traps a woman and her family in a poverty cycle," she said, "a living condition that as a general rule causes great physical, psychological, and many times moral damage not only to the woman but also to her children. Healing this damage is very often costly and sometimes impossible.

"I often accompanied the women to a doctor's visit, to a food stamp office, or on a visit to the welfare department. Finding transportation was the first problem; waiting in the welfare office or the doctor's office or in a food stamp line was another problem. Many times it took the complete day. Finding a babysitter to stay with the younger children or having someone stay at home to wait for those who come home from school was another problem. Then to top it all, the hostile attitude or treatment received from employees in these offices or agencies was exasperating. Additionally, all the families I lived with ran out of food in three weeks. In Texas a woman must support a family of four with only a $164 monthly grant ...

"Without a doubt women on welfare have serious mental and health problems. In my six-month stay in the housing projects I witnessed six suicide attempts .... The basic problem is inadequate income for support of basic family needs."

Although the Carter administration has pledged to provide more equitable and more adequate help for all those in need, its proposed welfare reform plan will not improve life for all these people. In some ways, it will make it worse. In addition, other proposals pending in Congress would cut back on even the limited aid now available.

Welfare reform   The administration-backed welfare reform bill (H.R. 9030/S. 2084) would replace the separate AFDC, SSI, and food stamp programs with one nationwide Federal program with cash benefits and a jobs program. The cash benefits would be a universal aid program, providing some benefits to all persons on the basis of their income and not limiting coverage, as present programs do, to certain groups such as single-parent families with children, or those over 65, the blind, or the disabled. Although the principle of a universal aid program has been widely applauded, its application in this legislation has been opposed by women on welfare because it would mean lower benefits than many now receive and the jobs program would cover only some needy people.

The administration bill separates persons into different categories with different benefit levels and eligibility conditions. The Federal benefits payable under the proposal to families with children would be lower than the combined value of AFDC benefits and food stamp benefits now available in approximately 40 States. For example, the proposed Federal benefit for a family of four "not expected to work" is $4,200 in 1978 dollars; for a family of four "expected to work," it is $2,300, even though the head of this family may not be able to find work. Federal benefits payable to the elderly, blind, or disabled would be $2,500 for an individual and $3,750 for a couple. This would be below the combined value of SSI benefits (including State supplements) and food stamps in some States. Benefits for childless couples or individuals who are 18 to 65 and not blind or disabled would be $2,200 and $1,100, respectively. The proposal permits but does not require States to pay additional benefits to supplement Federal benefits. Even if they did provide supplementary benefits, cash payments to families with children in the vast majority of States would be far below the 1978 poverty level of $6,400 for a family of four.

Individuals and families would be able to increase their income through paid employment or receipt of other nonassistance income, since some of that income will be disregarded in determining their eligibility for cash benefits. However, since welfare recipients are not guaranteed jobs, there can be no assurance that even everyone who is able and willing to work outside the home will be able to increase her income in this way. In addition, this factor offers no help to those who are wholly dependent upon the basic benefit for any length of time and to women who choose to stay home to care for their children.

Jobs for poor women Although women in AFDC programs must have the option of staying home, job opportunities are a key element in pulling women out of poverty. The administration proposal is supposed to assist women who are heads of families to become self-supporting if they are able to work outside the home. However, although the bill provides for public service jobs under a new Title 9 of the Comprehensive Employment and Training Act (CETA) if no private employment is available, these jobs would apparently replace rather than expand existing CETA commitments. Furthermore, the proposal does not even guarantee a public service job to all those who qualify. Moreover, despite the lack of a job guarantee, some families with children—two-parent families and single-parent families with children over 14—as well as single individuals and childless couples would be classified as "expected to work" and would receive lower benefits than others even though they are unemployed and actively seeking work.

The failure to guarantee a job together with the imposition of the work requirement and accompanying lower benefits would probably result in great pressure to give available jobs first to adults in families classified as "expected to work." This could mean that women heading single-parent families with younger children would be served last, if at all, by the jobs program even though they are theoretically eligible on the same basis as anyone else.

Women in two-parent families would also be largely disqualified from public service jobs because the program provides only one job per family, and the program specifies that the job would go to the "principal wage earner," the adult who had the highest earnings or worked the most hours during the last six months.

Under the administration proposal, persons "expected to work" would be required to accept minimum wage or slightly above minimum wage jobs in the private or regular public sector. Only if no such job was offered to the individual could she qualify for a public service job. That job would pay the minimum wage or slightly above, except that 15 percent of the positions could be classified as "work leaders" and receive up to 125 percent of the otherwise applicable pay rate.

In States that did not supplement the Federal benefits, the total combined gross income of benefits and wages available to a family of four in full-time minimum wage employment in the regular public or private sector at 1978 levels would be $7,432 in 1978 dollars, an amount barely above the poverty level and far below the Bureau of Labor Statistics lower living standard of $10,000 in 1976 for a family with an employed member. A family of four in a public service job in a nonsupplementing State would have a total gross income of $6,957.

The situation is even more bleak for individuals and childless couples. Their cash benefits under the proposal are so low that they are left in hopeless poverty without outside income. When they are able to get a job, they become eligible for cash benefits at earned income levels of $2,200 and $4,400, respectively, in nonsupplementing States.

At best, the administration proposal offers minimum wage jobs, but it fails to provide any stepping stones to higher paid employment. There is no provision for career education; no provision for ensuring that the jobs created will provide training for higher paying work in the regular economy; no emphasis on providing skills training for jobs other than those in the program; and no assurance that these subsidized jobs have counterparts in the regular labor market at adequate wage levels.

Although the categories of proposed public service jobs will provide needed services in local communities, they are not jobs with pay scales that will eliminate dependency unless some fundamental reappraisal of wage rates occurs.

'Workfare' plans Even more disturbing than the administration bill are other "workfare" proposals to force poor women into working off their family's grant as a condition of receiving public assistance. Some States are pushing strongly for authorization to start such programs for women who now receive AFDC payments, and legislation pending in Congress (H.R. 7200) would authorize such programs. Here is how they would operate:

Women would be assigned to unpaid work for public or nonprofit agencies and would work the hours necessary to pay off their family's grant. If a woman was receiving an AFDC check of $300 a month for her family's needs and she was assigned to work valued at $2.65 an hour, she would have to work 113 hours a month, or 26 hours a week, to work off her grant.

Under these programs, a woman would not receive any salary but would simply work as a condition of receiving the cash benefits. She would not be an employee of the agency or organization for which the work was performed and would not have any of the rights of an employee (collective bargaining, grievance procedures, etc.) or any fringe benefits (sick leave, vacation, health insurance). She would not even get social security coverage. She would not be an employee but a second class or "inferior" worker without any of the rewards or rights and benefits that a working woman has a right to expect.

The injustice of such "workfare" proposals is compounded by the fact that women could be assigned to jobs with little or no provision for skill development or training. In effect, they could just be used for whatever labor they were capable of and then later tossed aside without being any better qualified to enter the paid labor market and to support themselves and their families.

The Carter administration proposal does not provide any new funding for support services for those in employment or training. These services, including child care, are supposed to be provided under Title 20, but some States are already spending up to the ceiling in their Title 20 programs and therefore probably would not fund increased child care services.

The proposal does allow working adults to deduct child care expenses from their earnings before these are counted for purposes of determining eligibility for cash benefits. However, this does not apply to women who need child care for educational or training purposes and who do not have earned income sufficient to meet their child care costs.

While Congress ponders welfare reform, immediate action is needed to relieve the desperate poverty of women in the southern States where AFDC grants are indefensibly low as a result of the double race and sex prejudice of State governments. Federalizing AFDC at a decent level of family support must be a priority.

The purpose of welfare reform must be to bring millions of Americans out of poverty. For women in particular, welfare reform must include a comprehensive and multiple attack on the social and family problems that afflict poor women, enable them to exercise free choice on how they raise their children, and equip them, where possible, to become self-supporting members of a society that will benefit from their skills and participation.

CONTINUING COMMITTEE OF THE CONFERENCE

Whereas, Public Law 94-167 requires the establishment of a Committee of the Conference which will take steps to provide for the convening of a Second National Women's Conference to assess the progress made toward achieving the recommendations of this 1977 conference; and

Whereas, such Committee would constitute an important mechanism to consider steps to achieve the recommendations of this Conference.

It is hereby resolved that:

☐ A Committee of the Conference be selected by the National Commission on the Observance of International Women's Year after receiving recommendations of individuals to serve on the Committee in writing on or before December 30, 1977* from the delegates of this body following the Conference.

The Committee shall be composed of persons of diverse ages and racial, ethnic, religious, economic, social, and geographic backgrounds.

☐ This Conference calls upon the President to issue an Executive Order creating a commission to carry out our recommendations.

☐ The Committee of the Conference shall serve until such time as the President appoints such a commission.

☐ This Conference calls upon the President and the Congress to authorize and appropriate sufficient funds to enable these bodies to carry out this mandate.

*The Commission extended this date to January 15, 1978.

The National Commission appointed a Continuing Committee of the Conference, consisting of about 470 members from all parts of the country. The Committee held its first meeting in Washington, D.C. on March 22, 1978.

STATE MEETINGS: EVERY WOMAN HER SAY

The Groundwork for Houston

by Caroline Bird

From Eskimo villages to the Florida keys, every woman living under the American flag during the summer of 1977 had a chance to make her voice heard about what she thought should be done to remove the barriers "to the full and equal participation of women in the life of our Nation." Every woman 16 years or more—and every man, too—had a chance to vote for the delegates who would represent them at Houston.

More than 150,000 people took the opportunity Congress had provided to come to State and Territorial meetings. They came from metropolitan suburbs and inner city ghettos and midwest farms. They met on State fair grounds, college campuses, in hotels, civic centers, veterans' auditoriums, and under Hawaiian palm trees.

The law and its interpretive regulations set up simple ground rules. Meetings had to be open to the public. Parliamentary procedure had to be followed. Any duly registered female or male resident over 16 years old had the right to a vote. Women who do not ordinarily attend statewide meetings were to be recruited. Travel assistance should be provided for those who did not have the money for a trip away from home. Beyond that, each State or Territorial coordinating committee was free to plan its own program, although materials and other resources were available from the National Commission on the Observance of International Women's Year.

Each meeting was thoroughly planned and run by a local coordinating committee appointed by the National Commission. In addition to interested individuals and Congresspersons, more than a thousand national and State organizations concerned with women made nominations. The committees were chosen to be representative of the population of women they served and the special groups the law said the Conference had to attract: representatives of organizations working to advance the rights of women; members of diverse racial, ethnic, and religious groups; unions; publications; women of all incomes and women of all ages. The Commission also tried to include individuals competent in law, budgeting, public relations, conference planning, and the issues on the agenda.

More than half of the $5 million appropriated by Congress was allocated by the National Commission to the 56 State and regional committees. Based on a standard population and per capita income formula used by the U.S. Department of Health, Education and Welfare, grants ranged from $25,000 to $100,000 for the most populous States.

In order to provide common ground for the 56 meetings, the National Commission framed resolutions made on the basis of research and hearings set forth in its 1976 report, "To Form A More Perfect Union." The "core agenda" consisted of 16 resolutions on which all were asked to vote: resolutions on Arts and Humanities, Battered Women, Child Care, Credit, Education, Elective and Appointive Office, Employment, Equal Rights Amendment, Health, Homemakers, International Interdependence, Media, Offenders, Older Women, Rape, and Reproductive Freedom.

The Commission provided guidelines for workshop discussion and background material on these issues, but they were only suggestions. States were free to plan their own agendas on women's issues and programs, workshops, speeches, entertainment, and other complementary events. As a result, each meeting reflected the character and special concerns of its State or Territory.

Vermont led the way with a meeting in February. Neat, compact, with roots going back to the American Revolution, Vermont was an ideal pilot, just as its neighboring State, New Hampshire has been a good pilot for political primary campaigns.

The coordinating committee chosen by the National Commission planned a simple, neighborly 1-day "Vermont Women's Town Meeting" in its capital city. There was no expensive banquet or entertainment, but admission, bus service to Montpelier, and child care were all provided free. That meant that any woman in the small State could pack a brown bag lunch, take her children on the bus, spend the day at the meeting on the Vermont College campus at Montpelier while her children were cared for and fed, and get back home that night without spending a penny.

Like other small States, Vermont was allotted the minimum Federal grant of $25,000. Staff workers donated their services, the college donated the use of its facilities, and after the meeting, Vermont proudly returned $6,000 to the National Commission.

The kind of snow which makes Vermont a picture postcard had fallen the day before the meeting, but it did not prevent more than 1,000 women from attending, a greater number than anyone could remember coming together for any purpose in the State before. Nearly half said they belonged to no organization, and another 45 percent said they had never attended a meeting that discussed women. They came for all sorts of reasons, but the most poignant was given by a woman in a wheelchair: "I came to see if everything was really free and whether a disabled person could really participate."

The program the committee had planned contained the elements that all the State meetings were to include: workshop discussions on topics chosen by the State's own committee; a keynote speech; and a formal plenary session at which resolutions were voted and delegates elected.

Snow did not deter women from coming to Vermont College, site of first State meeting.

In Vermont, informal friendliness prevailed. People in boots drank the free coffee at the registration desk in Noble Hall while agonizing over which of eight morning workshops to attend and then sloshed through newly cleared campus walks to classrooms. In the morning, the most popular workshop was the one on "Women's Health Resources in Vermont." Another addressed the problems of French-speaking women in the sparsely settled "northeast kingdom" section of the State. "Alternate Lifestyles" was popular with refugees from the cities seeking the simple life. Informal cooperation reached a new high when a male reporter from the *Boston Globe* served as recorder for a workshop on the problems of homemakers.

Everyone crowded into the Vermont College gym to hear Frances "Sissy" Farenthold, president of nearby Wells College in Aurora, New York, describe the slow progress of equality for women under the law. Then another session of workshops, and back to the gym for the plenary meeting. After a spirited round of campaigning, most of the slate of delegates suggested by the committee were elected, and the body adopted resolutions from the floor on scholarships for continuing education for women, the rights of lesbians, diminution of violence and

Oral historians tape personal stories of Vermont women.

Governor Richard Snelling and Mrs. Barbara Snelling were among the early registrants at Vermont meeting.

Vermont coordinating committee plans State meeting.

Women from the villages came out in numbers for the Guam meeting.

Bush caucus at Alaska meeting.

Governor Ricardo Bordalla signs Guam's Equal Rights Amendment.

sex on television, and many other issues not addressed by the National Commission's core agenda.

In evaluating the meeting, the chair of the coordinating committee, Dr. Lenore W. McNeer, director of human services at Vermont College, said she hoped it would help women support each other and assert their interests to lawmakers. Two weeks later the Vermont legislature acted on a revision of the rape law that feminists previously had been unable to enact.

Vermont was the early bird. During the spring of 1977, State coordinating committees raced against time. The

More than 700 people turned out for state meeting at University of Alaska.

National Women's Conference had to be held no later than November 1977, and so that its agenda could reflect the decisions made in the States, those meetings all had to be held no later than July.

During the weekend of May 6, 780 Alaskan women crowded into the largest meeting room in Anchorage, a University of Alaska auditorium designed for 600. They had come in unexpected numbers in spite of an airline strike that could have stranded the isolated population of this huge State. Small children tagged around with their parents and were unceremoniously put to bed in sleeping bags in private homes. As in Vermont, it was the largest number of women ever to gather for a meeting in the State. Those attending adopted the core agenda by large majorities and elected 12 women of a variety of skin colors to represent them in Houston: four whites, three Tlingits, two Eskimos, one Athabascan, one black, and one Japanese American.

The same weekend 1,200 Georgians were formally squaring off to debate the Equal Rights Amendment in Atlanta's elegant Sheraton-Biltmore Hotel and were listening to Presiding Officer Bella Abzug of the National Commission tell them why they needed it. In this unratified State, the ideological split had begun in the carefully balanced Coordinating Committee. Conservative women presented their views in workshops on homemaker rights, child care, health, international interdependence, teenage pregnancy, and sex-role stereotyping in textbooks. More than 100 women nominated on the spot competed with the slate of 30 proposed

Commissioner Beverly Everett (left), Patricia Hutar and Chair Tay Thomas at Alaska meeting.

by the Coordinating Committee, and the meeting finally elected a racially and ideologically mixed delegation to Houston.

Two weeks later, in Boise, Idaho, women heard Valerie Harper, the actress who plays "Rhoda" on television, urge equal rights for homemakers, a popular issue in this ranching State. They also voted for the ERA even though the Idaho legislature had rescinded its ratification of the amendment, a move of doubtful legality.

Seven of the eight States that held early June meetings adopted all the core resolutions and elected delegations to Houston which were committed to equality for women. Otherwise they differed widely in geography, style, and concerns. In Arizona, where migrant labor is an issue, women refused to eat lettuce cultivated by non-union labor. Colorado's meeting was built around the theme, "Moving Mountains Together."

Indian women traveled long distances from their reservations to the New Mexico meeting and their men came to help them. In Oregon, Governor Robert Straub promised the meeting he would appoint a woman judge, and he later named Betty Roberts to the bench. In North Dakota, IWY Commissioner Koryne Horbal confessed that she became a feminist when as chair of the Minnesota Democratic Party she was asked to sew curtains for a party function. In Madison, women attending the biggest women's meeting ever held in Wisconsin heard Karen Grassle, television actress in "The Little House on the Prairie," tell why she was a feminist. They watched the University of Wisconsin women's crew race on Lake Mendota.

Women line up to register for Missouri meeting.

In these seven States, as well as in those which had held meetings earlier, women opposed to the program had attended or protested from the outside, and while they had sometimes made headlines and television news, they had not elected many delegates to Houston.

In Missouri, a State that has not ratified the Equal Rights Amendment, the anti-change viewpoint prevailed. The meeting was held at Washington University in St. Louis where Phyllis Schlafly, a leader of the Stop ERA movement, was attending law school. She did not attend this or any other State meeting, and other women publicly opposed to the ERA refused special invitations to serve on the Missouri Coordinating Committee. However, Ann O'Donnell, president of Missouri Citizens for Life, did serve.

Though members of the Committee were not of a single mind on the controversial issues, they did cooperate in planning a meeting around the historical theme, "Missouri Women, a Strong Past, a Confident Future." There were feminist speeches, a women's symphony, and a slide show of the history of women in Missouri. Chair Jean Berg saw to it that films and materials representing the anti-abortion view were available for the workshop on Reproductive Decisions.

The high point of the opening ceremonies was the appearance of six suffragists who had reproached the Democratic National Convention held in St. Louis in 1920 by staging a "Walkless, Talkless Parade" outside the convention hall. The Committee voted to give them yellow corsages in memory of the yellow banners they had waved at the male politicians 57 years before.

"The Missouri State meeting is an open meeting," Chair Berg announced. "There is no intent to create a uniform pattern of thinking or speaking." As expected, scores of women with conservative views were put in nomination for the 30 delegates to Houston who would be chosen on Saturday.

Fewer than 400 people had registered for Friday evening ceremonies

Women suffragists were honored at Missouri meeting.

and discussions, but on Saturday morning, when the election was scheduled, a coalition of anti-abortion and anti-ERA groups brought in more than 500 men and women who registered at the door. They brought along a handbill and a list of their own "New Suffragist" candidates printed on yellow paper. The sheets were offered to each registrant going in to vote. After a total of 861 had voted, insuring election of the anti-change "New Suffragist" slate, the visitors went back to St. Louis in their chartered buses without attending any of the workshops or entering into any dialogue with the women whose views they opposed.

Sunday morning, only 369 accredited registrants remained. They adopted some of the core agenda resolutions and passed a motion attempting to bind the elected delegates to vote for them at Houston. Knowing the attempt was useless, Chair Jean Berg pleaded with the

Long lines form to vote for delegates at Missouri meeting. Many people registered only for the voting.

elected delegates to be "open to other ideas and try to represent the diversity of opinion that was expressed at this conference." Privately, she cherishes the memory of a personal encounter with a Stop-ERA woman who sought her out during the confusion on Saturday to congratulate her on presiding "clearly and fairly" and to confess that she would have marched with the six suffragists if she had lived in their time.

The great majority of meetings were forums open to lively discussion and meaningful encounters between women of varying backgrounds and views. Most coordinating committees took very seriously the mandate of the law to attract women who do not ordinarily come to meetings of any kind, and they were conscientious in setting aside funds to pay the expenses of some women who would otherwise not be able to attend.

Both enterprises required ingenuity. Advance press notices were seldom compelling enough to bring out

105

Art sprouted on posters used to attract women to State meetings.

"Celebrating Women," a three-hour show, opened New York Meeting. Actresses Celeste Holm, Ruby Dee and Kim Hunter are in center.

women who were not used to going to meetings. Some States used alternate ways of spreading the word. In New Jersey, the telephone company inserted a notice of the meeting with bills to subscribers. In California, program flyers were placed in San Francisco buses.

Extraordinary efforts were made to recruit bilingual women, many of whom come from cultures that discourage women from participating in activities outside their homes. Notice of the meeting was translated into Portuguese in Rhode Island and into French in Maine. Special campaigns recruited Spanish-speaking women both in cities and in the agricultural areas of the Southwest. In California bilingual teams went into the fields in every county to tell workers about the program.

The really hard to reach responded only to a personal appeal. In South Dakota the outreach chair was an American Indian who visited her sisters living on reservations. In Connecticut coordinating committee teams visited homes for the elderly, mothers on Aid to Families with Dependent Children (AFDC), PTA meetings, handicapped women, and women offenders. In rural Nebraska planners made the rounds of farm and ranch meetings. In West Virginia they visited the wives and widows of coal miners and talked with hairdressers and neighborhood businesswomen who could spread news of the meeting by word of mouth. North Dakota mailed IWY posters to 600 beauty shops.

Many States whetted interest in a women's meeting by giving women a taste of what they could expect. The Arkansas outreach committee released a series of research papers on various aspects of the condition of women in the State that were reported in the press. The District of Columbia Committee held a two-day "hearing" at which it took public testimony on the problems of women. Oregon, North Carolina, Indiana, and Puerto Rico staged regional meetings at which women were invited to speak their minds. Utah outdid itself with 50 simultaneous mass premeetings, each co-chaired by a high school student and a local woman. New York sponsored a statewide "art on paper" competition.

Union women caucus during New York State meeting.

Alabama sent "Voices and Faces of Alabama Women," a pictorial account of the lives of 25 women important in the history of the State, on tour along with a gallery of women's art and a theatrical show of songs, poems, and sketches about women. Mayors in communities near the circuit proclaimed an International Women's Day, and a textile mill donated 100 IWY T-shirts to teenagers who distributed posters advertising the show. One visitor to the traveling exhibition wept when she spotted the picture of her mother, Idiana Little, leader of a 1927 march for the registration of black voters.

Conscious of the widespread belief that the "women's movement" downgraded women in the home, many States publicized studies on the legal status of homemakers. The National Commission, beginning in 1976, had sponsored these studies in every State.

Many States helped women financially by providing free or low cost bus transportation from distant parts of the State and using college campus lodging to keep expenses down.

Although meetings all over the country grappled with the same basic problems, there were regional differences in priorities and style. In Puerto Rico, for example, where the women's movement is not as advanced as it is on the mainland, the coordinating committee early decided that one of the goals of the meeting had to be consciousness-raising.

In order to encourage women to speak up for themselves, the organizers planned five regional meetings with a minimum of formal speeches but chaired by a leader specially trained in eliciting discussion. At a workshop in Ponce, the leader asked how many of the women who came had asked permission of their husbands or fathers and almost every hand in the audience shot up.

At the Territorial meeting on the campus of Sacred Heart College in Santurce, the workshop on "Female Sexuality and Sex Education" drew the largest number of participants. There were workshops on employment, marriage, divorce, media, and other IWY topics too. More than 800 women talked about some of the unique barriers facing Puerto Rican women. On the mainland, for instance, social security benefits are available for persons over 72 who have never earned money, but this amendment to the social security law has not been extended to Puerto Rico, where a far higher proportion of women reach retirement age without any record of earning. And though the island has a version of the Equal Rights Amendment in its constitution, married women can't file separate income tax returns.

The meeting was useful, but sedate. According to one reporter, young women attending seemed timid, and 17 professional women were elected delegates without organized campaigning.

The weekend after Puerto Rico' came California, the State where the women's movement is big, highly organized, diverse, socially advanced, politically sophisticated, and boisterous—and the California State meeting reflected that spirit. The 6,500 people who attended the many events, some of them outdoors, on the campus of the University of Southern California at Los Angeles belonged to scores of groups organized on the basis of ethnicity, occupation, ideology, and special interest. Among the many workshops was a "white ladies caucus" billed as a session to teach white women how to get along with black women.

Everything from the site and the date of the meeting to the counting of the ballots in the election of delegates was hotly and formally contested. Among others, blacks, Chicanas, and lesbians pursued conflicting concerns. Conservative women came too. They filled workshops on child care, family planning, and birth control; in one workshop half of the women present appeared to feel that the women's movement itself was the problem facing women.

The California meeting was a political arena for many polarized groups, and there were times when the coordinating committee despaired of getting anybody to agree on anything.

Women of all ages turned out for New York meeting.

Discussion was serious at Louisiana plenary session.

After nights of caucusing and many pleas for unity, the Californians elected their 96 delegates, the largest number from any State and as diverse as its population. There were among them 45 whites, 14 blacks, 21 Hispanic Americans and 10 Asian Americans. Thirteen declared themselves to be lesbians, and 30 described themselves as low income.

"We did it! Suzanne Paizis, the recorder of the California meeting, exulted. In the final pages of her report, she pointed out that agreement had been unrealistically expected of a body as diverse as that meeting in California simply because women are still stereotyped as a class. "What would happen," she inquired, "If you brought men together from all walks of life to discuss 'Credit Factors Influencing Your Life'? Who would expect bank presidents and hard core unemployed to attend or interact in those circumstances? Visualize thousands of neurosurgeons, truck drivers, school administrators, interior decorators, custodians, management consultants, tennis players, and sales-

108

men spending three days in a parliamentary session to come up with recommendations on 50 different subjects."

As the meetings followed each other in rapid successsion during June and July, the confrontation between women who wanted change and those who belonged to organizations opposing it sharpened. Both "sides" learned to present their case within the framework of the meetings.

Almost every one of the early meetings heard from the groups which had dominated the Missouri meeting: anti-ERA, anti-abortion organizations; some religious leaders; and right-wing Eagle Forum and Birch Society activists. Ann O'Donnell, the leader of the Missouri victory, went to some other meetings, and National Commission staffers recognized some of the male floor strategists at several meetings. But in some States only local conservatives showed up.

In Ohio a split among feminists enabled the "right to life" coalition to elect 80 percent of the delegates, but 10 of the anti-abortion delegates favored the ERA and individual "antis"

Sugar cane workers listen intently at Louisiana meeting.

Louisiana women vote on recommendations.

deserted the coalition to support many IWY planks at Houston. In Oklahoma a church-organized group elected a conservative slate, passed a resolution calling homemaking "the most vital and rewarding career for women," and then called for an end to the meeting, defeating the core agenda in a single block vote. Nebraska elected 16 delegates opposed to abortion but passed the ERA resolution in a highly charged plenary session.

The most spectacular victory of the conservatives was in Utah, the largest of all the meetings leading up to Houston. In this sparsely populated State, with little more than a million people, 14,000 men and women jammed the Salt Palace in Salt Lake City to attend "The Voice of Womankind: Utah's First State-wide Women's Meeting." They came at the call of some leaders of the Mormon Relief Society to stand up for "correct principles," to oppose Federal funding of child care, abortion, sex education in the schools, and employment "quotas" to secure equal opportunity for women. Although they reversed the intent of all the workshops designed by the pro-IWY State coordinating committee, the delegates they elected voted their compassion and

supported resolutions for the disabled, older women, and minorities when they got to Houston.

At the Mississippi meeting July 8 and 9 the Ku Klux Klan was added to the anti-change forces, which now comprised Stop ERA, Right to Life, the Birch Society, the Eagle Forum, the Conservative Caucus, and many local groups sympathetic with their point of view, as well as members of some fundamentalist and other church groups. Joining them were dozens of anti-feminist women's groups: the three "W"s, ("Women Who Want to Be Women"), the FIGs ("Factually Informed Gals.") With the exception of one black woman, who later resigned, all the delegates elected from Mississippi were white.

In Kansas, "Operation Wichita" flyers listed 809 parliamentary points on how to disrupt meetings. In Illinois, Ohio, Mississippi, Alabama, Hawaii, and Indiana, men acted as floor leaders and instructed their charges how and when to vote, when to speak,

109

and even handed them written notes. Whenever they could, they voted all the IWY suggested resolutions down en masse. Anti-feminists voted against aid to the handicapped in Connecticut, against reform of rape laws in Nebraska, and against world peace in Utah.

In Washington, where Mormons are less than two percent of the population, the *Seattle Post-Intelligencer* estimated that they were nearly half of those registered to vote at the State meeting. They came to vote against ERA, but they found themselves supporting other IWY goals. When a resolution supporting minority rights carried an endorsement of ERA, many opposition women were so torn that they abstained, but a few rose slowly and tearfully to vote "yes" for the minorities, ERA and all. Black women rushed over to embrace them. After a stormy session and a recount of ballots that took days, a majority of delegates favoring ERA was elected.

Although the "War Between Women" dominated headlines, the meetings accomplished their purpose of giving women, as individuals and in groups, a forum for the discussion of the issues that interested them and a showcase for their talents.

Many State meetings had exhibits featuring women artists and photographers. Women's history was a favorite theme. Crafts and other women's products were displayed. Idaho had a Women's Hall of Fame. South Carolina promoted its women of accomplishment by giving them badges titled, "I Broke a Barrier. Talk With Me." Entertainment ranged from cheerfully amateur to highly professional. The weekend meeting in New York's State capital, Albany, opened with a privately funded, professionally mounted three-hour show, "Celebrating Women," produced by Madeline Gilford, and featuring actresses Helen Hayes, Diane Keaton, Celeste Holm, Ruby Dee, Kim Hunter, Kitty Carlisle Hart, Hattie Winston, an Hispanic dance troupe, and a black rock group. New Mexico

Maine women talk issues over lunch.

featured multicultural entertainment: an Indian women's "Cultural Pageant," a black women's "200 Year Sojourn," and an Hispanic "Ballet Folklorica."

Workshops on ERA, homemaker rights, education, employment, and health were generally the most popu-

110

lar. Those on child care, reproductive freedom, international issues, and the ERA were most frequently disrupted by the opposition. In plenary sessions, 43 meetings adopted all or almost all of the 14 core resolutions. But the core resolutions were only a start. Everywhere, women came bursting to talk about issues that were not on the agenda. An additional 4,500 resolutions emerged from the 56 meetings.

Many resolutions reflected the concerns women brought to State meetings. Some were regional. In Louisiana, women wanted help for workers on sugar plantations; in New Mexico, for migrant workers; in Kansas, for family farmers. Arizona women wanted to eliminate the provision of their State constitution that restricted the highest offices of the State to "male persons." The Virgin Islands women demanded public hearings on a proposed agreement between their Government and the Hess Oil Company. Guam wanted local laws amended so that the Chamorro people could continue their customary practice of catching octopuses with sea slugs.

A large number of resolutions strengthened or added to the topics addressed by core resolutions. Minnesota asked the Governor to issue yearly public reports on recruiting and hiring of women in executive and judicial positions. New Hampshire asked for social security to fund schooling for widows and divorcees. Colorado urged measures that would encourage part-time and flexible work schedules.

The long list of new topics was aimed at practices that hurt those who have been silenced or are defenseless: volunteers, disabled women, rural women, lesbians, abused

Mississippi meeting aroused controversy. Male speaker opposes recommendation.

Wille Mae Latham Taylor, President of Southeastern Assn. of Colored Women, only black women elected to Mississippi delegation, resigned before Houston meeting.

children, and especially the racial minorities. Hispanics said that their problems were ignored because the census didn't count all of them. Arizona questioned placing Native American children in Anglo foster homes because "running water and utilities" were provided there, and they were angered by the unnecessary sterilization of Indian women. "Sometimes all you need is a Band-Aid," one spokeswoman said, "and what you get is a hysterectomy."

Resolutions calling for better housing, improved diet and nutrition, and stronger Government control of safety, energy, and natural resources, and for an end to violence both in word and in deed attested to the continuing concern of women for the health and well-being of all people. Women demanded simple justice for women in the military, in insurance coverage for pregnancy and pregnancy-related disabilities, in Government aid for small business enterprises, and in access to rental housing.

There were declarations of sentiment that put some meeting on record for specific moral principles. Colorado voted to support efforts towards "relationships based on the true equality of parenthood." Kansas encouraged men to take an active role in child rearing. Iowa women

111

Henrietta Roth leads workshop discussion on discrimination in the job market at Florida meeting.

were so offended by a sexist entertainment in the Ramada Inn where they met that they voted to boycott Ramada motels everywhere. Virginia women voted to boycott all consumer products made in their own State until it ratified ERA. Colorado recommended that education in pharmacology include information on the use of herbs in cultural folk medicine.

All these resolutions were forwarded to Washington and were used as a guide for the Commission in building the agenda to be considered at Houston.

After the meetings were over, an analysis showed that the great majority had supported all or some of the resolutions proposed by the National Commission and had endorsed the goals of the Federal legislation to promote the equality of women. Eleven State meetings—Alabama, Hawaii, Indiana, Kansas, Mississippi, Missouri, Montana, Nebraska, Ohio, Oklahoma, and Utah—had elected delegations that were predominantly against these goals, with several other State delegations split.

The organized nature of the opposition in some State meetings alarmed not only avowed feminists but also the great middle majority of American women who favor improvements in the status of women. Many began to rally to rebut the false or exaggerated charges anti-change groups had been making to the press and even in Congress.

In August, the American Association of University Women invited 40 organizations to form a loose Women's Conference Network for the purpose of supporting the IWY program and the goals of the legislation. It was the first time such a broad coalition had undertaken a cooperative venture.

The Network included groups with contrasting outlooks and national organizations with broad constituencies: the National Council of Catholic Women and the National Abortion Rights Action League; the Women's Divisions of both the Democratic and Republican National Committees; the League of Women Voters, the Federation of Business and Professional Women's Clubs and the Girl Scouts of America; the National Organization for Women and the National Gay Task Force; Church Women United, the United Methodist Board and major Jewish women's organizations; the National Women's Political Caucus, the AFL-CIO, Common Cause, and many other groups.

112

At well-researched press conferences in major cities, Network-sponsored "Truth Squads" presented data supporting the National IWY Commission program and the recommendations of the State meetings and evidence on the tactics used to oppose them. Jean Stapleton appeared on television talk shows in her private capacity as an IWY Commissioner, a visible refutation of the charge that the Commission was run by "misfits of society" without family feeling. At a press conference in Washington in October, Bella Abzug described the disruptive tactics of the Ku Klux Klan who, she said, "still want to keep their women home washing their sheets." Network organizations kept Members of Congress informed and urged their supporters to go to Houston as sympathetic observers, if they were not already delegates.

By the end of October, thousands of women were planning to go to Houston. They were going with hope and with a desire for the kind of unity exemplified in a resolution overwhelmingly approved by women at the Minnesota meeting: "Recognizing that we will never all agree on every issue, we pledge to bind ourselves together in love, to continue to work on the concerns of universal importance—the need for our personal dignity, the relief of our suffering, the achievement of our aspirations—so that we can go on to that great victory: equality for all women, not only in Minnesota, but around the world."

Special events at meetings ranged from concerts to demonstrations of martial arts.

**NATIONAL COMMISSION
ON THE OBSERVANCE
OF INTERNATIONAL WOMEN'S YEAR
STATE MEETINGS, 1977**

State	Place	Date	Number Attending	Approved Core*	Elected Delegates
Alabama	Montgomery	July 9	2,000	defeated all	24
Alaska	Anchorage	May 6-8	780	adopted all	12
American Samoa	Pago Pago	June 16-18	300	no action	12
Arizona	Phoenix	June 3-4	1,000	adopted all	18
Arkansas	Little Rock	June 10-12	569	adopted all	18
California	Los Angeles	June 17-19	6,500	adopted all	96
Colorado	Boulder	June 3-5	3,100	adopted all	20
Connecticut	Bridgeport	June 10-11	1,000	***	22
Delaware	Dover	June 17-18	699	adopted all	12
District of Columbia	Washington	June 10-12	1,138	adopted all	12
Florida	Orlando	July 15-17	2,700	defeated all	40
Georgia	Atlanta	May 6-7	1,257	****	30
Guam	Agana	July 8-9	1,500	no action	12
Hawaii	Honolulu	July 9	5,100	****	14
Idaho	Boise	May 21-22	1,016	adopted all	14
Illinois	Normal	June 10-12	2,500	***	58
Indiana	Indiana	July 15-16	3,712	defeated all	32
Iowa	Des Moines	June 10-12	1,500	adopted all	22
Kansas	Wichita	July 15-17	4,620	***	20
Kentucky	Lexington	June 10-12	1,277	adopted all	24
Louisiana	Baton Rouge	June 16-18	1,227	adopted all	26
Maine	Bangor	June 17-18	500	***	14
Maryland	Baltimore	June 12-13	750	adopted all	26
Massachusetts	Regional Mtgs.**	June 25	2,500	adopted all	34
Michigan	Lansing	June 10-11	2,100	adopted all	48
Minnesota	St. Cloud	June 2-5	4,500	adopted all	26
Mississippi	Jackson	July 8-9	1,500	defeated all	20
Missouri	St. Louis	June 3-4	1,164	***	30
Montana	Helena	July 8-10	1,787	defeated all	14
Nebraska	Lincoln	June 24-25	1,700	***	16
Nevada	Las Vegas	June 17-19	1,341	***	12
New Hampshire	Plymouth	June 10-11	750	adopted all	14
New Jersey	Princeton	June 10-11	3,500	***	40

State	Place	Date	Number Attending	Approved Core*	Elected Delegates
New Mexico	Albuquerque	June 3-5	802	adopted all	14
New York	Albany	July 8-10	11,000	adopted all	88
North Carolina	Winston-Salem	June 17-19	828	adopted all	32
North Dakota	Bismarck	June 3-5	400	adopted all	13
Ohio	Columbus	June 11-12	2,800	adopted all	56
Oklahoma	Stillwater	June 16-18	1,400	defeated all	22
Oregon	Salem	June 3-5	1,200	adopted all	18
Pennsylvania	Pittsburgh	June 24-26	3,700	adopted all	60
Puerto Rico	Santurce	June 10-12	1,200	no action	12
Rhode Island	Providence	June 11-12	2,103	adopted all	14
South Carolina	Columbia	June 10-11	1,100	***	22
South Dakota	Mitchell	June 17-18	800	adopted all	14
Tennessee	Clarsville	June 24-26	800	adopted all	26
Texas	Austin	June 24-26	2,600	***	58
Trust Territories	Regional Mtgs.**	July/August	—	***	12
Utah	Salt Lake City	June 24-25	14,000	defeated all	14
Vermont	Montpelier	February 26	1,000+	***	12
Virgin Islands	St. Thomas	June 24-25	597	***	12
Virginia	Richmond	June 10-11	1,277	***	30
Washington	Ellensburg	July 8-10	4,000	mostly no action	24
West Virginia	Huntington	July 22-23	1,500	adopted all	18
Wisconsin	Madison	June 3-5	1,500	adopted all	28
Wyoming	Casper	June 10-12	500	adopted all	12

*The IWY core recommendations submitted to the States for their consideration were on these subjects: Arts and Humanities, Child Care, Credit, Education, Equal Rights Amendment, Female Offenders, Health, Homemakers, International Interdependence, Media, Older Women, Rape, Teenage Pregnancy and Elective and Appointive Office.

**Massachusetts regional meetings were held in Boston, Worcester, Springfield, Fall River, and Methuen. The Trust Territories held meetings in seven regions.

***Indicates that State meeting passed most of the IWY core recommendations, with no action on some.

****Indicates that State meeting defeated some IWY core recommendations and failed to act on others.

Women and men wait in line at Texas meeting to vote for delegates to Houston Conference.

Top — Oldest participant in Texas meeting, with her daughter.

SUMMARY OF RESOLUTIONS ADOPTED BY STATE MEETINGS
(In Addition to Core Agenda Resolutions)

Topic	Total Number Adopted	Number of States Submitting	Total Workshop Recommen-dations	Number of States Submitting
Arts and Humanities	75	22	12	3
Battered Women	235	35	35	7
Child Care	250	42	29	8
Commission on the Status of Women	12	8	0	0
Credit	38	18	18	10
Education	458	43	146	9
Elective and appointive office	107	29	21	6
Employment	529	43	148	10
ERA	39	19	18	6
Female offenders	252	30	6	2
Handicapped	41	15	21	4
Health	429	37	106	9
Homemaker	147	34	50	8
Housing	89	18	13	2
Insurance	67	19	5	4
International	204	33	119	9
Lesbianism	178	34	31	7
Media	168	35	24	8
Minority women	164	23	34	5
Older women	184	36	39	7
Prostitution	13	11	0	0
Rape	205	36	32	8
Reproductive freedom	182	41	33	7
Rural women	44	19	15	5
Volunteerism	64	18	19	4
Welfare	94	27	45	5
Women and the military	30	10	0	0

HOUSTON DAY BY DAY

By Caroline Bird

In November 1977, close to 20,000 people left homes all over the country to travel to the National Women's Conference in Houston. Two thousand were delegates charged with telling the President and Congress what ought to be done to help American women achieve equality with men in all aspects of American life. It may well have been the most diverse and representative conference of delegates ever assembled.

THE DELEGATES

They were of all colors, cultures, and heritages: whites, blacks, Asian Americans, Hawaiians, Samoans, Eskimos, Aleuts, American Indians from many different tribes, and Hispanics of Mexican, Puerto Rican, and Latin American origin. They were of all occupations: secretaries, teachers, nuns, nurses, lawyers, doctors, ministers, factory workers, farmers, waitresses, students, scientists, migrant workers, Members of Congress, mayors, business owners, and at least one astrologer. Many were homemakers. As a matter of fact, whatever else they did, most of them did housework too.

They were single and married, divorced or widowed, and a small number were lesbians. The overwhelming majority of delegates were or had at some time been traditional wives and mothers. Illinois delegate Susan Catania, a member of her State legislature, nursed the youngest of her seven daughters during plenary sessions. One delegate was an 11th grader, and several were in their eighties.

One of the most heroic delegates was Judy McCarthey of Arizona, an Indian from the White Mountain tribe and a student at Arizona State University, who insisted on coming even though her labor pains had started. She stayed through the Conference and managed to get home before the birth of a daughter whom she named Era, in honor of the Equal Rights Amendment. The doctor she had

defied said he had known a lot of strong-willed women in his time, "but never one who could control labor pains."

Of the 2,005 delegates who came to Houston, 1,403 had been elected in State and Territorial meetings, 186 were alternates, and 47 were IWY Commissioners. There were also 370 delegates-at-large appointed by the National Commission on Observance of International Women's Year to comply with the law requiring the Conference to reflect the demographic composition of women in the country and to include representatives of organizations that "work to advance the rights of women."

The provision for delegates-at-large was a safety precaution against an unbalanced delegate body. The States had been so successful in reaching out to women who are usually underrepresented that only 64.5 percent of the elected delegates were white, as opposed to 84.4 percent in the general female population; 14.1 percent of the elected delegates had incomes of more than $20,000, compared to 25.7 percent nationally. This meant that some white middle in-

Kathryn Clarenbach, executive director of National Commission, has pre-session chat with Liz Carpenter.

come women had to be appointed to achieve demographic balance.

The Commission used its appointment mandate to achieve balance in other ways: it appointed blacks as delegates-at-large from States like Mississippi and Alabama, where white anti-IWY groups had flooded the meetings and elected overwhelmingly white delegations.

The Commission also appointed as delegates-at-large presidents of national women's organizations and women of notable achievement. The law did not require that any delegates be appointed on the basis of their views, only that they be people who "work to advance the rights of women." However, some people who belonged to organizations that opposed equal rights for women as well as the IWY Conference itself were going to Houston as elected delegates.

THE REAL SILENT MAJORITY

During the summer, the State meetings had attracted attention to the Houston Conference, and some of it was hostile.

"Houston will finish off the women's movement," Phyllis Schlafly, a leader of the Stop ERA movement, predicted on television. "It will show them off for the radical, antifamily, prolesbian people they are." She claimed that a "silent majority" opposed the ERA and the Congressional mandate of the IWY Conference.

But the facts were otherwise. Poll after poll showed that most women really favored change. According to a 1975 national survey of women prepared by Market Opinion Research for the IWY Commission, women with an "expanding outlook" appear to be the wave of the future. The survey found that a broader choice of life-

Illinois legislator Susan Catania, holding youngest of her seven daughters, said she hoped to have a son, "but not until ERA is passed."

style was favored by the increasing proportion of women who are under 35, employed, single, and educated beyond high school. It also found that large majorities of *all* women favored many of the proposals to be discussed at Houston. For instance, nearly two-thirds of all women thought the Government should assist in providing child care on the basis of ability to pay. And the most recent sounding on ERA, a Harris poll taken in the spring of 1977, had shown that 54 percent of women, and an even larger majority of men, were in favor of the amendment. An October 1977 poll by CBS News and *The New York Times* found 74 percent of all Americans agreed that "the right of a woman to have an abortion should be left to a woman and her doctor."

There were many reasons why some women and men disagreed with these majorities. Some were mobilized by ultra-conservative religious and political forces whose leadership they accepted. Others were women who were opposed as a matter of religious conviction or who believed ERA would undermine their roles as

wives and mothers. Still other women knew only that the issues were "controversial" and were glad of a chance to hear them debated.

As a vocal minority stepped up its attacks on the IWY Conference, the real silent majority began to feel that the delegates at Houston would need their support. In Peoria, Illinois an auto worker who had watched the Stop ERA forces pack her State meeting asked her union to send her to Houston. The union refused. So when her shift ended on Friday night, she drew on her savings, packed her bag, flew to Houston, and caught a plane back in time to punch in on the job Monday morning.

Though most delegates had their expenses paid, raising money was a problem for many others who wanted to come. Women put on bake sales, fashion shows, raffles, rallies, wine-tasting parties, and even a quilting bee to raise the fare for friends. The children of a woman from Nevada gave her the trip for Christmas. In California, a lesbian group paid the way for a disabled black woman who was concerned with the needs of both blacks and the disabled. A student organization in Albuquerque contributed transportation for Professor Joyce Trebilcot and 10 of her students at the University of New Mexico. On her return, she pronounced the

Delegates from Utah proclaim their arrival.

"I had always kept silent about the way that women are treated," said a nurse from the Midwest. "But when I heard Phyllis Schlafly speak on television for the 'silent majority' I felt I had to do something to show that she wasn't speaking for me." What she did was to borrow money and buy a ticket to Houston.

educational experience "worth four years of college."

Bea Rodriguez, a Chicana from Salinas, Kansas, decided she had to skip Parents Day at Kansas University, where two of her children were students. She feared too few Chicanas would be at Houston, and she wanted to learn how to get more of them involved in activities outside of their homes. "I could almost feel my heart beat because I wanted to be there and I didn't know whether I'd be able to arrange a flight." Later she said that she couldn't "have lived with myself if I had missed it."

Not everybody came to work for a cause. Many came for more personal reasons. A mother came because her husband disapproved of her working, and she wanted to find out "whether other people are feeling the same way I feel." She found that they did.

Another woman came after a brutal session with her drunken husband, who had been beating her regularly. She stuffed her clothes into a shopping bag and set off for Houston to get help. She found it: Women she had never seen before put her up in their hotel and located services she needed.

A television show predicting "confrontation" at Houston convinced a black woman in Oregon that Houston was going to be like the 1963 March on Washington when Martin Luther King made his "I Have A Dream" speech. Acting on impulse, she took her children out of school, packed them in the car, and started driving toward Texas.

Like so many others, she came to see history made and to play some part in making it.

THE OBSERVERS

More than 2,000 people came to the Conference as invited guests, official observers, and resource people. They came to lead workshops, give lectures, run exhibit booths, and provide entertainment. About 100 women from other countries were also official guests.

Some observers came because the aspirations of women were important to their work—social workers, equal employment officers, educators, elected officials, corporate policymakers, and publishers.

About 1,500 reporters, writers, photographers, television people, and broadcasters wanted press passes, twice the expected number. Many were media professionals, and about 60 percent were women journalists, some of whom were so eager to record history that they came at their own expense.

Nearly 3,000 came as volunteers. More than 2,000 of these were Houston women who took tickets, guided visitors, carried messages, made lists, went for coffee, answered phones, and did whatever had to be done to keep operations moving. Eight hundred women employed by the Federal Government volunteered to do everything from registering delegates to handling money.

None of these people knew quite what or whom to expect. The Ku Klux Klan had threatened to come. "I will be in the vicinity of the national IWY meeting in Houston," proclaimed Robert Shelton, Imperial Wizard of the United Klans of America. "Some of our women members and sympathizers will be in the meetings to oppose what is going on. Our men also will be there to protect our women from all the militant lesbians. It's not safe for a decent woman to be there."

YWCA delegates describe themselves as "Pro-Plan and Pro-Family."

The Commission holds a business session.

George Higgins, self-styled Grand Dragon of the Realm of Mississippi, United Klans of America, Inc., whose wife was a delegate, told a reporter that the Klan had controlled the State meeting in Mississippi. "I plan to go to Houston and do the same there," he added.

Newsweek had predicted that Houston would pit "women against women." The *Washington Post* had said that it might "create a public impression of even more discord than actually exists" so that citizens could just sit back to watch a brawl that would confirm "the most harmful stereotypes of women in politics."

Members of the IWY Commission who had media experience had worked for more accurate coverage.

At the suggestion of Commissioner Sey Chassler, editor of *Redbook,* 23 women's magazines carried positive stories or references about the meeting in their November issues. Word spread that Houston was the place to be.

THURSDAY, NOVEMBER 17:

Early Arrivals On Thursday women from all over the country began to converge on Houston by plane, car, and bus. Caught up in a common mood of excitement, many made friends on the way. At New York's LaGuardia Airport, an American Indian in traditional braids chatted easily with a proper New England matron with blue-rinsed hair. Like many delegates, they expected something big to happen, not only to

women in general, but to themselves.

At the Hyatt Regency Hotel in Houston, where delegates were being registered, the lobby was full of women whose faces were familiar from television. Early arrivals spotted members of the Commission who had been in town for several days. Presiding Officer Bella Abzug was easy to recognize in her hat. Many of the women in Congress were expected. Barbara Jordan of Texas was to be the Conference keynote speaker; Margaret Heckler a key figure in the struggle for ERA, was to address a plenary session; Lindy Boggs of Louisiana, sponsor of a bill to help battered wives, was to attend a workshop; Elizabeth Holtman of New York, known to many Americans for her role in the impeachment hearings, was a Commissioner; Pat Schroeder of Colorado and Yvonne Burke of California were to lead a special Sunday morning hearing on peace and disarmament.

Some of the best known women in the country were coming: Rosalynn Carter, Betty Ford, Lady Bird Johnson, Billie Jean King, and Margaret Mead.

There would be women from Government: Esther Peterson, currently consumer affairs adviser to the President; Eleanor Holmes Norton, the new chair of the critically important Equal Employment Opportunity Commission; Commissioner Mary Anne Krupsak, who as Lieutenant Governor presides over the New York State Senate; Sarah T. Hughes, the Federal judge who had sworn in Lyndon Johnson as President on Air Force One; Mary Crisp, co-chair of the Republican National Committee, was coming as a delegate from Arizona.

There would be relatives of political leaders: Judy Carter, the President's outspoken daughter-in-law; Sharon Rockefeller, wife of the new Governor of West Virginia and board member of the Public Broadcasting Corporation.

There would be the women other women wondered about: Midge Costanza, top woman on the White House staff; Ellie Smeal, the homemaker president of NOW; television actress Jean Stapleton, who portrays that archtraditional wife, Edith Bunker, while serving as an IWY Commissioner off-screen.

Commissioner Jean Stapleton, TV's Edith Bunker.

Commissioner Carmen Delgado Votaw.

Commissioner Bernice Frieder.

Commissioner Mildred Jeffrey chats with Presiding Officer Bella Abzug.

123

Mary Crisp, co-chair of the Republican Party National Committee, was Pro-Plan delegate from Arizona.

The Commissioners Thursday noon, Presiding Officer Bella Abzug presented the Commissioners to the press. They were from every part of the country, of different ages and backgrounds, women and men with records of personal achievement and service.

One was a young Japanese-American, Rita Elway of Seattle, Washington, a founder of the Asian Pacific Women's Caucus. Three were Hispanic: Carmen Delgado Votaw, president, National Conference of Puerto Rican Women; Cecilia Preciado-Burciaga, assistant provost of Stanford University; Rhea Mojica Hammer, publisher of *El Clarin*, a Spanish-language newspaper.

Eight were black: Maya Angelou, poet; Audrey Rowe Colom, director of women's activities, Corporation for Public Broadcasting; Jeffalyn Johnson, management consultant; Coretta Scott King, civil rights leader; Ersa Poston, Commissioner, U.S. Civil Service Commission; Gloria Scott, national president, Girl Scouts of America; Addie Wyatt, vice president, Amalgamated Meat Cutters and Butcher Workmen of North America.

And finally, one of the Commission's three male members, law professor Harry T. Edwards, who co-chaired the Commission's Rules Committee.

The other male Commissioners were editors Sey Chassler of *Redbook* and John Mack Carter of *Good Housekeeping*.

Other women's magazine editors on the Commission were Gloria Steinem, editor of *Ms.* magazine, and Lenore Hershey, editor of the *Ladies' Home Journal*.

There were policymakers from national women's organizations: Ruth Clusen, president of the League of Women Voters; Jane Culbreth, former president, National Federation of Business and Professional Women's Clubs; Beverly Everett, Iowa State president, American Association of University Women; Mildred Jeffrey, chair, National Women's Political Caucus; Eleanor Smeal, head of NOW.

There were Catholics, Protestants, and Jews: Margaret J. Mealey, immediate past executive director, National Council of Catholic Women; Claire Randall, general secretary, National Council of Churches of Christ in the U.S.A.; Bernice Frieder, former officer, National Council of Jewish Women. (Names and biographies of all the Commissioners appear elsewhere in this report.)

"We range from the young to the not so young," Bella Abzug noted. "Thirty-four of us are married. Four are widows. Seven are single, and one is

Commissioners Claire Randall, Connie Plunkett, Addie Wyatt and Ersa Poston (left to right).

Commissioners Ruth Abram, Beverly Everett and Mildred Persinger (left to right).

124

Commissioners Lenore Hershey and John Mack Carter, editors of women's magazines, read Conference briefing book.

Commissioners Sey Chassler and Mary Anne Krupsak show off their "Women on the Move" T-shirts.

Commissioner Harry T. Edwards chats with Alberta Henderson, who worked on housing arrangements.

engaged. There she is." Audrey Colom rose, and smiled at the applause.

Among them, Abzug added, the Commissioners were the parents of 74 children and 17 grandchildren. "And one is the mother of eight children," she continued, indicating Gerridee Wheeler of North Dakota, past president, National Association for Mental Health.

Denying claims that the Conference would be the "death knell" of the women's movement, she wound up: "We are a multitude. We are alive and kicking, and we shall get even livelier. The women's movement has become an indestructible part of American life."

In the lobbies of the delegate hotels, celebrities turned out to be easily accessible. Jean Stapleton seemed genuinely pleased when fans told her it was comforting to see a familiar face at the meeting. Gloria Steinem insisted on getting the autographs of the women who asked her for hers. "It's not feminist," she explained, "if it's not an equal exchange." A young admirer saw Elizabeth Holtzman "standing in line just like everyone else—and she's a Congresswoman!" Gail Sheehy, author of the best selling book, *Passages*, took furious notes on everything her neighbors said.

Women who knew one another only by reputation greeted each other with hugs and smiles. The scene reminded the *Washington Post*'s Sally Quinn of "registration day at a woman's college, with people lugging their suitcases, waiting for room assignments, singing songs, and making new friends. It was nice."

Nice, but a new experience. Steinem described the delegates as "so exposed, so vulnerable out there on the edge of history. No one will go away unchanged." Delegates and observers talked worriedly about the predicted showdown in Conference sessions between women who wanted change and those who did not. Even more worrisome were reports that men and women outside the meeting had come to Houston to stop it.

Women's rights advocates worried as much about divisions within their own ranks as they did about disagreement with the antichange forces. Not all of the women who favored change agreed on all of the 26 planks in the National Plan of Action. Some didn't want to jeopardize the ratification of ERA by linking it with controversial social issues that affect both sexes (though women more so), such as full employment, a national health plan, or help for battered children. And almost everyone had a deeply felt issue she hoped to advance.

Commissioner Margaret Mealey.

Commissioner Liz Carpenter, former press secretary to Lady Bird Johnson, warned that it wasn't going to be like a "white-gloved meeting of the colonial dames." But some delegates were praying for unity—literally. Barbara Conable and Ann McKay of Rochester, New York had composed a prayer entitled "Women Praying For Women," which they reproduced on small lapel tags secured by red, white, and blue ribbons.

Commissioner Liz Carpenter with former Commissioner Ellen Groves Kirby (left).

FRIDAY: NOVEMBER 18, 1977

Press Conferences, Caucuses, and Coalition   On Friday morning, Tom Brokaw of NBC's "Today Show," interviewed Liz Carpenter and Margaret Mealey. Although the two IWY Commissioners disagreed on a number of issues—for instance, Commissioner Mealey opposed the ERA and Reproductive Freedom planks— both emphasized their mutual interest in supporting the majority of recommendations in the National Plan of Action. Brokaw noted their unity and enthusiasm.

Meanwhile, in the cavernous and drafty basement of the Hyatt, other Commissioners and former IWY Presiding Officer Jill Ruckelshaus joined Bella Abzug in briefing the press. Abzug didn't think that the opponents of the ERA had any right to call themselves "Pro Family," since the ERA would actually strengthen the rights of women who work in the home. "No one has a monopoly on the family," she added. "Only 14 percent of American families have the traditional one breadwinner and one nonbreadwinner. Most of the women here have filled or are filling both roles." She promised that all views would be heard in an orderly way at the plenary sessions. "We have dissent among us," she said bluntly. "We respect, honor, and welcome it. It's the democratic way."

One of the potentially divisive issues most publicized by the press was the plank in the National Plan labeled Sexual Preference. Some delegates weren't sure how they felt about supporting the civil rights of lesbians, but the lesbians were accustomed to being a controversial minority. Right after the Commission briefing, reporters rode up the Hyatt's glass elevators to a small room on the top floor where a lesbian caucus had scheduled a press conference of its own.

Presiding was Commissioner Jean O'Leary, a former nun and co-executive director of the National Gay Task Force. She estimated that perhaps 60

Mary Keegan headed Houston committee.

126

of 130 lesbian delegates at the Conference were able to be open about their preference, but most were still forced into silence in order to protect their jobs or the custody of their children. They wanted to be a visible part of the Conference, however, so that they could refute myths about lesbians and explain the need for legal remedies against the discrimination they suffered.

O'Leary held up a half-page ad inserted in both Houston papers by opponents of the IWY. It pictured a little blonde girl clutching a bouquet of flowers and asking, "Mommy, when I grow up, can I be a lesbian?"

"This vicious and misleading ad," O'Leary said firmly, "is an attempt to exploit the lesbian issue, to divide women, and to discredit the IWY by making it seem that the Conference is totally focused on lesbians. As well as our own issue of sexual preference, we hope all lesbians will support *all* 26 resolutions and all women's issues."

Settling In All day Friday arriving delegates and their luggage piled up in the lobbies of the delegate hotels. Many of those who had come on Thursday had been sent to other hotels because their rooms were still occupied by men who had been attending an earlier convention. Roommates who arrived later had trouble finding them.

Tension mounted as hotel clerks tried to untangle the mixup and accommodate the rush of women arriving on Friday. Overloaded switchboards meant that friends and colleagues had to search through crowds to find each other in person. Roomless travelers had to line up for food, for toilets, for phones, and even for newspapers.

Delegates wondered whether the mixup was deliberate. Later, a Commission inquiry disproved rumors of sabotage and concluded that there were no "bad guys," only lots of problems. Hotels had overestimated the number of "no shows," underestimated the number who would arrive early; and they did not have the staff to handle inquiries from all the people who needed to find each other.

Women were tired, hungry, and grimy from travel, but surprisingly good-humored as they waited for rooms. They exchanged life histories and philosophies while standing in line. Commissioner Audrey Colom gave up her room to a delegate who walked with a cane. Florynce Kennedy, a black lawyer and lecturer famed in the women's movement for her verbal karate, slept on a hotel floor. Those who had rooms shared them with others. Betty Friedan bunked in a suite assigned to Bella Abzug. A white woman activist, discouraged about the progress of race relations in the South, got a pep talk about black feminism from roommate Libby Koontz without ever recognizing that the lively black woman who had taken her in was the former director of the U.S. Women's Bureau.

Women improvised systems. A Conference aide in a red T-shirt handed out numbers so that people

Thousands of suitcases fill the lobby of the Hyatt Regency as delegates waited for hours to register.

127

Susan B. Anthony, Bella Abzug, Betty Friedan and Billie Jean King accompany torch relay runners into Houston.

standing in line could get something to eat while they were waiting for room assignments.

Communications networks were improvised. A Chicana delegate walked slowly back and forth in a crowded lobby between orange sandwich boards bearing notes addressed to women with Hispanic names. Notices of meetings sprouted in elevators, on pillars in the lobby, on bathroom doors—everywhere a woman had to wait or even pass by.

The Torch Arrives   At noon on Friday a steady rain did not stop a thousand women from gathering in front of Albert Thomas Convention Center to welcome the torch. A total of more than 2,000 women runners had carried it in relays to Houston every step of 2,610 miles from Seneca Falls, New York, where the first women's rights conference was held in 1848.

For the dramatic last mile, three young Houston athletes ran together, accompanied by scores of delegates. A shout went up when the waiting crowd spotted the bronze torch being held aloft by the pale arm of Peggy Kokernot, marathon runner; the golden arm of Sylvia Ortiz, a senior at the University of Houston; and the

dark-skinned arm of 16-year-old high school track star Michele Cearcy. "ERA! ERA! ERA!" the crowd chanted. "Hey, Hey, What Do You say? Ratify the ERA! ERAERAERAERAERA."

News photographers could not resist snapping pictures of well-known feminists, including Bella Abzug in a hat, skirt, and high heels, jogging arm-in-arm with the young torch bearers in their bright blue T-shirts emblazoned with the words "Women on the Move."

The photos were so striking that they appeared on the front pages of newspapers in which the Conference was otherwise ignored.

The rest was equally great theater. Maya Angelou, an actress as well as a poet, delivered the dramatic Declaration of Sentiments which she had written to accompany the torch from Seneca Falls.

"Some of us run with a torch," said Bella Abzug. "Some of us run for office. Some of us run for equality—but none of us runs for cover." People laughed, feeling more cheerful as they huddled beneath coats and umbrellas. The three Houston runners then presented the torch to Billie Jean King, the tennis star, who passed it to Susan B. Anthony, namesake of the famous suffragist, who repeated her great aunt's famous words: "Failure is impossible."

The crowd roared. Well-wishers mingled with celebrities, hugging and kissing each other. Gloria Steinem's glasses misted as she stood with an observer from India and a trade unionist from Detroit. Few people noticed the fundamentalist preacher who announced his candidacy for governor of Oklahoma by raising two provocative placards: "Equal Rights for Christians" and "IWY Means Immoral Womens Year." Wisconsin members of NOW carried their own sign: "Women's Rights: American as Apple Pie."

The torch symbolized women on the move. To Peggy Kokernot, the woman athlete, it symbolized that women were indeed capable of getting to the finish line in an Olympic marathon. To Lenore Hershey, it was a lesson: "The one thing you can't do is to run backward."

Presidents for Era   After the arrival of the torch, women streamed back to see about hotel rooms, plan strategy, and exchange bulletins about the counter rally Phyllis Schlafly had said she would hold across town at the Houston Astro-Arena. Her followers called an ad hoc "hearing" at which speakers denounced the goals of the IWY Conference and ERA as "sick," "immoral," "unGodly," "unpatriotic," and "antifamily."

Most supporters of ERA were wives and mothers and even grandmothers, and all of them deeply resented the charge that they were somehow working against the family. "*They* are antifamily," retired Congresswoman Martha Griffiths exploded. "I have sat on legislative bodies for 25 years, and I've never seen any one of these people testifying on anything for the family."

SPIRIT OF HOUSTON

Griffiths, who had shepherded ERA through Congress, had come to Houston specifically to take part in a day-long Equal Rights Amendment Ratification Assembly, organized far in advance by the National Federation of Business and Professional Women's Clubs. The BPW had marshalled the presidents of six major women's organizations who had promised political and economic support for ratification.

"Our combined memberships number in the millions," BPW President Piilani C. Desha told a news conference. In addition to herself, the presidents were Dr. Marjorie Bell Chambers of the American Association of University Women (AAUW); IWY Commissioner Ruth Clusen of the League of Women Voters; IWY Commissioner Eleanor Smeal of the National Organization for Women (NOW); IWY Commissioner Mildred Jeffrey of the National Women's Political Caucus; and Marty Hatwood Futrell of the Virginia Education Association, representing the National Education Association (NEA).

The Panel of Presidents reported that more organizations were joining the boycott against States that had not ratified ERA by refusing to hold conventions in them. According to Ellie Smeal, Chicago had already lost more than $15 million in convention business, and both Miami and St. Louis had suffered substantial losses due to cancellations. "We're hitting

Presiding over Equal Rights Amendment Ratification Assembly, held day before conference opened, is President Piilani C. Desha of National Federation of Business and Professional Women's Clubs. Eleanor Smeal, head of NOW, is at right.

the pocketbook nerve where it hurts the most," Desha said.

Early in the evening more than a thousand women who had contributed at least $15 each to ERAmerica rallied under the glass chandeliers of the Hyatt's Imperial Ballroom. They came to pledge their resources to speed up ratification in three more States. It was an extraordinary gathering; women of every age and style came dressed in what each considered her best. For some it was pearls and furs. For others, embroidered jeans and boots.

The speakers were introduced by Commissioner Liz Carpenter, co-chair of ERAmerica with Elly Peterson, former assistant chair of the Republican National Committee. Congresswomen Elizabeth Holtzman and Margaret Heckler promised to support laws that would sweep away barriers to equality for women.

Then came two First Ladies, Betty Ford leading the way to the platform. Rosalynn Carter spoke first. Standing straight and very slim, the President's

Carol Bellamy was a leader of Pro Plan Caucus.

wife assured the audience that Jimmy was for the ERA also. To those "who are wavering because they are ill-informed or confused or because of shrill voices," she had a firm message: "Think of yourself!"

Former Congresswoman Martha Griffiths, who shepherded ERA through the House, speaks at ratification assembly.

Betty Ford said that ERA was "the first step in guaranteeing that every woman can be what she aspires to be." She ended with a message from her daughter: "Okay, let's go for it, girls."

Coretta Scott King linked the fight against sexism with the fight against racism. "We have a very great struggle ahead of us," she said, "but we women of this Nation, with the support of the brothers who believe in equal rights, can make this happen ... I challenge you to continue to struggle, my sisters, and not get weary."

Liz Carpenter had the last word, "If I should die, don't send me flowers. Just send me three more States."

The party was a high that came just at the right time. Most of the women who poured out of the glittering ballroom struggled past the crowds in the lobby to a night of caucusing before the opening session on Saturday morning.

Pro Plan　There was little fear that the ERA plank itself would be defeated. According to a pre-Conference telephone survey made by ERAmerica, the National Women's Political Caucus and the Women's Action Alliance, only 20 percent of the delegates actually opposed the amendment. This turned out to be a remarkably accurate reflection of the population at large. While the Conference was being held, the results of a new Roper poll were aired on the McNeill-Lehrer report: only 19 percent of those polled identified with Phyllis Schlafly and her anti-ERA stand. But delegates experienced in politics knew that majority support did not ensure clear sailing. The minority could not win, but they could paralyze the Conference in a shower of disruptive parliamentary maneuvers and discredit it with the nationwide audience that would be watching on television.

The possibility worried every woman who had witnessed the tactics of some of the organized opposition at State meetings. Several weeks before the national Conference began, delegates who favored all or most of the National Plan of Action had been asked to take part in a Pro Plan Caucus that would meet in Houston. The invitation was issued by the chairs of 11 State delegations: Arizona, California, Iowa, Kentucky, Maryland, Minnesota, North Carolina, New York, Vermont, Washington, and Wisconsin.

As delegates checked in on Friday, the most popular button in sight was the green one that said "PRO PLAN." And all day long, Commissioner Koryne Horbal of Minnesota, head of the Democratic National Committee Women's Caucus, had been meeting with special interest caucuses, State delegation chairs, and delegates-at-large to ask about their concerns and to assure them that they would be part

continued on page 133

Caucuses, Caucuses

Women who came to Houston made the most of the chance to meet with others who shared a special interest. Some caucuses were formal affairs planned in advance by well-staffed national organizations with thousands of members, but many emerged on the spot as like-minded women compared notes with each other.

Women who serve in the armed forces held a meeting, and so did women who had come to Houston to persuade the Conference to call for banning the neutron bomb. Disabled women, minority women, rural women, neighborhood women, young women, artists, and others found that their interests and outlooks varied widely, but the barriers they faced as women were surprisingly the same.

All of these special interest groups wanted to change some plank in the National Plan of Action or add an entirely new one. Because of the pressure of time, only a few amendments or substitutions could be made. The result was that many important perspectives were not able to reach the floor, but they were heard in other ways. In some instances, the women's demands were already covered in the National Plan but not in the context or with the emphasis they favored.

The National Congress of Neighborhood Women invited working class women of European ethnic origin to identify the National Plan's impact on women who are trying to maintain their cultural heritage and preserve their neighborhoods. Although they think of themselves as homemakers first, many have to work at paying jobs to help keep their families going; others are going to college for the first time.

They were concerned because there was nothing in the National Plan about affordable family housing. They also suggested amending the child-

care plank to include guarantees of parental control over federally funded services and amending the education plank to make it easier for a woman with family obligations to qualify for student financial aid. Finally, they wanted the guidelines of federally funded programs on health care, day care, job training, and housing amended to make these services available to women above the poverty level.

A *Youth Caucus* was called by Kari Lavalli, a high school senior from Dearborn, Michigan who at 17 was one of the youngest delegates. When she was in the seventh grade, she had filed a complaint with the Michigan Civil Rights Commission that led to desegregation of shop and home-making classes at her junior high.

In Houston, she assembled delegates between the ages of 16 and 21 to consider the impact the National Plan would have on young women. They were most concerned about lack of

money for college, lack of child-care facilities that keeps women "out of school and isolated and penniless in our homes," and rules restricting welfare recipients to two-year community colleges or training programs that direct them into low-wage jobs.

The caucus adopted a statement urging that "young women be included in all possible meetings and commissions which directly affect us, such as this Conference," and thanking the conveners "for the opportunity to demonstrate our opinions and laying the groundwork for the women's movement. We only hope that we can accomplish as much for women as you have."

An *Arts Caucus* chaired by Susan Schwalb of the New York-based Coalition of Women's Art Organizations discussed how women in the arts and humanities could get more political attention for their needs. They felt that the plank affecting them was weak because it called for women to be "more equitably represented on grant-awarding boards" and to "benefit more fairly from Government grants," instead of asking for equal representation and total justice.

They decided finally to put on record their request that Congress amend Title 6 of the Civil Rights Act of 1964 to bar discrimination in federally assisted programs on the basis of sex. This addition would extend to women working in museums, colleges, and on federally funded grants.

Women from a dozen farming states assembled in a *Farm Women Caucus* and assigned 15 women to draft an amendment to the Rural Women plank. "If you aren't now living on a farm," they told a woman farm lobbyist working in Washington, "you can't possibly understand the need we feel to be identified as farmers in our own right, rather than as farm wives. After all, we did not marry the farm!"

They drafted the following amendment: "American women should root out the false image of farm women; should acknowledge the true role many hold as an owner/operator of a farm; and should work for legislation that protects their rights of ownership. Programs of further training and preparation should be expanded or initiated to provide an opportunity for realization of their management skills."

Although there wasn't time to consider their amendment at the plenary session, they had the satisfaction of letting people know how they felt.

Because low income women were specifically recruited as delegates, an unusually large number of women with firsthand experience of welfare were able to talk with each other. They were invited to discuss the welfare resolution at a *Sex and Poverty IWY Poor and Low Income Women's*

Caucus called by the National Council on Women, Work, and Welfare, a listening post for low-income women in Washington. The caucus was chaired by Cathy O'Brien, a mother of four, who had earned her B.A. degree while on welfare.

The women who came objected to being treated by welfare authorities as if they were bureaucratic problems instead of people. Some women wanted to demand more and better jobs, while others were concerned that mothers of small children should not be made to work outside their

Commissioner Koryne Horbal.

homes. No one wanted to support "as is" the Carter administration welfare reform bill, but some opposed it entirely, while others found parts of it acceptable. The debate continued through three caucus sessions and finally produced on Sunday a substitute resolution that was approved by the Conference.

A *Peace Caucus* met on Saturday evening between plenary sessions to discuss the peace and disarmament resolution in the National Plan and to develop an ongoing peace network. More than 70 women from a dozen states crowded into a hotel room. They were delegates who belonged to

Women Strike for Peace, Women's International League for Peace and Freedom, and Another Mother for Peace, as well as to community groups.

One concern was pervasive among the women. The Conference must take a position against U.S. production of the neutron bomb, which kills people while preserving property. "Peace is a women's issue," said the caucus organizers. One woman asked: "How can we vote on issues to better our lives while ignoring threats to our existence?"

The caucus drafted an amendment opposing production and use of the neutron bomb and the "equality of death" it would bring. Although they were unable to present it as an amendment or as new business because of lack of time, 2,500 people at the Conference signed an anti-neutron bomb petition which they circulated.

A *Jewish Women's Caucus* agreed to support the goals of the National Plan of Action, although not all members agreed on all issues. The caucus was set up with the help of the Leadership Conference of National Jewish Women's Organizations. At a Friday meeting 100 delegates were briefed on strategy in the event anyone attempted to amend the National Plan to include an attack on Zionism, as had been done at the International Women's Year U.N. Conference in Mexico City in 1975. No one did. "As a method of spreading good will, there could have been no better forum," one caucus supporter said of the Houston Conference.

Women in Sports met to press their claims for equal opportunities for women athletes, and many other groups met to discuss a single issue. One such group was the Coyotes, advocates of decriminalizing prostitution. They were in Houston to protest sex discrimination in laws that penalized prostitutes but not their customers, and to urge that all laws on the subject be repealed.

of any decisions the Pro Plan Caucus would make that night. Commissioner Mildred Jeffrey and Jane McMichael

of the National Women's Political Caucus also briefed delegates.

After the ERAmerica party, more than 500 women jammed into the room where the Pro Plan Caucus was scheduled.

Carol Bellamy, newly elected president of the City Council of New York, called the Pro Plan Caucus to order. She announced a long list of organizations whose delegates had pledged to support the National Plan of Action in advance of the Conference. They included the American Association of University Women (AAUW), the National Organization for Women (NOW), the National Council of Jewish Women (NCJW), Women's Action Alliance, Coalition of Labor Union Women (CLUW), and the National Gay Task Force (NGTF).

A majority of delegates wanted to support the Plan as a minimum, but many had come to Houston with the hope of making some improvements in it. Some feminists wanted stronger legal protection for victims of rape. White ethnic groups wanted to be mentioned specifically. Artists wanted safeguards against discrimination, and there were a number of personal causes, such as the movement by some women from Puerto Rico to obtain the release of nationalist Lolita Lebron from a U.S. prison.

The disabled women were the first at the Caucus to win approval for change in the Plan. A woman in a wheelchair at the back of the room was close to tears when Bellamy recognized her. "We're in a moral dilemma," she said. "We want to beat the right wing. We agree with the Pro Plan Caucus that if everyone made amendments we'd never get finished, but as it is, we don't feel part of this group. We can't even get to the podium." Before she was through, many others were in tears, too.

Conference coordinator Lee Novick briefs Commissioners on meeting preparations.

Older women complained that the recommendation, as voted by State meetings, ignored their positive contributions and treated them as if their only problem were better nursing homes. "We are to be counted in," Dr. Elizabeth Welch, a retired college professor from Winston-Salem, told the Caucus. "If you don't, there will be others who will latch on to our productivity."

But changes had to stop somewhere. Dr. Allie Hixson, chair of the Kentucky delegation, pleaded for restraint. "We can hand down this National Plan of Action to our daughters and granddaughters with everything crossed out, marked up—some tattered old piece—or we can join together behind it, as it is, for victory!"

In the end, the Pro Plan meeting agreed to support substitute planks

"Signers" for the deaf were on platform throughout business sessions.

written by the caucuses of minorities, welfare advocates, and disabled women. Other changes were to be deferred in the hope that they could be brought up as new business in the last session on Monday morning.

Very few women slept that Friday night. There was plenty to do before

Women stream into Albert Thomas
Convention Center to register for
Conference.

the opening session the following
morning. Caucuses were rewriting
recommendations. Commissioners
were meeting to go over last minute
details with Bella Abzug and Executive Director Kay Clarenbach. A thousand chores confronted the staff,
which had been working in Houston
for weeks under the direction of Conference Coordinator Lee Novick. And
all over town, in hotels and homes,
women were talking with each other
about the coalitions they could build
to get action on the issues which had
meaning to their lives.

Photographers were everywhere.

135

Commissioner Gloria Scott uses historic gavel to open first plenary session.

Mayor Fred Hofheinz of Houston is flanked by Helvi Sipila (left) and Congresswoman Barbara Jordan.

SATURDAY, NOVEMBER 19

First Plenary Session At dawn observers began standing in line to get non-delegate tickets for the Coliseum where the first plenary session was due to begin at 9 o'clock. They were good-natured about it. "We've been waiting for over 100 years," said a member of the Church of God who had come to support the ERA. "I've been waiting all my life for this," a black woman said.

While they waited, they talked and sang and hoisted signs and banners. "ERA, Yes." A man carried a sign that he said his wife had given him: "Liberated Men Are More Fun." Her sign said, "Call me Ms., not Mrs. Him."

Anti-feminist pickets waved signs of their own. "Women's Lip: Follow Jesus Christ and Your Husband and Your Pastor ... REPENT." Men with bullhorns heckled the waiting women:

"You're not solving problems, you're causing trouble."

The women stayed calm, however, and the Houston police said it was the most orderly crowd they had seen. Later in the day there was a nastier street confrontation when a score of people representing the Christian Defense League tried to get into the Coliseum to "confront the enemy." They carried Confederate flags and anti-Semitic and racist placards.

Inside, the Coliseum had the familiar look of a national political convention. But instead of "Republican" or "Democratic Convention," the word "WOMAN" was spelled out in enormous letters on the blue curtain behind the officials on the stage. On the floor below, the delegates were seated by States, with delegates-at-large in the rear. On a huge platform straddling the center aisle, the TV cameras swiveled to monitor audience or stage.

There was plenty for the cameras and writers to see. Missouri delegates

held up red "Stop ERA" signs next to New York delegates with green "ERA-Yes" signs. Delegates wore their State identifications on their heads: "jibaro" sugarcane worker hats for Puerto Rico; "Free D.C." tricornes for the District of Columbia. Wisconsin delegates were in red cowboy hats with a white "W" and yellow neckerchiefs. New York delegates held up apples in honor of the Big Apple. California delegates waved golden bandanas.

When the bleachers were nearly full, there were 10,000 people inside, waving, carrying, or wearing a kaleidoscope of slogans and buttons, ribbons, T-shirts, hats, shopping bags, signs, banners, and balloons. Some of the signs seemed to talk to each other. On the floor, "Equal Rights for the Unborn"; in the bleachers, "If Men Got Pregnant, Abortion Would be Sacred."

A man wearing a button that said, "A Man of Quality Is Not Threatened by a Woman for Equality" seemed to be agreeing with the ERA button, "Human Rights Begin at Home." "Every Mother Is a Working Mother," said another button. "I own my own body," one T-shirt read, "but I share."

Signs advertised coalitions. A disabled woman hoisted her ERA sign on her crutch. Non-Hispanic delegates wore "Viva La Mujer" buttons, having learned from Hispanic delegates that it meant "Long Live Woman." Middle-class clubwomen supported civil rights for lesbians by wearing a button linking two female signs.

Ribbon colors proclaimed allegiances. Lavender for gay rights; green for giving the Plan a green light; gold for antichange delegates whose daisy-topped gold ribbon said "Majority" in defiance of the national polls' findings.

The sounds of the Conference floor were as lively as its sights. The roar of thousands of conversations, chanting, shouting above the din, official walkie-talkies, a stentorian public address system, and singing. Someone had written new words to the tune of "Alexander's Ragtime Band:" "Come on along, come on along. Come to Houston and we'll see. What can be done, what can be done, to promote equaliteee." And in honor of the host State, people sang, "The Yellow Rose of Texas."

When it was time to begin, commissioner Gloria Scott, national president of the Girl Scouts of America, brought the opening ceremonial session of the Conference to order with the gavel presented to Susan B. Anthony by the National American Women Suffrage Association in 1896. It had been lent for the occasion by the Smithsonian Institution's Division of Political History.

The San Jacinto Girl Scouts presented the colors and pledged allegiance to the flag. Shirley Baines of the Houston Opera Company sang the National Anthem.

A moment of silence reflected the commitment of the Conference to the right of each individual to ask for guidance in her or his own way.

Top—First Ladies applaud Congresswoman Barbara Jordan.
Center—Delegates hold up National Plan booklets to be autographed by Congresswoman Jordan.
Bottom—First Ladies Rosalynn Carter, Betty Ford and Lady Bird Johnson.

Houston's Mayor Fred Hofheinz welcomed the Conference, and Commissioner Scott introduced the presiding officer. Bella Abzug's introduction welcomed the three First Ladies. Their sheer physical presence was more moving than many women expected. To Rosalynn Carter, it was "significant that the three of us are here in Houston together on this platform today to affirm the continuity of our Government's efforts to improve life for all." It was the first time all three had shared the same platform.

Equally moving was the statement each First Lady made about herself as a woman, not only as a ceremonial wife.

"Jimmy asked me to be his personal emissary today and to talk to you briefly about his concerns and his goals. He and I have been partners for a long time—working together and separately," Rosalynn Carter said, praising the goals of the Conference. "Of course I am here for myself, too."

Of her own marriage, Betty Ford said, "We have both found a great deal of respect and appreciation in knowing that each of us can speak our own minds as we feel necessary."

Pat Kery displays "To Form a More Perfect Union" statement written by Maya Angelou and signed by First Ladies and delegates as well as thousands along torch relay route.

Betty Ford ended her remarks with a confidential wink that somehow took in the thousands in the Coliseum and the millions watching on television: "Let's keep it all together."

Lady Bird Johnson, accompanied by her feminist daughter, Linda Johnson Robb, confessed that she once thought the women's movement

Linda Johnson Robb joins in singing, "We Shall Overcome."

belonged more to her daughters than to herself, "but I have come to know that it belongs to women of all ages."

Next came the torch. It was formally presented to the Conference by runners who rushed it down the long aisle to a fanfare provided by an all-woman Drum and Bugle Corps wearing golden helmets with deep red plumes, that made them look like storybook Amazons. Tears welled up unexpectedly in the eyes of many delegates at this symbol of women's courage and endurance. With the torch, the runners presented the parchment scroll containing Maya Angelou's Declaration of Sentiments, which had been signed by all the runners. The First Ladies and the Commissioners signed it, and later the scroll moved around the Coliseum so that delegates could sign it too.

Then Bella Abzug explained the task of the Conference. "The mandate under which we meet does not tell us to consider whether women *should* seek to end discrimination or *should* seek full equality, full citizenship, and full participation in society," she re-

First Ladies and Bella Abzug hold torch aloft.

minded the delegates. "Instead, it takes a stand for equality, a position that I believe has the support of a majority of Americans.

"Our purpose is not to tell women how to live or what to do. It is simply to say that women must be free to choose what they do. Whatever women choose to do with equality, it must be ours as a matter of simple justice."

And she added, "Let us agree to disagree, if we must. It would be a dull weekend if we didn't feel free to state our beliefs."

First Lady Rosalynn Carter and Commissioner Coretta Scott King.

Commissioner Elizabeth Athanasakos (left) and former Commissioner Gilda Bojorquez Gjurich listen attentively to proceedings.

Commissioner Cecilia Preciado-Burciaga.

Mariko Tse (back row), Georgia McMurray, Marianne Bruesehoffe, Sharon Percy and Judy Carter were among delegates cited by Commissioner Liz Carpenter in speech at opening session.

Commissioner Liz Carpenter introduced some of the less well-known delegates who had come to Houston and who represented the diversity of the group:

"Sixteen-year-old Dorothy Arceneaux of Houma, Louisiana, Girl Scout leader, honor student, headed for college and anxious for women to learn how to walk hand in hand with life.

"Eighty-five-year-old Clara M. Beyer, retired Government worker, one of the valiant women who helped push the reform of child labor.

"Twenty-four-year-old Mariko Tse from California, leader of Chinese Women in Action, world traveler, graduate in anthropology, leader in Upward Bound programs for blacks, Chicanas, Indians, and the American Chinese."

She singled out other delegates: Sister Mary Agnes Drees, Director of Continuing Education at Marymount College, Kansas, who returns 60 percent of her salary to the college; Marge Jindrich of Illinois, a United Auto Worker member supporting an invalid husband and five children on a paycheck of $8,500; farm woman Marianne Bruesehoffe, who is putting three of her four children through college by raising poultry; Georgia McMurray, social welfare activist and former head of the Agency for Child Development in New York.

"America, look at us!" Carpenter concluded. "Listen to us. Have faith in us. Help us. Love us as we loved you."

Lady Bird Johnson introduced keynote speaker Barbara Jordan, Congresswoman from the Houston area, and noted that she and her husband had watched Jordan's star rise from the time of her debut in the Texas legislature.

Jordan's acknowledgement of this praise delighted everyone. "Thank you, Lady Bird Johnson, for an introduction of which I am worthy." And the delegates roared approval when she said, "Human rights apply equally to Soviet dissidents, Chilean peasants, and *American women*. Women are human. We know our rights are limited. We know our rights are violated. We need a domestic human rights program.

"This Conference could be the beginning of such an effort, an effort which would be enhanced if we would not allow ourselves to be brainwashed by people who predict chaos and failure for us.

"Tell them they lie—and move on."

Commissioner Harry T. Edwards explained the rules. Under the law, the rules for conducting the meeting had been adopted by the Commission after they had been published in the *Federal Register* and amended in response to public comment. The parliamentary procedure to be used was a combination of Robert's Rules of Order and Congressional procedures, designed to get a lot done by a large body in a short time. Speeches were limited to two minutes. Debate could be closed by majority vote. The chair could decide whether voting was to be by voice, standing, or the count of tellers, depending on the closeness,

Second Plenary Session When the delegates came back after lunch, eight microphones were placed at intervals around the floor. Deliberations—and the test of women's ability to work together—were about to begin. In the chair was Commissioner Ruth Clusen, national president of the League of Women Voters, familiar to many of the audience as the moderator of the Carter-Ford debates on television sponsored by the League during the 1976 campaign.

Two speakers set a tone of humor and cooperation. Judy Carter, the President's daughter-in-law, charged that in spite of lip service honoring the family, laws and attitudes do not adequately value women who are mothers. Jill Ruckelshaus, former member of the Republican National Committee and past presiding officer of the IWY Commission, pleaded for unity in support of the National Plan of Action.

"By a recent Gallup Poll," she said, "63 percent of all of the people in this country, male and female, young and old, support the goals of the women's movement. Yet the press and many politicians claim that women cannot agree on what they want. Why is total unanimity suddenly demanded on women's issues?"

Commissioner Ruth Clusen chaired second plenary session.

Former Presiding Officer Jill Ruckelshaus.

141

but rollcall votes had been ruled out. Because delegates were voting as individuals, not States, and because there were 2,005 of them, one rollcall vote could tie up the Conference for many hours.

Under the regulations, the Commission's decisions on the credentialing of delegates and the agenda were also binding on the body, having been published for public comment and amended before the Conference.

In spite of the concern and anger over the takeover of some State conferences by the ultraright—especially the overwhelmingly white delegation that resulted from an allegedly Klan-dominated conference in Mississippi—the IWY legal counsel had ruled that only election fraud was grounds for challenging a delegate's credentials. Since the law had provided that delegates-at-large could be used to balance the national delegate body, the counsel held this was a sufficient remedy.

The first voice from the floor was an objection to the seating of the Mississippi delegation by C. Delores

Dr. Homer G. Morgan, Mississippi delegate.

Tucker, former Secretary of State from Pennsylvania. She was registering the indignation of the delegates at the election of a white delegation from a State that was more than a third black.

While ruling the objection out of order, the chair noted that the Com-

mission had formally stated its "dismay and indignation" at the election results of the Mississippi meeting. The delegates hissed and booed their disapproval on behalf of their black sisters in Mississippi. It was an emotional moment and one that might have broken the Conference had the black delegates not had faith in the good will that had produced an unusually representative Conference.

The reading of the preamble to the National Plan of Action came next.

"We are here to move history forward," Commissioner Coretta Scott King began.

"We are women from every State and Territory in the Nation," Commissioner Jean Stapleton continued.

Lupe Anguiano, a founder of the National Women's Political Caucus, was the third voice: "We are women of different ages, beliefs, and lifestyles."

The entire body joined the readers in the pledge at the end of the Declaration of American Women: "We pledge ourselves with all the strength of our dedication to this struggle 'to form a more perfect Union.'"

When debate began, delegates lined up at the eight microphones, some to raise procedural questions on how amendments could be made, others to call the question before debate about procedures could begin. Each microphone was recognized in rotation, and microphone monitors raised color-keyed cards to tell the chair what kind of motion the next woman in line at that mike was requesting: blue to speak for the motion; green against; orange for amendments or substitutions; yellow for points of order; white for moving the question; and red for any disorder requiring a sergeant at arms.

There were problems. Since procedural questions had to be dealt with first, some delegates tried to use the yellow card to get the floor for speeches, amendments, or motions to end debate and vote. The chair urged them not to raise points of order so that the time could be used for substantive debate. Other delegates tried

C. Delores Tucker of Pennsylvania objects to seating of all-white delegation from Mississippi.

Parliamentarians were present on platform throughout the sessions to explain intricacies of procedures to delegates.

Congresswoman Elizabeth Holtzman reads plank on Battered Women.

to "pack" the microphones by standing in line for a resolution not yet under consideration, in hopes of being first when it came up.

In that first afternoon, however, ground rules were established, delegates learned how to use the color code, and it became clear that a comfortable majority favored the Plan. Reliance on procedural questions emerged as the tactic of anti-change forces.

The first plank on Arts and Humanities, urging equal opportunities for women in federally funded cultural institutions, was read by Commissioner Connie Plunkett of Georgia, a member of the Democratic National Committee. As one of the least controversial items, it passed without debate by voice vote.

Then the plank on Battered Women, which said elimination of violence in

the home should be a national goal, was introduced by Commissioner Elizabeth Holtzman and adopted by a voice vote after a speech in its favor.

The recommendation on Business, calling for an end to discriminatory practices against women entrepreneurs, was moved by Commissioner Ersa Poston, member of the U.S. Civil Service Commission, and after a short speech by a delegate opposing the involvement of the Federal Government in the problems of women in business, it passed by a standing vote. The "nays" were on their feet in the sections reserved for Missouri, Indiana, Mississippi, Ohio, Oklahoma, and other States that had elected delegates who had joined the anti-Plan coalition.

The plank on the prevention of Child Abuse was moved by Commissioner Ruth Abram, executive director of the Women's Action Alliance. Alice Ward of Ohio spoke against it. "Did you know spanking is now called child abuse? There is big publicity to turn in child abusers." Anti-IWY literature had argued that the Federal Government should not be allowed to intervene in family affairs, that anti-abuse legislation would interfere with the rights of parents.

Myrtle Pickering of Louisiana spoke in favor: "I say to you, two children in my own town were found dead last month."

A motion by Mary Gigandet of Ohio to "include those one million preborn children killed by abortion last year" was ruled not germane and out of order. An amendment that would have strengthened the resolution by calling for an urban system of "drop in" centers, operated fulltime for women and children in crisis, was also defeated. The Pro Plan network had not agreed to it and rural women thought it too limited. The resolution passed by a big majority, including some "yes" votes from anti-IWY delegates.

The plank on Child Care, recommending federally funded low-cost programs accessible to all who need them, regardless of income, was read by Commissioner Audrey Rowe Colom, former chair of the National Women's Political Caucus and current director of women's activities at the Corporation for Public Broadcasting.

Debate was limited to 10 minutes as it had been on preceding votes, and there were speeches on both sides. Among them were:

Elizabeth Koontz of North Carolina, former director of the U.S. Women's Bureau: "The issue of child care is no longer one of choice for wealthy women; it is a matter of necessity for all women."

Christine Marsten, a low-income delegate from Washington with four children, spoke in favor of the resolution "on behalf of children who need quality care and parents who worry about children while they are at work or training."

Gerri Madden of Hawaii spoke against: "The similarity between Hitler's camps and these youth camps might produce the same consequences."

A substitute recommendation that preschool child development programs should be controlled by the private sector was voted down, and the original recommendation was passed by a standing vote. Some of the opposition broke ranks to vote for it too.

The plank on Credit was moved by Commissioner Eleanor Smeal, head of the National Organization for Women (NOW). Not a single delegate rose to vote "nay."

"The critics who said we could never all agree on anything—we have just proved them wrong," Chair Clusen announced.

Commissioner Bernice Frieder of the National Council of Jewish Women read the original plank on Disabled Women, Vera Prearin, president of the American Coalition of Citizens with Disabilities, moved the substitution of the plank that the disabled women themselves had worked all night long drafting. It called, among other things, for funds to let disabled women live independently if they

choose, inclusion of the disabled in the Civil Rights Act of 1964, and full coverage under Medicaid and Medicare. Futhermore, the definition of the word "woman" throughout the National Plan of Action was to be read as including women with disabilities.

The substitute plank was adopted by an overwhelming standing vote. It was a triumph for disabled women who had been courageous enough to participate in the State conferences and for the national delegates who had made an eloquent plea to the Pro Plan Caucus the night before.

On the emotional high of seeing women in wheelchairs cheer and move close enough to each other for celebratory hugs, the session adjourned for dinner.

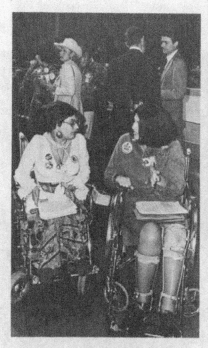

Third Plenary Session The evening session, chaired by Lieutenant Governor Mary Anne Krupsak of New York, opened with encouraging words from Patsy Mink, former Congresswoman from Hawaii; Margaret Heckler, dean of incumbent Congresswomen; and Helvi Sipila, Assistant Secretary General of the United Nations.

Congresswoman Margaret Heckler.

145

The plank on Education was read by Commissioner Alice Rossi, board chair of the Social Science Research Council and author of *The Feminist Papers*. Deborah Benzil of Maryland spoke in favor of the plank because "truly nonsexist equal opportunity education" would promote equality in all other areas. Ellen Gay Detlefsen of Pennsylvania spoke for it because it would help women school librarians attain administrative posts now held by men. Geraldine Rinehart of Ohio spoke against it, urging delegates to "consider very carefully before we allow our freedoms to be taken away and given to the Federal Government."

Three changes were voted down, including a substitute offered by Barbara Zapotocky of Nebraska to teach respect for a republican form of government, the free enterprise eco-nomic system, parents, all authorities, and absolute values of right and wrong.

The plank was passed by a standing vote with two additions. On the motion of Faith Mayhew, an American Indian from Oregon, school systems were asked to move against stereotyping on the basis of race as well as sex. The addition to the "male-defined" curriculum of "programs of study that restore to women their history and achievements" was moved by Amy Swerdlow of New York, and adopted.

The plank on Elective and Appointive Office, outlining ways to increase significantly the number of women in political office, judgeships, and Government policymaking positions, was moved by Commissioner Mildred Jeffrey, chair of the National Women's Political Caucus. It was passed by an overwhelming vote after defeat of an amendment, offered by Peggy Christensen of Montana, which would have restricted efforts to increase women in public life to

Congresswoman Lindy Boggs of Louisiana.

State Dept. official Patsy Mink, former Congresswoman, is escorted to platform by member of Hawaiian delegation.

Commissioner Mildred Jeffrey at podium, with Chair Mary Anne Krupsak seated at left.

Former State legislator Sissy Farenthold sits with Owanah Anderson, co-chair of Texas delegation.

"qualified" women. The word "qualified" is simply assumed of male candidates, but often used to create artificial barriers against women.

While the plank was being debated, some women in the back of the hall raised signs saying "Abortion Exploits Women;" "Rescind ERA;" and there were shouts of "We Want Phyllis!" But it was not Phyllis Schlafly, the Stop ERA leader, who had inspired the demonstration. It was Dr. Mildred Jefferson, the black Boston physician and leader of the anti-abortion forces at Houston. She had been appointed a delegate-at-large, but had not appeared until this moment.

"ERA now! ERA now!" Pro Plan delegates shouted as she walked slowly down the aisle. The nearest microphone monitor raised a red card. But photographers were disappointed. The chair asked "visitors" to "refrain from walking in the center aisles." Dr. Jefferson withdrew as unexpectedly as she had arrived.

If there was to be a dramatic confrontation between women who were for and against change, it would come when the Equal Rights Amendment was considered. Delegates and

photographers began positioning themselves in anticipation.

The detailed plank on Employment, including a call for a Federal policy of full employment, was moved by Com-

Chair Mary Anne Krupsak introduces Congresswoman Yvonne Burke, as Bella Abzug applauds.

147

Texas delegate Ann Richards was first to speak for ERA.

missioner Dorothy Haener, International Representative of the Women's Department, United Auto Workers, and passed after a speech favoring it by Robyn Remaklus of Oregon. Many delegates from Utah, a delegation that was solidly against the ERA and most other Plan issues, voted for it.

The Coliseum was tense and well filled when Commissioner Claire Randall, general secretary of the National Council of Churches of Christ, read the seven-word plank: "The Equal Rights Amendment should be ratified."

Pandemonium broke out. There were signs, chants, songs, and microphones jammed with women impatient to be heard.

Ann Richards, a county commissioner in her State of Texas, spoke for the ERA on behalf not only of "those few of us who are fortunate enough to be in the positions we are in but also for those who are speechless and voiceless, the divorced who may not

Commissioner Dorothy Haener presented plank on Employment.

get credit, the widows who are incapable of making a living ... my own daughter, who cannot find women in the history texts of this country in the elementary schools."

Dianne Edmondson of Oklahoma moved to amend the resolution by adding that the ERA should be ratified "only if done within the original seven-year period," a move against the extension legislation that had already been introduced in Congress.

Norma Paulus of Oregon yielded her place at the microphone to Betty Friedan of New York to speak for the Edmondson amendment, a surprise move since some people believed that defeating an extension would lessen the chances of ERA passage. But Friedan, an appointed delegate-at-large, supported the proposal for a different reason. "If the ERA is not ratified in the next year and three months," she argued, "it will be the

Calling for victory for ERA, delegate Susan B. Anthony tells crowd: "Failure is impossible."

signal to take away all that women have gained. If the President and his politicians do not pit their own power against the Far Right in the 15 Democratic States that have not ratified it, women will have been 'had' by the Government's $5 million." However, the delegates regarded the intent of the amendment as anti-ERA and voted to defeat it.

Coretta Scott King (seated left) listens attentively as Jean Westwood describes herself as a Mormon for ERA.

Government." (Section 2 reads: "The Congress shall have the power to enforce, by appropriate legislation, the provisions of this article." Constitutional lawyers point out that it does not give Congress any powers that it does not already have under the Constitution.)

"I am a Mormon woman speaking in favor of ERA," a delegate said when she was recognized by the chair. The hall went wild. When the hubbub died down, she continued, "I grew up in Utah, where women had the vote when it was a territory. They had the vote as a State, and in 1896, with the help of the Mormon Church, Utah passed in their Constitution an amendment which said, 'Women shall have equal civil, political, and religious rights with men.' I have devoted my life in politics to seeing that this privilege is extended to all women."

The unidentified woman was Jean Westwood, former chair of the Democratic National Committee, and the first woman ever to have held that position.

Rosemary Thomson of Illinois, chair of the IWY Citizens Review Committee, tried to introduce an amendment that would oppose ratification, but when it had been submitted to the chair in writing as the rules of the Conference required, it was incomplete.

After several unsuccessful attempts to write it properly to submit it to the Conference, Chair Krupsak gave up and ruled it out of order.

The ERA resolution was adopted by an enthusiastic and noisy standing vote that appeared to be almost five to one. "Ratify the ERA!" women chanted. "Three more States." They sang "God Bless America," and "The ERA Was Passed Today" to the tune of "The Yellow Rose of Texas." Karen DeCrow, former president of NOW,

continued on page 152

Susan B. Anthony of Florida, grandniece of "Susan B. Anthony the Great," spoke for the resolution, "the fulfillment of her lifetime work, her 51 years spent living and dying for women. Failure is impossible."

The audience echoed, "Impossible! Impossible!"

Evelyn Pitschke of Indiana, chair of the National Association of Lawyers Who Oppose the Equal Rights Amendment, spoke against the ERA because "section 2 of the amendment gives great power to the Federal

A New 'Era'

Era McCarthey was born shortly after her mother returned home to Phoenix, Arizona from the Houston Conference, which she attended as a delegate even though she was having labor pains.

"There are two reasons I named my baby girl Era," explained Judy McCarthey. "One is for our amendment since the ERA is the most important issue in our fight for true equality for all, and the second is because of the concept which arose out of the Houston Conference, the concept that it heralded the beginning of a new era for women."

Delegate McCarthey, a 31-year-old Apache Indian, and the mother of six children, has plans for a new life for herself, too. She is enrolled as a criminal justice major at Arizona State University and hopes to enter law school.

"I have been helping mature women reenter education and the job force via the Association for Women's Active Return to Education (AWARE) and the Department of Economic Security, Welfare Office," she told the National Commission. "As a welfare recipient, I am trying to get off the welfare merry-go-round, and I understand many of the problems facing other women in my position.

"I am very aware of what it means to be an ethnic minority, a divorced mother, a mature college student, and on a limited income. But I know, as we all do, that there can be a fuller life for all of us and our families. That is why I support the National Plan of Action and the Equal Rights Amendment."

Commissioner Rita Elway joins her sister delegates from Washington in celebrating approval of ERA plank.

Joan Gubbins, leader of anti Plan delegates.

led a happy chain of women down the aisles. Commissioners smiled and embraced each other on the stage. The New York delegates waved their symbolic apples over their heads, and the Californians waved their yellow scarves.

Women from Ohio, a State where the antichange forces had prevailed at the local conference, sat silent. They had voted against the ERA and some were in tears. Other delegates tried to explain to them that the ERA would not destroy their families, or integrate bathrooms (women's and men's), or force women out of their homes, as they had been told by anti-ERA literature and leaders, but they were not persuaded.

Congresswoman Margaret Heckler (left) confers with Jill Ruckelshaus.

For several minutes, the chair did not even try to restore order. It was clearly impossible. When the delegates finally settled down, it was nearly midnight. Some wanted to continue with the agenda, others felt adjournment was necessary. After a standing vote looked too close for decision, it was necessary to ask for a teller's count on the motion to adjourn.

The motion carried, 927 to 341.

It had been a long and productive day for the delegates, and Presiding Officer Abzug dismissed them gently.

"Good night, my loves," she said, after announcing the adjournment vote.

SUNDAY, NOVEMBER 20

Fourth Plenary Session Sunday morning, some delegates went to the peace and disarmament hearings, others went to religious services, still others continued to caucus and work on resolutions. Many were so exhausted from the hard work on Saturday and the postmidnight meetings that they were glad to sleep late. The plenary session convening at noon faced a nonstop agenda of 14 more planks, including the charged issues dealing with reproductive freedom (which included women's right to choose abortion), and protection for the civil rights of lesbians. Anne Saunier of Ohio, a leader of NOW, personnel executive and daughter of a woman parliamentarian, was to be the chair.

The opening ceremonies were brief. To honor the contributions of Hispanic women, they began with a bilingual dialogue between Commissioner Carmen Delgado Votaw, president of the National Conference of Puerto Rican Women, and Commissioner Cecilia Preciado-Burciaga, a Chicana and the assistant provost of Stanford University.

"Sisters, hermanas," Preciado-Burciaga began.

"Amigas, Compañeras," Votaw added.

Preciado-Burciaga: "We want equality."

Anne Saunier of Ohio chaired Sunday's long session.

Commissioners Cecilia Preciado-Burciaga and Carmen Delgado Votaw (at mike) in Spanish-English dialogue.

Votaw: "Buscamos la igualdad."

Their issues, they went on to say, "are the same as yours—empleo, educación, salud, vivienda." They seek, "nay demand, your recognition and respect for our cultural and linguistic heritage."

"We believe that blacks, whites, Chicanas, Cubans, Puertoriquenas, and Native and Asian Americans can join hands, and we urge you to join hands with your neighbor now."

They ended by repeating with the audience, "¡Que Viva La Mujer—Que Viva!"

Next came Margaret Mead. The audience greeted her with great warmth and applause, but the world-famous anthropologist was her usual no-nonsense self.

"I'm only allowed 10 minutes to speak," she said, "so let's not waste any of it in demonstrations ... demonstrations about me, I mean." She had come to urge women to work for peace.

"This Conference may well be the turning point, not only in the history of the women's movement but in the history of the world itself." Women were attaining political power, she explained, at a moment in history when the United States was "endangering

Margaret Mead.

the world" and at the same time "has the greatest chance to save the world" from nuclear proliferation, the arms race, and war.

"It has been women's task throughout history to go on believing in life when there was almost no hope," she concluded. "If we are united, we may be able to produce a world in which our children and other people's children will be safe."

The audience stood and sang, "Happy Birthday, Dear Margaret," in honor of her 75th year.

Commissioner Gloria Steinem read the Health resolution to the conference.

Commissioner Gloria Steinem, an editor of *Ms.* Magazine and a feminist organizer, read the Health resolution, which advocated a national health security system. Cheers punctuated the delegates' reception of this lengthy plank, particularly the sections

153

Commissioners Rhea Mojica Hammer (left) and Ethel Taylor share the torch at a Commission business meeting.

calling for the licensing of midwives, a patient's bill of rights, safeguards against hazardous drugs, and the establishment of a task force to investigate the increase in such surgical procedures as hysterectomy, mastectomy, and forced sterilization. It was clear that women deeply resented the inadequacies of a health system to which their reproductive capacity makes them particularly vulnerable.

The plank was overwhelmingly adopted as soon as the question was called.

Commissioner Lenore Hershey, editor of the *Ladies' Home Journal*, moved the plank on Homemakers, a resolution that said marital property, inheritance, and domestic relations laws should be based "on the principle that marriage is a partnership in which the contribution of each spouse is of equal importance and value." The plank was adopted after the chair ruled on questions about access to the microphones. "I am not a chair-*man*," Anne Saunier replied to an anti-change delegate who insisted on using the masculine form, "and I don't plan to become one."

Commissioner Cecilia Preciado-Burciaga moved adoption of the resolution on Insurance, which advocated the Model Regulation to Eliminate Unfair Sex Discrimination of the National Association of Insurance Commissioners.

Betty Wilson of New Jersey spoke in favor of it. "The current system of insurance is one where women pay more and get less."

Geraldine Rinehart of Ohio spoke against it as an impersonal Government-regulated system of providing help in which "the character building value which attends the voluntary response to the cry of the needy is lost." Nonetheless, the Insurance resolution received a large majority.

In urging that procedural motions be limited so that the time could be spent on debating the proposal, the chair complained that "some people get recognized on yellow cards to raise points which not only can I not answer, but God above cannot answer. *She* just doesn't have the answer." The delegates laughed and applauded understandingly.

The various sections in the long resolution on International Affairs were read by five commissioners in turn:

Koryne Horbal, U.S. delegate to the U.N. Commission on the Status of Women, read the section on Women and Foreign Policy.

Jeffalyn Johnson, former associate director of the Federal Executive Institute, read the section on Women in Development.

Coretta Scott King, founder of the Martin Luther King, Jr. Memorial Center, read the section on Human Rights Treaties and International Conventions on Women.

Ethel Taylor, national coordinator of Women Strike for Peace, read the section on Peace and Disarmament.

Mildred Persinger, representative to the United Nations for the Worldwide and National Board of the Young Women's Christian Association of the U.S.A., read the section on International Education and Communication, and moved the adoption of the entire plank.

Commissioner Jeffalyn Johnson presented International Affairs plank on Women in Development.

A motion to divide the question was defeated, and the International Affairs resolution was adopted.

At this point in the deliberation, a storm of points of order was raised by delegates from Nebraska, Kansas, Alabama, Missouri, Illinois, and Arkansas who felt that they were not being heard. When a Puerto Rican delegate wanted to be able to speak in her own language, an interpreter was found. Evelyn Pitschke of Indiana, one of the antichange delegates, finally acknowledged that "the chair has

tographers had to be cleared from the aisles, as they had been on earlier votes. "We are all women on the move," the chair said in an effort to hurry reluctant reporters. "Now what we want to see is media on the move." The Media resolution carried easily. Delegates were anticipating the next resolution.

The air was electric when Commissioner Jane Culbreth, former president of the National Federation of Business and Professional Women's Clubs, rose to the podium to

Commissioner Jane Culbreth moved the plank on Minority Women.

been very fair and has acted as fairly as possible, which we greatly appreciate."

Commissioner Sey Chassler, editor of *Redbook*, moved the resolution on Media, calling for "appropriate action to improve the image and employment of women in the communications industries." In response to a question from Rosemary Thomson of Illinois, Commissioner Chassler said the resolution intended women "of all viewpoints" to be included in policy-making positions in the media.

When it came time to vote on the Media resolution, reporters and pho-

read the next plank, the original, three-paragraph Minority Women's resolution.

Many delegates knew about the diverse caucuses that had been meeting before and during the Conference, and some didn't think that a coalition of all minority groups could happen. After all, Spanish-origin groups had not yet felt adequately represented or united by the title "Hispanic"; the black delegates covered the full range from conservative Republican to radical nonvoter; the Asian Americans included women whose countries had historic antagonisms (China, Japan, and the Philippines, for instance); and most American Indians had not had the opportunity to work together across tribal lines before. In addition, some

antichange delegates had been predicting trouble with a hint of anticipation. "If you think women are divided," said one stop-IWY activist to the press, "wait until you see these black people and the Mexicans. The Conference will either fall apart or blow apart."

All through Saturday, while the plenary sessions were in progress, a drafting coalition composed of representatives of all the minority caucuses had worked in a long, windowless coatroom, the only available room backstage at the Coliseum. (See section on Minority Caucus.)

When it was time to read the substitute resolution on the floor, even the delegates who knew about this drafting were not sure it had been completed. It had taken an early Sunday morning meeting to arrive at a final draft, and that left very little time to type it in triplicate for submission to the chair (as the rules required), distribute it to the various caucus members, and decide how it was to be introduced from the floor.

continued on page 158

THE MINORITY CAUCUS:
'It's Our Movement Now'

Of all the delegates in Houston who were drawn together by double discrimination—by a condition of powerlessness that multiplied their problems as women—the largest number were those from groups usually designated as minorities. There were black women from almost every State and Territory; Hispanic women, including Chicanas, Puerto Ricans, Cubans, and other Latinas; an Asian American caucus of Chinese Americans, Japanese Americans, Philippinas, and others; American Indians from many different tribes, as well as Alaskan natives; and Pacific Americans from Hawaii, Guam, Samoa, and other trust territories.

Together, they made up about a quarter of the delegates, a proportion greater than their percentage in the total population as counted by the U.S. Census, though it should be noted that these statistics have often been shown to undercount minority groups. In fact, its diversity was the most remarkable and distinguishing characteristic of the delegate body. In a country in which the majority group still dominates political and economic life, the unprecedented participation of minority women in the State meetings had turned the Houston Conference into a uniquely representative body: a nationwide, multiracial, multicultural town meeting of Americans.

Minority women in the State and Territorial meetings had voiced their concerns in a variety of ways. Some had included their needs and agendas in resolutions passed by the State meetings on a number of topics. Others had passed separate resolutions on minority issues. The National Plan of Action presented to the Houston Conference reflected these different approaches. A number of planks referred to minority needs; in addition, a separate three-paragraph plank on Minority Women was included in recognition of the distinctive importance of their concerns. In doing so, the National Commission had made clear that the minority delegates gathered in Houston were expected to present a more complete plank as a substitute if they wished.

Many minority delegates had been working long before Houston to do just that and to unite their own groups into much needed coalitions. The Government-funded Conference, like the preliminary State meetings, was regarded by many as an opportunity to meet their sisters and to form networks that could be crucial to their futures. Black delegates laid the groundwork, for instance, by polling their counterparts in other States by phone or by doing research through their existing organizations. A coalition started by the National Council of Negro Women and headed by Dr. Elizabeth Stone of Howard University had even prepared a mimeographed booklet entitled "The Black Women's Plan of Action."

In California, with its enormous distances and large Chicana population, Gracia Molina-Pick, a former professor of Third World studies and a longtime Chicana activist, brought together women from the northern and southern parts of the State. She also traveled to Texas in advance of Houston to share ideas with the Texas "host" delegation, which included more Chicanas than any other State did and whose co-chairs were both minority women: State Representative Irma Rangel, the first Chicana ever to serve in the Texas legislature, and Owanah Anderson, an American Indian spokeswoman.

Esther Kee, a Chinese American delegate from New York, canvassed her sisters by phone and helped to organize a meeting just before the Conference's opening session. To bring together members of all the minority caucuses, Kogie Thomas, an American Indian spokeswoman from California, helped to coordinate a coalition and statement among her

Women study Black Women's Plan of Action.

sisters before State meetings and before Houston.

In spite of possibly dozens more of such energetic, goodwill efforts, many minority delegates were meeting in Houston for the first time and bringing with them the diverse and crucial concerns of their own communities. Among them, as among the white majority, were many who had never before been to a large meeting; experienced political leaders and members of Congress; radicals who favored action outside the Conference and outside the electoral system itself; single-issue representatives who had never identified as feminists before; and separatists who felt the integrity of their particular minority group should not be compromised by coalition with other minorities, much less with more powerful groups. The polar extremes of their views were the determination of some to declare minority women's concerns completely separate from the Conference or its National Plan of Action and the conviction of others that the National Plan must be retained intact lest anti-change forces exploit any division.

That was the complex, hope-filled situation when minority women began arriving in Houston. In the midst of hotel room mix-ups, registration, and caucusing by State and other interest groups, it seemed as if only a miracle could achieve communication, much less coalition.

By the time the Pro Plan Caucus had its first big meeting Friday night, however, black delegates had met in several caucuses, and an Hispanic Caucus had separated into Chicana and Puerto Rican components to discuss issues. American Indian women from several States were trying to link up with their California sisters to form an organizing core, and Pacific and Asian American delegates were identifying themselves as groups.

Once most minority delegates were reassured by their Pro Plan representatives that they could indeed rewrite and expand the Minority Women plank, drafting committees began to spring up: one from the Racial/Ethnic

breakfast hosted by minority commissioners on Saturday morning, and one from additional delegates who met later that day. The Hispanic women inspired unity by coming up with an umbrella statement representing Chicana, Puerto Rican, Cuban, and other Latina delegates, the first time such a national coalition had ever been made.

By Saturday afternoon, a drafting committee of representatives of *all* minority caucuses was working together to coalesce each group's

statements. Members ranged from Dorothy Height, a respected black leader of 30 years' standing, to Colleen Wong, a 16-year-old Chinese American activist from San Francisco; from Dr. Ethel Allen, a Republican city councilwoman from Philadelphia, to Carmela Lacayo, an official of the Democratic National Committee; from Tin Myaing Thien, a young academician, to Billie Nave Masters, a Cherokee Indian and university teacher. After including Gloria Steinem, a non-minority Commissioner whom they had invited to help with hammering out coalition language (and cheerfully referred to by them as "the token"), the dozen or so members met nonstop throughout the second and third plenary sessions.

As each group read its statement, it became clear that most issues were shared. A Chicana delegate emphasized her group's suffering from coerced sterilizations; then black representatives cited similar tragic experiences, among their sisters, and an American Indian delegate brought tears to everyone's eyes by asserting

that 42 percent of that population's women have been sterilized, with or without informed consent. Asian American women explained that many of them suffer from monolingual education and health and social services just as Spanish-speaking women do. All agreed that culturally biased testing procedures and the lack of statistics based on sex and race were root problems for all those suffering from double discrimination.

In this careful, caring, organic way, umbrella issues emerged and were listed in order to write a basic statement. The remaining, more special issues—removal of American Indian children from their communities, for instance, or the isolation of Asian American women who have come to this country as wives of servicemen—were not dismissed but were allotted to special, smaller sections, one for each major group, that were to be appended to the introductory umbrella statement. The meeting continued until midnight and reassembled early Sunday morning to agree on final phrasing.

When the resulting statement was finally read on the Conference floor by members of each major caucus (see narrative), many felt it to be the most significant event of Houston and of all that had preceded it. For the first time, minority women—many of whom had been in the leadership of the women's movement precisely because of their greater political understanding of discrimination—were present in such a critical mass that they were able to define their own needs as well as to declare their stake in each women's issue. They were also able to make the media aware of their importance and to forge their own internal networks and coalitions in a way that was far reaching, inclusive, and an historic "first" for their communities, for women and men.

"Let this message go forth from Houston," said Coretta Scott King, "and spread all over this land. There is a new force, a new understanding, a new sisterhood against all injustice that has been born here. We will not be divided and defeated again." 🐾

Up to the last cliffhanging minute the drafters were unsure whether they would be allowed to have representatives of the largest groups take turns at reading the different sections (until then, one speaker each had been recognized for amendments and substitutions), and if so, at which of the many floor mikes they should gather.

As Jane Culbreth finished reading the original plank, the clear, strong voice of Maxine Waters, a young black assemblywoman from California, was heard demanding recognition from the back of the hall.

The noisy floor grew quiet as she began to read the umbrella statement applying to all minorities, an honor for which she had been chosen in recognition of the no-sleep energy she had put into helping the women come together in Houston.

"Minority women share with all women the experience of sexism as a barrier to their full rights of citizenship," she read slowly. "But institu-

tional bias based on race, language, culture, and/or ethnic origin ... have led to the additional oppression ... and to the conditions of poverty from which they disproportionately suffer." Reporters began to gather in the aisle where a rainbow of women waited their turn. When the next speaker was ceded her place at the mike, it was clear that something special, almost mystical, had begun.

"American Indian/Alaskan Native women have a relationship to Earth Mother and the Great Spirit," read Billie Nave Masters, one of the spokeswomen who had helped her American Indian sisters prepare for this meeting, "as well as a heritage based on the sovereignty of Indian peoples." Delegates began to stand on their chairs to see the source of this language, more poetic than had been heard in any other resolution.

Then Mariko Tse, a young Japanese-American actress, took her turn: "Asian/Pacific American women

are wrongly thought to be a part of a 'model minority' with few problems. This obscures our vulnerability due to language and culture barriers, sweatshop work conditions with high health hazards. ... "

She finished and turned the mike over to Sandy Serrano Sewell, president of the Comisión Femenil Mexicana, who stood in symbolic unity

Tears of joy as Conference overwhelmingly approved substitute resolution on Minority Women.

with Ana María Perera, a Cuban American, and Celeste Benítez a Senator from Puerto Rico, as she read the Hispanic statement. "Deportation of mothers of American-born children must be stopped ... " The delegates responded to her ringing tone with applause and shouts. "Legislation ... to provide migrant farm working women the Federal minimum wage ... classification of Hispanic American media as 'foreign press' must be stopped. ..."

The press now filled the wide aisle in front of the speakers and flashbulbs lit the faces around the mike as more and more reporters caught the historic importance of this moment.

Standing with a bodyguard at her side, a reminder of past tragedy, Coretta Scott King read the statement of black women that had been placed at the end, out of alphabetical order, in honor of her symbolic presence. "The President and Congress should provide full quality education, including special admission programs ... The President and the Congress should immediately address the crisis of unemployment which impacts the black community, and results in black teenage women having the highest rate of unemployment...."

When she ended by urging "the enthusiastic adoption of this substitute resolution on behalf of all the minority women in this country," the floor seemed to explode in applause and cheers and shouts. As the chair gaveled the delegates to order, however, there were some indications of opposition.

A delegate from Nebraska wanted to know if the minority delegates were going to support abortion, though an affirmative answer should have been clear from the resolution itself. The chair ruled the inquiry out of order. Delegates from Nebraska and Oklahoma stood up to object and to call for a "statement of monetary need" and "a price tag" for this resolution, but many other delegates booed these requests. An emotional tide of support had begun to surge through the hall, and no amount of objection or questioning could hold it back. A Missouri delegate requested that the resolution be read again, but a District of Columbia delegate, clearly wanting to get on with the voting, objected even to that. Nonetheless, the chair reread the resolution, and the floor grew quiet in anticipation of the vote.

When the delegates stood up to vote "yes," there was a moment's hush, and then shouts of joy. It was almost unanimous, and there were many surprises. Women from the almost totally white, anti-ERA delegation of Utah were also standing. So were members of the all-white delegation from Mississippi: one man and one woman reached across their seated, disapproving delegation

159

members to hold hands as they courageously stood to vote "yes" to the minority women.

A line of celebrating women began to form in the aisles and across the space in front of the stage. Others sang "We Shall Overcome," holding hands as they swayed in place. The readers of the resolution were swept off the floor to meet with the hundreds of media people who had been surrounding them.

At the impromptu press conference, speakers hailed the recognition of minority women, who had always been on the frontlines of the struggle for equal justice but had often been treated as "invisible women" by the press and sometimes by white women themselves. This victory belied the tired myth that only "white middleclass women" cared about equality. Even some of the toughest men among the reporters and TV camera crews were visibly moved.

The audience gave Anne Saunier a standing ovation when she tempo-

Dorothy Height and Maxine Waters at Minority Women press conference.

rarily relinquished the chair. She had steered the session deftly through some of its most difficult moments with her calm authoritative manner and clear instructions. Now vice chair Elizabeth Koontz, former director of the Women's Bureau, took over for the next two resolutions.

"Procedures are the same, rules are the same," chair Koontz announced. "Only the color of the presider up here has been changed."

The crowd roared appreciatively.

The spirits of celebrating delegates remained high as Commissioner Elizabeth Athanasakos, a former presiding officer of the IWY Commission, began to read the plank on Offenders.

There was some hint of the suffering of many women in prison in even the dry phrasing of requests for facilities within visiting distance of families, an end to sexual abuse inside prisons, and an end to the practice of calling young women delinquent for behavior that would not be punished in young men. Alice Travis of California, a former member of the California Council on Criminal Justice, spoke for the recommendation: "The criminal justice system provides cruel and unusual punishment for women who have committed crimes."

"Does this word 'discrimination' mean that our penal institutions will have to be coed?" a delegate from Illinois inquired, raising an issue that would not be affected by this resolution, since the right to privacy would prevail. The chair ruled her out of order and the plank was adopted.

Commissioner Carmen Delgado Votaw read for adoption the plank on Older Women, calling for improved services and funding, liberalized Medicare, continued efforts to hold down drug costs, efforts to promote a positive image of women in middle and later years, and an end to mandatory retirement.

An inquiry on the meaning of the word "discrimination" in this and every other plank of the National Plan was ruled out of order.

Priscilla Tuncap of Guam spoke in favor of the plank in her native language, which an interpreter translated for the delegates. She spoke in behalf of the many older American women who do not have enough food, shelter, clothing, and the right kinds of services.

Betty Hamburger, wearing "Pro God, Pro Family, Pro ERA" helmet, speaks for "dignity and respect" for older women.

Betty Hamburger of Maryland, a 73-year-old member of the Gray Panthers, an activist organization for the aid of older people, also spoke for the resolution: "What we want most is life with dignity and respect and an income on which we can live without having to hold out our hands and beg. We want to be part of the mainstream of life and not be put in golden playpens."

Elizabeth Welch of North Carolina introduced a stronger, more explicit substitute resolution which had the backing of the Gray Panthers and Elinor Guggenheimer, New York City Commissioner of Consumer Affairs. "The older woman should be recognized and acclaimed not only as a recipient of needed support and legis-

lation," she said, "but as a doer of a breadth and variety of creative productivity which will enrich not only her own personal life but the quality of life of her society, and I would like to remind the convention of one thing: We belong to a generation that doesn't have the time to wait. Take us now and make us a part of you."

Geraldine Rinehart of Ohio spoke against the substitute proposal: "Do we want to pay the bill directly and take care of our own and take care of those who are not able to take care of themselves, or do we want to send the money to Washington, D. C., and have *them* do it?"

Faire Edwards of Vermont spoke for it: "The elderly are the fastest growing poverty group in this county. More than half are widows, and a sizeable proportion of them are trying to exist on much less than $200 a month. Please . . . at least let us earn a living."

In response to a point of inquiry, the chair ruled that including legislation to help displaced housewives was germane to the resolution, since a large proportion of older women were in that category.

Irma Donnellon of Ohio spoke against the substitute resolution: "If a woman has the right over her own body in her early years, then why do we have to provide for her body in her later years?"

There were a few exasperated "boos" from the audience.

Gerri Madden of Hawaii spoke against the resolution: "I shall be 83 next month, the 6th of December, and I don't want any old folks' home, and I think the Government should not interfere with us."

The substitute resolution on Older Women was adopted by an overwhelming standing vote that included some antichange delegates as well.

Commissioner Margaret Mealey, retiring executive director of the National Council of Catholic Women, moved the resolution on Rape.

The plank, which proposed detailed revisions of criminal codes and case law dealing with rape and related offenses, was amended by Virginia Apuzzo of New York to provide that the past sexual conduct of the victim cannot be introduced into evidence. "The existing clause suggests that the rape of a woman is somehow more or less offensive depending on her sexual history," she argued. The resolution passed as amended.

Next on the agenda was Reproductive Freedom, a strong emotional issue because it included a woman's right to choose abortion, as upheld by the U.S. Supreme Court. The resolution also opposed the exclusion of childbirth, pregnancy-related health care, or abortion from federally funded programs, a reference to the ban on Medicaid coverage of abortion.

Photographers jockeyed for position. Delegates scrambled to line up at the microphones. Other groups caucused, readied signs and banners, or rushed though the aisles to confer on tactics.

After chair Saunier restored relative quiet and order, the Reproductive Freedom resolution was read by Commissioner Gerridee Wheeler, a Republican committeewoman, past president of the National Association for Mental Health, and mother of eight children.

As she spoke, enlarged color photographs of fetuses were raised around the hall by antichoice activists. So were signs on both sides: "Protect the unborn," "Keep Abortion Safe and Legal," and the coathanger symbol proclaiming the determination of women to provide legal, safe alternatives to this dangerous method of self-abortion.

The chair asked that all signs be put down "because people can't see me and that's critical." She announced that in the interests of fair debate, there would be two speeches for and two speeches against the motion.

The first speech for the resolution was made by Sarah Weddington of Texas, general counsel for the Department of Agriculture. She was the law-yer who had argued before the U.S. Supreme Court the landmark case resulting in the January 22, 1973, decision that a woman had the right to choose abortion as part of her constitutionally protected right to privacy.

"We would all agree that the best way to prevent the problem of un-wanted pregnancies is contraception ..." she said. "We do stress that we are for sex education; we are for the availability of family planning information and services ..., [but] there are some who refuse to continue pregnancy and ... we save our support for their choice."

Ann O'Donnell of Missouri speaks against Reproductive Freedom plank.

Despite her insistence that opponents be given an opportunity to speak, no green cards were raised. The chair had to appeal for speakers against the motion.

Ann O'Donnell of Missouri was the first to respond. "It is the antithesis of the feminist movement to oppress the less powerful," she said. "It therefore has to be absolutely ridiculous for people who call themselves feminists to suggest that they kill their unborn children to solve their social problems."

Jo Ann Medeiros of Hawaii wanted to know whether the resolution meant that teenage girls could get an abortion without telling their parents.

The chair ruled that she was asking a question rather than making a speech, so when Commissioner Wheeler answered the question with a single word "yes," the chair recognized Mary Fran Horgan of Missouri

as the second opposition speaker. She maintained that abortion abused "another minority in this country, the unborn children."

After the speeches, the resolution on Reproductive Freedom was adopted by a standing vote that appeared to be about five to one, the same division as in national public opinion polls.

The celebration was quieter than the demonstration for ERA the night before, with pro-choice delegates letting the songs and chants of the anti-choice minority go unanswered. They seemed to recognize how deeply those opposing them felt about the resolution and respected their feelings.

Commissioner Beverly Everett, a farm woman and Iowa State president of the American Association of University Women, moved the adoption of the plank on Rural Women,

Bea Kabler of Wisconsin, the wife of a doctor, was the second speaker favoring the resolution. She urged its adoption for the sake of the rising proportion of teenagers exposed to the high health, medical, and social risks of pregnancy. She pointed out that teenage mothers are more apt to have premature babies and babies with birth defects and that pregnancy is the main reason teenage girls drop out of school.

Opposition speakers were raising points of order, but none signaled a desire to speak on the substance of the resolution. In order to ensure debate, the chair called for speakers in opposition.

When the microphone monitor made a mistake and raised a white card calling for the close of debate, the outcry came not from the anti-abortionists who would be cut off, but from the Pro Plan delegates. "These people have a right to be heard," Bella Abzug cried, leaving the platform and striding down the aisle to the microphone.

Anti-abortion delegates bow their heads in prayer after Reproductive Freedom plank is adopted.

which spoke of their "special problems of isolation, poverty and underemployment." Lorna Bourg of Louisiana proposed amending the resolution to ask the President to appoint a joint committee from the Departments of Labor, Agriculture, and Justice to investigate the violation of human rights on Louisiana sugar cane plantations.

"There are 80,000 people living behind the 'cane curtain' on sugarcane plantations," she said. "Their mail is opened. They must get a permission slip to go to the doctor. Only a few years ago they were paid by tokens instead of United States currency."

Rowena Gamble of Kansas moved to amend the resolution to include "blacks, migrants, Native Americans, Alaskans, Asians, Hispanics, and all isolated minorities" in any programs adopted for rural women.

The plank was adopted with these two amendments before the Farm Women's Caucus had a chance to introduce a more detailed resolution which they had drafted in their caucus. Conservatives were split on the issue. Utah voted for the amended resolution; delegates from Missouri were against it.

Catherine East (hand upraised) speaks against plank on Sexual Preference.

It was long past the dinner hour, but tired and hungry delegates sat still and silent while Commissioner Jean O'Leary, co-chair of the National Gay Task Force, read the recommendation on Sexual Preference. Non-delegate lesbians watched from the bleachers.

The television cameras were poised at the ready.

Elimination of discrimination on the basis of sexual and affectional preference had not been one of the recommendations originally submitted by the National Commission to the States for action at their pre-Conference meetings. But over the long months, lesbians and other women who also believed in their rights had succeeded in getting sexual preference resolutions adopted by 30 State meetings. In response to this showing, Commissioners attending their pre-Conference meeting in Washington in October had voted overwhelmingly to add to the National Plan a plank barring discrimination on the basis of sexual preference.

During interviews, many delegates said they had never met a declared lesbian face to face before they came

to Houston. Women who thought that lesbians had a right to their choice of private sexual behavior worried about lesbian teachers. Some who had not thought about the subject were outraged by Anita Bryant's campaign against them in Florida. "After all, these people are women too," an observer from Louisiana said. "They have the same problems as straight women. They have reasons for their own feelings and philosophies."

Speakers pro and con explored many different aspects of the issue presented in the recommendation.

Speaking as "the president of the largest and strongest feminist organization in the world" and also as "a woman who has spent the last 14 years of her life as a homemaker and the mother of two," Eleanor Smeal of NOW declared that lesbianism was not only an issue of human rights but

of feminism. "We must not oppress any part of our society or of womanhood."

The first "con" speaker was Catherine East, retired coordinator of policy and planning for the IWY Commission. "In the interest of the future of the women's movement," she said, "we must limit ourselves to areas in which women are discriminated against vis-a-vis-men, or in which our services are undervalued, as they are in the home. I have no trouble distinguishing between gender and sexual preference."

Dorris Holmes, a leader in the fight for ratification of the ERA in Georgia, spoke against the resolution as an "albatross.... The States that have not ratified are conservative." And, she added, "it is not a unique woman's problem."

Charlotte Bunch, a leading feminist theoretician and editor of Quest, who described herself as being from "the not yet sovereign State of Washington, D.C.," argued that the resolution would help "all women, all women whose choices in life are in fact constrained by the fear and threat of being called a lesbian."

Winnie Matthews of Oklahoma was for keeping lesbians in the closet. "We would never advocate a stoning or a burning at the stake or throwing stones at a homosexual as long as homosexuals keep their sexual preference private, the same as adulterers and adulteresses."

The most unexpected support came from Betty Friedan. "I am known to be violently opposed to the lesbian issue," she began. "As someone who has grown up in middle America and as someone who has loved men too well, I have had trouble with this issue. Now my priority is in passing the ERA. And because there is nothing in it that will give any protection to homosex-

Delegates celebrate adoption of Sexual Preference plank.

uals, I believe we must help the women who are lesbians." Delegates cheered her remarks.

Among those who stood up to vote for the resolution were many women of conventional lifestyle and middle-of-the-road politics.

When the plank passed with a more than comfortable majority, the lesbians in the bleachers shouted, "Thank you, sisters," and released hundreds of pink and yellow ballons that said, "We Are Everywhere." Supporters of the resolution snakedanced across the front of the arena.

Meanwhile, at a whistle from Joan Gubbins, the opposition women and men from Mississippi turned their backs to the podium and bent their heads as if in prayer. "Keep them in the closet," their signs protested.

Adoption of the resolution on Statistics was moved by Commissioner Rhea Mojica Hammer, publisher of El Clarin. It called upon

166

the Federal Government to collect and analyze data on the basis of sex and was adopted without debate.

Commissioner Rita Elway of Washington, a public opinion research consultant, moved adoption of the original resolution on Welfare. It called for a Federal floor on aid to dependent families, job training to help women get off welfare, and a minimum guaranteed wage.

Advocates for welfare recipients wanted much more. They raised signs saying "Wages for Housework" and "Welfare is a Women's Issue." A substitute resolution prepared by the welfare caucus was introduced and read by three delegates who were or had been welfare recipients. To make its emphasis clear, they retitled it, "Women, Welfare, and Poverty."

Christine Marsten of Washington read the first three paragraphs, which called for recognition of the fact that poverty is a women's issue and must be attacked by eliminating discrimination against women in employment and in the home.

Frankie Jeter of Pennsylvania, chair of the National Welfare Rights Organization, read the paragraph which opposed the Carter administration's welfare bill, and also "workfare" proposals that would require women on welfare to work off their payments without getting any of the benefits of employment.

Beulah Sanders of New York, a past president of the Women's Welfare Rights Organization, read the concluding portion of the resolution which asked for specific action to give poor women alternatives to the dead-end, low-paid jobs that keep them in poverty.

The substitute resolution was adopted by an overwhelming vote after delegates defeated an amendment to eliminate censure of the Carter administration welfare reform bill. Delegates who had worked straight through without a supper recess were tired and restless after the welfare plank was passed.

Betty Friedan with Kate Millett.

167

Before adjournment, it was announced that any resolution to be offered as New Business the following day had to be submitted in writing before delegates left the hall. The plank to create a Cabinet-level Women's Department, and New Business were left for Monday morning, as was discussion of the implementation of the Plan of Action.

Presiding Officer Bella Abzug took the floor to make a few announcements. As she finished, some delegates good naturedly broke into song, to the tune of "Good Night Ladies." "Good night, Bella, good night, Bella ... we're going to leave you now."

"I'll see you in the morning bright and early," Abzug said, and the session adjourned. It was past 10 p.m.

MONDAY, NOVEMBER 21

Final Plenary Session   After three days of talk and excitement and mindchanging, the major recommendations had been agreed upon. Monday morning came with the inevitable letdown—checking out of hotels and worrying about catching planes and buses back to jobs and families.

Delegates drifted into the Coliseum. Those who had deferred their own proposals hoped to bring them up at the final session during New Business. The meeting opened late.

Chair of the session was Commissioner Addie Wyatt of Chicago, former President of the Coalition of Labor Union Women. She commended the delegates for their orderly dispatch of the long agenda Sunday and invited each one to shake hands with the sister next to her by way of congratulation.

Midge Costanza, assistant to the President, promised that "the response from Jimmy Carter will be sensitive." She urged the delegates to go home and defeat elected officials who do not share that sensitivity.

Women who introduced substitute Welfare plank congratulate each other after its adoption.

Brenda Parker of Happy, Texas, 17-year-old president of Future Homemakers of America, speaks at closing session.

Substituting for Commissioner La-Donna Harris, who was ill, was Billie Nave Masters, a Cherokee Indian and teacher of American Indian studies at the University of California at Irvine. She called on delegates to save Indians from termination of Government responsibility for protection of their traditional lifestyle.

Then Mary Keegan, chair of the Houston Committee, presented roses to Bella Abzug on behalf of the Houston volunteers. Brenda Parker, the 17-year-old national president of Future Homemakers of America, assured the Conference that young women were not afraid of the changes they face in the future.

Presiding Officer Abzug gave thanks to the IWY Commission staff, who had worked for months with little rest or reward, and called them up individually to the stage. She asked also for a round of applause for the Houston volunteers.

By the time these ceremonies were over, it was 11 o'clock, only an hour and a half before the mandated adjournment time.

After some altercation about the right of the Commission to change the order of business, the increasingly restive and time-pressed body of delegates voted down the 26th plank of the proposed National Plan of Action, which had recommended establish-

Billie Nave Masters, delegate-at-large, confers with John Ryor, president of the National Education Association.

The Presiding Officer gets a new hat from Puerto Rico delegation.

ment of a Cabinet-level Women's Department to coordinate social policy affecting women. Some delegates feared that a new Department would isolate women's concerns in a single agency. They approved a moderating amendment to make clear that the new Department was to "coordinate" not "consolidate" the work of advocates for women in existing Departments. But then on a standing vote, they rejected the entire proposal.

Voted down, too, was a NOW-sponsored resolution from the floor proposing that the Plan be implemented by a "Congress of Women" consisting of two women elected from each State. They then voted to approve a National Commission resolution to establish a continuing Committee of the Conference to "assess the

progress made toward achieving the recommendations of this 1977 Conference" and to take steps to provide for the convening of a Second National Women's Conference, as mandated by Public Law 94-167. The Conference also called on the President to issue an Executive Order creating a Commission "to carry out our recommendations."

Although the Commission had voted to extend the session until 3 p.m., a motion to adjourn carried before New Business could be considered. "I think we accomplished more in this meeting than we could possibly have hoped for," Presiding Officer Bella Abzug said in parting. She promised that the Commission would deal with the New Business

Bella Abzug and Chair Addie Wyatt embrace as Conference ends.

resolutions the delegates had left behind them. More than 100 resolutions on implementation and New Business had been submitted.

As delegates began to leave, Joan Gubbins, leader of the anti-change forces, tried to end the Conference on a note of protest. She marched out of the hall followed by delegates from Mississippi, Alabama, and Nebraska, singing "God Bless America." But many of her former supporters from Utah and unratified States like Georgia refused to join in, and rather than concede patriotism to the opposition, some feminists stood and sang "God Bless America" with them.

Many delegates held hands and sang along with Margie Adam, a California feminist songwriter, who sat at a grand piano on stage and sang her song: "We Shall Go Forth."

Delegates and observers drifted away from the Coliseum with a mix of emotions. Some were frustrated that there had not been time to take up their particular concerns under New Business. Others shed unashamed tears at the final moments of sisterhood that had touched them so much. Still others were overwhelmed by a sense of history in the making, and of personal growth and achievement. And many felt all these emotions.

The dire predictions that the Conference would fall apart in conflict had proved false. Even the anti-change delegates had walked out only after the Conference was over, not during it, as some had threatened.

As the great hall emptied out, the last sounds were the voices of stragglers singing "We Shall Go Forth" and "We Shall Overcome."

It was a life-changing and history-changing event. Neither individual women nor the country would ever be quite the same again.

We Shall Go Forth

© 1977
Words and Music
by Margie Adam

We shall go forth__ from this place Proud of the things we've done,

Shar-ing the things we've won We shall not fail.   We   shall go

forth__ from this place Wil-ling to o-pen wide, Shar-ing the light in-side,

We shall not   fail.   Bring-ing to-geth-er__ all we know_ For

oth-ers who are strug-gling a-lone, Bring-ing to-geth-er__ all we are,

Of-fer-ing those who want to find us__ A way to find__ us, A way__ to

see.   We shall go forth from this place Tak-ing with us the pride of

know-ing we can de-cide.We shall not fail.We shall go forth. We shall go forth.
Repeat...

Transcription by Erlys Jedlicka

EPILOGUE
The Spirit of Houston

Women who came to Houston in 1977 will remember the Conference not only for the decisions they made but also for the spirit in which they worked together to make them.

Superficially, the sights and sounds of Houston reminded veteran reporters of the national political conventions. No sleep but lots of excitement and noise. A great hall with State banners locating the delegates, the aisles clogged with strategists and press, the songs and buttons and ribbons and demonstrations and signs.

Even superficially, however, the difference was that the signs spoke to issues the male political establishment does not take seriously or tries to forget: Wages for Housework; Keep Your Laws Off My Body; Stop Rape; Make the Air Force Hold a Bake Sale to Buy a Bomber; Viva La Mujer; ERA Now; Equality Begins at Home.

More historically minded reporters likened it to a constitutional convention for women. Unlike political conventions, it was concerned with basic principles. There were no future jobs or rewards with which to make deals, so most women voted their convictions. The delegates did not vote by State at the order of some hierarchical boss but as individuals in coalitions born of convictions that changed in strength and membership with the issue at hand. And unlike the party platforms that are decided before they ever reach the floor, most resolutions adopted at Houston had been debated, amended, rewritten, or initiated in their entirety at State and Territorial meetings open to all residents from 16 years of age up.

But the biggest difference was that the delegate body had been far more representative by race, ethnicity, age, income, and social class than any political convention in history. It truly reflected the multicultural diversity that enriches America.

There were probably many more mind-changing encounters in Houston than in the State meetings. In some States anti-change women only participated when it came time to vote, sometimes even being called in by the hand signals or walkie talkies of male group leaders. At Houston, however, the delegates sat together for three days on the plenary floor, long enough to shatter stereotypes that had separated many from each other.

Unusual, too, were the logistics which were intended as a showcase. The program for children, for instance. In the future fathers may take as much responsibility for children as mothers, but the truth of most mothers' lives is that they still have the primary role in the care of their children. The Commission decided to pay for child care at Houston as a reminder that all public meetings should provide it as a matter of course for conference-goers of both sexes, and it decided it should be nonracist, nonsexist, and multicultural.

The system worked smoothly. A special shuttle bus ferried children from the hotels and the convention center to a child-care center where a health examination, breakfast, lunch, snacks, naps, and age-graded activities were provided for more than 150 children of delegates and volunteer staff on all four days of the Conference.

The professional child-care staff had been trained in nonsexist child

development. Multicultural field trips to points of interest in Houston were planned. And in order to clue the children in on what their parents were doing at the Coliseum, there were discussions of the role of women in history and the program of the Conference.

And then there were the disabled. Most conventionally-run conferences relegate the handicapped to the sidelines, if it is possible for them to participate at all. At Houston, ramps were built giving access to the Conference floor so that motorized "chairees" were able to propel themselves into the thick of demonstrations and were given precedence in the scramble for position at the mikes by a special request of the chair. At one point, a woman with a cane guided herself off the convention floor by grasping the back of a sighted woman's wheelchair. The disabled added their voices to the chants and their ideas to the proceedings. Arrangements for accommodating them were based on the suggestions they made to the Conference staff in advance.

The IWY Commission had determined early to make these arrangements a visible model. Two "signers," one on each side of the stage, translated the deliberations into sign language for the deaf and hard-of-hearing in the audience. Essential information was available on cassettes and in braille. The Houston Lighthouse for the Blind transcribed the proposed National Plan of Action into braille and sent it to blind delegates before the Conference so that they could study the agenda and follow it from the floor in a "blue book" of their own. They also provided braille transcriptions of signs for floor numbers that were posted in the elevators of the delegate hotels.

The physical arrangements at the Coliseum were made to comply with the 1977 regulations of the Architectural and Transportation Barriers Compliance Board. Ramps and other facilities had to be added to previously unequipped buildings and restrooms; elevators and Coliseum seating were inspected to be sure that they could handle wheelchairs. Wheelchairs and crutches were rented in advance as requested, and lift vans were provided to transport wheelchairs between the Coliseum and the hotels. Hotel rooms were checked to be sure that there were grab bars in the bathroom. There was one oversight: the Coliseum platform had been built without a ramp, and a delegate in a wheelchair had to be carried up the stairs to participate in the opening day's ceremonies.

The Conference differed from male-run events in some less visible ways. The Commission made it a point to solicit bids from women-owned or women-run services and often found that these were the most competent and most economical. Women in Production, for instance, a California-based, all-woman crew, did all the staging, lighting, and sound for the 35 hours of entertainment at Seneca Falls South.

Like many women's events, the Conference was underfinanced. The original request for financing 56 State and Territorial meetings plus a national conference had been $10 million. Managing on only half of that meant much pennypinching, ingenuity, and dependence on volunteers. At Houston alone, about 3,000 people donated their services. State meetings had also depended heavily on volunteers, because much money went into paying the way of women who could not otherwise have afforded to participate.

Night owl volunteers reported for duty after midnight each night to help get out the National Conference Daily Bulletin, which provided official summaries of each day's floor resolutions and Conference business. The volunteers typed, sorted pages, and stapled to have the Xeroxed Bulletin ready before sunup.

Busy and highly paid professional women volunteered their special services too. Dr. Constance Myers of the University of South Carolina recruited 27 oral historians from leading universities to tape interviews with a random cross section of women attending the Conference. Their tapes will be deposited in the National Archives for future historians to use in analyzing the Houston conference.

About a hundred media women came to the Conference and pitched in to make the Houston Breakthrough a daily for the duration. The regular Breakthrough, a monthly women's newspaper edited by Janice Blue and Gabrielle Cosgriff, issued a call to every women's publication in the country asking for help to produce an unofficial daily similar to one produced at the Mexico City conference in 1975. The 36-page Breakthrough provided the most detailed coverage of the dozens of meetings and personalities that the regular press did not have time or staff to cover.

But the most significant difference was an intangible one of style. Perhaps because women have been trained to adapt, they were remarkably good humored in the adversity of the hotel mixup and ingenious in organizing to cope with it. "Men wouldn't stand for this," women would exclaim when they found themselves standing for hours in line. But after the first flash of anger, they endured and made do.

Delegates seemed open and personal in reaching out to strangers and making new friends. Some went to the Astro-Arena to find out how anti-change women really felt about the issues. A great many took advantage of the opportunities to explore the lifestyles and cultures of women quite different from themselves.

An ultimate in cross-cultural exchange was the dialogue between two muumuu-clad Samoans who had never been to the mainland before and some activist prostitutes from the Coyote organization, reported by Lindsy Van Gelder in Ms. Magazine. The Samoans were interested in a frank exchange about prostitution. "How often do you do it? What's it like? What does it pay?" they wanted to know.

There was more compassion. "It's a hole in the road you happened to hit," a younger woman told an older one, embarrassed because she was stumbling from fatigue on the way back to the hotel after a late night session.

There was more sharing of food, of space, of experience, and of expertise.

Most significant for the future were the hints of what politics will be like when it will be as easy to elect a woman as a man. In spite of strong feelings, the women in this overwhelmingly female convention seemed more willing to compromise to achieve coalition, more responsive to the views of the other side, and far less likely to seek out confrontations. "We're trying hard to be nice to each other," Joanne Alter from Illinois said of the ideological split in her delegation. "We're all human beings." In her Redbook article, Gail Sheehy talked about the emergence of a female-based "politics of empathy."

"Despite strong feelings on both sides, there was a remarkable absence of aggression," wrote Joe Klein, covering the Conference for Rolling Stone. "There was real anger, but not even the slightest intimation of violence, not a push or a shove. There was intolerance, but not all that much yelling ... Try as they might, women had never been trained to be aggressive, and therefore weren't too good at it, which made for a far more civilized gathering. There was a wonderful emotional honesty, and even a spirituality that most men have yet to explore."

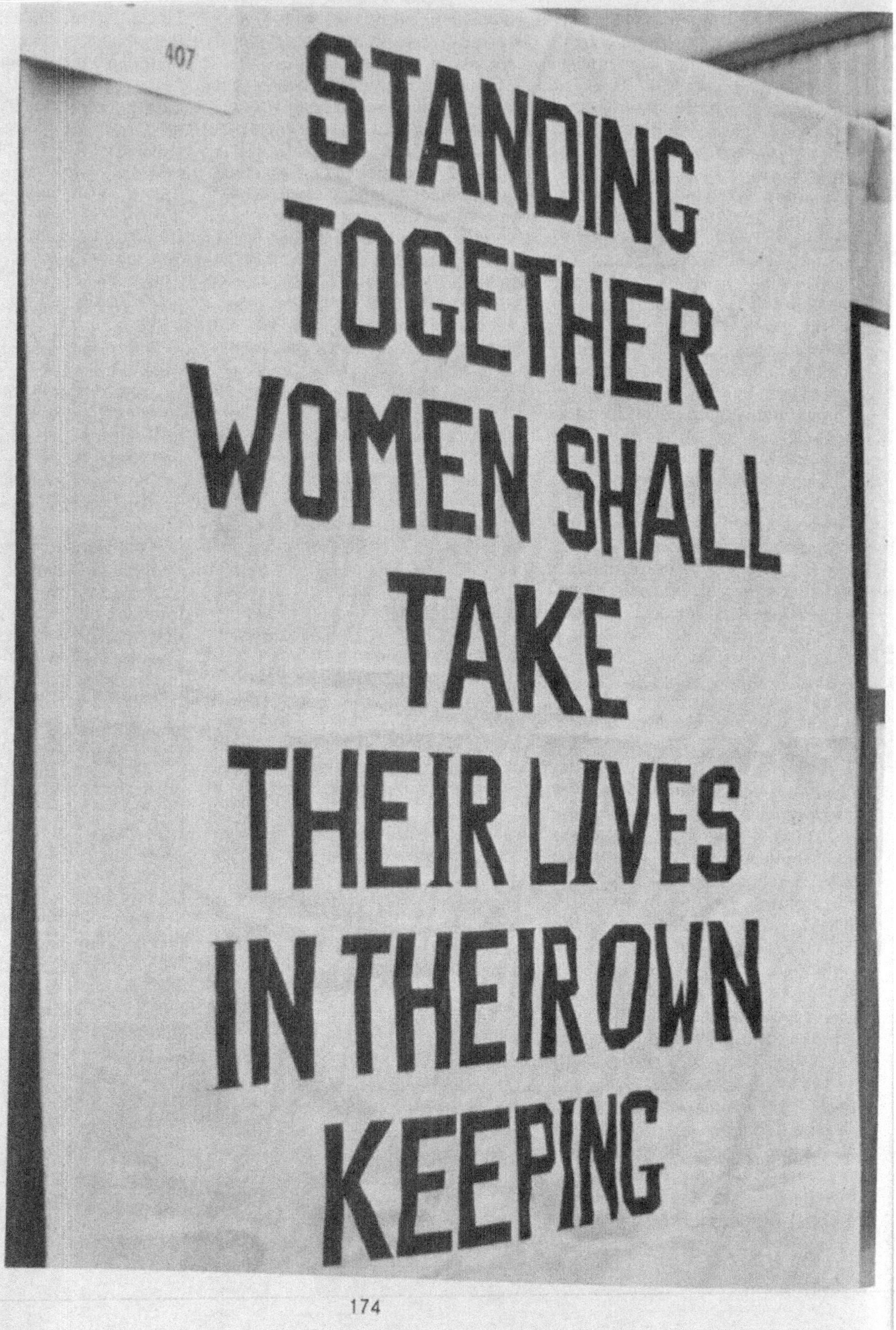
407
STANDING
TOGETHER
WOMEN SHALL
TAKE
THEIR LIVES
IN THEIR OWN
KEEPING

CONVENTION CENTER: SOMETHING FOR EVERY WOMAN

Crowd gathers outside Albert Thomas Convention and Exhibit Center.

While delegates were deliberating in plenary sessions, thousands of non-delegates at the Conference were taking part in events of their own at the Albert Thomas Convention Center just across the park from the Coliseum. Some of these events and activities were as important to the future of individual women as the resolutions being considered, and delegates sampled them when they could.

In the huge space provided by two floors of a building that itself stretched for two city blocks, visitors could choose from hundreds of offerings: skill workshops, lectures, classes, exhibits, literature, and entertainment for every interest and mood. The general effect was that of a county fair set down in the middle of a university campus.

There was something for every woman. She might ask advice of a successful woman in her own field in a skill workshop, put her problem before a clinic, learn how to make a speech on a subject she chose, or walk on stage to make the speech. She could listen to music produced by women, watch films, look at art, eat, meet friends, shop, or just relax. There was even a place where a woman could stop in and talk about whatever she had on her mind. It was called "Kum Baya" (come by here) and it was described in the Convention Center program as a "listening service provided by Houston-area women."

BRIEFINGS, WORKSHOPS, CLINICS

Briefings From the Top, coordinated and moderated by Federally employed women, were presented by some 38 distinguished women in Government, from Dr. Beth Abramowitz, Assistant Director of the Domestic Policy Council in the White House, to Esther Wunnicke, Federal co-chair of the Federal-State Land Use Planning Commission for Alaska.

So many people crowded the room in which Eleanor Holmes Norton was reporting on her restructuring of the Equal Employment Opportunity Commission that some had to listen out-

175

side to a speaker turned on loudly enough to be heard in the hall.

"I felt I had to set out to completely overhaul this agency," said Norton, the first woman to head it. "Piecemeal reform had been tried here and there and had proved highly ineffective. In my judgment, the machinery had to be taken apart and put back together again. The reforms under way at EEOC now conform to the recommendations of all the respected analysts who have studied this agency. First there is functional reform, then headquarters reform and then field reform."

Eileen Shanahan, Assistant Secretary for Public Affairs, U.S. Department of Health, Education and Welfare: "All wisdom does not reside in Washington. There has to be interaction with the people who will be administering out across the country, and with the people who will be the recipients across the country if programs are to succeed, if they are to be sound in concept."

Esther Peterson, Special Assistant to the President for Consumer Affairs: "What we're trying to do is to give the consumer a voice in the Federal Government."

Carin A. Clauss, Solicitor of Labor, U.S. Department of Labor: "We are trying to eliminate unsafe conditions, but if that means the right to choose work in unsafe conditions, then women should have the same choice as men."

Barbara Watson, Assistant Secretary of State for Consular Affairs, U.S. Department of State: "Developing countries have more women holding key positions in government because the countries' resources are limited and the talents of women have to be utilized."

Barbara Blum, Deputy Administrator, U.S. Environmental Protection Agency: "More women who volunteered in the environmental movement should seek paying positions. Volunteers are sometimes more qualified by experience than those educated in the field."

Success Stories, a series of workshops describing barriers that were overcome, attracted many women

who wanted to share experiences with panelists.

A workshop describing the Shelter for Battered Women set up by the Center for the Elimination of Violence in the Family, in Brooklyn, New York, brought together so many people concerned with the problem in their own communities that participants decided to keep in touch with each other through a newsletter.

"The prevention and treatment of domestic violence is a pro-family issue," said Judy Vandegriff, legislative aide to Representative Newton Steers. "When we get this issue out and we can discuss it and deal with it in our society, then we will no longer need the cycle of shelters and protective services and complete social rehabilitation."

Jan Peterson, an employee of ACTION with a special interest in the neighborhood women's groups, added, "If you can't make the house safe, you can forget about the streets."

About 150 women and five men attended the three sessions of the "suc-

cess story" describing the Minority Women's Employment Program that began in Atlanta in 1972. Since then it has placed more than 2,000 minority women in upper-level white collar jobs in 10 major cities. The story attracted blacks and whites, Chicanas, Asian Americans, and American Indians, as well as a student from Thailand and a woman from South Africa. Workshop leaders offered on-the-spot counseling for special employment problems.

Skills Clinics shared practical advice. At a clinic on "How to Influence Schools," Clelia Steele, an associate director of the Project on Equal Education Rights, told women that enforcement of laws barring sex discrimination has been "dilatory, slipshod, and cursory." She distributed 300 review kits to people who wanted to check up on their schools when they got home.

"Mothers, Inc.," a support group in Austin, Texas, led a workshop for women who wanted help in dealing with the conflicts of being a mother in a society that tells women—and

Presidential Assistant Midge Costanza spoke to standing room only crowd at "Briefings from the Top."

especially mothers—to put themselves second.

The skill clinic with the largest audience was "Marriage, Separation, and Divorce." Women were so eager to get legal advice that they gave up lunch to attend. Raising children is not inconsistent with feminism, said delegate Roxanne Barton Conlin, U.S. Attorney from Iowa who conducted the clinic, but she cautioned the standing room only crowd that family life is closely regulated by State law, which varies widely. She said that women who fear that the ERA will deprive them of the right to alimony if they divorce are in for a rude shock. Only a small percentage of women get any alimony at all, and payments are usually meager, sporadic, and short-lived, she reported.

Other popular clinics were "Communications Strategies," "Employment Discrimination," and a training session on how to influence legislators entitled "Getting Your Point of View Across."

SENECA FALLS SOUTH

A big assembly space in the Convention Center was called Seneca Falls South, a name chosen in honor of Seneca Falls, New York where the first women's rights meeting was held in 1848. Beanbag chairs, fuzzy carpets, plants and flowers, and a television set helped create livingroom comfort for Conference goers. Thousands at a time filtered through Seneca Falls South, sharing in a special women's culture.

On the Seneca Falls Stage there were continuous performances, beginning on Friday night with readings from the 1976 Brussels Tribunal on Crimes Against Women. Tribunal listeners understood the serious business of the weekend as they heard a terrifying and realistic appraisal of some of the lives of women around the world. One woman in the darkened audience cried out, "Stop it!" and left the room shaken. She said that women should stand up and fight for the right not to be harmed.

Saturday's stage program began with music and historical drama by the Co-Respondents of Washington State. The program continued until midnight with poetry reading, humor, music, films, classical and ethnic dance, mime, and historical fashion. There was also an electrifying demonstration of self-defense by Karen Sprintzin, a first degree black belt Tae Kwon Do expert who sparked the audience into practicing defensive techniques with her. Later, Karen overheard two women from the Midwest admit: "I never even thought of fighting back."

The Seneca Falls South scene had informal entertainment as well as formal programs. Boo-lu, a clown on stilts, strutted through the crowd engaging observers in her limericks and riddles. At least one little girl was visibly astonished when Boo-lu told her that women could be clowns—and even fire-eaters.

Saturday night's audience swayed and danced and laughed with the songs of Cryer & Ford, the comedy of Robin Tyler and Maxine Feldman, the music of Holly Near and Mary Watkins, the foot-stomping sounds of The Deadly Nightshade. During the concert, police officers, there to help guard against disturbances, slowly worked themselves close to the stage. They were drawn into the music, howled at the ribald humor, smiled at the goodhearted fun.

Entertainment opened on Sunday morning with T'ai Chi, the gracefully slow Chinese exercises, in a performance of absorbing discipline and power. That feeling permeated the day's program as dance, literary readings, classical music, comedy, and folk singing followed one another on the stage.

When the professional performers were not on stage, some of those attending the Conference were. The "Seneca Soapbox" gave women a chance to speak from the microphone about anything they wanted. Moderator Diane Gallagher of Massachusetts described the Soapbox as a "sharing and caring place." She told about one young woman from California who said at the mike, "I just wish that all the women who came here had taken the time to get dressed up. There are many people looking at us across the Nation. I think we should look as well as we can." A Wyoming cowgirl in the audience stood up to answer: "I felt the reason we came here was to share and not get costumed up. I want to learn from you what you think, not what you wear." Afterwards, Gallagher watched the two women approach each other. There was initial coldness, she said, but they went off together

talking about riding horses, something the Californian had never dared to do.

Delegates and observers were invited to a Music Hall Revue on Sunday night to listen to folk singer Malvina Reynolds, Sweet Honey in the Rock of Washington, D.C. and feminist songwriter Margie Adam. In the words of one observer who had been at the long plenary sessions, their songs "shared the frustrations and triumphs of being women and refreshed our worn enthusiasm."

Women's "Artspace" found a home in Seneca Falls South too. It was a magnet for women artists at the Conference, and it generated a two-day marathon encounter as observers came in crowds to talk with artists and watch films.

"Finding our History" offered 25 women's studies courses ranging from scholarly lectures such as "Historical Perspective on the Woman Teacher in America" to activist topics such as "The Politics of Women's Studies."

One woman summed up the reaction of many who had shared in the activities of Seneca Falls South: "This was a place to grow a little—and show it a lot."

EXHIBITS

In another wing of the Convention Center, more than 20,000 people visited the mammoth Exhibition Hall during the Conference. At the 231 exhibition booths, 45 States and Territories took space, as did approximately 22 U.S. Government agencies, 80 women's and nonprofit organizations, more than 40 women-owned-and-run small businesses, and seven unions. Women in the arts were represented, as were women in sports, women in business, women in recording, and women in publishing.

Exhibits in the Convention Center offered products for sale, literature on many issues, information on government and private agencies.

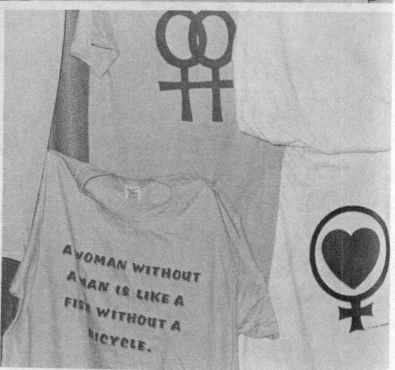

Many women displayed and sold their crafts. There were "ratified apples" from Washington, quilts from Idaho, Indian art from Arizona, and a Tlingit Indian woman from Alaska who sat weaving a raven-and-whale-patterned blanket with yarn made of mountain goat hair and cedar bark. There was even a booth where you could learn how to hammer nails properly.

Big companies bought space to tell their story to women. Small firms, many of them women-owned, rented booths to sell books, records, jewelry, clothing, and giftware. Some indicated their feminism in their names: Daughters Publishing Co., Inc., Women Made Products, Womantours, Womansplace, Feminist Forge, and Feminist Press, to name a few.

Government agencies were on hand, too. Among them were the Bureau of the Census, the Food and Drug Administration, the Office of Revenue Sharing, the Small Business Administration, the Indian Health Service, the Environmental Protection Agency, and the Alcohol, Drug Abuse and Mental Health Administration, as well as the Department of Labor and the Commission on Civil Rights. Women inquired about their services and suggested new ones. The Postal Service sold stamps picturing women as well as the 1975 United Nations International Women's Year stamp.

The nongovernmental organizations were there: the YWCA, the National Council of Catholic Women, the

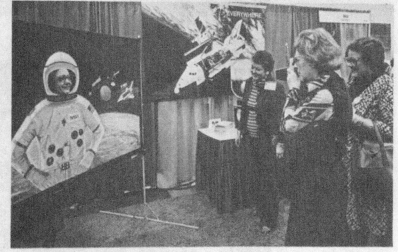

National Council of Jewish Women, the Girl Scouts, and the Women's International Bowling League.

Professional associations were there: the American Nurses Association, the National Association of Social Workers, and the National Association of Women Lawyers.

Activist groups of every persuasion handed out literature and tried to win converts. The Eagle Forum was present and so was the National Gay Task Force, Wages for Housework, the National Abortion Rights Action League, Houston Right to Life, and Women Strike for Peace.

Delegates wished they had been able to spend more time at the festival of women and women's activities. Some non-delegates spent the entire Conference there, without getting around to all of the events. For many, the Spirit of Houston will be remembered as the sights and sounds of Seneca Falls South.

Chief Pulu Peneuta, Mayor of Pago Pago, at Houston.

Helvi Sipila, of Finland, the first woman to hold the rank of Assistant Secretary-General at the United Nations, wearing the IWY design of Valerie Pettis, at the NY State Women's Meeting.
Photographs Copyright © Diana Mara Henry / www.dianamarahenry.com

INTERNATIONAL PERSPECTIVES:

World Peace is a Women's Issue

"If women are the civilizers of the world, why aren't they civilizing it?"

Margaret Mead put the question to the women of many nations attending an unofficial congressional hearing on peace and disarmament at Seneca Falls South in the convention center on Sunday morning.

Her answer: Because there aren't enough women in "positions of power and negotiations" to get action "for the things women care about." Women are nurturers, she added, and one of the things that they care about is life.

"Everything is done in the name of protecting women and children," Congresswoman Patricia Schroeder of Colorado said. "But no one gets around to asking the women and children how they want to be protected."

In their own countries, women have always been in the lead in urging peace and disarmament. As the nuclear arms race quickens, they remain a massive source of support for nonviolent, humanistic solutions to conflict among nations.

Women from different countries discovered how many concerns they shared when they met together officially and cross-culturally in 1975 to draw up a World Plan of Action for women at the United Nations World Conference of the International Women's Year in Mexico City. The National Women's Conference at Houston and the 56 State and Territorial meetings that led up to it were an American response to the call for a Decade for Women issued at Mexico City. One of the purposes of the Houston Conference as spelled out in the law was "the assessment of the participation of women in efforts aimed at the development of friendly relations and cooperation among nations and to the strengthening of world peace."

The Commission sought outside support for the "International Perspectives" program at Houston and the participation of women from other countries. Those who took part were not only to explore how women can work together for peace and disarmament but also to relate the Conference to the worldwide advancement of women.

Eighty-three women from 56 countries came to Houston. Some came on their own. Others were official observers for their governments. Still others were sponsored by various organizations, including the U.S. Department of State, the United Nations Educational, Scientific and Cultural Organization (UNESCO), the German Marshall Fund, and the African-American Labor Center. Cuba also sent its first delegation of women.

Margaret Mead at ad hoc disarmament hearing.

AD HOC HEARING

The role of women in achieving international peace and disarmament was the subject of the Sunday morning ad hoc hearing chaired by Congresswoman Schroeder, a member of the House Armed Services Committee, who was joined by Congresswoman Yvonne Brathwaite Burke of California, a member of the House Appropriations Committee.

These policymakers heard testimony from experts—all women—who were on hand to explain the intricate technical issues facing disarmament negotiators, issues on which it is sometimes claimed that women are not qualified to speak.

it will be a great day

when

our schools

get all the money

they need

and the air force

has to hold

a bake sale

to buy a

bomber

Randall Forsberg, a fellow of Harvard University's Program on Science and International Affairs, questioned the need for the size of the U.S. military establishment, now the single largest employer in the country. She suggested that this force is designed for intervention in international crises rather than for the defense of the continental United States against an invader. Our present system, she said, is designed to give us the capability to wage any kind of war anywhere in the world across the full spectrum of military power, including nuclear arms. In her view, this buildup makes us less safe than we would be if we settled for a smaller military force.

Dr. Helen Caldicott, a Boston pediatrician, described the clinical impact of nuclear radiation on human beings, including nursing mothers and unborn babies. The neutron bomb causes brain cells to swell, she said, creating a period of lucidity for the victim before she dies painfully— within 48 hours. She called on women to organize politically to ban this weapon.

Dr. Anne Cahn of the U.S. Arms Control and Disarmament Agency warned that the $370 billion spent collectively by all the countries of the world on military forces in 1975 was a drain on the pocketbook of every family on earth. She noted that on the average, 60 times more is spent to equip a soldier than to educate a child. The world's budget for military research is more than six times its budget for energy research. Developed nations spend 20 times more for their military programs than they do for economic assistance to developing countries.

Military spending is one of the *least* effective ways to create jobs, she added. It requires spending on technology and machinery rather than on wages for the kind of worker who is often unemployed.

Dr. Betty G. Lall, professor at the New York State School of Industrial and Labor Relations, defined the task as finding a safe and sure way to reduce the number of missiles, bombers, nuclear bombs and other weapons by building on the agreements reached between the United States and the Soviet Union at the Strategic Arms Limitation Talks (SALT). As citizens and members of organizations, women can raise their voices, do their homework, argue the case against massive weapons building, and put their money and their votes with those willing to display moderation in military spending, she said.

A number of women described citizens' efforts to promote public discussion and action. Peggy Carlin, Vice President of the United Nations Association, talked about "Operation Turning Point," sponsored by the Institute of World Order, which aims to inform the public on the issues coming up at the special United Nations Sessions on Disarmament in May 1978. Josephine Pomerance, U.N. observer for Americans for Democratic Action, spoke of the Coalition for a New Foreign and Military Policy. With a membership of more than 50 na-

tional organizations, it is one of many lobbying groups trying to develop support for limiting the arms race.

IWY Commissioner Ethel Taylor, national coordinator of Women Strike for Peace, urged women crusading for women's rights to include peace

campaigns in their agendas. Kay Camp, president of the Women's International League for Peace and Freedom, reported that international conferences of women's organizations are paying more attention to peace and disarmament.

Congresswoman Pat Schroeder.

A VOICE FOR WOMEN

A practical way to get the voices of women heard more directly in military and disarmament policy, as well as in foreign policy generally, is to encourage more young women to undertake the technical training that leads to high level Government positions. At a Saturday panel entitled "A Greater Voice for Women in Foreign Affairs," experienced professionals advised young women to study the newer fields of diplomacy such as food, population, energy, science and technology, environment, and arms control and urged that women Foreign Service officers be recruited on college campuses. They said women's organizations can help by recommending individual women for specific posts, urging Government agencies to put more women on U.S. delegations to international conferences, improving the flow of information on the world outside the United States, and monitoring U.S. aid to developing nations for their impact on women.

The other objective of the international program, to relate the Conference to the worldwide advancement of women, could advance the cause of peace as well. Some behavioral scientists now believe that polarized sex roles are the root cause of violence, and there is anthropological evidence that the least violent societies are those that make the least differentiation between the roles of men and women, while the most violent, such as our own, encourage a "macho" masculinity that glorifies war. If this is true, equality for women would reduce the root cause of violent attitudes that lead to military buildup and war.

In private conversations and panel discussions, American women learned how women in other countries deal with many of the issues under consideration at the Coliseum. Many American women were surprised, for instance, to learn that some of the less advanced countries had more women in elective and appointive office than the United States does.

Health care in some countries is organized so that childbirth is managed by women. Some believe that women are able to contribute more to the physical and psychological comfort of the mother than the male obstetrician can. American women who would like to see women trained as midwives for home deliveries can profit by the experience of foreign countries where this is the practice.

American women have learned that lack of child care is less of a barrier to women in traditional cultures because there are always relatives available to care for a child while the mother works outside the home. Women in these countries have been supported by their culture, too, in the personal sacrifice of leaving their children to go abroad for study or diplomatic assignment.

CHILD CARE ABROAD

In a panel discussion on International Child Care Services sponsored by the German Marshall Fund of the United States, specialists from Israel, France, and Sweden described the services provided by their countries, all of which differ from the United States in assuming that the community shares with parents a continuing responsibility for children from their birth.

Dr. Rivka Bar Yosef of Israel reported that her country holds itself responsible to and for every person in it, and that no distinction is made between the welfare of parents and the welfare of children. Factories give mothers special breaks for nursing.

In France comprehensive maternal and infant health care is provided through the national health insurance plan. *Creches* for children up to age 3 are run by the Ministry of Health Care, while 90 percent of the 4- and 5-year-olds and all of the 6-year-olds attend "Ecoles Maternelles," operated by the Ministry of Education.

Annika Baude of Sweden described the rapid growth of publicly founded services for children of working parents in Sweden, where quality child care is subsidized by the Government. Both parents are allowed paid leave and a stipend to care for their child.

All three countries were judged ahead of the United States in providing child care for working parents and in their commitment to the well-being of children by members of the Coalition of Labor Union Women who visited their child care facilities, according to a summary of their findings presented by Joyce Miller, head of CLUW. Only an insignificant amount of child care is provided for profit in these countries, because all of them support child care systems at Government expense.

American women learned that there was much they could do to improve the lives of women in other countries. Again and again, the foreign visitors urged that American women use their newly won political power to work for peace and disarmament and to stop all the nuclear testing that has polluted some of the areas in their homelands.

Congresswoman Yvonne Burke and Commissioner Mildred Persinger.

Americans learned too that they can help by monitoring the impact on women of U.S. development assistance programs and U.S. commercial development in poor countries. Women from developing countries described the effect of industrial development on their cultures. When a military base or other large installation is built, for example, the men are recruited to work on the project and receive training that brings them into an industrial economy, while the women are left at home to take over all of the work of family and village. Although they become conservators of the traditional culture, the women lose ground, and the gap between men and women widens.

WOMEN IN UNDERDEVELOPED NATIONS

At a symposium on "Women, Development, and Change," Mrs. Mary Kazunga of Zambia pointed out that women in her country rarely benefit from new technology because it is the men who are trained; "development" for the women too often means discouraging the production of native crafts which bring them income, she said.

Programs aimed at speeding the development of rural economies are directed by men who teach the new agricultural methods to the men rather than to the women who actually produce the food crops. In Kenya, for example, women grind the corn, but only men were taught to use an improved mechanized corn grinder because "women don't understand machinery!" In West Africa, men took over the management of stores that replaced the market stalls where women had traditionally sold their goods.

In a session on the media, many women complained that television programs from the United States have affected the native cultures by introducing Western stereotypes. Efforts of American women to limit violence and sex-role stereotyping on television ultimately help women in the developing countries where the imported shows have a big impact.

In formal presentations, the international guests described the uneven impact of change on women. In Mexico, for instance, there are good labor laws guaranteeing equal pay for women, pregnancy leave, and child care centers, but women are paid less than men in agriculture and they do not get equal treatment in family and property laws.

In Botswana, women are still expected to do the heavy work, to carry water and sand on their heads. In countries like Thailand and Indonesia, they are regarded as the "weaker sex." Law and custom have traditionally given women position and status in the family, but they have been largely denied the expression of their own individuality and independence anywhere else.

All the panelists agreed that the gap between "elite" women and women in rural areas is being widened by social and economic change and that they need better education to cope with the changes. For many, the priority was literacy at least equal to that of men.

Anthropologist Margaret Mead summed up the discussions. "Whether we come from a civilization that is a thousand years older than ours, or from a civilization that has only recently come into the United Nations society, we are all dealing with the same issues," she said. "But let us be ever alert to the danger in trying to force the same solutions on everyone."

FOREIGN GUESTS IMPRESSIONS

Much of the participation of the international visitors was informal. In the International Lounge set aside for them near Seneca Falls South, they could talk with American women and each other all during the Conference.

They talked of the multiple burdens and responsibilities of women in their countries seriously and with surprising optimism. Many talked about what meeting American women meant to them.

"I was really struck by the confidence of American women," a woman from South Africa said. "We must learn this if we are to get what we want."

"The entire experience has opened my eyes to what is involved in creating a women's movement," a woman from India said. "I was also struck by how many of your issues as seen in your National Plan of Action are central to us in other countries—issues like education, planning of families, training for jobs, concerns of rural women."

"I will take back this utmost honesty, frankness, courage of American women," a woman from Bangladesh said. A Zambian visitor was impressed with the enthusiasm of American women and wished she could convey it to the women in her country. "We can go back and emphasize that women must unite, do things together, and depend on themselves for the things that they want to do," a woman from Botswana added. "I hope the spirit of Houston will carry on."

Many women were impressed with the willingness of American women to tackle broad social problems. "I thought it would be purely cultural," a Nicaraguan confessed. "I thought the U.S. woman was too pampered and didn't realize she uses her liberty to help others."

Several were heartened by the promise of more understanding for their countries and the cause of world peace in general. "How wonderful it would be if an international conference of this sort could be made to solve issues that are truly global," a woman from Egypt exclaimed. "I'm thinking now of the food problem, overpopulation, and arms trade."

A Fiji woman summed up the feeling of most: "American women can do a lot for the world if they would make world peace their issue."

THE TORCH RELAY

During the two-month countdown before the National Women's Conference, a lighted torch was passed hand to hand across 2,600 miles and 14 States on the trail to Houston from Seneca Falls, New York.

Hundreds of eager runners in the southeast quadrant of the United States bore this symbolic flame down the highways as national and local media jogged alongside, commenting on the historic link between the 1848 Seneca Falls women's rights convention and the 1977 National Women's Conference to come.

The Torch Relay, one of the most dramatic features of the Conference, was an almost entirely voluntary effort stemming from a suggestion by Sey Chassler, editor of *Redbook*, one of three men Commissioners and a member of the sports committee.

Plans for the relay were developed by the sports committee, co-chaired by Tina Santi, vice president of corporate communications of Colgate-Palmolive, and Barbara Fultz, vice president of television programing for William Esty Company. This committee was an outgrowth of the fund raising committee chaired by Commissioner Lenore Hershey, editor of the *Ladies' Home Journal*.

The Torch was lighted in Seneca Falls, New York, at the site of the Women's Rights Convention held in 1848. Lt. Governor Mary Anne Krupsak holds torch. Sissy Farenthold at left.

Almost the very first problem was to find a torch. No such torch had been made in eight years, and the maker of the last torch had died. A New York expert finally made two torches, one as a spare.

The 13,000-member National Association of Girls and Women in Sports (NAGS) organized the Torch Relay with the cooperation of the 8,000-member Road Runners of America and the President's Council on Physical Fitness and Sports. At the request of Commissioner Hershey, the Charter Company of Jacksonville, Florida assigned a staff member, Patricia Kery, to serve as National Relay Coordinator. She was assisted by a fulltime Washington-based volunteer, Henley Roughton, from the Road Runners. Colgate-Palmolive donated 3,000 blue T-shirts bearing the IWY emblem and slogan "Women on the Move," and *womenSports* magazine contributed $3,000 for telephone calls and similar expenses.

Carole Oglesby, president of the National Association of Girls and Women in Sports and professor of physical education at Temple University, appointed NAGS relay coordinators in the 14 States and in New York City and the District of Columbia. These in turn enlisted daily planners to handle countless details.

Commissioner Maya Angelou, poet and playwright, wrote a new 1977 Declaration of Sentiments entitled,

Relay Coordinator Pat Kery.

"To Form a More Perfect Union . . . ." Ida Fidelman, a *Redbook* secretary, handlettered the Declaration on a scroll to be carried and signed by the runners and to be given with the torch to the Smithsonian Institution.

Judy Carter, daughter-in-law of President Carter, read Maya Angelou's moving words publicly for the first time at a candlelight ceremony in Seneca Falls the evening before the relay got underway. (The text appears elsewhere in this report.) Lieutenant Governor Mary Anne Krupsak, President Sissy Farenthold of Wells College, and Commissioner Sey Chassler joined in the ceremonial lighting of the torch. Newspapers throughout the country received Associated Press wirephotos and United Press International telephotos of the event.

The relay began formally the morning of September 29, a sunny autumn day, with Millicent Brady Moore, a descendant of Susan Quinn Brown, who attended the 1848 women's rights convention, handing the lighted torch to the first runner.

She was Kathy Switzer of New York City, who as a Syracuse University student in 1967 had been the first woman to compete officially in the

Sey Chassler (left) waits for relay to begin.

Boston marathon. She sped eastward along Routes 5 and 20 to the first of many green and white mileage markers. There she passed the torch to Donna deVarona, a winner of two Olympic swimming medals.

Carole Oglesby ran five miles. Betsy East of Cortland, a physical education instructor who coordinated the relay in New York, ran two miles and drove the accompanying car all day.

Mary Jayne Engel's children were excused from school to cheer their mother, a 39-year-old newspaperwoman, as she carried the torch a mile through the Montezuma Swamp in 10 minutes.

First-day runners carried the torch 54 miles through Auburn and Manlius to Chittenango. The flame moved 48 miles next day through Oneida and Utica to Herkimer, which boasts a statue of General Francis E. Spinner, who first employed women in government service after the Civil War. Women employed by the Department of Treasury had paid for the statue.

Rain and cold replaced the sunshine but the torch moved as planned

Judy Carter greets runners in Atlanta.

Runners stop to sign the Declaration.

Commissioner Maya Angelou

'...To Form A More Perfect Union...'

We American women view our history with equanimity. We allow the positive achievement to inspire us and the negative omissions to teach us.

We recognize the accomplishments of our sisters, those famous and hallowed women of history and those unknown and unsung women whose strength gave birth to our strength.

We recognize those women who were and are immobilized by oppression and crippled by prejudice.

We recognize that no nation can boast of balance until each member of that nation is equally employed and equally rewarded.

We recognize that women collectively have been unfairly treated and dishonorably portrayed.

We recognize our responsibility to work toward the eradication of

negatives in our society and by so doing, bring honor to our gender, to our species, and to ourselves individually.

Because of the recognition set down above we American women unfold our future today.

We promise to accept nothing less than justice for every woman.

We pledge to work unsparingly to bring fair play to every public arena, to encourage honorable behavior in each private home.

We promise to develop courage that we may learn from our colleagues and patience that we may attack our opponent.

Because we are women, we make these promises.

Maya Angelou
1977

through Albany, the capital of New York, and along rural roads lined with bright wet autumn foliage into Massachusetts. Coordinator Pat Griffin, a University of Massachusetts doctoral student, ran nine miles herself "without any sense of fatigue" and wrote a poem about her experience.

Connecticut runners carried the torch south to Hartford and New Haven. Secretary of State Gloria Schaffer cheered them on. Some women ran in "packs." Some sang and shouted college cheers as they rode in escorting buses. Many schools excused students to take part in and watch the relay. *The New York Times* pictured Fairfield and Norwalk high school students carrying the torch and an IWY banner along a wet roadway on October 6.

Schedules called only for daylight running, but a fatal trailer truck accident near Bridgeport that afternoon backed up traffic for miles on the Connecticut Turnpike and prevented a van of Southern Connecticut State College women from reaching a relay point on Route 1. To make up the lost hours, New York women ran until 11:30 p.m., carrying the torch through White Plains, Scarsdale, and Yonkers to the New York City line at Van Cortlandt Park.

Sister Dorie Smith, head of the College of Mount St. Vincent, lighted the torch on October 7. Students from John F. Kennedy and other high schools carried it south via Broadway and Riverside Drive and through Central Park. The day's coordinator, Dorie McCaffrey, Herbert H. Lehman College director of athletics, bore the torch down Park Avenue past the Pan American Airways Building.

Cheryl Toussaint, Olympic silver medalist, delivered it to a midday press conference at Cooper Union. Present were Helvi Sipila of Finland, Assistant Secretary General of the

Midge Costanza and Mbuangi Swed-Gingles run through Lafayette Park near the White House.

Runners came in all sizes.

Gail Sheehy, present as a reporter for *Redbook*, then carried the torch a mile north to Third Avenue and 22nd Street. Suzy Chafee, a former Olympic ski team captain, cheered by her mother, moved it to midtown. Two women from Cardinal Spellman High School carried it across the George Washington Bridge over the Hudson River. Escorted by New Jersey State Police, women from Lehman College then ran it to East Newark.

Coordinated by Sandy Petway, Rutgers University cross-country coach, New Jersey athletes carried

United Nations; Presiding Officer Bella Abzug; Commissioners Sey Chassler and Ruth Abram; Mary Burke Nicholas, head of the Governor's Women's Unit; Carol Bellamy, chair of the New York delegation; and, in a wheel chair, Ruth Begun, a delegate-at-large and member of the Disabled Women's Caucus. There the Ford Motor Company presented the relay with a $13,000 Lincoln Versailles car, as blue as their shirts, to accompany runners from New York to Houston.

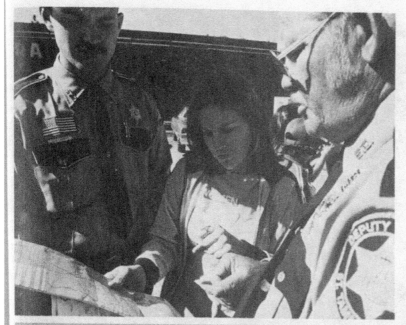

Runner stops to compare road maps.

the torch across the State, via Trenton
in 10 hours. Often running in the rain,
Pennsylvanians took it from the
Morrisville Bridge through Philadelphia and Harrisburg. Nikki Franke of
Temple University, a fencing champion, was Pennsylvania coordinator.
Ten members of the West Chester
College cross-country team carried
the torch from Bryn Mawr to Lan-
caster.

Rain continued as the torch was
carried across Maryland and into the
District of Columbia where the *Washington Post* frontpaged a picture of
"soggy relay runners" trotting into
Lafayette Park opposite the White

House on October 14. Midge Constanza, assistant to President Carter, spoke and joined the runners in circling the park for television cameras.

Among those carrying the torch away from the Park were 10-year-old Mbuangi Swed-Gingles and her mother, Sheryl Swed, a member of the IWY Commission staff.

Escorted by motorcycle police, IWY staff and students ran past the Jefferson Memorial and handed the torch to Virginia runners at the 14th Street bridge over the Potomac.

Rain slowed rush hour traffic as the torch was carried through Arlington, Crystal City, and past Mount Vernon. Driving the Lincoln Versailles for the first time, Catherine East, formerly of the IWY staff, had trouble keeping abreast of the runners. In Manassas, Officer K. Murray gave her a $30 ticket for "impeding a safe flow of traffic." This was the only difficulty with police during the 2,600-mile run. Many States and cities cheerfully provided police escorts.

Runners from George Mason College, Mary Washington College, the University of Virginia, and other schools carried the torch through Fredericksburg and Richmond across Virginia. A rally at Durham welcomed the relay to North Carolina. An elaborate program was arranged in Charlotte by Karen Popp, a 19-year-old sophomore basketball player who coordinated the 50-mile run from China Grove to Lowell. Mayor John M. Belk proclaimed October 21-23 "International Women's Year Weekend."

State police escorted the relay through South Carolina. While nearly

A soon-to-be mother runs a mile into Houston.

Over highways and byways.

Gloria Scott, IWY Commissioner and Girl Scout President, makes the early morning mile.

all runners were women, a Spartanburg insurance man earned press and television notice by running with his wife. Crowds cheered the torchbearers in Atlanta, Georgia, and those accompanying them were entertained by Mamie K. Taylor, local feminist leader. A front tire of the Lincoln Versailles went flat from driving on rocky road shoulders as the relay left Georgia. Runners changed it. Since several cars were then accompanying them, there was no delay.

There were difficulties in Alabama. Yielding to pressure from ERA opponents, Birmingham Road Runners, scheduled to supply runners in that area, cancelled them at the last minute. A high school principal also decided not to excuse from classes some girls ready to run. While Pat

Men join the run.

Field, official photographer, and spunky Catherine East, who is near retirement age, and others who had been accompanying the relay ran or walked with the torch, other runners were being recruited. Patricia Kery, Torch Relay Coordinator, flew from Houston to Birmingham with Peggy Kokernot, a 25-year-old physical education teacher and marathon runner. Both ran, Kokernot for 16 miles. (Her picture appeared on the cover of *Time* on December 5, when the magazine covered the National Women's Conference.) University of Montevallo women ran more than the planned 49 miles from Clanton to Montgomery. Additional runners came from the Anniston Track Club, McClellan Army Base, and Auburn University.

By November 3 the relay was back on schedule and *The New York Times* pictured Diane Westhoven happily

A special ceremony at the home of Babe Didrikson Zaharias in Texas.

Donna de Varona and Suzy Chaffee lead run into Houston.

passing the torch that warm day to Kate Milly between Montgomery and Selma, where Dr. Martin Luther King led a civil rights march in 1965. Runners from the Mississippi University for Women received the torch on Route 20 at the State line on Nov. 5. It was carried on schedule across Mississippi and Louisiana through Meridian, Jackson, New Orleans, and Baton Rouge.

As a band played "The Eyes of Texas," a sheriff's posse of orange-vested men and women on horseback and a parade arranged by Carol McGill, head of the Orange chapter of NOW, welcomed the torch to Texas the afternoon of November 16. "Orange did itself proud," reported the *Chicago Tribune.* A minister asked God to "evoke his blessings on the women of this country." Mike Hoke, a teacher who ran the first Texas mile,

said: "I proudly accept this torch in honor of my daughter, my wife, my mother . . . and liberty."

Women ran west on November 17 through Beaumont, birthplace of Mildred (Babe) Didrikson Zaharias, who starred in the 1932 Olympics and later was a champion golfer. They received roses and medallions at the memorial to the great woman athlete.

The final day's ceremonial entrance into Houston was coordinated by Col-

A Message to Women from Billie Jean King: Get Off the Sidelines

"The torch relay is one more indication of the recognition by women of the importance of their physical development," tennis star Billie Jean King said in a message to the National Commission.

"However, women's sports participation still lags far behind that of men, who for years have realized that sports are essential to their personal development. Our society and Government need to encourage girls and women to get off the sidelines and become participants for their health and enjoyment, and most importantly, to realize their full potential as individuals.

"Specifically, we need to provide equitable opportunities for women in international competition and in governance of local, national, and international sports organizations. We should make certain that all publicly supported sports programs, including educational sports facilities, public arenas, parks, and recreation programs and facilities, provide equal athletic opportunities for women. And we must take affirmative action to educate everyone on the value of developing lifelong habits of regular physical activity and sports participation.

"Sports have always provided men with a training ground for life. It is time the same opportunities were provided to women."

Top—Billie Jean King and Bella Abzug share the excitement of the arrival.

Bottom—Carole Oglesby (left) joins Sylvia Ortiz, Peggy Kokernot and Michele Cearcy.

Torch relay runners wave from the platform.

onel Evelyn Baker. Three Houston athletes carried the torch the final three miles into Houston the next day. They were Peggy Kokernot; Michele Cearcy, 16-year-old track star from Phyllis Wheatley High School; and Sylvia Ortiz, a senior at the University of Houston. (Their photo appears on the cover of this report.)

Joining them were Olympic gold medal winners Donna deVarona and Suzy Chaffee and more than 50 other athletes, some of whom had run earlier. There also were women, including six from Oregon, from States far from the relay route. Many more women—some present at the start in Seneca Falls, joined in for what was billed as "the last grand mile."

As the flaming torch ended its 51-day, 2,600-mile journey, about 1,000 women—mostly young, but some in their sixties—and many of the Commissioners ran or walked with it, bringing it to welcoming ceremonies at Albert Thomas Convention Center. The next morning they presented it to three First Ladies at the official opening of the National Women's Conference.

WHAT THE PRESS SAID

The Nation's media turned out in force for the Houston weekend, fueled by its own predictions of confrontation and disarray.

All three commercial television networks sent teams of reporters and crews. The Public Broadcasting Service and National Public Radio provided special programing throughout the conference and a one-hour PBS TV documentary was widely shown in the following weeks. Every major newspaper and news magazine in the country was represented. Journalists came from overseas.

Before it was over, those who had foreseen chaos witnessed substance, significance, and history.

The skeptical *Washington Post,* which had previously worried that "some of the most harmful stereotypes of women in politics could be confirmed," concluded that "women from all those regions, backgrounds and circumstances shared not only common concerns but an impressive amount of energy and organizing skill."

In a long and detailed December cover story. *Time* magazine described American women as having reached "some kind of watershed in their own history and in that of the nation."

Said *Time:* "What happened ... was an end to the psychological isolation that had constrained their activities and ambitions. They learned that many other middle-of-the-road, American-as-Mom's apple-pie women shared with them a sense of second-class citizenship and a craving for greater social and economic equality."

Gail Sheehy, author of *Passages,* analyzed the chemistry of Houston for *Redbook:* "Once having left the mainland for that long weekend on an island of women, once having seen and heard for themselves the burdens of inheritance, the accidents of birth and double discrimination that others and very different women brought with them, something fundamentally female took over: the politics of empathy."

For other commentators, the Conference was proof that the women's movement and women's issues had moved into the political mainstream. "The real significance of Houston," said David Broder of the *Washington Post,* "was to bury the idea that so-called 'women's issues' are a sideshow to the center-ring concerns of American politics."

KNOX Radio of St. Louis said the political savvy exhibited in Houston would have a global effect. In an editorial, KNOX said the meeting "proved that the women's movement is now a meaningful force in American politics, a force to be reckoned with at the local, state, national and even international levels." Columnist Ellen Goodman called Houston a "political training ground."

Even the most hard-boiled of skeptics were impressed. James J. Kilpatrick, the conservative columnist who had predicted "the liveliest brawl since John L. Sullivan licked Jake Kilrain in 75 bare-knuckled rounds," proclaimed afterward that the Conference had been "an interesting affair" that "may even have had its useful aspects. I have seen far more Federal money wasted in much worse ways," he observed.

In conservative Indiana, the *South Bend Tribune* concluded that "on balance, the Houston convention, which could have been a debacle, was in fact a solid gain for the cause of women." Although committed to traditional values, the *Sacramento Catholic Herald* applauded the Conference for addressing problems of discrimination, and declared that one of the great achievements was "that any dialogue took place at all."

The feminist press hailed the Conference as confidence building for women. "Houston transformed us all," wrote Lindsy Van Gelder in *Ms. Magazine.* "We learned that we could excel at serious parliamentary procedure, and still indulge in singing 'Happy Birthday' to speaker Margaret Mead; to knit and to nurse babies during debates; to laugh with Bella as she banged the gavel to adjourn and wished us 'Good night, my loves.' We were sensitized to minorities ... formed and fortified dozens of networks that will live beyond Houston and help implement the Plan, from a new national coalition to help battered wives, to an organization of feminist elected officials, to a continuing caucus of American Indians and Alaskan Natives."

To many, the Conference made clear that major social issues are transformed by the inclusion of women's concerns and a feminist understanding.

"Women's issues are not simply those of greater representation in political and other walks of life," Garry Wills wrote in the *Philadelphia Inquirer.* "Women have special problems and insights in many areas our culture must cope with—child care, education, welfare, health problems, alcoholism, aging, family life, farms, arts, the legal professions."

Others talked about the political consequences of this compassion. "It may be called the *Women's* movement," *Newsday's* David Behrens said of the National Plan of Action, "but it is also an egalitarian movement, an umbrella for the civil rights movement and the movement for economic equality, for the environmental and consumer movements and the movement for participatory democracy. ..."

The *London Evening Standard* offered a similar assessment.

"For better or worse, mainstream feminism has evolved into the most broadly based movement for egalitarianism that America possesses ... The women's movement is now a truly national, unified engine of change which could conceivably become the cutting edge of the most important human issues America faces in the next decade."

Some of those who noticed the broadening of the women's movement were divided about its political chances. In her *Nation* report, Lucy Komisar was hopeful: "The significance of the Houston Conference is that under the neutral sponsorship of the government and through the elected delegates and delegates-at-large, it gathered the major women's organizations and made it possible for them to approve a comprehensive national political program that belongs ... equally to all of them, because it was not proposed by any one of them."

Lukewarm comment tended to question whether the Conference would be taken seriously by the President and the Congress. "Direct results," said the *St. Louis Post-Dispatch*, "should not be expected overnight." The *Kansas City Times* saw "many more battles with officials who hold purse strings and make the laws before any of the goals will be achieved." The *St. Paul Dispatch* maintained the Conference would not change many minds. "It is unfortunate," the newspaper said, "to see so much energy and talent channeled into this event."

The Conference, as expected, drew poor reviews from those who were already openly opposed to the program. Among those urging the President to give the National Plan of Action a low priority was syndicated columnist Patrick Buchanan, who wrote in the *Chicago Tribune*: "If Carter is thinking of a second term, he will thank them for their work, promise to study the agenda, give the girls some milk and cookies and send them on their way. Why? Because the National Plan of Action adopted in Houston points Carter in precisely the opposite direction from where the national majority is headed."

Some detractors attacked the Conference for what they considered to be an anti-family concept. As an example, there was this comment from the *Cincinnati Enquirer*: "If there is any comfort to be derived from the weekend events, it is the knowledge that for every American woman fighting for abortion and homosexual rights in Houston, there were thousands in Cincinnati; New York; Lincoln, Nebraska; Santa Fe, New Mexico; and Portland, Oregon, tending to the concerns of their families, having babies, teaching Sunday School, working at their jobs and upholding the institutions—including the family itself—that give meaning and stability to American life."

Commenting on "the vigorous expression of opinion," the Houston *Chronicle* said only that "Houston was pleased to serve as host." The Houston *Post*, in a favorable editorial titled "Equality," said: "Those opponents of the National Women's Conference who try to label the whole 2,000-member delegation as 'lesbians and abortionists' are betraying their own inability to read and grasp facts. Starting with first lady Rosalynn Carter and former first lady Betty Ford, the conference is drawing some of the most distinguished women in America."

Time magazine concluded: "Certainly, Washington and the whole nation are watching the leaders of this increasingly vocal majority. As was echoed many times in Houston, it is a particularly exciting time to be a woman."

REDISCOVERING AMERICAN WOMEN

A Chronology Highlighting Women's History in the United States

1587
Virginia Dare, a girl, was the first baby born to English colonists in the New World. The daughter of Elenor White Dare and Ananias Dare, she was born on August 18 in Roanoke Island, Virginia.

circa 1600
The Constitution of the Iroquois Confederation of Nations guaranteed women the sole right and power to regulate war and peace. The women also selected tribal leaders.

1607
Princess Pocahantas saved the life of Captain John Smith, one of the founders of the Jamestown Colony, by interceding with her father, king of the Powhatan Confederacy.

1620
The Mayflower Compact was signed aboard ship by 39 men and male servants among the 102 passengers aboard the Pilgrim vessel. Women, who were not considered free agents, were not asked to sign. Only five of the 18 wives who arrived in Plymouth on the *Mayflower* survived the first harsh winter in the new land.

1638
Anne Hutchinson was excommunicated by the Puritan church in Boston for challenging its religious doctrines. One of her followers, Mary Dwyer, later became a Quaker and was hanged in 1660 in Boston for refusing to accept a sentence of banishment. Another woman who fought for freedom of conscience was Lady Deborah Moody, who moved from Massachusetts to Gravesend, Long Island where she and her companions established a community based on religious tolerance and self-government.

1648
The first attempt by a white woman to obtain political power in America originated with Margaret Brent. In a petition to the Colony of Maryland House of Delegates she requested two votes in the Assembly. She believed she merited one vote as a landowner, a vote a man would have obtained without question, and one vote as the executrix for the deceased brother of Lord Baltimore. Her request was denied.

1652
Elizabeth Poole formed a joint stock company in Taunton, Massachusetts to manufacture iron bars. This was one of the first successful iron production plants in the colonies.

1717
Twenty young women sent by King Louis XIV aboard a "brides' ship" to Louisiana to marry French settlers there refused to do so when they arrived in the primitive colony. Their revolt became known as the "petticoat rebellion."

1735
During the eight months that printer Peter Zenger was in jail in New York awaiting trial on charges of printing seditious materials, his wife, Catherine, kept his printshop running. She set type, read proof, wrote, and continued publication of his *New York Weekly Journal.* After her husband's death in 1746, Catherine Zenger continued to publish the newspaper.

The first woman publisher in the Colonies was believed to be Elizabeth Timothy, who took over her late husband's paper, the weekly *South Carolina Gazette,* in Charleston, South Carolina. An estimated 30 women were newspaper publishers in the 18th century Colonies.

1761
The first black poet whose work was to be preserved arrived in Boston harbor on a slave ship from western Africa. Then seven years old, Phyllis Wheatley was taught to read and write English and Latin, and her poetry became a focus for antislavery forces.

American Revolution
Women's groups, such as the Daughters of Liberty, organized to boycott tea and later to provide clothing and supplies for the Army. Deborah Sampson served as a soldier, for which she received a military pension, and Molly Pitcher assisted in the battlefield.

Groups of New Jersey women took vigorous action against husbands who abused their wives. Entering the home of a known wife-beater in the evening, they stripped the man and spanked him with sticks, shouting, "Woe to the men that beat their wives."

1777
Abigail Adams wrote to her husband, John Adams, and suggested, "... in the code of laws ... I desire you to remember the ladies and be more generous and favorable to them than your ancestors. Do not put such unlimited power into the hands of the husbands. Remember all men would be tyrants if they could. If particular care and attention is not paid to the ladies, we are determined to foment a rebellion and will not hold ourselves bound by any laws in which we have no voice or representation." The future President replied: "Depend upon it, we know better than to repeal our Masculine systems."

In the years immediately following the American Revolution, women had the right to vote in some parts of Virginia and New Jersey. Later, the adoption of State constitutions limited the franchise to white males and excluded women.

1788
Mercy Otis Warren, the first American woman historian, a political satirist and playwright, wrote her *Observations on the New Constitution* in which she deplored the absence of a Bill of Rights. The first 10 Amendments (the Bill of Rights) were added to the Constitution in 1791.

1800-1820
Deborah Skinner operated the first power. loom. In the first two decades of the 19th century, factories were established employing large numbers of women and children, particularly in the New England textile industry.

1804
Sacajawea, a young Indian woman, accompanied the Lewis and Clark expedition to the West. Her skill and courage were credited with helping to make the exploration a success.

1805
Mercy Otis Warren published a three-volume history of the American Revolution which is still used by historians.

1810
Mother Elizabeth Bayley Seton founded and became head of the first sisterhood in America, the Sisters of Charity of St. Joseph's. She was canonized as the Catholic Church's first U.S.-born Saint by Pope Paul VI in 1975.

1821
Emma Willard founded a female seminary at Troy, N.Y., the first effort to provide secondary education for women. In 1837 Mary Lyon founded Mt. Holyoke Seminary (later College), which provided education similar to that offered to men at the better men's colleges.

1828
The first known strike of women workers over wages took place in Dover, N.H. Similar strikes were waged in Lowell, Mass. in 1834 and 1836 by women textile workers protesting reduced real wages.

1833
Prudence Crandall opened a school for black girls in her Connecticut home. She was arrested, persecuted, and forced to give up the school to protect her pupils from violence.

1837
First national Anti-Slavery Convention of American Women met in New York City. This was the first national gathering of women organized for action without the assistance or supervision of men.

1839
After this time, most states began to recognize through legislation the right of married women to hold property. In New York State, Ernestine Rose and Susan B. Anthony led a petition campaign for women's rights. Mrs. Rose, Polish-born daughter of a rabbi, addressed the New York state legislature on at least five occasions until the body enacted a married women's property law in 1848.

1841
The first woman graduated from Oberlin College, having completed an easier "literary" course. At Oberlin, female students were required to wash male students' clothing, clean their rooms, serve them at meals, and were not permitted to recite in public or work in the fields with male students.

1845
Woman in the Nineteenth Century, written by Margaret Fuller, was an early and influential publication urging women's rights. Fuller wrote: "We would have every path laid open to Woman as freely as to Man."

1847
Trained by her father as an astronomer, Maria Mitchell at age 29 discovered a comet while standing on a rooftop scanning the sky with a telescope. In 1848 she became the first woman elected to the American Academy of Arts and Sciences in Boston.

1848
The first Women's Rights Convention was held in Seneca Falls, N.Y., led by Lucretia Mott and Elizabeth Cady Stanton. Its Declaration of Sentiments, paraphrased from the Declaration of Independence, stated that "all men and women are created equal." Eleven resolutions were approved, including equality in education, employment, and the law. A resolution advocating the right to suffrage passed by a narrow margin, with some delegates feeling that it was too daring a proposal.

The first issue of *The Lily,* a temperance paper, appeared with an editorial by Amelia Bloomer, later known for her experiment in clothing reform.

1849
Elizabeth Blackwell received her medical degree at Geneva, N.Y., becoming the first woman doctor in the United States.

1851
Sojourner Truth, ex-slave, electrified an audience in Akron, Ohio by drawing a parallel between the struggle for women's rights and the struggle to abolish slavery. In answer to arguments that women were delicate creatures who necessarily led sheltered lives, she described the hard physical labor she had done as a black woman slave and demanded, "And ain't I a Woman?"

1854
The first American day nursery opened in New York City for children of poor working mothers. In later years, licensing standards were established, but only minimal Federal funding was provided, except during the Depression and World War II.

1860
Elizabeth Peabody, a teacher, writer, and associate of the Transcendentalists, organized in Boston the first formal kindergarten in the United States. It was modeled on the Froebel kindergarten system in Germany.

Civil War

Women were responsible for the establishment of the U.S. Sanitary Commission. Dorothea Dix, Clara Barton, and Mother Bickerdyke served as nurses and trained others. Dr. Mary Walker was one of several women who served as doctors and surgeons at the front.

Susan B. Anthony organized the National Women's Loyal League to collect signatures for passage of the 13th amendment abolishing slavery. Women's rights leaders were prominent in the struggle to end slavery.

Women entered government offices to replace clerks who went to war. This established women not only in Government service but in clerical work. After the invention of the typewriter in 1867, women flocked to white collar office work, which began to be considered a women's specialty.

1864

Working Women's Protective Union was founded in New York to ensure fair treatment for women wage earners. Thousands of women were working in factories.

1865

Vassar College opened, offering the first college-level curriculum for women. Five years later, Wellesley and Smith Colleges were founded. Although women were admitted to some coeducational institutions, their opportunities to study with men were limited until the University of Michigan admitted women in 1870 and Cornell University became coeducational in 1872.

1866

Elizabeth Cady Stanton became the first woman candidate for Congress, although women could not vote. She received 24 votes.

1868

The first women's suffrage amendment to the Constitution was introduced by Senator S. C. Pomeroy of Kansas. In 1878 another proposal for woman suffrage, which came to be known as the Anthony Amendment, was introduced.

1869

After passage of the 14th and 15th amendments granting suffrage to all males, both black and white, leaders of the women's movement determined to press their own claims more vigorously. Because of differences over strategy, two organizations were formed. The National Woman Suffrage Association was led by Elizabeth Cady Stanton and Susan B. Anthony while the more conservative American Women Suffrage Association was directed by Lucy Stone and Julia Ward Howe. Unification of these two groups was not achieved until 1890.

1870

Women gained the right to vote and to serve on juries in the Territory of Wyoming.

1872

Susan B. Anthony attempted to vote in Rochester, N.Y. She was tried and convicted of voting illegally but refused to pay the $100 fine.

1873

Belva Lockwood was admitted to the bar of the District of Columbia and in 1879 won passage of a law granting women lawyers the right to practice law before the U.S. Supreme Court. She ran for President in 1884 as candidate of the National Equal Rights Party and got 4,149 votes.

1874

Under the leadership of Frances Willard, the Women's Christian Temperance Union became the largest women's organization in the Nation. During this same period, the Young Women's Christian Association evolved to meet the needs of working women away from home. Other women organized for cultural purposes and by 1890 the General Federation of Women's Clubs was formed. The Association of Collegiate Alumnae, organized in 1882 to investigate the health of college women, eventually became the American Association of University Women.

1878

The Knights of Labor advocated equal pay for equal work, the abolition of child labor under age 14, and in 1881 opened their membership to working women. By 1886, 50,000 women were members.

1880's

Lucy Gonzalez Parson, a labor organizer, traveled in 16 states to raise funds to help organize women garment workers and others. She founded *The Alarm* newspaper and edited *The Liberator.*

1890

Elizabeth Cady Stanton was elected first president of the unified suffrage organization, the National American Woman Suffrage Association. She also studied organized religion as a major source of women's inferior status and in 1895 published *The Woman's Bible.*

1893

Rebelling against an invitation to organize a Jewish women's committee to serve at receptions during Chicago's big Columbian Exposition, Hannah Greenbaum Solomon invited Jewish women from all over the country to attend a conference at the same time as the Exposition. The result was formation of the National Council of Jewish Women, dedicated to education, social reform, and issues of concern to women.

1896

The National Association for Colored Women, the first national organization of black women, was established, and Mary Church Terrell served as first president.

1898
Charlotte Perkins Gilman published *Women and Economics*, in which she decried the wasted efforts and the low economic status of the housewife. Gilman advocated the industrialization of housework and the socialization of child care.

1899
Florence Kelley became general secretary of the National Consumers League and worked for legislation in behalf of working women and children.

1900
The first decade of the 20th century showed the greatest increase in the female labor force of any period prior to 1940. New groups were formed to protect women and children from exploitation by industry. Several unions were organized at this time composed largely of women in the garment trades. Mother Jones, a labor organizer, led a march of children who worked in the Pennsylvania textile mills to the home of President Roosevelt in Oyster Bay, Long Island to call public attention to their plight.

1902
Carrie Chapman Catt organized the International Suffrage Alliance to help establish effective women's groups in other countries.

1904
Mary McLeod Bethune founded Bethune-Cookman College in Daytona Beach, Florida.

1907
The landmark case, *Muller v. Oregon*, established sex as a valid classification for protective legislation. The sociological type of evidence assembled by Florence Kelley and Josephine Goldmark to convince the court that overlong hours were harmful to the future of the race provided a model brief for later laws. While labor laws applying only to women were on the whole beneficial to women in the early part of the century, when jobs were largely sex segregated, the laws did result in loss of job opportunities for those seeking "male" jobs.

1908
A poem, "The New Colossus," written by Emma Lazarus, a poet who had died in 1887, was inscribed on a tablet in the pedestal of the Statue of Liberty in New York harbor. Its most famous lines: "Give me your tired, your poor, Your huddled masses yearning to be free ..."

1909
The first significant strike of working women, "The Uprising of the 20,000," was conducted by shirtwaist makers in New York to protest low wages and long working hours. The National Women's Trade Union League (founded in 1903) mobilized public opinion and financial support for the strikers.

1911
The Triangle fire on March 25, in which 146 women shirtwaist operators were killed, dramatized the poor working conditions of immigrant women. A report of the Senate Investigation of the Condition of Women and Child Wage Earners led to establishment of the Children's Bureau (1912) and later the Women's Bureau of the Department of Labor (1920).

Liga Feminil Mexicanista was founded in Laredo, Texas to insure that the Mexican American culture and heritage would be preserved and transmitted.

1913
Harriet Tubman, ex-slave and most famous "conductor" on the Underground Railroad, died in poverty. Before the Civil War, she made 19 rescue trips to save hundreds of slaves. During the war, she served as a nurse, spy, and scout and led daring raids into the South.

1914
The Alaska Native Sisterhood was formed as an auxiliary of the Alaska Native Brotherhood, the most powerful union of native peoples in Alaska.

1915
Jane Addams, "the angel of Hull House," Carrie Chapman Catt, and other women leaders held a meeting of 3,000 women in Washington, D.C. on January 10 which organized the Women's Peace Party. They called for the abolition of war.

Margaret Sanger, having studied birth control clinics abroad, returned home to campaign against the legal barriers to the dissemination of contraceptive information. She and other women, including Emma Goldman, were jailed for their efforts.

1916
Impatient with the slow pace of the woman suffrage campaign, Alice Paul organized the National Woman's Party to conduct a more militant strategy. Its followers organized suffrage parades, picketed the White House, and chained themselves to its fence. Repeatedly arrested and imprisoned, the women protested their illegal and harsh confinement by going on hunger strikes. They were force-fed by prison authorities. Their suffering aroused widespread public outrage and was credited with hastening ratification of the suffrage amendment.

1917
Jeannette Rankin, a Republican from Montana, was the first woman elected to serve in Congress. The first vote she cast opposed American entry into World War I. She was the only woman to serve in Congress before adoption of the Federal suffrage amendment.

1919
An outgrowth of women suffrage organizations, the League of Women Voters was set up to educate women for their new political and social responsibilities. The National Federation of Business and Professional Women's Clubs was also organized.

1919
Jane Addams led a delegation of American women to a Women's Conference in Zurich, which paralleled the official peace conference in Paris. They formed the Women's International League for Peace and Free-

dom, with Jane Addams as president and Emily Green Balch as secretary-treasurer.

1920
On August 26, the 19th amendment was ratified and 26 million women of voting age finally gained the right to vote.

1923
The Equal Rights Amendment, advocated by Alice Paul and the National Woman's Party, was introduced in Congress for the first time. Most women did not support this effort because they feared it would threaten protective legislation for women workers who labored in sweatshop conditions.

In the following years, the momentum of women's campaigns for access to equal education, employment, and professional achievement waned. Discrimination against women intensified. From 1925 to 1945 medical schools placed a quota of five percent on female admissions. Columbia and Harvard law schools refused to consider women applicants.

1928
Doris Stevens became the first president of the Inter-American Commission of Women, the Organization of American States.

1930
The Depression encouraged reaction against any change in women's traditional domestic role. Legislation restricted the employment of married women, and there was strong public disapproval of women working when men were unable to find employment. Nevertheless, many women performed low-paid labor to support their families. Opportunities for women to obtain college educations and graduate training were limited by lack of financial support.

1931
Suma Sugi, the first Nisei lobbyist (American born of Japanese ancestry), succeeded in amending the Cable Act of 1922 to permit American-born Asian women to regain their American citizenship upon termination of their marriage to an alien.

1933
Frances Perkins, the first woman to hold a Cabinet post, was appointed to head the Department of Labor by President Roosevelt and served in his cabinet for 12 years.

Eleanor Roosevelt turned her 12 years in the White House into a model of activism and humanitarian concern for future First Ladies.

1935
The National Council of Negro Women was founded in New York, with Mary McLeod Bethune as its first president.

1940
The percentage of working women was almost the same as it had been in 1900, when one of every five women worked for wages. After the U.S. entered World War II, wartime needs required the employment of large numbers of women. "Rosie the Riveter" became a national symbol. After the war, many women remained in the labor force, although many were displaced by returning veterans. Between 1940-60, the number of working women and the proportion of working wives doubled. More women over 35 were employed in rapidly expanding business and industry. Inequities in pay and advancement opportunities became more obvious limitations affecting large numbers of women. Economic conditions produced a favorable environment for the increasing demands for equity voiced by the women of the 1960's.

1950
A repressive decade for Chicana activists. Several were deported for their attempts to organize communities. Also deported was film actress Rosaura Revueltas, featured in the film, "Salt of the Earth," about striking miners in the Southwest.

1952
The Constitution of the Commonwealth of Puerto Rico was enacted, embodying the Equal Rights Amendment.

1953
Simone de Beauvoir's The Second Sex, a scholarly and historical analysis of the inferior status of women, was published in the United States.

1956
Rosa Parks, a black seamstress, refused to give up her bus seat to a white man and was arrested, touching off the Montgomery, Alabama bus boycott.

1957
Daisy Bates, coeditor with her husband of a black newspaper and president of the Arkansas National Association for the Advancement of Colored People, acted as spokesperson and counselor for the nine black youths who desegregated Little Rock Central High School.

1960
Women Strike for Peace was formed as an outgrowth of protests against resumption of nuclear testing by the Soviet Union and United States.

1961
The President's Commission on the Status of Women, chaired by Eleanor Roosevelt, was established by Executive Order 10980, with a charge to study seven areas: education, private and Federal employment, social insurance and tax laws, protective labor laws, civil and political rights and family law, and home and community. Esther Peterson, Director of the Women's Bureau, was the moving force in its establishment, with the assistance of then Vice President Lyndon Johnson.

1962
In Michigan, the Governor's Commission on the Status of Women became the first State commission. Union women Mildred Jeffrey and Myra Wolfgang were the leaders in obtaining its establishment.

1962

Acting on a recommendation of his Commission on the Status of Women, President Kennedy issued an order requiring Federal employees to be hired and promoted without regard to sex. Prior to this order, Federal managers could restrict consideration to men or women.

1963

The National Federation of Business and Professional Women's Clubs adopted as its top priority the nationwide establishment of State commissions on the status of women. By June 1964 when the first national conference was held, there were 24 commissions, and by the end of the year there were 33.

The Equal Pay Act was passed in June, effective June 1964, after formation of a coalition of women's organizations and unions to support it in Congress.

The Feminine Mystique by Betty Friedan was published. Describing social pressures that sought to limit women to roles as wives and mothers, it became a national and influential best seller.

The Interdepartmental Committee on the Status of Women and Citizens Advisory Council on the Status of Women were established by Executive Order 11126, with Margaret Hickey as its first chairperson. The Committee and Council sponsored national meetings of the State commissions, issued annual reports on issues affecting women, and made legislative and administrative recommendations. Subsequent chairpersons were Maurine Neuberger and Jacqueline Gutwillig. (The Council was terminated on August 22, 1977 by Executive Order 12007.)

1964

The Spring issue of *Daedalus*, Journal of the American Academy of Arts and Sciences, devoted an entire issue to "The Woman in America," enhancing the academic respectability of the subject. Alice Rossi's "Equality Between the Sexes: An Immodest Proposal," probably the most widely reproduced article in the women's movement, first appeared here.

Title 7 of the Civil Rights Act, enacted in 1964, prohibited discrimination in employment because of sex, race, color, religion, and national origin.

The first meeting of the First National Institute on Girls' Sports was held "to increase the depth of experience and expand opportunities for women."

1965

The U.S. Supreme Court found that a Connecticut law banning contraceptives was unconstitutional because it violated the right to privacy. *Griswold v. State of Connecticut,* 381 U.S.C. 479.

1966

A Federal court declared that an Alabama law excluding women from State juries was in violation of the equal protection clause of the 14th amendment, the first time in modern times a Federal court had found a law making sex distinctions unconstitutional. *White v. Crook,* 251 F. Supp. 401.

The National Organization for Women (NOW) was organized at the Third National Conference of Governors' Commissions on the Status of Women as a culmination of dissatisfaction with the failure to enforce Title 7 of the Civil Rights Act. Among the 28 women who founded NOW were: Betty Friedan, Aileen Hernandez, Dr. Kathryn Clarenbach, Dr. Pauli Murray, Marguerite Rawalt, Catherine Conroy, Dorothy Haener, and Dr. Nancy Knaak.

1967

The first "women's liberation" group was formed in Chicago, partially in rebellion against the low status of young women in civil rights and "new left" campus movements. Similar groups were independently organized in New York, Toronto, Detroit, Seattle, San Francisco, and other cities. Initially concerned with analyzing the origins, nature, and extent of women's subservient status in society, some groups used the technique of "consciousness-raising" sessions to help women liberate themselves from restricting inferior roles. Most of the groups were small, egalitarian and opposed to elitism. They called for far-reaching and radical change in almost all aspects of American society.

Executive Order 11246, prohibiting discrimination by Federal contractors, was amended to include sex discrimination, with an effective date of October 1968.

A law repealing arbitrary restrictions on military rank held by women was signed by the President.

1968

The Church and the Second Sex by Dr. Mary Daly, a scholarly critique of Catholic Church doctrine, influenced Protestant as well as Catholic women. The first stirrings of Catholic feminist dissent occurred at the Second Vatican Council. The American branch of St. Joan's Alliance, an international Catholic feminist organization, had been formed in 1965 by Frances McGillicuddy.

Beginning in 1968, a number of distinguished Native American women, including Lucy Covington (Colville), Ramona Bennett (Puyallup), Joy Sundberg (Yurok), and Ada Deer (Menominee), were elected as tribal chairs.

Federally Employed Women was organized in September to press for equality in Federal employment, with Allie Weedon, a black attorney, as first president.

The Women's Equity Action League was organized in December by Dr. Elizabeth Boyer and other members of the National Organization for

Women and concentrated on attacking sexism in higher education.

Women liberationists picketed the Miss America beauty pageant in Atlantic City. Contrary to myth, they did not burn bras. They carried signs that said: Women are People, Not Livestock.

1969
Shirley Chisholm, Democrat of New York City, was the first black woman elected to Congress.

Weeks v. *Southern Bell Telephone Co,* 408 F. 2d 228, was the first appeals court decision interpreting sex provisions of Title 7 of the Civil Rights Act of 1964. The lawsuit was brought by a blue collar union woman protesting discriminatory effects of State labor laws applying only to women. Marguerite Rawalt, NOW legal counsel, located a Louisiana lawyer, Sylvia Roberts, to represent Mrs. Weeks, and NOW paid court costs. The excellent decision, the great courage of the plaintiff, and the important victory of a volunteer woman lawyer and a women's organization over highly paid corporation lawyers were a great boost to the women's movement.

An equally important Title 7 case was decided by the Seventh Circuit Court of Appeals. *Bowe* v. *Colgate Palmolive,* 416 F. 2d 711. Union women and volunteer women attorneys were the pattern in this case, too. These and later Title 7 cases illustrated the real effects of State labor laws applying only to women and led to their early demise and broadened support for the Equal Rights Amendment.

The first Commission on the Status of Women appointed by a professional association began to function inside the Modern Language Association. In its early years, that Commission assumed responsibility for collecting and disseminating data on women's studies courses and programs. In December 1970 the Commission published a list of 110 women's studies courses taught at 47 colleges and universities. There were by then two Women's Studies Programs at Cornell University and San Diego State University.

In Fall 1972, the *Women's Studies Newsletter,* edited by Florence Howe, began to appear quarterly on the SUNY College at Old Westbury campus, published by The Feminist Press. Annually, the newsletter lists Women's Studies Programs; in 1977, there were 276. There are also groups of women's studies courses on more than 1,000 other campuses. The total number of courses now offered exceeds 15,000.

A women's caucus was organized at the Chicano Liberation Conference held in Denver.

The Boston Women's Health Collective was organized, one of a number of women's self-help groups that emerged in various parts of the country. The group researched and wrote *Our Bodies, Ourselves,* which later became a worldwide best-seller.

The four Republican Congresswomen—Florence Dwyer, Margaret Heckler, Catherine May, and Charlotte Reid—asked for an unprecedented audience with President Nixon to discuss women's issues. They presented a letter which outlined a proposed administration program and provided data on discrimination. Their program became the agenda of the President's Task Force on Women's Rights and Responsibilities, which the President later established with Virginia Allan as chair.

Women in the American Sociological Association formed the first caucus within a professional association, after presentation of a survey by Dr. Alice Rossi on the status of women in graduate departments of sociology. By the end of 1971 every professional association had an activist women's caucus or official commission to study the status of women.

1970
Women's Equity Action League officer, Dr. Bernice Sandler, filed the first formal charges of sex discrimination under Executive Order No. 11246 against the University of Maryland. The charges were well documented. By the end of 1971 women professors had filed formal charges of sex discrimination against more than 300 colleges, largely through the efforts of Dr. Sandler and WEAL.

The first statewide meeting of AFL-CIO women was held in Wisconsin in March. The women endorsed the ERA, opposing AFL-CIO national policy. The next month the United Auto Workers became the first major national union to endorse ERA. Later the AFL-CIO executive council changed its position and announced its support for the ERA.

The Subcommittee on Constitutional Amendments of the Senate Judiciary Committee, chaired by Senator Birch Bayh, held three days of hearings on the ERA in May. Leaders of women's organizations and unions, women lawyers, and Members of Congress testified.

The NAACP adopted a women's rights platform at its annual national convention in June.

The first national commercial newsletters to serve the women's movement— *Women Today,* published in Washington by Myra and Lester Barrer, and *Spokeswoman,* published in Chicago by Susan Davis—were issued.

The Interstate Association of Commissions on the Status of Women was organized to provide a national voice and greater autonomy for the State commissions. Elizabeth Duncan Koontz, newly appointed Director of the Women's Bureau, arranged the organized meetings, and Dr. Kathryn Clarenbach was elected first president.

The Women's Bureau held its 50th anniversary conference, attended by more than 1,000 women. The Conference endorsed the ERA and other recommendations of the President's Task Force on Women's Rights and Responsibilities.

On the first day of the Women's Bureau Conference, Congresswoman Martha Griffiths filed a petition to discharge the ERA from the House Judiciary Committee, where it had rested without hearings since 1948. The petition was successful, and the ERA was debated in the House on August 10, passing overwhelmingly. It was then defeated in the Senate by the addition of unacceptable amendments.

Hearings on discrimination in education were held in June and July by Congresswoman Edith Green, chairing a special House Subcommittee on Education. The two-volume report is a classic in documenting discrimination against women in education.

The Women's Affairs Division of the League of United Latin American Citizens was organized at the convention in Beaumont, Texas, with Julia Zozoya and Ada Pena in the forefront.

The National Conference of Commissioners on Uniform State Laws published the Uniform Marriage and Divorce Act, based on the assumption that marriage is an economic partnership and recognizing homemakers' contributions as having economic value.

A nationwide celebration of the 50th anniversary of the suffrage amendment, including a mammoth parade in New York City, was held in all major cities on August 26 by a wide spectrum of organizations and individual women. The parade became an annual event.

Sixty-three Native American women from 43 tribes and 23 States met at Colorado State University to discuss their common concerns. They organized the North American Indian Women's Association.

Patsy Mink, Democrat of Hawaii, was the first and only Asian woman elected to Congress. In New York City, Democrat Bella Abzug was the first woman elected to Congress on a women's rights platform. They were among only 11 women in the 435-member House of Representatives.

1971

The National Women's Political Caucus was organized at a meeting in Washington in July, with Congresswoman Bella Abzug, Gloria Steinem, Aileen Hernandez, Fannie Lou Hamer, Edith Van Horn, Liz Carpenter, Koryne Horbal, Congresswoman Shirley Chisholm, Brownie Ledbetter, Betty Friedan, Bobby Kilberg, Jo Ann Gardner, LaDonna Harris, and Virginia Allan among the early leaders.

The U.S. Supreme Court held in *Reed* v. *Reed* that an Idaho law giving preference to males as executors of estates was invalid under the 14th amendment, the first in a series of Supreme Court cases expanding the application of the 5th and 14th amendments to sex discrimination, 404 U.S. 71, 1971.

A preview issue of *Ms.* magazine was published in December with Gloria Steinem as editor. Established to give voice to the ideas of the women's movement, it was an immediate success.

The Women's National Abortion Coalition was organized to work for repeal of anti-abortion laws.

1972

The Equal Rights Amendment was overwhelmingly approved by the Congress and submitted to the States for ratification. Hawaii was the first State to ratify.

The Equal Employment Opportunity Act of 1972, extending coverage and giving the EEOC enforcement authority, passed. The EEOC issued greatly improved sex discrimination guidelines.

Title 9 of the Education Amendments of 1972 was passed, prohibiting discrimination on account of sex in most Federally assisted educational programs. The Equal Pay Act was extended to cover administrative, professional, and executive employees, and the Civil Rights Commission was given jurisdiction over sex discrimination.

The Democratic and Republican Party platforms endorsed the ERA and vigorous enforcement of anti-discrimination laws. As a result of campaigns by the National Women's Political Caucus, the participation of women as convention delegates was higher than in previous conventions. At the Democratic convention, women were 40 percent of the delegates; at the Republican convention, 30 percent.

The National Conference of Puerto Rican Women was organized in Washington, with Carmen Maymi and Paquito Viva in leading roles.

The November elections brought more women into elective office. The number of women elected to State legislatures was 28.2 percent higher than those serving in the preceding year. In the House of Representatives, the number of Congresswomen increased to 16, but with the retirement of Margaret Chase Smith, the U.S. Senate once again became all-male.

Members of the National Council of Jewish Women conducted a study of day-care facilities in 176 areas. The NCJW report, written by Mary Keyserling, concluded that while the need for day-care centers was enormous, facilities were nonexistent in most places or were of poor quality, underfunded, and understaffed.

1973

AT&T signed an agreement with the EEOC and the Labor Department providing goals and timetables for increasing utilization of women and minorities. About $15 million in back pay was paid to some 15,000 employees.

In a historic decision on January 22, the U.S. Supreme Court held that during the first trimester of pregnancy, the decision to have an abortion must be left solely to a woman and her physician. The only restriction a State may impose is the requirement that the abortion be performed by a physician licensed by the State. In the second and third trimesters, the Court held, the States may impose increasingly stringent requirements. Lawyers for the plaintiffs were Sarah Weddington and Marjorie Hames. *Doe* v. *Bolton and Roe* v. *Wade*, 93 S. Ct. 739 and 755.

The National Black Feminists Organization was formed. Eleanor Holmes Norton, leading attorney and head of the New York City Human Rights Commission, was one of the leaders.

The Foreign Assistance Act (Public Law 93-189, 87 Stat. 714) included the Percy Amendment providing that in administering financial aid, particular attention be given to "programs, projects, and activities which tend to integrate women into the national status and assisting the total development effort." Dr. Irene Tinker and the Federation of Organizations for Professional Women were leading proponents.

Billie Jean King beat Bobby Riggs in straight sets in their "Battle of the Sexes" tennis match.

1974

The Coalition of Labor Union Women was organized in Chicago with over 3,000 women in attendance. Olga Madar, former UAW vice president, was elected president.

More than 1.5 million domestic service workers were brought under the coverage of the Fair Labor Standards Act by Public Law 93-259, approved April 8. A rate of $1.90 per hour was effective May 1, 1974, with increases slated for later periods.

The Wisconsin Commission on the Status of Women, chaired by Dr. Kathryn Clarenbach, inaugurated a series of six regional conferences to examine the status of the homemaker.

A national newsletter, *Marriage, Divorce and the Family*, edited by Betty Blaisdell Berry, began publication.

The Mexican American Women's Association (MAWA) was founded.

A study by Dr. Constance Uri, a Cherokee/Choctaw physician, revealed the widespread use and abuse of sterilization of Native American women in Indian health care facilities. The expose led to the investigation of excessive sterilization of poor and minority women and to the 1977 revision of the Department of Health, Education, and Welfare's guidelines on sterilization.

Congresswoman Bella Abzug's bill to designate August 26 "Women's Equality Day" in honor of the adoption of the Suffrage Amendment became Public Law 93-392.

The Housing and Community Development Act of 1974, Public Law 93-383, prohibited sex discrimination in carrying out community development programs and in making federally related mortgage loans. The Civil Rights Act of 1968 was also amended to prohibit sex discrimination in financing, sale or rental of housing, or the provision of brokerage services.

The Equal Credit Opportunity Act became Public Law 93-495 after Congresswomen Bella Abzug, Margaret Heckler, and Leonor Sullivan led the fight for it in the House. It prohibited discrimination in credit on the basis of sex or marital status. Later, Congresswoman Abzug led a delegation of women members of Congress to meet with Chairman Arthur Burns of the Federal Reserve Board to protest unsatisfactory regulations designed to implement the new law. The regulations were revised.

The Screen Actors Guild reported a nationwide survey of 10,000 viewers on their opinions of women in the media. The majority wanted a more positive image of women, wanted to see women appearing on TV in positions of authority and in leading roles, and felt the media did not encourage young girls to aspire to a useful and meaningful role in society.

Following a "Win With Women" campaign by the National Women's Political Caucus, 18 women were elected to the 94th Congress. A 19th member was elected in a special election in early 1975. In the State legislatures there was a 29.5 percent increase in the numbers of women (465 to 604). The first woman governor to be elected in her own right, Ella Grasso, was elected Governor of Connecticut. Mary Anne Krupsak was elected Lieutenant Governor of New York, and many more women were elected to statewide offices.

1975

The U.S. Supreme Court held in *Wiesenfeld* v. *Wineberger* that a widower with minor children whose deceased wife was covered by social security is entitled to a social security benefit under the same circumstances as a widow would be. The Court held unanimously that the fifth amendment prohibited the present difference in treatment. 43 USLW 4393.

The Supreme Court also held that, in the context of child support, a Utah statute providing that the period of minority extending for males to age 21 and for females to age 18 denies equal protection of the laws guaranteed by the 14th amendment. *Stanton* v. *Stanton*, 43 USLW 4167.

Ms. magazine published a petition for sexual freedom signed by 100 prominent women. They pledged to work for repeal of all laws and regulations that discriminate against homosexuals and lesbians.

The National Commission on the Observance of International Women's Year, 1975, was appointed by President Ford with Jill Ruckelshaus as presiding officer. Elizabeth Athanasakos became presiding officer in 1976. Members of the Commission represented the United States at the United Nations International Women's Year Conference in Mexico City in June.

The First American Indian Women's Leadership Conference met in New York City, sponsored by the International Treaty Council in conjunction with IWY.

A bill introduced by Congresswoman Bella Abzug directed the National Commission to organize and convene a National Women's Conference, preceded by State meetings. The bill was passed by both Houses, was signed by President Ford and became Public Law 94-167.

1976

The number of women delegates to the political party conventions rose to 31.4 percent at the Republican convention and declined to 34 percent at the Democratic convention. A large and effective women's caucus at the Democratic convention in New York met with Presidential nominee Jimmy Carter and obtained pledges from him to appoint significant numbers of women to his administration, to take other steps to improve the position of women, and to campaign for ratification of the ERA.

The major parties nominated 52 women for the House of Representatives, eight more than in 1974, but 31 ran against incumbents. Eighteen were elected, one less than in the previous Congress. Although women won seats in Maryland and Ohio and all incumbents won reelection, Congresswomen Bella Abzug and Patsy Mink gave up their seats to make unsuccessful campaigns for the Senate, and Congresswoman Leonor Sullivan retired. The number of women in State legislatures increased to 685, representing nine percent of legislative seats.

1977

President Carter named a new National Commission on the Observance of IWY and appointed Bella Abzug presiding officer. He named two women, Patricia Harris and Juanita Kreps, to his Cabinet and made other major appointments of women. An analysis of the Presidential personnel plum file appointments list in October, however, showed that of 526 top positions in the Carter administration, only 60 (11 percent) were held by women.

The drive for final ratification of ERA was stalled at 35 States, with three more States needed to meet the 1979 deadline for ratification.

The National Women's Conference met in Houston, Texas, November 18-21, attracted almost 20,000 people, including 2,005 delegates, adopted a National Plan of Action, and was acclaimed a success.

Editor's Note: In highlighting some of the notable women and events affecting women in American history, this chronology makes no pretense to being complete or even comprehensive. It is intended rather to remind readers that the role of women in America has too often been overlooked and that the struggle for equality for women is as old as our Nation.

Among the books which the editors found particularly useful in compiling this chronology were:
Chafe, William. The American Woman: Her Changing Social, Economic and Political Roles, 1920-1970. Oxford University Press.
DePauw, Linda Grant. Fortunes of War, New Jersey Women and the American Revolution. New Jersey Historical Commission.
Flexner, Eleanor. Century of Struggle. Atheneum.
Freeman, Jo. Women: A Feminist Perspective. Mayfield.
Hole, Judith, and Ellen Levine. Rebirth of Feminism. Quadrangle.
Lerner, Gerda. "The Lady and the Mill Girl: Changes in the Status of Women in the Age of Jackson." American Studies Journal, spring 1969.
Lerner, Gerda. Black Women in White America. Vintage.
O'Neill, William. Everyone Was Brave. Quadrangle.
Papachristou, Judith. Women Together, A History in Documents of the Women's Movement in the United States. A Ms. Book.
Wertheimer, Barbara. We Were There: The Story of Working Women in America. Pantheon.

Special thanks to Catherine East for compiling the original chronology on which this is based, which appeared as an IWY publication in 1975.

WHAT THEY SAID: Excerpts From Major Speeches

SPEECH BY COMMISSIONER GLORIA SCOTT
FIRST PLENARY SESSION
NOVEMBER 19, 1977

I am Gloria Scott, member of the Presidentially appointed National Commission on the Observance of International Women's Year. I am a Texan and a native Houstonian. It is my pleasure to welcome the First Lady, Rosalynn Carter, former First Lady and Commissioner Betty Ford, former First Lady Lady Bird Johnson, the National Commission, Members of the Congress, the executive branch of government, delegates, official visitors, observers, international guests, Mrs. Helvi Sipila from the United Nations.

On behalf of the Commission I wish to thank Public Broadcasting for providing gavel to gavel coverage of this historic meeting so that the public beyond these walls may observe the deliberations of this body.

The late President John Fitzgerald Kennedy had the foresight to establish a President's Commission on the Status of Women in the early sixties.

The late President Lyndon Johnson continued that vision by appointing a Citizens' Advisory Council by Executive order to assure continued advancement of the status of women. He said in 1966: "The time has come for the American woman to take her rightful place in American society."

In January 1975, former President Gerald Ford issued an Executive order establishing a National Commission on the Observance of IWY.

And in April 1977 President James Earl Carter reappointed the Commission to continue work to organize and implement the State meetings and the national conference. It is now November 19, 1977, and that conference is a reality.

We live in a time where the rate and quality of change combine to produce a sometimes formidable combination. Increasingly, there is the request and demand for the enactment of a change in societal mores which addresses the true realization of a pluralistic culture in which variables that describe or define individuals have fundamental equal status. We are "in passage" and our fates are inextricably bound. The aim is the fostering of the well-being of people—not of women alone or of men apart—but a society of diverse talents.

For a brief period in our lives we will deliberate across variables which might tend to isolate, stereotypes which tend to separate—yet we will share the same experiences.

As we approach this delegate assembly, let us keep ever before us the concept that the unexamined issue is not worth holding on to forever.

As our country has just celebrated its Bicentennial, it is appropriate that we now focus nationwide attention on a most important resource that has helped to make and keep America great from the time of its founding—our American women.

In 23 short years—at the turn of the century—the year 2000, those of you in the audience today who are 16 to 25 will be 39 to 48; 26 to 35 will be 49 to 58; 46 to 55 will be 69 to 78; 56 to 65 will be 79 to 88.

It is important that decisions we make are tempered by our full knowledge that their impact will have influence on generations to come after us—yet unborn.

It is against this background that we assemble this weekend. It is in the true spirit of American democracy that we have come together to debate issues and not people.

It is a sobering experience to preside over the opening ceremonies of the most significant and far-reaching event in this century. This National Women's Conference will insure that we the people of the United States of America, in order to form a more perfect union, do move closer to the possibility of what America can be.

In this opening session there will be no business conducted. The discussion and debate of issues in this democratic forum will begin in the second plenary session. It is now my official pleasure to open this meeting of American women on the move.

SPEECH BY BELLA ABZUG, PRESIDING OFFICER
FIRST PLENARY SESSION,
NOVEMBER 19, 1977

We've waited almost two years for this moment, and it was worth it.

The road to Houston started more than a century and a half ago when American women began organizing to win the rights of citizenship.

The torch of freedom has been handed from generation to generation of women, and the torch we see here today is a symbol of our past victories and our hopes for future ones.

The road has twisted and turned, gone down byways and made detours at times, but today we're on the high road to equality.

Our present journey started with a bill—Public Law 94-167—that I introduced in Congress as a followup to International Women's Year in 1975. Congresswomen Patsy Mink and Margaret Heckler and the other Congresswomen united around the bill and spoke for it, as did many of the male members of Congress.

Our conference is a first in many ways.

It is the first time the Federal Government has sponsored a National Women's Conference and the 50 State meetings and six Territorial meetings that preceded this event.

It is the first time the Congress and the President have mandated American women to identify and help remove the barriers that stand between us and full equality with men.

The mandate under which we meet does not tell us to consider whether women *should* seek to end discrimination, or *should* seek full equality, full citizenship, and full participation in society. Instead, it takes a stand *for* equality, a position that I believe has the support of a majority of Americans. The law under which we meet is rooted in the belief that men and women should share equally in the rights, responsibilities, and opportunities that our democracy offers.

How could it be otherwise 200 years after our nation was born in the great struggle for the rights of the individual?

And so the law directs us to examine the past and the present. It directs us to examine the status of American women, our needs, our problems, and the diversity of our lives. It directs us to seek change and improvements in the lives of women who have been held back by discriminatory practices.

That is our mission here this weekend.

We will be debating and voting on a National Plan of Action that includes dozens of recommendations on ways in which equality between men and women can be made a living reality.

Many of us see a future in which women will be free to live and work as individuals, as members of families, as members of society without the constraints of narrow customs and prejudices that demean our self-worth or laws that treat us as inferiors or weaklings.

Some among us may prefer a future that simply continues the past. Our purpose is not to tell women how to live or what to do. It is simply to say that women must be free to choose what they do.

Let us agree to disagree, if we must. It would be a dull weekend if we didn't feel free to state our beliefs. But I hope all of us here will remember our common interests as women who have for too long been treated as merely auxiliary human beings.

The National Plan of Action we shall be discussing comes from you, from the State meetings, from the members of the National Commission. It reflects the breadth of your concerns and needs and interests. ...

Throughout the history of our nation women have worked, but today more women than ever before are working.

Many are housewives who work part-time or on night shifts to help pay the mortgage and the grocery bills. Many work to support themselves and their children or work because they are single women, widowed, or divorced.

But despite the fact that women compose 40 percent of the work force, the wage gap between men and women gets wider, not smaller. A woman with a college education still earns less, on average, than a man with a high school education. And minority women earn less than white women.

Housewives, or homemakers, if you prefer, earn nothing at all, though this nation could not function for a day if the millions of women who work exclusively in the home were to stop doing what they do so lovingly for their families.

No objective value is placed on their sun-up to sun-down labor, and the result is that homemakers are placed at a serious disadvantage in inheritance and social security laws, in divorce and separation cases.

If so many women are concerned today about our status in the family, on the job and in our educational system, it is because more and more women realize that we are responsible for ourselves.

The economist Sylvia Porter reported recently that of 100 typical American women now 21 years of age, six will never marry. Of the 94 who will marry, 33 will get divorced, and of the remaining 61 who stay married, 46 will outlive their husbands.

Like it or not, that means that 85 out of 100 women will be on their own at some time during their adult lives. It is this realization that we do indeed have the responsibility for our own lives that brought more than 130,000 women out to the State meetings and brought you here to Houston. ...

What we are doing here in Houston is part of an irreversible worldwide movement in which women are speaking out for our needs and trying to create a better world in which men and women do not victimize each other, but work together for a decent life for all people.

There can be no turning back to a time when women were segregated in auxiliaries, prevented from using their skills and abilities, barred from places of power.

We can no longer accept a condition in which men rule the Nation and the world, excluding half the human race from effective economic and political power. Not when the world is in such bad shape.

We can argue about whether women, if we arrive at the stage where we do share power with men, will create a better world. I believe we will. I believe, if we had the opportunity, we could figure out ways to spend some of the $300 billion spent on armaments each year for more rational and humane purposes—like feeding the hungry, housing the homeless, creating jobs, preventing disease, ignorance, and illiteracy.

Personally, I am not interested in seeing women get an equal chance to push the nuclear button. I do want to see women and men work equally together for a peaceful world in which my daughters and your sons and daughters can live without fear.

But whatever women choose to do with equality, it must be ours as a matter of simple justice.

Our journey is far from over. We have much to do when we leave Houston. We have to see that the recommendations we support here become reality—and that will be long, hard work. We have to reach out to millions more women and men to enlist them in our cause. And we have to win real political power for women because as long as the Congress, the State legislatures, and city councils are dominated by men, we have to come as supplicants rather than as decisionmakers.

A reporter asked me yesterday whether Houston was going to be the death of the woman's movement.

Well, look at us!

We are a multitude. We are alive and kicking, and we shall get even livelier.

After this weekend, the whole Nation will know that the women's movement is not any one organization or set of ideas or particular lifestyle. It is millions of women deciding individually and together that we are determined to move history forward.

The women's movement has become an indestructible part of American life. It is the homemaker deciding that raising children, cleaning, cooking, and all the other things she does for her family is work that should be accorded respect and value. It is the young woman student asserting she wants to play baseball, major in physics, or become a brain surgeon. It is the working woman demanding that she get the same pay and promotion opportunities as a man. It is the divorcee fighting for social security benefits in her own right, the widow embarking on a new career, the mother organizing a daycare center, the battered wife seeking help, the woman running for public office.

It is all of us here and all of the women out there who say the time for equal rights has come.

I think of what a southern woman named Nell Battle Lewis wrote after the suffrage amendment to the Constitution was finally ratified.

"The pedestal has crashed," she said. "There are many even now who would patch the idol together. It was only an image after all ... In its place is a woman of flesh and blood, not a queen, or a saint, nor a symbol, but a human being with human faults and human virtues, a woman still only slowly rising to full stature, but with the sun of freedom on her face."

Let the sun shine on our deliberations, and let us celebrate womanhood and woman power.

SPEECH BY FIRST LADY ROSALYNN CARTER
FIRST PLENARY SESSION
NOVEMBER 19, 1977

It is a pleasure to welcome you to the National Women's Conference.

Jimmy is sorry that he could not be here today. His concern about the outcome of your agenda is deep. He cares about what is going on here this weekend. And I trust that you don't think he's sent a woman to do a man's job!

I would like to address myself to that issue. The substance of this conference is much, much more than a man-woman thing. Or symbolism.

There is a lot of talk about style and substance these days. But they are not mutually exclusive—in men, women, or government. I think that our two former First Ladies here this morning have shown us that.

Mrs. Johnson, you left behind a national legacy that blooms with the seasons and inspires us all to enjoy, cherish, and want to improve our environments. And your memorable style helped to point up the need for community action.

And Mrs. Ford, I know that your courageous—yes, your outspoken—acceptance of your illness prompted untold numbers of women and men to seek help and information about cancer. You brought hope and alleviated fears—and left an imprint in the White House by your enthusiastic style.

Both of you are admired throughout the world for your dedication to your role—your job—as First Lady. And I think it is significant that the three of us are here in Houston together on this platform today to affirm the continuity in our government's efforts to improve life for all.

Jimmy asked me to be his personal emissary today, and to talk to you briefly about his concerns and his goals. He and I have been partners for a long time—working together and separately to raise our children, start a business, undertake the duties of elective office, and to fulfill our shared commitment to improve the lives and possibilities for happiness of the women and men in this country. Of course, I am here for myself, too.

This conference holds promise for so many—around this world. I flew out last night with four women from the White House whose responsibilities in government reflect Jimmy's recognition that women are good leaders.

These women are among the assistants and special assistants—key decisionmakers—to the President of the United States. I was proud to be with them. There have been very few in those jobs before.

There are more than 40 other women who are here from the administration, women who make and direct policy in management jobs throughout the government. This is an indication of how far women have come. Did you know that the general counsel of the Department of Defense is a woman in the Carter administration? And the general counsel of the Department of Agriculture is a woman—from Texas?

In just 10 months we have—
—Two women in the Cabinet;
—Four women ambassadors;
—One out of every four professionals on Jimmy's domestic policy staff is female;
—A top woman advises him on the National Security Council.

These are building blocks.

Here are some initiatives that Jimmy has already taken on behalf of women:

Just this week, he sent a directive to all department and agency heads about the Executive order signed by President Johnson 10 years ago banning sex discrimination in Federal employment. In this directive he said that government officials should develop "innovative programs to recruit and hire qualified women" at all levels—including top levels—of the career and noncareer Federal service.

He has already—voluntarily—brought the Executive Office of the President under Title 7 of the Civil Rights Act of 1964. And he has taken steps to give government women workers—and the government is the largest major employer of women—better opportunities through part-time work, flexitime schedules, and better mechanisms for handling discrimination complaints.

He is concerned about equal employment enforcement, sex discrimination in Federal laws, barriers to women in business. I think these are important building blocks toward equal participation in national life. That is what we are here for today. Equal participation is our goal.

I am proud to be a part of the National Women's Conference. Never before in our history has there been such a women's meeting: in numbers, in preparation, in diversity, in long-range effect. The breadth of opinion, ethnic group, income, and occupation represented here is remarkably reflective of our whole country.

That diversity among women is itself indicative of how completely we are a part of America. The strength of our country from its very beginning has been the wide variety of people and ideas that have worked together for the good of all.

There have been a lot of disagreements and conflicts. There will be a lot of disagreements and conflicts. But I agree with my daughter-in-law Judy that we must guard against obscuring valid issues with defensiveness and anger. The glue that holds us together is the firm knowledge that our basic goals are the same.

All of us cherish our freedom to live, to worship, to vote, to work as we please. We are all searching for ways to create a better future for our children. Here in Houston, we have that chance. And we must consider carefully our responsibilities.

We are responsible to the American people, who, through their taxes, have supported this Conference.

We are responsible to the hundreds of thousands of women who attended State meetings in good faith.

We are responsible to the Congress and to the President, who will use the report generated by the Conference for many years to guide them in their efforts to solve the problems identified and discussed here.

Above all, we are responsible to ourselves—and the future generations of American women—and men.

Because we are making history. I think we all are aware that we are making history—as we come together here in this huge gathering.

It is a privilege we share these next few days.

SPEECH BY BETTY FORD
NATIONAL COMMISSIONER
AND FORMER FIRST LADY
FIRST PLENARY SESSION
NOVEMBER 19, 1977

It is absolutely thrilling to see such a tremendous crowd here this morning, to act as ourselves, and I want everybody in the world to know it.

Mrs. Carter, Mrs. Johnson, and all of you who are here on behalf of the IWY, the first thing I would like to say is that I am honored by the company I'm with.

This points out how dramatic are the common cause and hopes of so many people of so many different persuasions. I told Jerry I was determined to go to Houston and have my voice here. Jerry answered to me, "Well, naturally. Okay, Betty. I expected it."

Well, that lighthearted exchange really has a serious side for Jerry and for me. We have both found a great deal of respect and appreciation in knowing that each of us can speak our own minds as we feel necessary. Jerry sends his warmest regards and certainly his best wishes for this Conference.

I am sure a great many of you, perhaps, read about Amelia Bloomer and perhaps know who she was. Well, it was way back in the 1800's that Amelia Bloomer designed the first pants. And now some of you may also recall that my maiden name, if you'll pardon the expression, was "Bloomer."

We haven't had time to determine for sure that we're relatives, but I don't think there are many of us around. However, if she came up with the idea of pants for women, she sounds like my kind of gal.

Very seriously, I am proud to be here, and I am very honored by the privilege to participate with each and every one of you. However, in terms of advice let me say this: we must keep focus on our goals in business, education, employment, and politics, or in the home. We may have different interests, but we shouldn't be dismayed by the clash of opinion and ideas. It has been said the "evils" of controversy will pass, but its benefits are permanent.

Thank you again for having me here. I'm proud to be part of it. So let's keep it all together.

COMMISSIONER LIZ CARPENTER: FACES AND VOICES
FIRST PLENARY SESSION
NOVEMBER 19, 1977

The eyes of the Nation are on Texas today. As a native-born daughter, I assure you we like it that way!

Let the good news ring out! There is no energy shortage here in Houston—the Philadelphia of 1977. Here is a supply of America's greatest untapped energy resource—set aside for 201 years—misused and unused (a fuel that comes with brains)—the women of America.

This year something quite wonderful happened. Every woman living under the American flag had a chance to attend a meeting, vote her mind, and send a delegation here to this national summit of women.

So here we are, the faces and voices ignored and silenced too often by the decisionmakers. . . .

We are the map of America. Some of us think the country's moving too slowly. Some fear it will move too fast. Our roots are privileged and they are humble. So here we are inside this hall and out—women of many faces and voices. We are not all as passionate as Bella, as perceptive and photogenic as Gloria, as judicious as Judge Shirley Hufstedler, as futuristic as Betty Friedan, as impish as Amy or mellow as Miss Lillian, as caring as Rosalynn, dedicated as Lady Bird, gentle as Pat Nixon, or courageous as Betty Ford.

But something of all of them is in all of us. We are not look-alikes, and think-alikes, and God forbid that we ever will be.

Look at us. Who are we today? Some homemakers—some breadwinners—some both. How many homemakers are here? All homemakers, hold up your hands.

Any breadwinners out there? All you people who earn a salary, big or small, hold up your hands.

We come from all ages. Let's see how many are under 30? How many are somewhere between 40 and death?

Who else are we? We are voters, since 1920, and there was a lot of "brouhaha" about that! We are volunteers and rising new voices at city hall and the State capitals.

We are in public office by election and appointment! Republicans, Democrats, Independents, nothing.

Let's see how many public office holders out there. Hold up your hands. Who are we, delegates? We are young and old: Sixteen-year-old Dorothy Arceneaux of Houma, Louisiana. Honor student, Girl Scout leader, member of the school band. Would you deny this young girl the right to equality of education and opportunity? Not me.

Eighty-five-year-old Clara M. Beyer of Washington, D.C.. Retired government worker of 60 years, protege of Justice Frankfurter, teacher at Bryn Mawr College, one of the handful of valiant women who with Eleanor Roosevelt and Florence Kelly pushed reform of child labor. Mother of three sons and 12 grandchildren. Would you deny this senior citizen mother the social security rights due her—or deny women like her their inheritance rights? Not me!

Twenty-four-year-old Mariko Tse, delegate from California. Actress, leader in Chinese Women in Action. At the age of eight, she was a world traveler, standing before a judge to get her citizenship, now a leader in upwardbound programs with blacks, Chicanas, Indians, and the American Chinese. She came to meet the Asian women in all the delegations. "That gives me a terrific thrill—to see them moving ahead," she said. Would you deny this ethnic American, or any other ethnic American women, the rights of equality under the law? Not me!

Politically active wives of governors like delegate Helen Millikin of Michigan and Sharon Percy Rockefeller of West Virginia, who do their volunteerism in environment and the crafts of Appalachia. Would you deny these women and many like them, housewives and mothers, the right to do magnificent things for their communities and their states? Could their communities survive without their volunteer time?

Vida Haukass, trial judge from Wind River Reservation in Fort Washaske, Wyoming. Her Indian name is Sinopahki. "I have come to hear what everybody else thinks." Would you deny this Native American any right from the country which was her land long before it was ours? Not me!

The delegate from Kansas, Sister Mary Agnes Drees, director of continuing education at Marymount College, a member of the Sisters of St. Joseph and the network lobby of Catholic sisters working for social justice. "The Sisters of St. Joseph were always in the vanguard of change on the frontier. We are still there working in our precincts, active politically in city hall." She returns 60 percent of her salary to support Marymount College, where she teaches. Would you deny this religious woman, or any religious woman of any creed, a voice or the right to move ahead in their religious group? Not me!

The delegate from Illinois—Marge Jindrich—14 years with the United Auto Workers, Local No. 954 of Region 4. She helps support her semi-invalid husband and five children on a paycheck of $8,500. "My husband and my children believe like I do—that things aren't moving fast enough for women in the legislature at Springfield or in the unions. There's too much foot-dragging. Something needs to happen. I want to help make it happen." Would you deny this mother and wife the right to attempt to move the unions forward in the matter of equality of opportunity for women? Not me!

Delegate-at-large from Georgia—Mrs. Jack Carter—Judy, young homemaker, and mother of a two-year-old son, and babysitter for his five friends quite frequently, as you can detect over the phone.

We are Margie Flores, of El Paso, Texas, chair of the Chicana Women's Caucus, mother of four and now back in school herself studying elementary education so she can teach. "I want women to learn they can work together with the commonality that binds us together." Would you deny this woman and the thousands like her their full rights as citizens of this great nation? Not me!

The delegate from Minnesota, farm woman Mary Ann Bruesehoffe, who runs her own poultry farm on route 2 near Watkins. She was butchering ducks when I called. While her husband raises pigs, cattle, and sheep,

she just fell into raising 3,000 broilers, ducks, and geese each year because "we like good old-fashioned food that's uncontaminated. Everyone else did, too, and it helps pay the college tuition of three of four children." Why did she want to come? "I demand of our society that attitudes be the same toward the sexes and the races. It is inconceivable to me in a democracy that we cause anyone pain because of preconceived notions about the way people should feel toward one another." Would you keep this woman out of business because she couldn't get equal credit to run a business—or unfair taxes that prevent her from deductions that are allowable to her counterparts? Not me!

The delegate from New York, Georgia McMurray, longtime leader in movements for civil rights and the disabled, brings head and heart to New York's community services. Would you deny this and any of the millions of black women the right to go as far as their dreams and magnificent talents can take them. Not me!

That's who we are—this great women's movement. Progress always begins with a movement. But all movements of people become movements of individuals, and that is where we are today, establishing a belief in ourselves, gaining the courage to walk in the sunshine of our own souls.

That is the final greatness a nation dêrives from the movements of its times: the gift of individual courage in people to be their own selves and speak their own thoughts.

America, look at us! Listen to us. Have faith in us. Help us. Love us as we loved you.

INTRODUCTION OF CONGRESSWOMAN BARBARA JORDAN BY LADY BIRD JOHNSON, FORMER FIRST LADY
FIRST PLENARY SESSION
NOVEMBER 19, 1977

How pleased I am to add my voice of welcome to you who have come here to Texas to help move history forward and to say how honored we are to have Betty Ford and Rosalynn Carter!

I once thought the women's movement belonged more to my daughters than to me, but I have come to know that it belongs to women of all ages. I am proud to say and I want you to know that Texas was the ninth State to ratify the right to vote and the seventh State to ratify the Equal Rights Amendment.

While you are here I hope you will meet many of the Texas women who are today's doers. We have an impressive share of bright, articulate women in every part of this State—women who are mayors of cities, large and small, county clerks, presidents of great universities, deans of schools, lawyers, and doctors, and artists.

Certainly one of the brightest stars in this galaxy is the woman I have the privilege of introducing today.

Texas has known for some time that it was watching someone quite remarkable as Barbara Jordan kept enlarging her claim on our attention. . . . back when she was an outstanding student in Phyllis Wheatley High School here in Houston; back when her debate team at Texas Southern University tied with Harvard, and she graduated magna cum laude.

Texas watched with growing interest when she made her first races for the State legislature in the early sixties and lost. Later we cheered when she ran for the State senate in 1966 and won.

By the time she claimed her seat in the United States Congress in 1972, we knew—and the nation itself began to sense—that a star was born.

She no longer is ours exclusively. Her voice is an American voice now, speaking with compassion and with wisdom ... speaking for justice ... speaking with a compelling eloquence that has gripped this nation's heart and held its people spellbound.

My husband once said of her: "I don't know where her future's going to take her, but wherever she goes, we'll be right behind her."

As we follow her, we are pleased to share her leadership with the nation ... but we are proud to claim her as our own.

KEYNOTE SPEECH BY CONGRESSWOMAN BARBARA JORDAN
FIRST PLENARY SESSION
NOVEMBER 19, 1977

... If you read the 31st Chapter, it begins a litany of praise for the worthy woman. It begins this way: "Who can find a virtuous woman for her price is far above others." From virtue to power. What we are about here now will require no small amount of virtue and a great deal of power.

The value of women mostly in a narrowly construed fashion has been recognized throughout the ages, but the value of women has been periodically re-evaluated and is sometimes devalued.

American history is peppered with efforts by women to be recognized as human beings and as citizens and to be included in the whole of our national life.

This Conference is one more effort on the part of women for total recognition and total inclusion.

The success or failure of this Conference is our responsibility and we should not waste one moment trying to find scapegoats.

If this Conference succeeds, there will be ample accolades for everybody, and, if it fails, all of you may look into your mirror and identify a contributing culprit. ...

The goals of this Conference are as logical and reasonable to me as the goals President Carter talks about of human rights in America's foreign policy.

If Americans were asked to differentiate or distinguish between what characterized other countries and what characterizes us, we would say our high regard for the individual. That's the thing which makes us different.

We endorse personal and political freedom as a national right of human pride. Human rights are more than abstractions, particularly when they are limited or non-existent. Human rights apply equally to Soviet dissidents, Chilean peasants and American women.

Women are human. We know our rights are limited. We know our rights are violated. We need a domestic human rights program.

This Conference could be the beginning of such an effort, and we should not allow ourselves to be brainwashed by people who predict chaos for us and failure for us.

Tell them they lie and move on. ...

This Conference is inclusive; everybody is here and everyone must be free to define the meaning of total woman, for herself.

The differences among us at this Conference cannot and should not be ignored. They are rational; the difference is economic, cultural, social, political, ideological—the differences are there.

The delegates to this Conference are certainly not of a single mind. We should not be of a single mind. No one person and no sub-group at this Conference has the right answers. "Wonder Woman" is not a delegate. The "Bionic Woman" is not here either.

American representatives are here to try to work through the problems of this Conference. Of course we will debate, of course we will differ. We will plead and placate ... We will persuade and dissuade, and, when a debate becomes heated, I hope you will remember Lyndon Johnson's invocation, and, Isaiah's invocation: "Come now, let us reason together."

This statement was made by Hubert Humphrey recently on the floor of the United States Senate, and, he was talking about the Senate when he said: "There are no problems between the different points of view, and this body that cannot be reconciled if we are willing to give a little and share a little." Do that. We can't expect it all to be our way.

At a time when this country is drifting, if it is not shifting to the right, civil rights and affirmative action efforts are lagging.

This is the time for foot soldiers, not "Kamikaze" pilots. What occurs here and what does not occur here can make a difference in our personal and selective lives.

The legislation which authorized this Conference mandated a course of future action. One hundred and 20 days after we finish here, a report is to be submitted to each house of the Congress. What will you have in it?

A hundred and 20 days after that, President Carter is to submit recommendations to each house of the Congress based on the report which emanates from this body. What will he recommend? Eight months from the time we leave here, something is supposed to happen.

Recommendations will be submitted. Well, I have no doubt that legislation which emanates from this Conference ... will have a better chance of passage if support for that recommendation is widespread.

Congress approved $5 million with its congratulations, but, if we do nothing here productive, constructive or healing, we will have wasted much more than money.

We will have wasted, lost, negated an opportunity to do something for ourselves and for generations which are not here.

Not making a difference is a cost we cannot afford.

The cause of equal and human rights will reap what is sown November 18th through November 21st, 1977.

What will you reap?
What will you sow?

SPEECH BY JUDY CARTER
SECOND PLENARY SESSION
NOVEMBER 19, 1977

I am honored to be asked to speak with you. I hold no office, and I have no title. I write things for *Redbook* magazine when my two-year-old will let me. Mostly, I am a housewife, and as Jason says, "just a plain old Mommy." I work hard. Most of the women in this room are also homemakers and mothers who have all mopped floors and wiped noses like every other plain old Mommy. It is an important choice, carefully made.

Whatever our other differences, we all care a lot about our families. When you have chosen to build a life with a husband and children, you are extremely protective of the stability and security of that family. The basic decisions made in each home about how to make enough money and how to spend time are never made lightly or without regard to the well-being of the children there. Our goal invariably is to provide the best possible life, and the most opportunities for our children.

We will never, in this country, be able to provide the best possible life and the most opportunities as long as woman are denied equal legal rights under the Constitution. Our daughters are second-class citizens the moment they are born, and mothers are prevented from contributing fully to their families.

Our society gives great lip service to the preservation of families, but by its laws and attitudes it does not in fact adequately value women who are mothers. In many states, women are not considered legal guardians of their own children. They cannot take any legal action in behalf of their children. Often, women are not the legal owners of anything, such as a home, purchased during marriage, even if they worked to make the payments on them. In that situation, women are also not allowed to will anything directly to their children. In most states, a husband is not legally required to support his wife and children as long as his marriage remains valid.

If the husband squanders the family income on himself or simply refuses to provide for his wife and children, the wife's only legal recourse is divorce. That is a drastic step indeed for the mother concerned about holding her family together.

The lack of protection women have under the law is not usually evident to the housewife whose husband adequately provides for her. For most homemakers, life goes along just fine until something happens to the husband. What happens if he dies? Men have traditionally spent a great deal of money on life insurance to care for their families in case something happens to them. They usually overlook the fact that the wife's legal status without him will severely hinder her efforts to maintain for her children any semblance of the life they formerly had.

Inheritance laws vary widely from State to State, but rarely does a widow have full authority over her husband's estate, even when she has worked diligently with him for many years to build it. Other laws which discriminate against women become evident when the wife becomes head of the household, as 18 million women are right now. Fair wages, equal credit opportunities, insurance, retirement benefits are much more important when she bears the total responsibility for her family. A widow is faced with the full responsibilities her husband had, without the same legal rights.

A woman who is divorced faces essentially the same problems a widow faces when she becomes head of the household. It is virtually certain that she will have to begin working to support her children. Her chances are about 50-50 that she will ever collect any alimony or child support from her former husband. The legal system, both the laws themselves and the enforcement of them, has not adequately assisted women who must raise children by themselves.

There is one change in our system that will help us all, regardless of our feelings on other women's issues. The most basic, elementary, legal change that needs to be made is to include women in the Constitution. Until women are accorded adequate legal rights, we cannot hope to make the other changes we all know are necessary. We cannot preserve our families and churches and other things precious to us without being a legal part of the system which protects them.

I believe that the most important vote that can come from this National Women's Conference is a resounding affirmation of our united determination to become part of the legal processes of this country.

Let us make it clear to the people of our country that a vote for ERA is a vote for a better life with greater opportunities for all our citizens.

Let us make it clear that we are proud to be the mothers and wives, the women of America, that we care deeply about our families and their future.

Let us make it clear that we will not be intimidated by lies or loud voices.

Let us make it clear that we will not be divided in our struggle to gain the simple fairness our country stands for around the world.

We are strong, and we are determined, and we will not fail.

SPEECH BY
JILL RUCKELSHAUS
FORMER PRESIDING OFFICER,
NATIONAL COMMISSION
SECOND PLENARY SESSION
NOVEMBER 19, 1977

The yearning of American women for some say in their destiny, some control of their lives, some choice, is as old as our country.

We had, in fact, a very unfortunate beginning. Abigail Adams wrote John in the Continental Congress: "Don't forget the ladies." He did.

So, women were resigned, from those first moments in our Nation's history, to a system of laws based on the Common Law of England in which women were listed this way: Idiots, lunatics, convicts, mental defectives, and women.

I think what I mind is being last. So, no women could vote; no women could own property; no women could make a contract in her own name.

The history of American women has been one of pushing back continually the very narrow limits that defined our lives, our actions, and our words, and, you can feel sympathy with the early women in this country who often faced great scorn and public ridicule for talking about women's rights, for talking about what they yearned to do in society and were kept from doing—because each one of you, by your presence here, and, by your involvement in the women's movement, has taken personal risk, has received personal scorn, has felt the pain and the misunderstanding and the criticism, sometimes, of those you love.

We are seeking, in fact, pretty fundamental change, and no change is ever made without struggle because there are always those who fear change, who prefer to accept conditions as they are instead of taking a risk, and, of course, there are those who are benefiting from the status quo.

It is important to know that not all the women who work for the advancement of women's role in society agree on every issue. So, let's not be surprised that we are not of one mind here. How boring if we were. Let's celebrate our diversity.

There is no one credo for all the women in this country. I find our individual opinions, our passions, our dissension, to be very healthy. We are not controlled; we have not been dictated to.

Take a look at the resolutions. They have come forward from 50 State conventions.

There is no scheme involved with these resolutions.

Your presence amidst such great controversy expresses the openness of those State meetings.

What has always seemed so strange to me is the curious standards imposed by leaders and the media on issues which involve women.

When a national problem, such as the energy crisis, or inflation, or housing, or the environment, or the consumer movement or human rights, has the support of over 50 percent of the people, according to George Gallup or anybody else's poll, it is called the "national will," and anything over 55 percent is overwhelmingly national support. If a politician wins an election by even 51 percent of the vote, he is accepted as the winner and new leader.

Why is it that the support of over 50 percent of the people in this country for women's issues is held up to a different standard?

According to a recent Gallup Poll, 63 percent of all the people in this country, male and female, young and old, support the goals of the women's movement.

Yet, the press and many politicians claim that women can't agree on what they want. Why is total unanimity suddenly demanded on women's issues?

Over 60 percent of the general public, by many polls I have seen, support the Equal Rights Amendment. Yet, politicians continue to dodge, and weave, and say, "Well, women themselves can't agree on this issue. What do you expect us to do?"

We live with a double standard. There is no doubt about that. But, we have a chance here in Houston to mortally wound that standard by our words and by our actions.

In Mexico City, at the United Nations Conference for Women, the aims and goals of that conference were badly reported by the media.

They covered the shouting confrontations, the furious debate, the expressions of impatience, and they reported to the audience in the United States a conference of conflict and disorder.

That is not how it happened, but that is how it was reported, and that is how most of the people in the United States still think about the conference in Mexico City. So, the leaders say: "Well, you women don't know what you want." And, they did nothing. That must not happen here.

My good, good friends, over a very long journey, everything we believe in and have worked so hard for is at risk here. All the hours we have spent together, all the lessons we have learned, all of the progress we have made, all the understanding we have earned from our families and friends, all the momentum of our successes, our honor as women, all is at risk here in Houston.

The weight of the lives of our grandmothers and great-grandmothers is very heavy on our shoulders. The words they might have spoken are whispers in our minds.

The hopes of those young women, hundreds of thousands like them, who ran those 2,000 miles and carried the torch from Seneca Falls to Houston, is a care wound around our hearts.

We have before us an historic task; make no mistake about that. Just as we now speak of Seneca Falls and the suffrage movement, women from now on will speak of the Women's Conference in Houston.

We have a very, very difficult task. Those of us with concerns which have been excluded from the consideration or acceptance by the established bodies must have them heard here. Those people must find our sensitivity and care.

We must listen with concern to those whose faces have been turned from by the Establishment. They must find love and support here.

We must be open to one another's concerns. We must put aside our defensiveness, our fear, put aside ourselves and listen very hard.

Every issue in our plan of action is just as important as the others. Those at the end of the alphabet have equal importance as those at the beginning.

We must have a full hearing for each recommendation, but we will need to impose discipline on ourselves to achieve that end. The responsibility is entirely ours.

We have been moving toward this day for 200 years. We must leave here with a message that is unmistakable to the country that is watching. We must show such courage and gallantry and maturity that America will watch this Houston Conference and feel respect for the song that we are singing and admiration for the singers.

I would like to ask you all to stand and join hands with one another right now and to join with me in an affirmation of this Conference. Will you follow me?

We are here, America. We are here in America at last, at last, to move history forward. With patience we will listen. With wisdom we will decide. With vision and courage we will seek equality and liberty. And this time, America, we will not be denied.

SPEECH BY CONGRESSWOMAN MARGARET M. HECKLER
THIRD PLENARY SESSION
NOVEMBER 19, 1977

Picture a young law school graduate, one who had been published in the *Law Review,* one who was well qualified as a beginning lawyer.

She answered an advertisement for a part-time legal opportunity and was interviewed by the hiring partner. She was told: "Your credentials are excellent, but we would never hire you. You're a mother. You can't be serious about being a lawyer."

I was that young lawyer and young mother. I am still a mother. I am a God-loving, pro-family woman. I am a member of the Commission on the Observance of International Women's Year. I am a Member of Congress and a vigorous supporter of the Equal Rights Amendment. Those qualifications are not incompatible.

If each of you sketched a profile of herself, she would portray characteristics that identify the self-uniqueness of each one of us.

This Conference reflects the women of this country, with their differing personalities, varying backgrounds, different philosophies, and various goals. This Conference offers an opportunity for the sharing of our uniqueness and our diversity. It is not a melting pot; it is a potpourri.

We have a similar situation in Congress, where 15 of the women members have joined together to form the Congresswomen's Caucus. I have the honor of chairing that caucus with my distinguished colleague, Congresswoman Elizabeth Holtzman of New York.

The caucus transcends political, philosophical, and regional viewpoints in the sharing of information about the problems of women. It is moving on many fronts—to correct inequities in the laws as they relate to women.

The women in Congress united a week ago to win veterans' benefits for a group of women pilots who had

been struggling 33 years to achieve those benefits despite their obvious qualifications to receive them.

This underscores a basic political lesson that there is no limit to what women can achieve when they work together. This Conference will deal with a potpourri of issues. The question in my mind is this: What is the lowest common denominator among the needs of women in America? My answer is: economic equality.

What has Congress done to encourage economic equality? The Equal Pay Act, in effect since 1963, is enforced by the Equal Employment Opportunity Commission. When it was passed, women represented one-third of the work force and earned 60 percent of the wages of men. Today women comprise 56 percent of the work force and earn 57 percent of the wages of men.

It is a fact, sad enough to make me shudder, that the EEOC has a backlog of 130,000 cases. This was brought home to me dramatically when a woman sought my help during office hours in my district. She is a 57-year-old college professor. She has done all the right things—published in professional journals, represented her institution in the community.

Yet she earns $10,000 a year less than her male colleagues. This woman has filed a complaint with the EEOC, but there is no guarantee it will be adjudicated within her working years.

Social security legislation is replete with sex discrimination. The married woman realizes few benefits from her social security payments because she can only collect from one account, usually her husband's. Therefore, she loses the contribution she has made to the social security system—billions of dollars.

I sponsored and worked vigorously to achieve passage of the Equal Credit Opportunity Act to prohibit discrimination on the basis of sex or marital status. But that act is not vigorously enforced.

These are the facts. One might suggest: Why not ask Congress to change the laws and impose enforcement? As a Congresswoman with 11 years of experience, I am here to report to you that it will take too many Congresses to amend the existing laws and achieve the equality we seek.

Although I respect my colleagues in Congress and I respect the institution itself, I know there are too many issues facing Congress. There is not sufficient commitment on the part of Congress to place women's issues in the forefront.

Furthermore, these laws, no matter how well intentioned, are mere band-aid solutions. Women will not achieve true equality—equal justice under law—until we have a constitutional basis for that equality. Only the Equal Rights Amendment can do that.

Comparing the ERA with these piecemeal solutions reminds me of the beginnings of the age of flight, when individuals first attempted to fly, strapping wings to their backs, flapping their arms, inventing contraptions which they felt would enable them to soar, like the creatures of the air. But these devices barely got off the ground. It was only when the inventors added the engine—the power—to the emerging structure that the flying machine began to succeed. The surge of power propelling the wings lifted it up, above the forces that held it earthbound.

The Equal Rights Amendment is the power of constitutional protection that will allow women's equality to become airborne. Without the ERA, women's equality will continue to flap its wings, making small leaps forward, struggling against the forces that hold us down. With the ERA, we will have the power, the constitutional foundation to soar above our current limitations, limitations which have bound us to limited choice of opportunity.

There must be greater commitment if we are to pass the ERA. Your commitment to constitutional action can awaken the conscience of the country and of those who hold the power to ratify the ERA.

A country that can put men on the moon can put women in the Constitution. If we really believe in the inscription engraved on the Supreme Court building, equal justice under law, the ERA is the only way to achieve it. Put your power behind the ERA—now!

SPEECH BY HONORABLE PATSY MINK ASSISTANT SECRETARY OF STATE (FORMER CONGRESSWOMAN AND CO-SPONSOR PL 94-167)
THIRD PLENARY SESSION
NOVEMBER 19, 1977

Your presence at this National Conference for Women attests to the importance you give to the changing role of women and the need to resolve a dynamic agenda for our future.

No matter who argues to the contrary, I believe there is a cross-section of America present here tonight and that your deliberations will reflect the major forces for change and reform in our society to the end that women shall be finally equal under the law.

Thousands of women who vied for your delegate's badges are not here but we are acutely aware they are vitally concerned that this event not only achieve a high place in history but that it record accurately the current attitudes and aspirations of women in our contemporary society.

Two hundred years have gone by to shape this nation, to give its institutions direction and purpose, to enable its citizens to flourish and enjoy the blessings of liberty and freedom. Each step of the way towards the building of our democracy has been hard fought.

The struggles of the blacks and of all minorities to be accepted and accorded the fullness of opportunity and recognition has been etched in blood and anguish and the struggle still continues.

This meeting of women is unique in that unlike the true minorities, you possess the numerical majority to make this country whatever you choose.

This is the obvious anomaly as well as the challenge of this historic convocation.

Our destiny is in our own creation. Do we want change? How shall we achieve it? How do we mobilize this numerical majority of women to act? How do we appeal to their self-interest and gain their support for issues which are so vital to our full birth as human beings?

How do we generate a common understanding that the mere denial to a single woman on account of sex of a job, of a promotion, of a scholarship, of a recognition, of an opportunity to be a self-supporting individual is an abrogation of the rights of all women for which we cannot remain silent, for silence is acquiescence to our own derogation.

There are some who would ridicule our efforts to improve the status of women here and elsewhere. They will try to radicalize simple efforts to state the fundamental principles of equality and our efforts to apply them to all persons, including women.

Anti-ERA attitudes are generated because equality is feared and the goal of status for women as persons under our Constitution to them threatens the basis of their preference for subordination.

So under the guise of "save the home," women are being told that equality will threaten their rights as homemakers. It is unproductive, it seems to me, to debate that issue with its advocates. What we need to do is take our cause affirmatively to the American woman. We need to dramatize the reality that you and I are homemakers, too, that you and I have struggled separately for the most part of our entire adult lives to breathe life into equality, that we have pushed our way into the centers of business, of science, of government, of politics, despite the barriers that have only recently begun to be lifted because of our newly achieved collective strength.

This Conference, for me, is the culmination of a life's work—no small part of it being motivated by the intense wish that somehow all the personal affronts, put-downs, and outright discriminations which I endured to make my own way as a human being can be spared my daughter and yours.

I am therefore all the more incensed by those who would paint as anti-family, women who have lived hardships and out of their personal experiences are now committed to finding solutions for their children's future security and happiness.

We, each of us, have a great challenge to permit this Conference to express the will and determination of women who do desire equality before the law and who seek changes in status so that women can obtain positions of responsibility.

Women are needed as active participants in all institutions and forums of public policy. Women need to have a more direct voice in the formulation of policies and programs that vitally affect their lives and the lives of their family. Until we do, the maxim of our democracy "of the people and by the people" is diminished by half.

This is the high goal which this Conference must obtain. It must serve as a significant event of the coming together of women across this land, charged with a sense of importance and deeply committed as a group to achieve positive gains for women in all aspects of living. There can be no equivocation on this point.

No matter how vigorously we may disagree and debate procedures and strategies, the bottom line for this Conference must be a serious attempt to provoke meaningful change so that American women of the future can be assured justice, equal protection under the law, and full participation in their own government as proclaimed by our Constitution.

We know that we are at the most critical juncture of our Nation's history. The country is watching you tonight. What is the public verdict to be on this meeting? What we do here will determine whether we will be joined by the public in what could be this century's most significant policy platforms for the future.

I place my life, my future, and that of my family in the wise and effective deliberations which I have every expectation will highlight this Conference beyond all predictions.

With faith, perserverence, and personal commitment, the cause of justice and sisterhood will triumph at last.

SPEECH BY HONORABLE HELVI SIPILA ASSISTANT SECRETARY GENERAL, UNITED NATIONS
THIRD PLENARY SESSION
NOVEMBER 19, 1977

Two years ago, at the end of International Women's Year, there was a cartoon in a town in Finland. This cartoon showed me, the Secretary General of the International Women's Year, washing up the dishes and perspiring and my husband sitting in a rocking chair reading the newspaper and saying to me, "Now, Helvi, it's the end of the year. Go to the fridge and bring me some beer."

The 129-year long history of the role of women in the United States, from the first nationwide meeting at Seneca Falls to today's National Conference, is the American version of a global story of changes in the status, situation, and role of women who have all shared a common fate.

For thousands of years, most of the world's women have lived in society structured and dominated by men, as dependents whose value was in their reproductive capacity and in their labor. Traditions and customs, constitutions and laws, all bear evidence to this.

Women who were bound to their restricted roles by circumstances or lack of awareness or lack of choice and whose situation remained the same through generations were hardly aware of any possibility for change.

In this respect, the first meeting at Seneca Falls in 1848 was a great contribution to a development in the status and role of women in many societies and in many fields.

Look at the situation in 1848. No woman in any country had political rights. Women had very limited access to education and none at all to higher education.

Women had very limited opportunities in the economic field. Women, especially married women, had an inferior status in civil law.

Much has been changed, although slowly, but we have to be grateful to your country for having paved the way for many changes, and we have to be grateful to women in the Western hemisphere who brought the principles of equal rights to the United Nations Charter.

The Proclamation of the International Women's Year 1975 and the present decade for women are direct results of the work of the United Nations and especially the Commission on the Status on Women.

One difference between the past efforts and today's efforts is the fact that government nowadays realizes that unless there will be changes in the situation of women, political, economic, social, and cultural targets of development will not be met.

The situation and needs of the two billion women of the world are varied both in kind and degree. These differences became increasingly clear during International Women's Year.

Some of us in the industrialized countries have our main emphasis on the equality of men and women. Women from the developing countries, where over 70 percent of the world's population lives, emphasize that without changes in the situation of women and development there can be no future for humanity.

In many ways, International Women's Year was a pioneer year. It was a year for fact-finding and for planning and now it is a time for action.

We have a first direction, which is the first social, economic and political plan that men and women all over the world have ever had together.

It was drafted by women. It was adopted at the conference where women formed majorities, and perhaps this is the reason why it's so practical.

National action is, naturally, most important, and this is why your action here is important for your country, but it's equally important for every other country, because we are interdependent . . . .

Our interdependent world is faced with an increasing number of problems which cannot be solved by any country alone. They require joint efforts. And in many of the problem areas, women can play the key role. The quality of life of all people and the future of humanity depend on the action of hundreds of millions of women. Their behavior and their action is of crucial importance in bringing new life, in the maintenance of life, and in assuring the human rights and basic needs of everyone.

I would like to say to you, my friends, it depends on you and us and hundreds of millions of other women what the future of women, men, and children in the world will be, and we need each other.

In conclusion, I would like to say I wish that the National Conference of Women of the United States, once again as it was in Seneca Falls, will be an inspiration and the unifying factor for all the women in our joint endeavor to assume increasing responsibility for the development of our nations and our world and for the peace and security of humankind.

**COMMISSIONER
CECILIA PRECIADO-BURCIAGA
COMMISSIONER
CARMEN DELGADO VOTAW
HISPANIC DIALOGUE**
FOURTH PLENARY SESSION
SUNDAY, NOVEMBER 20, 1977

CPB—Sisters, hermanas,

CDV—Amigas, Compañeras, We would like to share with you, as we have shared in the past, the struggles that accompany any major strides or improvements in the conditions that affect our lives.

CPB—And what, may you ask, are the aspirations of Hispanas?

CDV—¿Que metas persiguen las Hispanas?

CPB—We, the Hispanic women of America, can repeat forcefully, in unison, with you: *WE WANT EQUALITY.*

CDV—*BUSCAMOS LA IGUALDAD.*

CDV—We are the fastest growing segment of the population and in the coming decade the strength of our numbers will be felt.

CPB—Nuestra población aumenta rápidamente y para el 1980 seremos la minoría mas numerosa en este país.

CDV—What are our issues?

CPB—¿Cuales son nuestros problemas?

CDV—They are the very same issues you are trying to resolve, to move women forward.

CPB—Nuestros problemas son empleo, educación, salud, vivienda.

CDV—Our problems are the age-old ones of employment, education, health, housing, etc.—the whole list of issues covered in the draft Plan of Action.

CPB—What do we seek to convey as Hispanas?

CDV—¿Que deseamos ustedes comprendan?

CPB—Que necesitamos el reconocimiento de ustedes, con respeto a nuestra herencia cultural y linguística y el aprecio a nuestra contribución al enriquecimiento de este pueblo, de esta nación.

CDV—We seek—nay—demand, your recognition and respect for our cultural and linguistic heritage, your appreciation of our contribution to the enrichment of this nation.

CPB—Why do we claim double jeopardy?

CDV—¿Por qué creemos el discrimen es mas agudo contra nosotras?

CPB—Because discrimination against us is two-pronged: because of sex and because of origin.

CDV—El discrimen que afrontamos es doble: por nuestro sexo y por nuestro origen.

CPB—What do we want to stress?

CDV—The tenacity and dedication of all minority women to walk apace with the rest of society in dignity and collaboration, to proclaim that we have Unity-Unidad. Please shout these key words with us—UNITY-UNIDAD! That we seek EQUALITY-IGUALDAD!

CPB—La tenacidad y determinación de todas las mujeres minoritarias de caminar a la par con el resto de ustedes en dignidad y colaboración. We believe in a common destiny that will bind us together in our efforts for the advancement of women.

CDV—Creemos en un destino comun que nos unirá en nuestros esfuerzos por el mejoramiento en la condición de la mujer.

CPB—We believe that blacks, whites, Chicanas, Cubanas, Puertoriqueñas, Native and Asian Americans—*the whole pluralistic spectrum of our society—can join hands and we urge you to join hands with your neighbor now and, as we will do, join your voices with ours in proclaiming the greatness of American women:*

CDV—Unánse con nosotras y extiendan la mano a la persona que esté cerca de ustedes para proclamar en coro, al unísono, la grandeza de la mujer americana:

CPB—¡QUE VIVA LA MUJER AMERICANA—ARRIBA—ARRIBA!

CDV—UNITY—EQUALITY!

CPB—UNIDAD—IGUALDAD!

CDV/CPB—¡QUE VIVA LA MUJER!—¡QUE VIVA!

SPEECH BY HONORABLE MARGARET MEAD
FOURTH PLENARY SESSION
NOVEMBER 20, 1977

Women of America, I am only allowed 10 minutes to speak, so let's not waste any of it in demonstrations until the end because I want to use it as fully as possible.

Demonstrations about me, I mean.

This Conference may well be a turning point, not only in the history of the women's movement, and not only in the history of the movement of the world, but, in the history of the world itself.

We have a chance, at last, to act as women in a way that women have not been able to act, virtually since the paleolithic period.

Someone talked last night about restoring women to full partnership with men. They haven't been there since the development of large-scale civilization, when they were left behind at the hearth as the men organized up and up and up until now they have got to the position where they can cook millions of tons of food without ever remembering that anybody eats it.

Women's traditional tasks through history, during which they cooperated with men to make a full society, were to care for the young and the old and the weak and the poor and the preservation of society. When they were left behind and robbed of any political power for the last 10,000 years, civilization has been in charge of only one sex.

Men know a lot about dying but they don't know enough about living. It has been women's biological and social and cultural task through history to live.

It is true that women risk their lives in childbirth and men risk their lives on the borders protecting their country. Men had to be willing to die and to kill for the safety of their women and children and their land and their faiths, but women had to be willing to live day after day, year after year, caring for the everyday needs of children who would have died without them.

At this moment in history, the United States is the richest and strongest country in the world. It is the country ... that has the greatest chance to save the world.

The women's movement has at least succeeded in placing enough women in strategic positions of power so that our disarmament discussions this morning came from women in strategic positions.

We have women on Congressional committees; we have women in disarmament agencies; we have women in all the points that are essential for an understanding that we must stop this arms race and we must stop the proliferation of nuclear power if we are going to protect the people of the world.

So, it may be thought that we have now reached "take-off" point. We have a President who is willing to undertake leadership in stopping nuclear weapons proliferation and deescalating the arms race and stopping ourselves from being "merchants of death."

It is not, I say, without historic significance that we share the news today with an attempt to solve the problems between Israel and the Arabs by human friendliness instead of by giving weapons to both sides. It is amazing what it is possible now to do. I think if we can ask, on the one hand, why women have arisen to the call for peace, and then, gone home again and risen, and then, gone home again and risen, and then, gone home again, we can say we have never had a concerted movement before because most of the appeals that have been made to us have been threats and women are very hard to scare.

It has been women's task throughout history to go on believing in life, when there was almost no hope, and they are unable to deal only with despair. What we must present to every woman in this country today is that if we will act unitedly, forget every other consideration on earth, as we do when our children are at stake, we may be able to turn this world around and produce a world in which our children and other people's children will be safe.

SPEECH BY COMMISSIONER ADDIE WYATT
CLOSING PLENARY SESSION
NOVEMBER 21, 1977

"Sisters, sometimes I wish my eyes hadn't been opened. Sometimes I wish I could no longer see all of the pain, the hurt and the longing of my sisters and me as we try to be free.

"Sometimes I wish my eyes hadn't been opened just for an hour; how sweet it would be not to be struggling, not to be striving, but just completely secure in our slavery.

"But now that I have seen with my eyes, I can't close them because deep inside me somewhere and somehow I will still know the road that my sisters and I have to travel. My heart would say yes and my feet would say no.

"Sometimes I wish my eyes hadn't been opened, but now that they have I am determined to see that somehow my sisters and I will be this day the free people we were created to be."

I want to thank Carol Ederly for those beautiful words penned in her poem, "Sometimes I Wish My Eyes Hadn't Been Opened," because I think it so very well expresses the sentiment of so many of us who have been involved in this struggle and other struggles of this kind for so many years.

We have arrived here this morning, I hope sincerely, for the intent of doing what is necessary to bridge the gap between the promise and the fulfillment of freedom, equality and the fullest opportunities possible for all women in America and women in the world.

So on that basis, on those bases we greet you and we ask God's blessings upon all of our efforts today.

It is my hope and my desire that we will meet here today, realizing that most people fall into at least three major categories: namely, there are some people who go through life watching things happen; they just watch.

There are some people who go through life just wondering what is happening.

Then there are some people who go through life making things happen.

I am proud this morning to be among so many of you who are very capable of making things happen, and especially our Plan of Action as we rededicate and recommit ourselves to move American women forward.

I want to commend you for the manner in which you conducted yourselves yesterday under the most strenuous circumstances.

We met, we debated, we agreed, we disagreed, we acted and some reacted, but still we remained intact and I have yet to see an assembly as large as this that can conduct themselves in the manner that you, my sisters, conducted yourselves yesterday.

I want you to take time to shake hands with your sister next to you to congratulate her as you congratulate yourselves. If there is a brother next to you, shake his hand. Wasn't that wonderful? It gives you a good feeling to be able to shake hands with a sister or a brother.

SPEECH BY HONORABLE MARGARET "MIDGE" COSTANZA ASSISTANT TO THE PRESIDENT
CLOSING PLENARY SESSION
NOVEMBER 21, 1977

We have spent four days together, and after 25 years of active political and public life, I can stand before you and I can say I am a woman and somehow it has a new meaning. It has a new feeling. It has a new power. It has a whole new identity and a hell of a lot of pride.

What I love most about these days is that I continually learn from those who have gone and still are going ahead of me. I learned from those who are coming behind me and it was a learning process that I am taking back to my community and sharing with those who could not be here with us.

I feel so strongly about the ERA and the fact that I want to be legalized in this Constitution of the United States. I am woman and I want the right to choose my own destiny and whether that destiny be housewife or mother or assistant to the President, it is not what you choose but the right to make that choice.

The message has gone out loud and clear that I am woman. I may be poor, I may be black, I may be Hispanic, I may be Asian, I may be a Native American or, I may be an Italian American or any other ethnic; but I'll tell you I want my human dignity. Not as a privilege, but as a right.

I am not a mother, but if I were a mother I would want a decent education for my children. If I were a mother and if I were on welfare I would not want anyone to think I am lazy and shiftless and that I do not want to work. I want them to know I want to work when they will give me decent child care so I can go out and get a job. If I have children and they are abused, I want a safe place to put that child. The message has gone out loud and clear. I am woman and I am handicapped and I don't want your pity. I want to be part of the mainstream of life, the equal opportunity to be part of everything that you are, as a total human being.

I am woman and I want the right to love whomever I please without any harassment. And without discrimination and the fear of losing my job.

I am a woman who also happens to be assistant to the President of the United States. I have trust and confidence in the depth of Jimmy Carter's commitment to women. I know that the response from Jimmy Carter will be sensitive as he will respond to the messages that we send out to the Nation and to the world from this Conference. To use his phrase, you can depend on that.

But what now? I have gone through some of the issues and the sensitivity and the priorities that we have set here in the last four days; but what now?

What happens when you leave this Conference and you go back into your communities to your organizations?

What happens with the information and the renewed strength and commitment that you got here the last four days?

Will it become just a great exhilarating memory? Will it become something you will always remember as being a historic event and nothing more? It cannot be. You must go back to your community. You're going to have to defeat those elected officials who do not share a sensitivity.

You will elect those who do share a sensitivity and commitment and you will give support to those appointed and elected officials who have the courage to stand up for what they believe, even though it may be uncomfortable and controversial. But more fully, you will stay alive.

I have had the most exhiliarating four days of my life and the most meaningful and I think it is because I have had an opportunity to share myself, my life—my most valuable commodity—with all of you.

There were many people who served as Commissioners on International Women's Year. All of them are committed to other professions and activities. They have given so much of their time and efforts. To them as women, to them as sisters, as an assistant to the President who named them, I thank you all so very much for sharing with us.

SPEECH BY BILLIE MASTERS CHAIR, NATIONAL AMERICAN INDIAN AND ALASKAN NATIVE WOMEN'S CONFERENCE
CLOSING PLENARY SESSION
NOVEMBER 21, 1977

I bring you greetings from the American Indian and Alaskan native women that are here with you today. We have participants, delegates, and observers from the Indian world and the native peoples of this land here.

There are very special items in our lives that remain with us as the best memories and the best experience of our lives, and those are the times when we are accepted, recognized, and appreciated for our efforts and our concerns.

This is one of the times that we feel that we have been accepted here, that we have been heard and our efforts have been appreciated and we thank you.

What is an Indian? That is a question we have to face so often, and I would like to tell you today that we have Federally recognized Indians and we have non-Federally recognized Indians.

We have tribal Indians and we have fullbloods and we have BIA-recognized and we have HEW-recognized; we have quarterbloods and halfbloods, and the divide and destroy concept is at work all the time.

The concept of divide and destroy cannot be something that we fall prey to. I have never heard of my black sisters being asked if they are fullbloods.

An Indian is an Indian. We are all together. Termination is a word that might be new to some of you here today, but it is a word that remains as a constant threat to the American Indian woman and the Alaskan Native woman in this country.

Termination is the destruction of all government responsibility and the destruction of the traditional lifestyle of the native people; and we ask you to take an active part to dedicate yourselves to eliminate the threat of termination that exists in the Indian world. We would like you to do that personally, to accept that as your charge, as you leave here today. I wish to make you aware. I wish you could look into the issues. I wish you could ask embarrassing questions of your Congressmen and your Congresswomen and ask what is being done to protect these lifestyles and to assure the existence of the traditional way of the Alaskan Native people and their reservations. Reservation, by definition, is all the Indians have left. One-tenth of one percent of their original land. We need

you to be aware that no Indian people want to give up their reservations. The land base that we have today, even though inadequate for our people and even though low in economic standards, job opportunities, and schools, is the very core of the lifestyle for the American people, and the reservation land base must be secured to the American Indian woman and to all the future generations so that we can have this always, for our own sovereignty.

Something that America feels strongly about is sovereignty—the right of people to govern themselves, to be recognized—and now the sovereignty of the American Indian people is threatened.

I cannot begin to tell you the importance of this issue, but I would like your support. I would like you to become aware, to ask questions about sovereignty, and to protect the sovereignty for the native people of this land.

SPEECH BY BRENDA PARKER PRESIDENT, FUTURE HOME-MAKERS OF AMERICA
CLOSING PLENARY SESSION
NOVEMBER 21, 1977

We have it in our power to shape change. We may choose one future over another. We cannot, however, be content with the past in our family forms as well as in our economics, science, technology and social relationships.

We will be forced to deal with change and movement. I have been delighted that this Conference has dealt so strongly with the roles of women and especially the homemaker. Women and men should be guaranteed equality of rights, both in the home and the world of work.

I feel a good definition of a homemaker is anyone who shares in the responsibility of making the home a nurturing self-value, goal-setting, self-fulfilled environment. It is not a label to pin on any one person. Indeed, men, as well as women, children, grandparents, single people, can and do fill this role.

The Future Home Makers of America have worked very hard to help people accept the changing roles of women and to adjust to the roles of men and women in today's society.

We feel that individuals should mold their own lifestyles, not according to a fixed pattern or stereotype. We do demand as a human right a full voice and a role for women in determining our world, our nation, our families, and our individual rights.

I urge all women, especially you, to become involved in helping achieve this goal and to help form a more perfect union.

We will continue our struggle for equality. Yes, from the leadership of Susan B. Anthony and Elizabeth Cady Stanton in Seneca Falls in 1848 to go on to achieve the right to vote to the leadership of Eleanor Roosevelt and then on to the seventies to Esther Peterson, Bella Abzug, and Barbara Jordan.

In the Future Home Makers of America we stress cooperation. Each of us, as we leave this National Women's Conference, must master the art of cooperation. We must cooperate to make our vote truly democratic, and bring the promise of a bright future, not only for women but for men as well, for our children and our families.

HEARING ON DISARMAMENT AND PEACE ISSUES

(Held in conjunction with National Women's Conference)

U.S. MILITARY FORCES, ARMS REDUCTIONS AND SECURITY

Randall Forsberg, Fellow, Program for Science and International Affairs, Harvard University
November 20, 1977

If we are going to have a safe and reasonable military policy in this country, the majority of the people have to have a hand in shaping that policy. Today, practically the only people who can tell you where our defense dollars go are those with a personal stake in the matter. The military establishment is the single largest business in the country, providing full income to 5,000,000 employees of the Defense Department and the arms industries, and supplementing the income of another 2,000,000 reservists and retired officers. Naturally, these people have an interest in seeing that the military budget is not cut.

What powerful group is there on the other side, who have a personal interest in paying attention to our military policy and making sure that the budget and forces are kept to the minimum needed for peace? There is no such special group. There are only the citizens at large, whose taxes, quality of life, political and social order, peace and, ultimately, survival are at stake. For this reason, it is essential for you and for women throughout America to know what military forces the United States has and what the rationales for these forces are; to form your own opinion about a safe military force and budget; and to spread information and work for political action on these issues.

Concretely, I would like to start this process by describing the main components of U.S. forces and their rationales, and then showing why I think there is a wide margin for arms reduction. Let me begin with the surprising view that the Defense Department is rather like the emperor whose new clothes were invisible, in the sense that practically none of the defense budget is spent, speaking quite literally, on national defense. What this means will become clear as I run through the various components and their functions.

The Defense Department divides our military forces into two kinds, which they call the strategic forces and the general-purpose forces. Strategic, in this context, means concerned with the vital interests of the homeland. General purpose, obviously, is a catchall for everything else. If research and reserves and other support activities are divided between the two, then out of the $120 billion Carter defense budget for 1978, only $20 billion or so goes to the strategic forces, while about $80 billion goes to the general-purpose forces. The remaining $20 billion is divided between retired pay and Intelligence and Communications.

Within the strategic category are what are called offensive forces and defensive forces. The offensive forces are the long-range nuclear weapons that we hear and talk most about. These include 400 B-52 bomber aircraft, built between 1958 and 1962, which can each carry four to six nuclear bombs or air-to-surface missiles. They also include the long-range ballistic missiles.

We have about a thousand land-based intercontinental ballistic missiles, ICBMs, located underground, in concrete-reinforced silos, in eight Western and Midwestern states. These were built between 1960 and 1967. A similar force of Soviet ICBMs, 1,500 rather than 1,000, was built between 1964 and 1971. We also have similar missiles, somewhat smaller, based on submarines and called submarine-launched ballistic missiles or SLBMs. The United States has 41 strategic submarines with 16 ballistic missiles on each, making about 650 SLBMs. These were also built between 1960 and 1967. The Soviet Union started building similar submarines in 1967 and they are just finishing a production run of 54 subs, some with 12 missiles and some with 16, making about 800 Soviet SLBMs. In all, both sides have around 2,000 long-range delivery vehicles, that is, missiles and bombers.

Between 1970 and 1977, most of the original American missiles were replaced by new missiles which have several small (Hiroshima-sized) nuclear warheads in the nose cone, instead of one giant H-bomb. The nose cone acts like a bus, aiming individual warheads at different targets and letting them fly off alone. These multiple reentry vehicles, called MIRVs, have increased the number of nuclear warheads on the land-based missiles from 1,000 to 2,000. On the submarines, where there are 10 warheads per missile, the increase is much bigger: the force has gone from 650 bombs to about 5,000, giving the United States an overall total of about 9,000 deliverable warheads. The Soviet Union, lagging five or six years behind, started a MIRV program like ours in 1976 and will probably finish with comparable numbers of nuclear warheads in the early 1980s. At the same time, the United States already has programs underway to replace the current forces with new submarines, called Trident, which will carry 24 missiles instead of 16, and new land-based missiles, called MX, which will also carry larger warheads.

These offensive nuclear weapons, which absorb about $18 billion of the $20 billion bill for the strategic forces, are not meant to *defend* this country in the traditional sense. Their main function is to *deter* an attack on us, by threatening retaliation in kind. In contrast, the remaining $2-$3 billion of the strategic bill does go to strategic defense, which is the only component of the military budget aimed strictly at national defense. This defensive component, which accounts for less than five percent of the budget, is made up of five things: (1) radars, to warn of bomber or missile attack and, in the case of the missiles, give us 20 minutes or so to evacuate the cities; (2) a small number of interceptor aircraft, in case the Russians decide to use their 100 obsolete bombers instead of their missiles; (3) research on short-range missiles to intercept the incoming missiles (no way has been found to do this reliably); (4) civil defense shelters, about one-tenth of one percent of the budget; and, finally, (5) the Coast Guard, which protects our coastal waters but which is financed by the Department of Transportation rather than the Department of Defense, in essence because there is no military threat to the coasts.

Before commenting on the rationale for our nuclear policy, I would like to touch on the three main parts of the general-purpose forces, which take up most of the defense budget and are tied up with the nuclear rationale. These are the traditional World War II, or Vietnam-type, nonnuclear forces, also called conventional forces. First, there are ground troops, about one million men in the Army and the Marines, whose function is to seize,

hold, and keep territory. Second, the Air Force has tactical combat planes to give the ground troops air cover, attack enemy troops, and prevent enemy planes from attacking our troops. And third, there are the traditional naval forces, which, like the tactical air forces, comprise about one-half million men.

These forces are not maintained to defend the United States, for the simple reason that there is no nonnuclear military threat to this country. Neither the Soviet Union nor any other country has the transport ships and aircraft, the logistic support, the firepower cover, or the foothold on the continent which would be required to launch some sort of invasion or conventional attack on this country. If not national defense, then what are the functions of the general-purpose forces?

About half of the Army consists of what are called heavy divisions, with a lot of tanks and armor. These are meant to help defend Western Europe in the event of a nonnuclear war with the Soviet Union. The rest of the Army and the Marines are lighter divisions, with fewer tanks and armored vehicles. These are oriented mainly toward the Pacific and intervention in developing countries like Vietnam, Korea, or perhaps Angola. The Navy's roles are split like the Army's, though with greater emphasis on Third World intervention. Attack of weaker military powers is the main use of the aircraft carriers and amphibious landing ships, which would be highly vulnerable to Soviet action; these are needed only for areas where we don't have access to friendly bases; and, together with their defensive escorts, supply ships and aircraft, they account for over half the Navy budget. The rest of the Navy is composed of patrol aircraft, antisubmarine submarines, and convoy escorts, which

are supposed to defend the supply lines to Europe from Soviet submarine attack in case we have a long, nonnuclear World War II-type war. The tactical air force is flexible: it might be used either in Europe or in the Third World. In all, then, it seems that about half of general-purpose spending is oriented to aid Western Europe in a repeat of a nonnuclear, World War II-type war with the Soviet Union; and the other half is oriented mainly toward Vietnam-type conflicts in the Third World.

One thing that must be added to this picture is that while the general-purpose forces are equipped to fight without any nuclear weapons, as they did in Vietnam, they also have the capability to use short-range nuclear weapons. These are called tactical nuclear weapons and their supposed function is to attack other military forces: aircraft, ships, submarines, tanks, troop concentrations, supplies, and the like. These weapons are often ignored in the nuclear debate because they are not expected to be used on U.S. or Soviet territory; the countries in Europe and the Far East where they might be used cannot be so sanguine, however. In addition to our 9,000 strategic warheads, the United States is estimated to have about 20,000 tactical nuclear weapons, most Hiroshima-sized or larger. The Soviet Union also has several thousand of these weapons.

Taken together, it appears that U.S. military forces have very little to do, directly, with the defense of this country, and are much more concerned with having the capability to intervene in international crises and conflicts across the full spectrum of military power from guerrilla warfare through big conventional wars, supposedly contained tactical nuclear war, and up to intercontinental nuclear exchanges. To the extent that it is based on rational considerations, rather than just vested interests and generalized fears, this policy derives from a militarized response to international relations. It permits an interventionist position, which relies on being one-up, militarily, in every type of force and every sort of crisis. In my view, this is a dangerous and unnecessary military policy for three reasons.

First, it links the nuclear forces—and various advantages, disadvantages and war-fighting capabilities in nuclear weapons, above and beyond the basic, undeniable capability of the United States and the Soviet Union to destroy each other's urban population—to possible conflicts of interest and even conventional confrontations over relatively small issues. Having the danger of escalation to nuclear warfare behind our small moves on the international scene may give us some influence, but it does so by increasing the danger and the risk of nuclear war.

Second, as the leader in armaments technically and the world's strongest military power in an all-round sense, the United States contributes to perpetuating a high level of conventional arms, in a world where almost no one believes that a major conventional war among the industrialized countries is possible any longer. Maintaining these arms may increase the likelihood of such a war and dampen or obstruct the development, which is growing anyway, of constructive international relations and institutions.

Third, with regard to both nuclear and conventional arms, the resources absorbed by the military in the United States and the Soviet Union, and increasingly in other countries, particularly Third World countries, have represented a much larger portion of the national product since World War II than was ever the case in peacetime before then: 5-10 percent now as against at most 1-3 percent earlier. There seems to be no rational cause or excuse for the present degree of militarization, except perhaps the failure of the populations to insist that it is not necessary to be heavily armed in order to deter war. Indeed, the poised balance of excessive arms, particularly nuclear arms, poses a far greater threat than much smaller military forces would do.

This conclusion is, of course, a matter of judgment. I hope you will, during and after this meeting, listen, read, and consider further on the matter; and, if you come to the same conclusion, encourage other women to find out what's going on and play an active part in reducing the danger and the waste.

THE ECONOMIC CONSEQUENCES OF THE ARMS RACE

Dr. Anne H. Cahn
Head, International Social
Impact Section
U.S. Arms Control
and Disarmament Agency

The divisions within the women's movement, between pro- and anti-abortionists, pro- and anti-ERA, pro- and anti-gay rights are reflections of deeper divisions existing within our society. The American public at large is just as divided about questions of national security—are we spending too much or too little on national defense? Can the Russians be trusted to abide by international agreements or not? Do more planes, missiles and tanks increase or decrease national security?

These divisions and the uncertainties arising from the complexities of the world in which we are living mean that those of us who are deeply committed to one point of view or the other have a formidable job ahead of us. We who are committed, as I am, to the cause of arms control and disarmament, who believe that the strength and security of the United States depend as much upon internal stability, justice, and equality as they do upon armaments or uniformed men or women, need to convince our neighbors, friends, and co-workers of the righteousness or the superiority of our point of view, as opposed to the others!

In order to do this, I am convinced that we must speak from the knowledge, as well as from emotions, that facts do matter and most importantly that national security is not primarily a technical issue which can only be understood by theoretical physicists. National security and arms control policies affect each and every one of us in very profound and fundamental ways and therefore we owe it to ourselves to be as informed and involved in these matters as we are in environmental issues or in local or school matters. One of the most fundamental ways is economic. National discussions on new and bigger weapons systems, or on arms control measures, directly affect the pocketbook of every one of us. The B-1, for example, which was going to cost over $100 million for each plane before the President cancelled the system. The ABM treaty is a case where a negotiated arms control agreement most likely resulted in substantial savings. Estimates range from $6 to $11 billion. Thus, I view my task here today to help familiarize you with this important aspect of the arms race—economic.

First of all, the United States is apparently not the number one military spender in the world. That dubious honor must be reserved for the Soviet Union. According to official U.S. Government estimates, the Soviet Union spent the equivalent of $119 billion on military expenditures in 1975 while the United States spent $91 billion. Our present estimates for 1976 are about $125 billion for the Soviet Union and $91-$95 billion for the United States. By comparison, the Peoples' Republic of China, the third largest military spender, spent about $33 billion in 1975 and other countries like West Germany and France lag far behind, spending a mere $15 or $12 billion. Together, the United States and the Soviet Union account for about one-half of the world's total military expenditures.

Second, I doubt that many of us have a real appreciation of what these numbers really mean—$370 billion—the amount the world spent on military expenditures in 1975, is about $370 every single minute since the year 1 A.D.

Third, if you accept my definition of national security as dependent upon internal stability, justice and equality, then it is apparent that military expenditures need not necessarily buy you national security. President Carter recently commented on the fact that the world today spends more than 60 times as much equipping each soldier as educating each child. The world's budget for military research is more than six times its budget for energy research; developed nations spend 20 times more for their military programs than for economic assistance to developing countries; and the equivalent of a year's budget for the United Nations and its agencies is spent in two days on arms.

Underneath all these statistics, there is a widespread perception that military spending is good for the economy. Many Americans believe that military spending creates jobs, cures recessions, and that arms exports help our sagging balance of payments. But as John Kenneth Galbraith has put it, "To talk about this publicly is never thought permissible; to say that the arms race is good because it sustains income and employment, adds usefully to innovation and gross national product, verges on the obscene." Galbraith goes on to say, "It would greatly clarify our political discussion if economic interest could be openly recognized and discussed." So let's look for a few moments at the facts. What do we and don't we know about military spending and the economy? How does it affect jobs and the balance of payments?

There is a widespread belief that the economy needs military spending, exemplified on the right by John Connally, who defended the bail-out loan to Lockheed in 1971 by stating it would "provide employment for 31,000 people throughout the country at a time when we desperately need that type of employment," to Tom Hayden on the left, who said in 1976:

"I don't believe that any defense contract ought to be cut in the face of mass unemployment." Despite these statements, studies of the number of jobs created by various government programs are in general agreement on one point: military spending is one of the least effective ways to create jobs. This should not be surprising. Defense contractors are usually the highest paying employers in their communities and defense firms have a disproportionately higher share of highly paid engineers and scientists compared to nondefense firms. In addition, the defense industry is capital intensive in its utilization of expensive equipment and materials. If the primary objective of the Federal government were to generate employment it could create the maximum number of jobs by employing low paid people in service activities, not through defense contracts. Job creation is clearly a weak argument for military spending. As for balance of payments, any goods that the United States or any other country exports help balance of payments. Civilian goods do this just as well as military exports. In fact, this administration is committed to reducing our gross military sales abroad. This brings me to the question of alternatives.

What alternatives are there to the present scheme of things? Is it possible to design a defense policy which permits and indeed encourages a national defense industry which is fully responsive to America's legitimate defense needs but is able to expand

and contract in conjunction with the flow of events? More and more people are coming to the realization that we need to improve developed planning mechanisms to facilitate such ebbs and flows. Several bills are now before Congress dealing with the issue of economic conversion.

Within the executive branch, too, there is a growing awareness of the need to deal with this issue more adequately. I encourage each of you to think about the problem and what solutions you propose. One might consider, for example:

(1) Requiring defense contractors to pay a percentage of their defense contracts into a government-operated trust fund. Proceeds from the fund could assist workers who lose their jobs because of defense cutbacks.

(2) What about requiring several years advance notification to affected employees and communities of contract cancellations?

(3) Or providing readjustment assistance, including retraining of workers affected by the termination of major government procurement programs.

(4) How about providing tax incentives to industry to hire retrained defense workers?

I would urge you to think not only about this important subject of economic conversion but about the broader subject of arms control in general, for in order to realize any significant reductions in military budgets, we and the other major spenders are going to have to reach meaningful arms control agreements—agreements which substantially reduce nuclear and conventional arsenals. Such agreements will only be possible if there is widespread support for them and that is where we most need your help. We need you to be knowledgeable about these issues, to understand what the acronyms like SALT and MBFR are all about—to be willing to get involved in these issues and together we hopefully can leave a peaceful and secure legacy to our children and our children's children.

WHAT DISARMAMENT POLICY FOR THE UNITED STATES?

Dr. Betty G. Lall
Faculty, N.Y. State School
of Industrial and Labor Relations
Cornell University

Our task is to find a safe and sure way to disarm—to reduce the missiles, bombers, nuclear bombs, and the rest of the weapons of war.

Short of a world war, some argue, there is no way to persuade the men who make decisions in the United States, U.S.S.R., and other nations concerning national security to disarm rapidly. Distrust is still a cornerstone of international relations. Bureaucracies are loath to change. And governments fear that rapid disarmament will unleash new forces in the world, causing uncertainties with destabilizing consequences. Many governments are apprehensive about their internal affairs and the lack of tranquility among the citizenry, many of whom live under conditions of suppression, hunger, and terrible inflation.

National leaders seek stability. Change is anathema. These are the realities. Realism, however, is not the opposite of idealism. Stating the realities only provides the framework for our goal and enhances our determination to achieve results.

To move toward comprehensive disarmament in a world fraught with hostility as well as timidity requires a concept and a plan. It demands conviction and perseverance as well as patience and skill. The plan I present to you has three parts covering (1) disarmament of strategic vehicles; (2) reduction of nuclear warheads, bombs, and other nuclear explosives; and (3) limitations of conventional armaments production and sales.

To reduce strategic arms we must build upon the agreements reached between the United States and the Soviet Union at the Strategic Arms Limitation Talks. These two countries have made to date definite but very modest tentative agreements to limit the number of missiles and bombers capable of delivering nuclear weapons on each other's territory from thousands of miles away. The total number of vehicles to be retained by each country, somewhat exceeding 2,000, over half of which would be equipped with multiple nuclear warheads independently targeted, is over 10 times what would be needed to deter the other side from initiating an aggression in a first strike attack. These conclusions, still valid, are based on an important paper prepared in the government several years ago for President Kennedy which has now been released. Thus, our objective should be at the least to reduce this 2,000-or-so-figure by half.

In addition, the development and production of new strategic systems must stop. The goal of disarmament and arms control is not only to reduce the implements of war. It is to release resources. The new, very large missiles of the Soviet Union, and the projected development of a mobile MX missile and the highly adaptable cruise missile of the United States are even more dangerous than what both sides have now and should be abandoned. Other new strategic systems also should be stopped.

But it is the momentum of the arms race that propels us constantly forward—the Soviets concentrating on big weapons and increasing their production of them and the United States emphasizing advanced technologies. As the leader in the race, the United States can safely show restraint. Let us argue with military officers, the defense planners, the industry executives and lobbyists, and their supporters in the Congress. Of the $41 billion we will spend in the current fiscal year for all research, development, and procurement for weapons, $13 billion will be for strategic weapons. Let us now take a few billion from this amount and call on the Soviet Union to join us in a downward trend in the building of weaponry.

I dwell on a reversal of the strategic arms race for three reasons. First, because these weapons can cause millions of deaths once they are used; second, because the reduction of strategic weapons and the curtailment of the development and production of new ones can be observed, and thus, an essential element of arms control and disarmament, namely the verification of agreements and mutual restraints, will be satisfied; . . . third, because these weapons can be reduced by the United States and the Soviet Union acting alone. No other country has such quantities of these weapons.

Now I come to the second part of the plan: measures to achieve some reduction of nuclear warheads, bombs, and other nuclear explosives.

One measure is that the United States and the Soviet Union should stop production of fissionable materials for nuclear weapons. Not only will this foreclose adding to the stockpiles of warheads in strategic delivery vehicles aimed at killing innocent populations, but it will also help stop the accumulation of tactical or small nuclear weapons such as the neutron bomb, which will make nuclear war more likely. This step can be verified without much intrusion into the territory of the U.S.S.R.

The second measure is to reduce the nuclear weapons stockpiles of the U.S.S.R. and the United States. These number over 50,000 for the two countries, with the United States having a substantial lead over the U.S.S.R. A few thousand weapons—1,000, 4,000 or 10,000 as a beginning—can be taken from the arsenals and deposited at an agreed location where observers can check their dismantling. It will not be easy to reprocess and find alternative uses and safe storage places for so much nuclear material. The Uranium 235 can be used in nuclear power reactors, but the plutonium must be stored. To undo what we have made in over 30 years can consume the ingenuity of some of the scientists and engineers who built these weapons in the past.

The United States has rightly invested enormous efforts to persuade countries not to go nuclear—not to make even a single or a few nuclear bombs. How can we convince these nations when our own stockpiles remain intact with new additions every year? Our position is inconsistent, and some among the world's leaders may think it arrogant.

A third measure toward nuclear disarmament is to stop nuclear testing. The Soviet Union and the United States have been negotiating to achieve this single relatively simple act for 20 years. Six American Presidents (three Democrats and three Republicans) and two Soviet rulers have failed to agree to stop testing. Once again we can state with assurance that the cessation of nuclear testing can be verified by using national instruments to "look into" the Soviet Union and record any cheating that would be significant.

A fourth measure for nuclear disarmament should be an agreement among all five of the nuclear weapons powers not to use or threaten to use nuclear weapons against nonnuclear weapons states, particularly those without nuclear weapons or troops of a nuclear weapons power on their territory. To the uninitiated this sounds like a modest proposal. But no, national leaders have made it into a task so difficult that the United States has yet to propose it. Such a step would free all parts of the world from nuclear warfare, except the territories of nuclear weapons states, Europe, and South Korea—these are the areas where nuclear weapons or troops of nuclear powers are stationed. It would be a significant step toward persuading other countries to decide not to make nuclear weapons.

The final part of my recommendation on disarmament is a scaling down by the United States of its conventional armaments production and sales. This will have to be followed by similar action by the other leading producing powers—the Soviet Union, France, Great Britain, and China. This fiscal year we will spend up to $28 billion for the development and procurement of conventional weapons. Our government will also sanction sales of about $10 billion in weapons to the Middle East and elsewhere.

We should urge the United States to cut its own budget for these fighter bombers, reconnaissance planes, tanks, and similar weapons. This in itself would be incentive to weapons industries to transfer capital and resources to other pursuits. If only $3 billion a year for five years could be cut from the billions spent for these so-called conventional weapons, this would be a significant accomplishment.

In addition to cutting our own budget for new sophisticated conventional weapons, we can put teeth into President Carter's objective to cut arms sales. We can move from a $10 billion annual sales to $8 billion, $6 billion, and ultimately to only several million dollars to be sold abroad.

These disarmament measures affecting strategic nuclear delivery vehicles, nuclear weapons, and conventional weapons production and sales abroad would, if adopted, effectively stop the arms race. They would not bring about comprehensive disarmament. We would still be supporting an armed forces establishment of almost four million persons. About $100 billion of our $116.4 billion budget for fiscal 1978 would not have been touched.

In other words, stopping the arms race is one thing; comprehensive disarmament is quite another.

Are the measures I propose all that can be achieved? For the short run—10 years perhaps—my answer is this would be the greatest combination of acts to enhance our national security and the security of other nations since the end of World War II.

More can be done and must be proposed. But the world must evolve into new systems of international security, and new ways for states to maintain internal order with social justice and economic well-being for their citizens. Comprehensive disarmament cannot be achieved in a vacuum. Settling international disputes peacefully and enhancing respect for human rights are intimately related to a world without arms. Devoting our energies to making progress toward these goals will also be required. But the measures outlined to you today could create momentum toward a new world security order, and that is what we most need.

Can women be the vital element in realizing these goals? Why not? With few exceptions, men make the decisions to go to war, to produce weapons, to divert our taxes. We have been largely excluded. As private citizens and as members of private organizations we can raise our voices, do our homework, argue the case against massive weapons building, and place our money and votes for those willing to display moderation and restraint and to support initiatives including stepped-up negotiations to reach these relatively modest ends.

Above all, we women must not be deterred because some with more power wish to discourage us and dominate the field. Let us not be dissuaded when many declare that no disarmament is possible because we face a dangerous and intractable adversary in the Soviet Union. The Soviet people have suffered from war and hardship more than we have. Many millions of Soviet civilians were killed in World War II. There is no need to fear, for we have plenty of weapons to protect us. We and the Soviet Union can agree not to fight and instead cooperate toward solving the world's problems, at the same time admitting that we do not like each other's political and economic systems. We cannot avoid the responsibility that the United States and the Soviet Union are essential partners in building a more peaceful world.

We must distinguish what action can be safely taken by ourselves, what steps require the Soviet Union as a partner, and what measures must await concurrence by several other countries.

Only if we act can the world be saved from the catastrophe of a nuclear war. Only if we speak will our representatives in Congress work with the President to curtail and ultimately eliminate the weapons. Only if we organize together and with those of our menfolk who believe as we do can we make the difference in diverting billions from arms to building our society into a more just and even greater democratic country.

NUCLEAR WAR—
THE HUMAN DIMENSION

Helen Caldicott, M.D.
Pediatrician, Cystic Fibrosis Clinic
Boston, Massachusetts

Nuclear war is an insanity. Nuclear weapons are a diabolical force which threaten the existence of the human race. The bomb dropped on Hiroshima had the explosive power equivalent of 12,500 tons of TNT and killed approximately 200,400 people. Not all died immediately, however. The sequence of medical events was this: Thousands died immediately from burns and the blast effect. Two weeks later, thousands more died of acute radiation illness. This means that all of the actively dividing cells of the body died—hair fell out, skin sloughed off in big ulcers, vomiting and diarrhea occurred. As the red and white blood cells and platelets died, people died of infection and/or massive hemorrhage.

Five years later an epidemic of leukemia appeared among the survivors. It increased five times above the normal incidence, and 15 to 30 years later an epidemic of solid cancers of lung, bowel, breast, etc., occurred. There was an increased incidence of microcephalic (small-headed) babies born to women who were pregnant during the explosion. It is predicted in future descendants of the survivors that there will be an increased incidence of inherited disease and babies born deformed.

The atomic bombs made today are 6,000 times bigger than the Hiroshima-type bomb. America has enough nuclear weapons to overkill the Russian population 40 times, and Russia has enough to overkill America 20 times. There is as much explosive power in the combined arsenal of the USA and Russia as in 15 tons of TNT for every man, woman, and child on earth.

There is no way to survive a nuclear war. It would only take several hours from the initial press of the black button to extinction of most life in the Northern hemisphere and much life in the Southern hemisphere. Those human beings who did fortuitously survive the initial blast by way of shelters, etc., would then enter a world polluted by radiation—the air, water and food would be so contaminated that the bodies of the survivors would quickly become polluted by radioactive elements like Strontium 90, radioactive iodine and plutonium. Most would die of acute radiation illness two weeks later, and if there were long-term survivors, they would contract leukemia five years later or cancer 15 to 40 years later. That is, if they could survive in a totally destroyed world, with no medical help, no transport, no food, etc.

The neutron bomb is perhaps the most illustrative weapon of mankind's diabolical imagination and ingenuity. It has an extremely high radiation output of neutrons, but has a low blast effect, so buildings are left standing. It is designed to be used on invading armies. The dose of radiation must be extremely high so that the soldiers do not survive intact for two weeks to fight before they die of acute radiation illness. The disease they will die from is called the acute encephalopathic syndrome. Within 48 hours after the explosion of the neutron bomb, the brain cells of the victims will be so damaged by radiation that they will swell and enlarge, producing increased pressure inside the skull. The symptoms are confusion, delirium, stupor, ataxia (abnormal gait), fever, then a period of lucidity before sudden death occurs. Surely a most hideous and diabolical way to die. Could man devise a more effective inhumane way to kill his brother?

The dose of radiation emitted from the bomb will be so high that although the buildings will remain intact, they will be so radioactive that they will be uninhabitable for hundreds of years.

Because of man's destructive brilliance, the future of our children, grandchildren and descendants is in grave jeopardy. We are the curators of life on earth. With a press of the button, we can effectively destroy civilization and the human race.

I see no good reason why we as women and mothers should be so concerned about immunizing our children against disease, giving them good food, love and a good education, when they may have no future. Women are the civilizers of the world. We understand the genesis of life. We care about our children. We won the right to vote years ago, but have stood back and allowed the male politicians to rush like lemmings toward virtually assured destruction. We must use our political force to save the world for our children and descendants. More than half the adults in the world are women. Let us rise up and eliminate all nuclear weapons on earth. This is the ultimate in preventive medicine. This must be the universal goal of all women in all countries of the world.

NATIONAL COMMISSION ON THE OBSERVANCE OF INTERNATIONAL WOMEN'S YEAR

PRESIDING OFFICER

Bella S. Abzug, of New York, New York; author of Public Law 94-167, which designated the National Commission as sponsor of the National Women's Conference; member of Congress, 1971-1976; attorney, lecturer, author; convener and former chair, National Women's Political Caucus; Congressional Adviser to U.S. Delegation to U.N. World Conference on IWY in Mexico City, July 1975; former member advisory board, National Organization for Women, Americans for Democratic Action; member, B'nai B'rith, Hadassah, American Civil Liberties Union, Women's Forum; 1976, Democratic Party platform committee; named third most influential member of Congress by her colleagues and one of 10 most important woman leaders in a *U.S. News and World Report* poll in 1976; Honorary degrees, Hunter College, Manhattanville College, Hobart College.[1]

COMMISSIONERS

Ruth J. Abram, of New York, New York; Executive Director, Women's Action Alliance Inc.; former program director, American Civil Liberties Union, New York City; former executive director, Norman Foundation; Board of Trustees, National Council on Philanthropy; Board of Advisers, National Women's Political Caucus.

Bella S. Abzug

Ruth J. Abram

Maya Angelou, of Sonoma, California; poet, actress, playwright, author of *I Know Why the Caged Bird Sings, Gather Together in My Name, Singin' and Swingin' and Gettin' Merry Like Christmas,* a musical, *And Still I Rise;* two volumes of poetry, *Oh Pray My Wings Are Gonna Git Me Well* and *Just Give Me a Cool Drink of Water 'Fore I die;* film industry's first black woman writer-director; scored numerous motion pictures, television productions, and two records; distinguished visiting professor at various U.S. universities; Member, American Revolution Bicentennial Council.

Elizabeth Athanasakos, of Fort Lauderdale, Florida; practicing attorney; Presiding Officer, IWY Commission, 1976; former municipal judge; member, Broward County, Florida and American Bar Associations; President, Florida Association of Women Lawyers, 1976-78; Presidential appointment to Task Force on Women's Rights and Responsibilities, 1969; Atlanta Regional Panel for the President's Commission on White House Fellowships, 1974-76; member, Zonta International; first vice-president, Florida Federation of Business and Professional Women's Clubs, Inc.; American Association of University of Women; Co-chair, ERA Florida, 1977; National Federation of Republican Women Board of Directors, 1976-78; Board of Directors, United Way of Broward County; Chair, Secretary's Advisory Committee on Rights and Responsibilities, Department of Health, Education, and Welfare, 1972-74.[2]

Maya Angelou

Elizabeth Athanasakos

Birch Bayh, of Indiana; U.S. Senate since 1962; member, Judiciary and Appropriations Committees; chair, Judiciary Subcommittee on the Constitution; chair, Transportation Subcommittee of the Appropriations Committee; member, Subcommittee to Investigate Juvenile Delinquency; member, Subcommittee on Anti-Trust and Monopoly; member, Senate Select Committee on Intelligence; chief sponsor of the Equal Rights Amendment to the U.S. Constitution.[1]

Betty Blanton, of Nashville, Tennessee; First Lady of Tennessee; member, Tennessee Federation of Democratic Women; 51.3% Committee for Women; Honorary chair, Tennessee Citizen Involvement for State Bicentennial Commission.

Birch Bayh

Betty Blanton

Cecilia Preciado-Burciaga, of Palo Alto, California; Assistant Provost for Faculty Affairs, Stanford University; former researcher and writer, U.S. Commission on Civil Rights; equal employment opportunity counselor; teacher and educational consultant; board member, Mid-Peninsula Urban Coalition, Center for Research on Women, Stanford University, National Conference on Women in Education, National Chicano Council on Higher Education; member, Mexican American Women's National Association, Project on the Status and Education of Women.

Liz Carpenter, of Austin, Texas; National co-chair ERAmerica; convener of National Women's Political Caucus; consultant to Friends of LBJ Library; columnist, author, lecturer; named Woman of the Year for Government and Public Affairs by Ladies Home Journal, 1976; named Distinguished Alumna, University of Texas, 1974; former president, Women's National Press Club; member, George Peabody Awards Selection Committee, Board of Trustees, College of the Virgin Islands.[2]

Cecilia
Preciado-Burciaga

Liz Carpenter

John Mack Carter, of New York, New York; editor-in-chief, *Good Housekeeping* magazine; former editor-in-chief, *The Ladies' Home Journal, McCall's, American Home;* former assistant editor, *Better Homes and Gardens;* member, National Commission on Working Women; named Publisher of the Year, 1977, by Brandeis University; 1978 Headliner Award, Women in Communications, Inc.; designated as one of the "10 Outstanding Young Men of the Year" by U.S. Junior Chamber of Commerce; veteran of service with U.S. Navy as Lieutenant (J.G.).[2]

Sey Chassler, of New York, New York; editor-in-chief, *Redbook* magazine since 1975; senior vice president of Redbook Publishing Company; former associate editor of *Collier's* and *Coronet;* former editor of *Pageant;* editorial director, *This Week Magazine;* vice president, American Society of Magazine Editors; member, Advisory Board, Institute for Education and Research on Women and Work.

Ruth C. Clusen, of Green Bay, Wisconsin; President, National League of Women Voters of the United States; alternate delegate to U.N. World Conference on IWY in Mexico City, July 1975; member, 1976 U.S. delegation to U.N. Habitat conference in Vancouver, Canada; member of 1974 U.S. delegation to U.S.-U.S.S.R. Joint Committee on Environmental Protection in Moscow; director, Board of Joint Center for Urban Environmental Studies; member, Board of Counselors for Center for Habitat and Human Settlements; sponsor of Policy Forum, Inc. In May 1977 honored as a Woman of the Year by *Ladies Home Journal* magazine as a result of her work on the 1976 Presidential debates produced by the League of Women Voters Education Fund.

Audrey Rowe Colom, of Washington, D.C.; immediate past chair of National Women's Political Caucus; Director of Women's Activities, Corporation for Public Broadcasting; formerly national vice-chair and president of the D.C. Women's Political Caucus; one of the "Outstanding Young Women of America" for 1976; former schoolteacher, helped develop and direct reading programs for black children and high school equivalency programs for women incarcerated in D.C. Women's Detention Center.[2]

John Mack Carter

Sey Chassler

Ruth C. Clusen

Audrey Rowe Colom

Jane Culbreth, of Leeds, Alabama; immediate past president 1976-77, National Federation of Business and Professional Women's Clubs, Inc.; administrative officer and corporate secretary, Moss-Thornton Company, Inc.; former teacher, telephone company and Federal employee; served two terms as elected alderman on Leeds, Alabama City Council (only woman ever elected); two terms as first woman executive committee member, Alabama League of Municipalities; member, Alabama Advisory Council for Comprehensive Health Planning; chaired State Subcommittee on Jury Service for Women, Alabama Commission on the Status of Women; member and past president, Zonta Club of Birmingham.

Harry T. Edwards, of Ann Arbor, Michigan; professor of law, University of Michigan School of Law; formerly law professor, Harvard University; specialty, labor law; extensive arbitration work; Board of Governors, National Academy of Arbitrators; secretary, Labor Law Section, American Bar Association; chair, program committee of National Academy of Arbitrators; board of directors, American Arbitration Association; published works include co-authorship of *The Lawyer as a Negotiator* and *Labor Relations Law in the Public Sector.*[2][3]

Rita Elway, of Seattle, Washington; communications researcher, consultant in public opinion research; past chair, Washington State Women's Council; vice chair of Washington State coordinating committee for International Women's Year; active in Asian-American community; founder of Asian Pacific Women's Caucus; board member, Japanese American Citizen's League.

Beverly Everett, of New Sharon, Iowa; State president, American Association of University Women (AAUW); member of International AAUW Liaison Committee; activist, agricultural and rural development issues; member, National Planning Association Agricultural Committee, Iowa Department of Environmental Quality Board of Certification, and Iowa Commission on the Future; member, Advisory Committee, College of Home Economics, Iowa State University; past chair, Environmental Resources Committee; member, United Methodist Church, Iowa Conference, Status of Women Commission and Bishop's Legislative Committee.[2]

Betty Ford, of Palm Springs, California; former First Lady; honorary chair, Palm Springs Desert Museum; board of trustees, Eisenhower Medical Center; trustee, National Symphony Orchestra; advisory board member, Rosalind Russell Medical Research Fund.

Bernice S. Frieder, of Lakewood, Ohio; State conference coordinator, Arts, Education and Americans, Inc.; former national officer, National Council of Jewish Women; past president and honorary life member, National Association of State Boards of Education; member, Colorado State Board of Education, 1959-72; former executive director, United Parents Associations of New York City, Inc.; only woman appointed by President Lyndon B. Johnson to National Advisory Council, Title 3, Higher Education Act, U.S. Office of Education; executive committee member, National Coalition for Public Education and Religious Liberty; former vice chair, Clearinghouse on Women's Issues, Washington, D.C.

Betty Ford   Bernice Frieder

Jane Culbreth   Harry T. Edwards

Rita Elway   Beverly Everett

Martha W. Griffiths, of Romeo, Michigan; member, Griffiths and Griffiths law firm; member of Congress, 1955-75; recipient of 21 honorary degrees; trustee of Detroit Education Television Foundation, Fund for Henry Ford Hospital, and Mercy College of Detroit; member of advisory boards to State of Michigan, Department of Social Services, the Institute for Socioeconomic Studies, United Foundation, and Urban Institute; member of Committee for National Health Insurance, Comptroller General's Consultants Panel, Tax Foundation Incorporated, and Conference Board; chair of the Institute for Congress.[2]

Dorothy Haener, of Detroit, Michigan; Representative, International Union, United Auto Workers (UAW) Women's Department; board member, National Committee on Household Employment; founder and past board member, National Organization for Women (NOW); NOW Legal Defense and Education Fund; convener, National Women's Political Caucus; organizer and negotiator, Engineering and Shop Employees, UAW Local 142, 1946-52, and first woman elected to negotiating committee; co-chair, Michigan ERAmerica; member, National Democratic Platform Committee, Michigan State Central Committee, Michigan Advisory Committee of American Civil Liberties Union, Women's International League for Peace and Freedom, Catholics for a Free Choice; recipient of 1973 Michigan Distinguished Women's Award from Michigan Federation of Business and Professional Women's Clubs; member, Presidential Task Force on Women's Rights and Responsibilities, 1969; panel member, Women and Infants' White House Conference on Food, Nutrition ahd Health, 1969; participant, White House Conference on Equal Employment Opportunity, 1965.

Rhea Mojica Hammer, of Chicago, Illinois; former vice chair and member, National Advisory Board, National Women's Political Caucus; founder and publisher of *El Clarin;* award-winning television producer in Spanish-language programing; founding member of National Latino Media Coalition; member of Chicago chapters of National Academy of Television Arts and Sciences and Chicago Women in Broadcasting; board member, Illinois division, American Civil Liberties Union; board chair, Spanish Coalition for Jobs, Inc.; charter member and first president, Mexican American Business and Professional Women's Club of Chicago; member of 1980 Census Advisory Committee on Spanish-origin population; board trustee, El Congreso.

LaDonna Harris, of Albuquerque, New Mexico; president and founder, Americans for Indian Opportunity; member of original National Indian Opportunity Commission; former chair of Women's National Advisory Council on Poverty; 1973 Outstanding Woman of the Year in human rights, *Ladies' Home Journal;* board member, Common Cause, National Urban Coalition, National Urban League, National Committee Against Discrimination in Housing, National Rights Housing Conference; executive board of Southwest Center for Human Relation Studies; board of visitors of University of Oklahoma; board of trustees, Antioch College; advisory committee of National Organization for Women; co-convener and member, National Women's Political Caucus; board of directors, National Association for Mental Health.

Margaret Heckler, of Wellesley, Massachusetts; representing 10th District of Massachusetts in Congress since January 1967; former member, Massachusetts Governor's Council; member, Republican Platform Committee, 1972 National Convention; member, Joint Economic Committee and House Select Committee on Ethics; member, Boston Bar Association, Massachusetts Trial Lawyers Association, Women's Lawyers' Association, and the American Bar Association; co-chair, Congresswomen's Caucus.[1]

Lenore Hershey, of New York, New York; editor-in-chief, *Ladies' Home Journal;* vice president of Downe Publishing, Inc.; member of 1972 Presidential Advisory Committee on Economic Role of Women; board member, Center for Voluntary Action and Child Study Association of America; named as one of 25 most influential women in America by the

Rhea Mojica Hammer   LaDonna Harris

Margaret Heckler   Lenore Hershey

Martha Griffiths   Dorothy Haener

Newspaper Enterprises Association and World Almanac; elected to Board of Women's Forum, 1977; the 1977 winner of the Women in Communications National Headliner Award.[2]

Elizabeth Holtzman, of Brooklyn, New York; third-term Representative from New York's 16th District, youngest woman ever elected to House of Representatives; member of Judiciary Committee and its subcommittees on Immigration, Criminal Justice and Crime; House Budget Committee member and chair of committee's task force on State and local finance; founder of Brooklyn Women's Political Caucus; Harvard University Board of Overseers; founder of Law Students Civil Rights Research Council; co-chair, Congresswomen's Caucus.[4]

Koryne Horbal, of Minneapolis, Minnesota; U.S. Representative to United Nations Commission on the Status of Women; chair, Women's Caucus, Democratic National Committee; Democratic National Committeewoman; Minnesota Metropolitan Airports Commissioner; former chair, Democratic State Party; member of WEAL, National Organization for Women; MS Foundation Board, National Women's Political Caucus Board, Project ELAN; Genesis II; National Deputy Coordinator of Carter/ Mondale 51.3% Committee.

Mildred M. Jeffrey, of Detroit, Michigan; chair, National Women's Political Caucus; chair, Democratic Task Force, National Women's Political Caucus; founder of Coalition of Labor Union Women; life member, National Association for the Advancement of Colored People; co-convener, Michigan Women's Political Caucus; *Detroit Free Press* 1976 award as one of 10 outstanding women; board of governors, Wayne State University; Michigan Consumer Council; Wayne County Advisory Committee on Substance Abuse.

Jeffalyn Johnson, of Alexandria, Virginia; president, Jeffalyn Johnson and Associates; management and organization specialist; formerly associate director, dean and senior professor, Federal Executive Institute; lecturer, University of Southern California, School of Public Administration; policy analyst and planner, Carter-Mondale campaign; member, Carter-Mondale Transition Group; 1978 National Conference, chair, American Society for Public Administration; chair, 1975 National Conference Program, National Conference of Minority Public Administrators; member, Committee on the Status of Blacks, American Political Science Association; board member, Women's Education Fund.

Coretta Scott King, of Atlanta, Georgia; U.S. Representative to the U.N. General Assembly; civil rights worker; founder of the Martin Luther King, Jr. Memorial Center, Atlanta; Dag Hammarskjold Award, 1969; international lecturer; author of *My Life with Martin Luther King;* member, board of directors, Southern Christian Leadership Conference; trustee, Robert F. Kennedy Memorial Center, and Ebenezer Baptist Church; *Who's Who in America.*

Mary Anne Krupsak, of Canojoharie, New York; Lieutenant Governor, State of New York; former State Senator and former assemblywoman, New York State Legislature; chair, New York State delegation to White House Conference on Balanced Growth and Economic Development, 1978; co-chair, New York State delegation to Democratic National Convention, 1972 and 1976; chair, National Leadership Conference for Polish-Americans; Doctor of Law, University of Chicago.

Margaret Mealey, of Washington, D.C.; immediate past executive director, National Council of Catholic Women; former member, Citizen's Advisory Council on the Status of Women; White House Conferences on Children and Youth; on Aging; on Food, Nutrition and Health; adviser on the status of women to four presidents; Churchwoman of the Year 1975, Religious Heritage of America, Inc.

Coretta Scott King   Mary Anne Krupsak

Elizabeth Holtzman   Koryne Horbal

Margaret Mealey

Mildred Jeffrey   Jeffalyn Johnson

Jean O'Leary, of New York, New York; co-executive director, National Gay Task Force; a former nun; founder of Lesbian Feminist Liberation; delegate to 1976 Democratic National Convention; member, 51.3% Committee for Women, Advisory Board to the New York State Human Rights Commission; Advisory Board of National Women's Political Caucus; Board of Gay Rights National Lobby and New York City Health Systems; member, N.Y.C. Community Planning Board 4.

Charles Percy, of Illinois; U.S. Senate since 1967, currently ranking Republican on the Senate Governmental Affairs Committee; member, Foreign Relations Committee and Special Committee on Aging.[1]

Mildred Emory Persinger, of Dobbs Ferry, New York, national board member for 20 years, Young Women's Christian Association (YWCA) of the U.S.A.; U.N. Representative for the YWCA; organizing chair of the parallel nongovernmental Tribune during the U.S. World Conference on International Women's Year in Mexico City, July 1975; member, World YWCA's Council; president, International Women's Tribune Centre, Inc.; member, United Nations Association National Board; member, President's Commission for the 25th Anniversary of the United Nations (1970-71) and the Commission on Social Insurance and Taxes; former member, President's Commission on the Status of Women.

Connie Plunkett, of Carrollton Georgia; member, Affirmative Action Committee of the Democratic National Committee; former city councilwoman, Carrollton, Georgia; former vice chair and member, executive committee, Georgia Democratic Party; Deputy Campaign Director, Campaign Staff, Carter-Mondale campaign; Carroll County Board of Elections; former teacher of American and world history; member of Democratic National Charter Commission and Credentials Committee for National Democratic Convention, 1972.

Ersa Poston, of McLean, Virginia; member of U.S. Civil Service Commission; member, International Civil Service Commission; former commissioner and past president, New York Civil Service Commission; former member, U.S. Delegation to 31st U.N. General Assembly; former vice presiding officer, National Commission on the Observance of International Women's Year; president, International Personnel Management Association; former vice president, National Urban League; presiding officer, International Symposium on Public Personnel Administration, Salzburg, Austria.[2]

Claire Randall, of New York, New York; general secretary, National Council of Churches in the U.S.A.; former associate executive, Church Women United; church educator; artist; designer; an ordained elder in the United Presbyterian Church in the United States.

Alice S. Rossi, of Amherst, Massachusetts; professor of sociology, University of Massachusetts; chair, board of directors, Social Science Research Council of New York; former chair, Committee on the Status of Women, American Association of University Professors; vice president, American Sociological Association; organizer of Sociologists for Women in Society; author, *The Feminist Papers, Academic Women on the Move,* and many articles.

Gloria Scott, of Houston, Texas; Assistant to President and Professor of Higher Education, Texas Southern University; National President, Girl Scouts of the U.S.A.; member, Board of Trustees, National Urban League; member, Board of Directors, Southern Education Foundation; 1977 Honorary Doctorate, Indiana University; 1977 *Ladies' Home Journal* "Woman of the Year" award for humanitarian and community service; former National Officer, Delta Sigma Theta, Inc.

Mildred Emory Persinger   Connie Plunkett

Jean O'Leary   Charles Percy

Ersa Poston   Claire Randall

Alice S. Rossi   Gloria Scott

Eleanor Smeal, of Pittsburgh, Pennsylvania; president, National Organization for Women; homemaker.

Jean Stapleton, of Los Angeles, California; actress, two-time Emmy winner for "All in the Family"; recipient of two Golden Globe Awards and two American Academy of Humor Awards; appeared in both Broadway and motion picture versions of *Damn Yankees* and *Bells Are Ringing;* other motion picture credits include *Klute* and *Up the Down Staircase.* Other Broadway appearances were in *Funny Girl, In the Summer House, Rhinoceros,* and *Juno.*[2]

Gloria Steinem, of New York, New York; an editor and co-founder of *Ms.* magazine; chair of the board, Women's Action Alliance; convener, National Women's Political Caucus and Advisory Committee member; founder and member of the Coalition of Labor Union Women; National Advisory Board member, National Organization for Women.

Eleanor Smeal

Jean Stapleton

Gloria Steinem

Ethel Taylor

Ethel Taylor, of Bala-Cynwyd, Pennsylvania; national coordinator and spokeswoman, Women Strike for Peace; sculptor; a founder of Committee of Liaison for Families and Servicemen Detained in North Vietnam; WSP representative to 1975 International Women's Year Conference on Equality and Disarmament in East Berlin; former national board member, Committee for Sane Nuclear Policy, and a founder of Philadelphia branch of SANE.

Carmen Delgado Votaw, of Bethesda, Maryland; U.S. delegate to Inter-American Commission of Women of the Organization of American States; president, National Conference of Puerto Rican Women; Board of Overseas Education Fund, League of Women Voters; advisory board member of Puerto Rican Family Institute in New York; Aspira of America Fellowship Program; Women's Educational Equity Action League Fund and Public Members Association of the Foreign Service; member, Coalition for Women in International Development, Coalition for Women's Appointments, National Women's Political Caucus, and Women's Agenda.

Gerridee Wheeler, of Bismarck, North Dakota; member of Republican National Committee; past president, National Association for Mental Health; member, Department of Health, Education, and Welfare Secretary's Advisory Committee on the Rights and Responsibilities of Women; vice chair, Commission on Prevention of Child Abuse; member of National Committee of Human Concerns, Republican National Committee; mother of eight children, including three adopted Korean Americans.[2]

Addie Wyatt, of Chicago, Illinois; national vice president, Coalition of Labor Union Women; international vice president and director of Women's Affairs Department, Amalgamated Meatcutters and Butcher Workmen of North America; first woman elected to the union's International Executive Board; minister of music, Vernon Park Church of God;

Adviser and labor instructor, Roosevelt University; member of Coalition of Black Trade Unionists; adviser and member, Citizens for Day Care; member, Cook County Schools Advisory Board; adviser and member of women's organization, National Association of the Church of God; labor committee adviser to Chicago Urban League; *Who's Who Among Black Americans,* 1975; selected as one of 12 Women of the Year by *Time* magazine; member, board of advisers, Alliance to Save Energy; member, National Council of Negro Women; Selected by *Ladies Home Hournal* as one of 10 Women of Year awards for 1976; one of *Ebony's* nine profiles of Black Womanhood in August, 1977.

Carmen Delgado Votaw

Gerridee Wheeler

Addie Wyatt

[1]Served on previous IWY commission as Congressional representative.
[2]Served on previous IWY commission as appointee of President Ford.
[3]Resigned December 1977.
[4]Congressional representative.

APPENDIX

PUBLIC LAW 94-167

Ninety-fourth Congress of the United States of America at the first session begun and held at the City of Washington on Tuesday, the fourteenth day of January, one thousand nine hundred and seventy-five.

AN ACT

To direct the National Commission on the Observance of International Women's Year, 1975, to organize and convene a National Women's Conference, and for other purposes.

Be it enacted by the Senate and House of Representatives of the United States of America in Congress assembled,

FINDINGS

SECTION 1. The Congress hereby finds that—

(1) International Women's Year, and its World Plan of Action, have focused attention on the problems of women throughout the world, and have pointed to the need for an evaluation of the discrimination which American women face because of their sex;

(2) The Bicentennial year of 1976 is a particularly appropriate time for the United States to recognize the contributions of women to the development of our country, to assess the progress that has been made toward insuring equality for all women, to set goals for the elimination of all barriers to the full and equal participation of women in all aspects of American life, and to recognize the importance of the contribution of women to the development of friendly relations and cooperation among nations and to the strengthening of world peace; and

(3) A national conference of American women, preceded by State conferences, is the most suitable mechanism by which such an evaluation of the status of women and issues of concern to them can be effected.

DUTIES OF COMMISSION

SECTION 2. (a) The National Commission on the Observance of International Women's Year, 1975, established by Executive Order 11832 on January 9, 1975 (hereinafter in this Act referred to as the "Commission"), is hereby continued. The Commission shall organize and convene a national conference to be known as the National Women's Conference (hereinafter in this Act referred to as the "Conference"). The Conference and State or regional meetings conducted in preparation for the Conference shall be held in such places and at such times in 1976 as the Commission deems appropriate.

(b) The Commission shall consult with such National, State, and other organizations concerned with women's rights and related matters as the Commission considers necessary to carry out the purpose of this Act.

COMPOSITION AND GOALS OF THE CONFERENCE

SECTION 3 (a) The Conference shall be composed of—

(1) representatives of local, State, regional, and national institutions, agencies, organizations, unions, associations, publications, and other groups which work to advance the rights of women; and

(2) members of the general public, with special emphasis on the representation of low-income women, members of diverse racial, ethnic, and religious groups, and women of all ages.

(b) The Conference shall—

(1) recognize the contributions of women to the development of our country;

(2) assess the progress that has been made to date by both the private and public sectors in promoting equality between men and women in all aspects of life in the United States;

(3) assess the role of women in economic, social, cultural, and political development;

(4) assess the participation of women in efforts aimed at the development of friendly relations and cooperation among nations and to the strengthening of world peace;

(5) identify the barriers that prevent women from participating fully and equally in all aspects of national life, and develop recommendations for means by which such barriers can be removed;

(6) establish a timetable for the achievement of the objectives set forth in such recommendations; and

(7) establish a committee of the Conference which will take steps to provide for the convening of a second National Women's Conference. The second Conference will assess the progress made in achieving the objectives set forth in paragraphs (5) and (6) of this subsection, and will evaluate the steps taken to improve the status of American women.

(c) All meetings of the Conference and of State or regional meetings held in preparation for the Conference shall be open to the public.

POWERS OF COMMISSION

SECTION 4. The Commission shall—

(1) designate a coordinating committee in each State which shall organize and conduct a State or regional meeting in preparation for the Conference;

(2) prepare and make available background materials relating to women's rights and related matters

for the use of representatives to the State and regional meetings, and to the Conference;

(3) establish procedures to provide financial assistance for representatives to the Conference who are unable to pay their own expenses;

(4) establish such regulations as are necessary to carry out the provisions of this Act;

(5) designate such additional representatives to the Conference as may be necessary and appropriate to fulfill the goals set forth in section 3(b) of this Act;

(6) grant technical and financial assistance by grant, contract, or otherwise to facilitate the organization and conduct of State and regional meetings in preparation for the Conference;

(7) establish such advisory and technical committees as the Commission considers necessary to assist and advise the Conference; and

(8) publish and distribute the report required under this Act.

ADMINISTRATION OF COMMISSION

SECTION 5. (a) The Commission may appoint such staff personnel as it considers necessary to carry out its duties under this Act. Such personnel shall be appointed without regard to the provisions of Title 5, United States Code, governing appointments in the competitive service, except that no individual so appointed may receive pay in excess of the annual rate of basic pay in effect for grade GS-18 of the General Schedule. Appointments shall be made without regard to political affiliation.

(b) The Commission may accept, use, and dispose of contributions of money, services, or property.

(c) The Commission may use the United States mails under the same conditions as other departments and agencies of the United States.

(d) The powers granted the Commission by this section shall be in addition to those granted by Executive Order 11832. The powers granted the Commission by Executive Order 11832 may be employed to fulfill the responsibilities of the Commission under this Act.

(e) The Commission, to such extent as it deems necessary, may procure supplies, services, and personal property; make contracts; expend funds appropriated, donated, or received in pursuance of contracts hereunder in furtherance of the purposes of this Act; and exercise those powers that are necessary to enable it to carry out efficiently and in the public interest the purposes of this Act.

(f) The powers granted the Commission under this Act may be delegated to any member or employee of the Commission by the Commission.

STATE AND REGIONAL MEETINGS

SECTION 6. (a) A meeting in preparation for the Conference shall be held in each State in accordance with regulations promulgated by the Commission, except that in the event the amount of time and resources available so requires, the Commission may combine two or more such State meetings into a regional meeting.

(b) Any State or regional meeting which receives financial assistance under this Act shall be designed and structured in accordance with the goals of the Conference set forth in section 3(b) of this Act.

(c) (1) Each State or regional meeting shall select representatives to the Conference in accordance with regulations promulgated by the Commission and consistent with the criteria set forth in section 3(a) of this Act.

(2) The total number of representatives selected under this subsection shall be apportioned among the States according to population, except that despite such apportionment no State shall have fewer than ten representatives.

REPORT

SECTION 7. The Commission shall submit a report to the President and to each House of the Congress not later than one hundred and twenty days after the conclusion of the Conference, and shall make such report available to the general public. Such report shall contain a detailed statement of the findings and recommendations of the Conference with respect to the matters described in subsection (b) of section 3. The President shall, not later than one hundred and twenty days after the receipt of the report, submit to each House of the Congress recommendations with respect to matters considered in such report.

TERMINATION OF COMMISSION

SECTION 8. The Commission shall continue in operation until thirty days after submitting its report pursuant to section 7, at which time it shall terminate, but the life of the Commission shall in no case extend beyond March 31, 1978.

AUTHORIZATION OF APPROPRIATION

SECTION 9. There are authorized to be appropriated without fiscal year limitation, such sums, but not to exceed $5,000,000, as may be necessary to carry out the provisions of this Act. Such sums shall remain available for obligation until expended.

No funds authorized hereunder may be used for lobbying activities.

DEFINITION

SECTION 10. For the purpose of this Act, the term "State" includes the District of Columbia, the Commonwealth of Puerto Rico, Guam, American Samoa, the Virgin Islands, and the Trust Territory of the Pacific Islands.

Speaker of the House of Representatives
Vice President of the United States and President of the Senate.

EXECUTIVE ORDERS

EXECUTIVE ORDER 11832 ISSUED BY PRESIDENT FORD

THE WHITE HOUSE
EXECUTIVE ORDER

Establishing a National Commission on the Observance of International Women's Year, 1975

There is increasing recognition of, and interest in, the contributions of women to the national life of this country in all its important aspects—cultural, political, economic, and social. Significant progress continues in advancing the rights and responsibilities of women, in opening new opportunities, and in overcoming political, legal, social, and economic handicaps to which women have long been subject. Americans must now deal with those inequities that still linger as barriers to the full participation of women in our Nation's life. We must also support and strengthen the laws that prohibit discrimination based on sex.

The United Nations General Assembly, by proclaiming 1975 as International Women's Year, has offered us an exceptional opportunity to focus attention throughout the country on the rights and responsibilities of women. Presidential Proclamation No. 4262 of January 30, 1974, called upon the Congress and the people of the United States, interested groups and organizations, officials of the Federal Government and of State and local governments, educational institutions, and all others who can be of help to provide for the national observance of International Women's Year with practical and constructive measures for the advancement of women in the United States.

I have now determined that it would be in the public interest to establish a National Commission on the Observance of International Women's Year, 1975.

Now, therefore, by virtue of the authority vested in me as President of the United States, it is ordered:

SECTION 1. Establishment of a National Commission.

(a) There is hereby established a National Commission on the Observance of International Women's Year, 1975.

(b) The Commission shall consist of not more than 35 members to be appointed by the President from among citizens in private life. The President shall designate the presiding officer, who may designate from among the members of the Commission as many vice presiding officers as necessary.

(c) The President of the Senate and the Speaker of the House of Representatives are invited to designate two Members of each House to serve on the Commission.

(d) The members of the Commission shall serve without compensation, but shall be entitled to receive travel expenses, including per diem, in lieu of subsistence as authorized by law (4 U.S.C. 5703).

SECTION 2. Functions of the Commission.

(a) The Commission shall promote the national observance in the United States of International Women's Year. To this end, it will focus attention on the need to encourage appropriate and relevant cooperative activity in the field of women's rights and responsibilities.

(b) The Commission shall take as its action agenda the relevant parts of the resolution adopted by the United Nations General Assembly proclaiming 1975 as International Women's Year:

(1) To promote equality between men and women.

(2) To ensure the full integration of women in the total development effort, especially by emphasizing women's responsibility and impor-

tant role in economic, social and cultural development at the national, regional and international levels, particularly during the Second United Nations Development Decade.

(3) To recognize the importance of women's increasing contribution to the development of friendly relations and cooperation among States and to the strengthening of world peace.

(c) The Commission shall keep itself informed of activities undertaken or planned by various organizations and groups in the United States in observance of the Year and shall consult with such groups including the United States Center for International Women's Year.

(d) The Commission shall encourage the public and private sectors to set forth objectives to be achieved as part of the program observing International Women's Year, as provided in the Presidential Proclamation.

(e) The Commission shall, through close liaison with appropriate Government agencies and their public advisory committees, keep itself informed about and make known to the public all major programs and special efforts during International Women's Year which are supported by those agencies.

(f) The Commission shall hold meetings at such times and places as the presiding officer shall determine. It may assemble and disseminate information, issue reports and other publications and conduct such other activities as it may deem appropriate to provide for effective participation of the United States in the domestic observance of International Women's Year.

(g) The Commission may establish, within the limits of available funds, such subcommittees or working groups as may be necessary for the fulfillment of its tasks. The membership may include persons not members of the Commission.

(h) The Commission shall conclude its work by the end of the year 1975 and make a report to the President within thirty days thereafter. The Commission shall then be terminated.

SECTION 3. Assistance and Cooperation.

(a) The Commission may request any agency of the Executive branch of the Government to furnish it with such information, advice, and services as may be useful for the fulfillment of the Commission's functions under this Order.

(b) The agencies of the Executive branch are authorized, to the extent permitted by law, to provide the Commission with administrative services, information, facilities and funds necessary for its activities.

(c) The Commission may procure, subject to the availability of funds, the temporary professional services of individuals to assist in its work, in accordance with the provisions of Section 3109 of Title 5 of the United States Code.

SECTION 4. Responsibilities of Government Departments.

Each agency of the Executive branch shall designate at least two persons, preferably a man and a woman, to be responsible for planning and implementation of projects and programs within such departments and agencies for the domestic observance of International Women's Year. Persons so designated shall constitute membership of an interdepartmental task force for International Women's Year. The Department of State shall designate the presiding officer. The task force will coordinate the activities undertaken by the Executive branch of the United States Government as well as those undertaken by the Commission in the domestic observance of International Women's Year.

Gerald R. Ford
THE WHITE HOUSE,
January 9, 1975

THE WHITE HOUSE
EXECUTIVE ORDER

Amending Executive Order No. 11832 of January 9, 1975, To Extend the Existence of the National Commission on the Observance of International Women's Year, 1975

By virtue of the authority vested in me by the Constitution and the statutes of the United States of America, including Section 204 of the Supplemental Appropriations Act, 1975 (P.L. 93-554, 88 Stat. 1784) and the State Department appropriations act for 1976 (P.L. 94-121), and as President of the United States of America, Section 2(h) of Executive Order No. 11832 of January 9, 1975, is hereby amended to read as follows:

"The Commission shall, to the extent funds are available, continue its work through June 30, 1976, and shall submit a final report on its activities to the President within thirty days thereafter, at which time the Commission shall terminate."

Gerald R. Ford
THE WHITE HOUSE,
November 25, 1975

EXECUTIVE ORDER
ISSUED BY
PRESIDENT CARTER

National Commission on the Observance of International Women's Year, 1975

By virtue of the authority vested in me by the Constitution and statutes of the United States of America, and as President of the United States of America, in accord with Section 2 of the Act approved December 23, 1975, to direct the National Commission on the Observance of International Women's Year, 1975, to organize and convene a National Women's Conference, and for other purposes (Public Law 94-167, 89 Stat. 1003), and in order to increase the number of members on the Commission, it is hereby

ordered that Section 1(b) of Executive Order No. 11832, as amended by Executive Order No. 11889, is amended to read as follows:

"(b) The Commission shall consist of not more than 45 members to be appointed by the President from among citizens in private life, except that not more than 10 members may be officials of State or local governments. The President shall designate the presiding officer, who may designate from among the members of the Commission as many vice presiding officers as necessary."

THE WHITE HOUSE
March 28, 1977

EXECUTIVE ORDER

National Commission on the Observance of International Women's Year, 1975

By virtue of the authority vested in me by the Constitution and statutes of the United States of America, and as President of the United States of America, Section 1(b) of Executive Order No. 11832, as amended, is further amended by substituting "42 members to be appointed" for "45 members to be appointed."

THE WHITE HOUSE
March 29, 1977

SUMMARY OF SOME ACTIONS TAKEN BY NATIONAL COMMISSION PRIOR TO HOLDING OF NATIONAL WOMEN'S CONFERENCE NOVEMBER 18 to 21, 1977

In behalf of the Commission, Presiding Officer Bella Abzug sent the following letters and statements to various government officials and bodies to implement policy positions of the Commission:

March 28, 1977: Letter to Secretary Joseph Califano of the Department of Health, Education and Welfare urging inclusion of questions about the economic arrangements at divorce and separation in the 1976 Census on Income and Education. The commission had recommended such a survey in its 1976 report to the President.

March 31, 1977: Letter to HEW Secretary Califano protesting proposed cuts on funding for alcohol abuse treatment programs and pointing out that only three percent of existing funds for treatment of alcoholics is spent on the special needs of women alcoholics.

April 20, 1977: Letter to HEW Secretary Califano requesting information about plans to improve management of the Office of Civil Rights in light of a GAO report which found a pattern of nonenforcement of the civil rights laws for which HEW had responsibility.

April 29, 1977: Presiding Officer Abzug testified before the Senate Committee on human resources in support of S. 995, which would extend the protections of Title 7 of the 1964 Civil Rights Act to prohibit discrimination based on pregnancy.

May 23, 1977: Letter to Secretary Marshall of the Department of Labor requesting further information concerning statistics showing a decline in the number of employees and the amounts found to have been underpaid under the Equal Pay Act, and calling attention to the Commission's recommendation that the Act be vigorously enforced.

June 22, 1977: Letter to President Carter drawing his attention to two Commission recommendations: that he direct all Federal agencies to review the relevant recommendations contained in the 1976 Commission final report to the President; and that Federal departments and agencies be encouraged to supply the Commission with funds, staff, and resources in accordance with Section 3 of the Executive Order 11832.

July 25, 1977: Presiding Officer Abzug testified before the House Subcommittee on Employment Opportunities in support of the Displaced Homemaker Bill, HR 28. She pointed out that the Commission, in its 1976 final report to the President, had supported such legislation and continues to do so.

August 4, 1977: Letter to Representative Charlie Rose, chairman of the Policy Group on Information and Computers, asking his assistance in obtaining wide publicity for the commission booklets on the legal status of homemakers in every State.

August 24, 1977: Letter to Frank Cylke, Chief of the Division for the Blind and Physically Handicapped, The Library of Congress, thanking him for having made "... To Form a More Perfect Union ..." (Commission report issued in 1976) available to the blind as a talking book cassette recording.

August 30, 1977: Letter to President Carter protesting the proposed dependency test for receipt of social security benefits by spouses not covered in their own right. The letter called attention to the Commission's recommendations in its 1976 report that HEW establish a task force to study earnings-splitting and develop recommendations with the Justice Department's Task Force on Sex Discrimination.

September 22, 1977: Statement by Presiding Officer Abzug appeared in *Congressional Record* reporting on State Meetings for women sponsored by the Commission and efforts by anti-change groups to disrupt these meetings.

September 23, 1977: Letter to Labor Secretary Marshall urging him to take steps to increase the number of women who participate in public service employment programs. Presiding Officer Abzug noted that more than 90 percent of the persons receiving AFDC payments are women, and it is shocking that less than 40 percent of those hired for public employment are women.

October 24, 1977: In response to request from the Joint Economic Committee of Congress, Presiding Officer Abzug submitted statement for hearing on record on women in a full employment economy. She pointed out that women have the highest unemployment rate in the Nation and that the proposed National Plan of Action called for a national policy of full employment.

October 31, 1977: Letter to the Small Business Administration urging that agency to reconsider its policy of excluding women from the benefits of the 8(a) program for socially disadvantaged small business owners.

RULES OF ORDER FOR HOUSTON CONFERENCE

§1901.1 Definitions of terms used in this chapter.

(a) "Commission" means the National Commission on the Observance of International Women's Year, 1975 established by Executive Order 11832, 3 CFR 106, 40 FR 2415, January 13, 1975; Pub. L. 94-167, 89 Stat. 1003, December 23, 1975.

(b) "Conference" means the National Women's Conference to be organized and convened by the Commission in accordance with Pub. L. 94-167.

(c) "Coordinating Committee" means the Coordinating Committee in each State designated by the Commission to organize and conduct a meeting in the State in preparation for the National Women's Conference.

(d) "State" includes the fifty States and the District of Columbia, the Commonwealth of Puerto Rico, Guam, American Samoa, the Virgin Islands, and the Trust Territory of the Pacific Islands, unless otherwise specified.

(e) "State Meeting" means the meetings organized and conducted in each State by the Coordinating Committee in preparation for the National Women's Conference.

(f) "Act" means Pub. L. 94-167, 89 Stat. 1003, December 23, 1975.

(g) "Conference session," "plenary session," or "session" refers to the meetings which may be held at the following times:

Session I. November 19, morning.
Session II. November 19, afternoon.
Session III. November 19, evening.
Session IV. November 20, afternoon.
Session V. November 21, morning.

§1901.2 Words importing gender.

As used in this chapter, unless the context requires a different meaning, words importing the feminine gender include both genders.

PART 1905—NATIONAL WOMEN'S CONFERENCE RULES OF ORDER

Sec.

Subpart A—Call to Conference
1905.1 Call to Conference

Subpart B—Voting Delegates and Voting
1905.2 Voting Body.
1905.3 No proxy voting.
1905.4 Method of voting.
1905.5 Identification Badges.

Subpart C—Registration for Plenary Session
1905.6 Registration.

Subpart D—Conduct of Conference Sessions
1905.7 Order of Business.
1905.8 Designated Seating.
1905.9 Quorum.
1905.10 Discussion and debate.
1905.11 Making Motions.
1905.12 Credentials Committee.
1905.13 Timekeepers.
1905.14 Floor Tellers.
1905.15 New Business.
1905.16 Minutes.
1905.17 Interpretation of Rules.
1905.18 Parliamentary Authority.
1905.19 Conference Officials.
1905.20 Committee of the Conference.

AUTHORITY: E.O. 11832, 40 FR 2415, January 18, 1975, Pub. L. 94-167, 89 Stat. 1003, December 23, 1975.

Subpart A—Call to Conference

§1905.1 Call to Conference.

The Commission shall determine the time, place and the agenda of the Conference and shall issue official notice thereof to the Chair and to the Recording Secretary of each Coordinating Committee, to all delegates, and to the general public.

Subpart B—Voting Delegates and Voting

§1905.2 Voting Body.

The voting body of the Conference shall consist of the following voting delegates:

(a) State delegates, certified as having been duly selected in accordance with applicable regulations;

(b) All current and past members of the Commission;

(c) Additional delegates-at-large designated by the Commission deemed necessary and appropriate to fulfill the requirements of Section 3(a) of Public Law 94-167;

(d) Alternate State delegates who have been properly certified in one of the following two ways:

(1) If the Commission receives proper notification by November 1, 1977, that a State delegate is unable to attend, the ranking alternate selected at the State Meeting will be permanently certified by the Commission as a State delegate; or

(2) The chair of the State delegation shall notify the Credentials Committee if she has been informed by a delegate in her State's delegation that such delegate is unable to attend or can no longer continue to participate in one or more sessions. Upon notification by the chair of the State delegation, the Credentials Committee will then certify the appropriate ranking alternate delegate present at the Conference as a delegate for her State for the appropriate session or sessions.

(3) In implementing the aforementioned rules, the following principles shall be controlling:

(i) An alternate has no right to participate as a voting delegate unless properly certified pursuant to §1905.2(d) (1) or (2) above.

(ii) If a delegate has notified the chair of her State's delegation that she is unable to participate in any session and if she has been replaced by an alternate for that session according to the procedure in this section, she may not return and be recertified as a voting delegate during any such session.

(iii) There shall be no alternate delegates for current and past members of the Commission and delegates-at-large.

§1905.3 No proxy voting.

There shall be no proxy voting. No individual shall have more than one vote.

§1905.4 Method of Voting.

The regular method of voting shall be by standing vote, except that individuals with physical limitations may vote by raising their hands. A majority vote of those present and voting shall be required in order to overrule any ruling of the chair. There will be no secret ballots or roll call votes.

§1905.5 Identification Badges.

Voting delegates and alternates shall have photo identification badges.

Subpart C—Registration for Plenary Sessions

§1905.6 Registration.

All persons who attend the plenary sessions (including press) must comply with registration requirements, including registering with name, address, identification, and payment of any required fee. Upon compliance with registration requirements each registrant shall be issued an identification badge as voter, special guest, observer, press or staff. Badges shall not be transferable and they must be visible at all meetings. Badges shall not be altered in any fashion.

Subpart D—Conduct of Conference Sessions

§1905.7 Order of Business.

The Commission shall establish the order of business for the Conference when it issues the Call to the Conference according to §1905.1. New business may be submitted and adopted in accordance with §1905.15.

§1905.8 Designated Seating.

Separate seating spaces shall be provided and clearly designated as follows:

(a) Current and past Commission members,

(b) State delegates, seated by State delegation,

(c) Delegates-at-Large,

(d) Alternate State delegates,

(e) Special guests,

(f) Official observers,

(g) Operational committees and Commission and Conference staff,

(h) Duly registered press and,

(i) Duly registered observers to the capacity of the meeting room.

Only persons wearing an appropriate badge shall be admitted to the plenary sessions by the Credentials monitors, and only to designated areas and at designated times in accordance with procedures established by the Commission and the Credentials Committee. Only voting delegates, authorized media personnel and authorized Commission and Conference staff shall be admitted to the floor for Conference sessions.

§1905.9 Quorum.

One-third of the duly registered voting delegates shall constitute a quorum for the plenary voting sessions.

§1905.10 Discussion and debate.

(a) In order to address the Conference, a voting delegate must address the chair, await recognition, give her name and identification and state whether she is speaking in the affirmative or the negative.

(b) Discussion on a motion or agenda topic shall be limited to two minutes for each speaker.

(c) No one may speak a second time on an issue until all others who wish to speak have had an opportunity to do so.

(d) Debate may be limited or terminated by a majority vote of those voting delegates present and voting.

(e) The Chair shall have the authority to call an executive session when she deems it necessary to insure the orderly conduct of the Conference. In the event the Chair exercises this authority, the hall shall be cleared of all observers.

§1905.11 Making motions.

(a) Only properly certified voting delegates may speak to issues, make motions or vote. All motions, except on procedural matters, shall be written and signed by the person who makes the motion. The Chair may require such written motion before action is taken.

(b) A majority vote of those voting delegates present and voting shall be required to table, or to postpone indefinitely, or to object to consideration.

§1905.12 Credentials Committee.

A Credentials Committee shall be appointed by the Rules Committee. The Credentials Committee shall have authority and responsibility to resolve any question of registration, voting rights, or admission to the Conference, and to report registrations to the Conference upon request of the Chair. List of State delegates and of delegates-at-large shall be provided to the Chair of the Credentials Committee prior to the opening of Conference registration. Duplications of such lists shall be prepared to facilitate the registration.

(a) No registrant will be permitted to obstruct the view or hearing of any other registrant by any device. Only persons authorized by the Commission shall be permitted to bring any electronic or sonic devices into the Conference. Any person violating these rules may be denied all Conference privileges and removed from the Conference.

(b) Any registrant may be requested at any time by the Credentials Committee to provide additional identification. The Credentials Committee may deny any or all Conference privileges to any registrant who lacks appropriate identification or abuses any Conference privilege or obstructs the orderly conduct of the Conference.

257

(c) The Credentials Committee shall appoint sergeants-at-arms and credentials monitors as necessary to assist the enforcement of the rules of the Conference.

§1905.13 Timekeepers.

Timekeepers shall be appointed by the Rules Committee to serve at all sessions. Their duty shall be to indicate to each speaker an appropriate warning before expiration of the time allowed.

§1905.14 Floor Tellers.

Floor tellers shall be appointed by the Rules Committee to count, tabulate and report standing count votes. The floor tellers shall be assigned to definite sections of the conference floor. A record of the vote shall be entered in the minutes. During a vote count only floor tellers will be permitted to move about. All other persons except voting delegates shall leave the voting area.

§1905.15 New business.

Subject matter not embraced within the established order of business, in the judgment of the Chair, may be brought up under the heading of new business at the final session. Any such new business shall be submitted to the Recording Secretary in writing prior to the close of the session before the last plenary session in order that it may be read to the Conference body at the start of the last plenary session. A majority vote of those voting delegates present shall be required to consider such new business.

§1905.16 Minutes.

The recording secretary, who shall be appointed by the Rules Committee, shall be responsible for the preparation of the official minutes for all plenary sessions. Tape recording shall be provided for all plenary session discussions to aid in the preparation of accurate minutes by the designated Recorder or Recorders. Minutes shall be approved by the Chair of the Session and by the Presiding Officer of the Commission or her designate.

§1905.17 Interpretation of Rules.

Any question regarding the interpretation of these rules shall be resolved by the Rules Committee.

§1905.18 Parliamentary Authority.

(a) The Rules Committee shall appoint the parliamentarians who shall be advisors to the Chair. The rules in Roberts' Rules of Order Newly Revised shall govern the plenary sessions of the Conference in all cases when not inconsistent with these rules.

(b) The format, agenda, order of business and seating arrangements shall be determined in all cases by the Commission. All discussion groups or other meetings of the Conference shall be governed by Roberts' Rules of Order Newly Revised whenever open debate is scheduled.

§1905.19 Conference Officials.

At each plenary session there shall be in attendance a Chair, Vice-Chair, Federal officer, appointed pursuant to the requirements of the Federal Advisory Committee Act, the Chair of the Rules Committee or her designee, the Chair of the Credentials Committee or her designee, an official parliamentarian, timekeepers, tellers, a recording secretary and credentials monitors. The Chair and Vice-Chair for each plenary session shall be appointed by the Commission.

§1905.20 Committee of the Conference.

Pursuant to Section 3(b) (7) of Public Law 94-167 the Conference shall establish a Committee of the Conference which will take steps to provide for the convening of a second National Women's Conference.

Elizabeth Athanasakos
Co-Chair, Rules Committee
National Commission on the
Observance of International
Women's Year.

Harry T. Edwards
Co-Chair, Rules Committee
National Commission on the
Observance of International
Women's Year

NATIONAL COMMISSION ON THE OBSERVANCE OF INTERNATIONAL WOMEN'S YEAR

FORMER MEMBERS PRIOR TO FEBRUARY 1977 (APPOINTED BY PRESIDENT FORD)

ALAN ALDA, of New York, New York—actor.

ETHEL D. ALLEN, of Philadelphia, Pennsylvania—Physician, Surgeon; City Councilwoman-at-large, Philadelphia.

ANNE L. ARMSTRONG, of Armstrong, Texas—Former U.S. Ambassador to the United Kingdom.

MARGARET LONG ARNOLD, of Washington, D.C.—Executive Assistant for Women's Activities, National Retired Teachers Association/American Association of Retired Persons.

RANDY BACA, of Phoenix, Arizona—Executive Director, Arizona Small Businessmen's Association.

BARBARA R. BERGMANN, of Bethesda, Maryland—Professor of Economics, University of Maryland.

PATRICIA T. CARBINE, of New York—Publisher and Editor-in-Chief, *Ms. Magazine.*

NORA JIMENEZ CASIANO, of Santurce, Puerto Rico—Business Manager, Caribbean Business; Past President, League of Women Voters of Puerto Rico.

WESTON CHRISTOPHERSON, of Lake Forest, Illinois—President, Jewel Companies.

MARY STALLINGS COLEMAN, of Battle Creek, Michigan—Justice, Michigan Supreme Court.

HELEN K. COPLEY, of La Jolla, California—Chair and Chief Executive Officer of Copley Newspapers.

RICHARD CORNUELLE, of New York—Author.

WINFIELD C. DUNN, of Nashville, Tennessee—Vice President, Hospital Corporation of America.

CASEY EIKE, of Lawrence, Kansas—Co-director, Douglas County Rape Victim Support Service.

MARCH K. FONG EU, of Sacramento, California—Secretary of State for California.

MARY GERMANY, of Meridian, Mississippi—Election Commissioner; Civic and Political Activities.

PAULA GIBSON, of Spokane, Washington—Field Underwriter, Life Insurance.

GILDA BOJORQUEZ GJURICH, of Montebello, California—President and Senior Partner, Robert Parada Construction Co.

ELLA T. GRASSO, of Windsor Locks, Connecticut—Governor of Connecticut.

HANNA HOLBORN GRAY, of New Haven, Connecticut—Provost (Acting President), Yale University.

KATHARINE HEPBURN, of New York, New York—Actress.

BARBARA WALTERS, of New York, New York—Television News Co-anchor, ABC Network.

ANNIE DODGE WAUNEKA, of Ganado, Arizona—Member of the Navajo Tribal Council.

VELMA MURPHY HILL, of New York, New York—Assistant to the President, United Federation of Teachers.

MING HSU, of Westfield, New Jersey—Director of International Trade Relations, RCA; Member, National Women's Political Caucus and W.E.A.L.

PATRICIA HUTAR, of Glenview, Illinois—President, National Federation of Republican Women; Former U.S. Representative to the U.N. Commission on Status of Women.

RITA Z. JOHNSTON, of Bethesda, Maryland—Former U.S. Delegate and Vice Chair of Inter-American Commission of Women, OAS.

ELLEN GROVES KIRBY, of Petersburg, West Virginia—County Public Health Nurse.

DOROTHY VALE KISSINGER, of Mesa, Arizona—President of Soroptimist International of the Americas.

CLARE BOOTHE LUCE, of Honolulu, Hawaii—Former Congresswoman; Former U.S. Ambassador to Italy; author, playwright.

WILLIAM CRAWFORD MERCER, of Wellesley Hills, Maryland—President, New England Telephone and Telegraph Co.

SHIRLEY PRICE, of Louisville, Kentucky—Member of County Executive Committee, Republican Party; Former Teacher.

SISTER JOEL READ, of Milwaukee, Wisconsin—President, Alverno College.

JILL RUCKELSHAUS, of Medina, Washington—First Presiding Officer, IWY; Member, Board of Trustees, University of Puget Sound; Former Special Assistant to Anne L. Armstrong, Counselor to the President.

DORIS ROYAL, of Springfield, Nebraska—Farmwife; Member of Agriwoman; Extension Club; Nebraska Feeders Auxiliary.

PATRICIA SAIKI, of Honolulu, Hawaii—Member, Hawaii State Senate; Member, Citizens' Advisory Council on Status of Women; Board of Trustees, Hawaii Pacific College.

BETTY SMITH, of Eugene, Oregon—Member, National Board of Directors, YMCA; City Councilwoman, Eugene.

MARY LOUISE SMITH, of Des Moines, Iowa—Former Chair, Republican National Committee; Active in civic and political organizations.

JOCELYN DAN WURZBURG, of Memphis, Tennessee—Member, Tennessee Commission for Human Development; Advisory Committee to the Minority Business Resource Center of the Federal Railroad Association.

NATIONAL COMMISSION STAFF

EXECUTIVE DIRECTOR:
Kathryn Clarenbach

CONFERENCE COORDINATOR:
Lee Novick

COORDINATOR, POLICY AND PLANS:
Mim Kelber

LEGAL COUNSEL:
Linda Dorian
William Wallace

CONSULTANT, POLICY AND PLANS:
Catherine East

SPECIAL CONFERENCE CONSULTANTS:
Helen Cassidy
Poppy Northcutt

PRESS OFFICE:
Kathy Bonk
Priscilla Crane
Elvira Crocker
Glenn Ellefson-Brooks
Judy Frie
Alice Hayes
Pat Hyatt
Brynda Pappas

POLICY AND PLANS:
Shelah Leader
Susan Rubin
Sheryl Swed

INTERNATIONAL:
Maxine Hitchcock
Marian Higman

CONFERENCE STAFF:
Joy Bennett
Nancy Dolan
Dorothe Dow
Alberta L. Henderson
Fran Henry
Rose Marie Roybal
Dorothy Spinks
Gisela Taber
Priscilla Weatherly

ADMINISTRATIVE:
Reuben Lev, Executive Officer
Bernice Baer
Dolores Brotherton

Paulette Carmon
Sandra Cunningham
Ann English
Ellen Ivie
Marian Lebowitz
Sally Monroe
Rita O'Fiinn
Margot Reiner
Phyllis Rich
Shoshana Riemer
Inez Sadur
Aida Schoenfeld
Vanna Shields
Agnes Sutphin
Betsy Thom
Lillian Wallace
Patricia Walters

CONFERENCE REPORT WRITER:
Caroline Bird

TORCH RELAY COORDINATOR:
Pat Kery

CONFERENCE SECURITY
COORDINATOR:
Barbara Cigainero

HOUSTON OFFICE MANAGER:
Joy Groseclose

CONFERENCE VOLUNTEERS
IN WASHINGTON:
Joan Biordi
Lisa Burns
Martha Chubb
Charlotte Conable
Doreen Dow
Audrey Ghizzoni
Michael P. McCarry
Yvonne McDonald
Mary Albert O'Neil
Henley Roughton
George Shields
Nancy Shue
Sharon Spinks
Denise Surber
Cindy Jo DeVibliss

CHIEF PARLIAMENTARIAN
FOR CONFERENCE:
Marcia Romberg

ASSISTANT PARLIAMENTARIANS:
Lila Crowley
Bettie Mooney
Gloria W. Resnick
Dr. Francine Merritt

OFFICIAL REPORTER:
Bobbie Ames

HOUSTON COMMITTEE

Executive Committee

CHAIR
Mary Keegan

VICE-CHAIRS
Elma Barrera
Helen Cassidy
Dr. Hortense Dixon

VOLUNTEER COORDINATORS AND
HOUSTON COMMITTEE OFFICE
ADMINISTRATOR
Reverend Sara Seeger
Derby Hirst

CITY LIAISON
Dr. Nikki R. Van Hightower

IWY HOTEL COORDINATOR
Helen Nelson

INTERNATIONAL
Alice Pratt
Dr. Margaret Melville
Allee Mitchell

Board of Directors

Vice-Chair Elma Barrera's Committees

FIRST AID
Sister Ambrose
Sister Carmella, CCVI
Dixie Brown

MEDIA
Odelia Mendez
Brenda Loudermilk

PARLIAMENTARY PROCEDURES
Margaret Acosta
Linda May

SPEAKERS
Dee Bishop

INFORMATION
Yvette Calloway
Mollie Parkerson
Eileen Wall

FINANCE
Ann Kaufman

SPECIAL SERVICES
Lillian Pasternak
Geraldine Rougagnac
Margaret M. Lopez

TRANSPORTATION
Barbara Lange
Poppy Northcutt

REGISTRATION
Guanita Reiter
Marjorie Randal
Charlotte Motley
Vikki Damrei

COLISEUM ARRANGEMENTS
Claire Noonan
Sherry Collier

CHILD CARE
Juanita Harang

SPECIAL EVENTS
Barbara Dillingham
Dr. Alice Whatley
Terry Lin

USHERS
Betsy Johnson

And Hundreds of other Houston Area
Volunteers

LEGAL REPORT
by Linda Colvard Dorian
General Counsel

Commission Litigation

The National Commission on the Observance of International Women's Year confronted novel legal problems from its earliest existence. Its powers, its expenditures, the composition of the Commission, the State meetings, and the National Women's Conference were all challenged in court. As of March 1978, nine lawsuits had been brought against the Commission. All of the cases that have been finally disposed of by the courts have been resolved in favor of the Commission.

One action brought in Federal court alleged that the Commission had misused its appropriated monies when, in fact, Congress had not yet appropriated any monies for the Commission. This lawsuit, typical of several such suits brought against the Commission, charged the Commission with unlawful lobbying activities, misusing Federal monies, and violating the requirements of the Federal Advisory Committee Act.

Plaintiffs in these court actions charged that the Commission was in violation of the lobbying restriction in the public law. That provision states that no funds authorized under the public law can be used for lobbying activities. Plaintiffs interpreted this provision to mean that the Commission was barred from taking positions on matters that may be pending in legislative bodies, such as the Equal Rights Amendment, and that Commissioners and staff were barred from stating their views on such matters in public meetings.

The courts and the Comptroller General were unanimous in their judgment that the plaintiffs were

erroneous in their interpretation of the lobbying restriction contained in the public law. The Comptroller General set forth his interpretation of lobbying in a response to a persistent congressional critic of the Commission:

"We explained that the term 'lobbying' and the advocacy of a particular point of view are not necessarily synonymous, and that in our view, 'lobbying' means 'direct communication to a member or members of a legislative body, State and Federal, to influence the vote on legislation pending before or proposed to that body or the vote on the ratification of constitutional amendments.' "

The Comptroller General further described the nature of the Commission's role:

"In our view, the Commission has been specifically directed to play an active role in encouraging and promoting 'women's rights,' as it sees them and there is nothing inconsistent with its advocacy position so long as it refrains from engaging in direct lobbying activities . . . ."

As to an alleged violation of the Federal Advisory Committee Act (FACA), plaintiffs argued that the Commission, the State coordinating committees, the State meetings, and the National Conference were not balanced in terms of points of view and were therefore in violation of the FACA. Rejecting this argument, the Comptroller General noted that the Commission was in large part operational rather than advisory in its functions, and that the State coordinating committees existed solely to plan and conduct a State meeting for women, not to perform an advisory function.

In assessing the nature of the State meetings and the National Women's Conference, the Comptroller General found that the requirements of the public law and the Commission's regulations "do not restrict the balance of the membership, but afford an extremely broad base for participation. In fact, the necessary practical

result of these provisions and requirements is to leave the degree of 'balance' essentially to the participants in the State and regional meetings themselves through the normal democratic process."

The Commission required each State coordinating committee to maintain records regarding its grant monies. Although the Commission was charged by its critics with mismanaging its monies, no credible evidence of any irregularity or specific allegations were ever brought to the attention of the Commission, the courts, or the Government Accounting Office. In fact, the fiscal records of the State coordinating committees were maintained with great care and with the continuous assistance of the Commission's budget and grant personnel in the national office.

Another line of litigation to which the Commission was a party involved the election of delegates at the State meetings held under the public law. After State meetings were held and delegates elected, some participants at the State meetings filed challenges with the Commission alleging that the elected delegates should not be certified as that State's delegation to the National Women's Conference. Bases for such challenges included claims that the delegates were not sufficiently diverse as to viewpoints or age, income, religion, or ethnicity, as required by section 3(a) (2) of P.L. 94-167; that the delegates were opposed to the purposes of the law, namely, achieving equality for women; and that there were technical defects in the election process such that the election should be considered null and void. Challenges were submitted in 36 States.

The Commission reviewed each challenge at an administrative proceeding after it gave notice to the public in the *Federal Register* and through other means that it would review all challenges and accompanying documentation submitted by August 8, 1977. The Commission determined that the only grounds on which it would deny delegates their certification at the national Conference was fraud in the election process. Finding no evidence of election fraud or unfairness, the Commission denied all challenges.*

Subsequent to the Commission's rejection of challenges, three separate lawsuits were filed in Federal courts challenging the election of delegates in three States—Hawaii, Ohio, and Washington. Two challenges were filed by pro-change groups and one challenge was filed by an anti-change faction. Hearings were held in all of these cases and legal memoranda were submitted by the parties. These actions were ultimately resolved, all in favor of the Commission, the week prior to the national Conference.

The remainder of the litigation to which the Commission has been a party involves contract disputes and legal problems encountered by the several State coordinating committees. A total of 12 lawsuits have been filed against the Commission; all decisions to date have been in favor of the Commission.

Interpretive Regulations The public law conveyed broad powers upon the Commission, including the power to issue regulations interpretive of the law. In exercising this responsibility the Commission initially issued two sets of regulations. The first set of regulations invested the State coordinating committees, members and employees, with certain responsibilities and powers. This set of regulations also set forth detailed financial procedures to govern the allocation and expenditure of grant monies and the reporting of expenditures. The second set of regulations governing the State coordinating committees established rules of conduct for the State meetings. These

rules attempted to insure the broadest possible democratic participation consistent with an orderly parliamentary process and fair election procedures.

The Commission issued a final set of regulations governing the conduct of the National Women's Conference. These regulations were based on standard parliamentary procedure as well as Congressional models governing debate.

Legislative Liaison The Commission was involved, throughout its tenure, with frequent coordination and exchange of information with the Congress. These contacts included congressional inquiries seeking information on the Commission's activities as well as congressional requests that the Commission state its views in testimony and written comments on issues of concern to women presently awaiting legislative action. Two such legislative matters on which the Commission stated its views are the pregnancy amendment to Title 7 and the Displaced Homemakers' Bill.

In an effort to fully inform the broadest segment of the public, the Commission, through its presiding officer, issued statements explaining the State meetings process and events associated with the State meetings in the *Congressional Record*. The Commission also listed the elected delegates in the *Federal Register* so that interested members of the public would know the identities of delegates from their State who would be attending the national Conference.

---

*The Commission did, however, deplore the lack of diversity in the composition of certain delegations, particularly when the imbalance involved significant under-representation of a racial minority in a State's population.

REPORT ON RESOLUTIONS

In voting on the 26 subject area recommendations in the National Plan of Action, delegates to the National Women's Conference voted to support 18 without change: arts and humanities; battered women; business; child abuse; child care; credit; elective and appointive office; employment; Equal Rights Amendment; health; homemakers; insurance; international affairs; media; offenders; reproductive freedom, sexual preference; and statistics. Four subject area recommendations were amended: education; older women; rape; and rural women. Substitute recommendations were approved in three subject areas: disabled women; minority women; women, welfare and poverty. One subject area recommendation calling for creation of a Cabinet-level Department of Women Affairs was defeated.

More than 90 resolutions were submitted by delegates before the required time of the close of the Sunday evening (November 20, 1977) plenary session for consideration the following day. The Resolutions Committee recommended that about 24 resolutions could be considered under the implementation or new business items on the agenda.

Under implementation in the final plenary session November 21, delegates defeated a resolution calling for creation of a Women's Congress consisting of two delegates elected by each state delegation to monitor implementation of the National Plan of Action. The delegates voted to approve a resolution authorizing the National Commission to select a Committee of the Conference, as required under Public Law 94-167. The committee is to take steps to provide for the convening of a Second National Women's Conference and to assess the progress made toward achieving the recommendations of the 1977 conference.

The conference adjourned without having the time to act on most resolutions submitted by delegates. The National Commission voted at its December 14, 1977, meeting to include in this final report a listing of all resolutions that were not acted upon at Houston. An analysis of these resolutions showed that they fell into the following general categories.

Proposals for ending discrimination against women in various activities:

A sports resolution recommending that the President and Congress implement all aspects of the report of the President's Commission on Olympic Sports to further equitable opportunities for women in international competition and in governance of national and international organizations; take specific steps to apply the principle of equal athletic opportunity to all publicly supported sports programs, including use of all educational sports facilities, public arenas, and parks and recreation facilities; develop a public education program on the importance of physical activity and fitness for women as well as for men.

A resolution on women in the military recommending that the President instruct the Secretary of Defense to submit to the Congress legislation to rescind Sections 6015 and 3549 of Title 10, U.S. Code. These sections preclude the assignment of women to duties aboard ships of the Navy and on aircraft of the Navy and Air Force, whereas the Army does not impose such constraints on the assignment of women.

A resolution asking the Congress to amend Title 6 of the Civil Rights Act of 1964, which prohibits discrimination on the grounds of race, color, or national origin in federally assisted programs to include prohibition of discrimination on the basis of sex, affectional preference, and age, particularly as it affects the National Endowments on the Arts and Humanities.

A resolution on women and housing asking the President and Congress to direct the vigorous and expeditious enforcement of all laws and regulations prohibiting discrimination in housing; enact comprehensive fair housing legislation adding marital status, presence of children and sexual preference to prohibited forms of sex discrimination in the sale or rental of housing; assurance of additional funds to increase the supply of low and moderate income housing; tax advantages for renters (frequently single or elderly women or women heads of households) similar to those now granted only to homeowners; reform of Federal and State laws relating to domicile, property and family that adversely affect a woman's right to acquire, hold, improve, insure, maintain and transfer shelter of her choice; Federal and State guarantees that views and needs of women are taken into account in planning rural and urban housing developments, revitalizing neighborhoods, supporting new communities and new towns in-town, and other forms of planned development that can systematically address the issues of adequate public transportation, location of jobs near homes, and provisions for child care; special programs to train women to work in all parts of the male-dominated housing industry, including construction, financing, management, planning, and policy.

Resolutions calling for the decriminalization of prostitution; condemning pornography; and erasing the criminal records of former drug addicts.

Proposals to implement the National Plan of Action:

These resolutions included support for economic boycott of states that have not ratified the ERA; and making

ERA a priority of the conference, the President and Congress; sending letters of thanks to members of Congress for authorizing the Conference; creating a National Task Force on Research and Information on Women; setting up continuing committees; increasing powers and funding of Women's Bureau; asking the President to order comparable worth study in executive branch and directing Civil Service Commission to set salaries based on comparable worth; requesting President to set timetable for implementing the National Plan within 30 days of receiving it.

Proposals on human rights and extension of democratic rights:

A resolution, accompanied by more than 1,000 signatures, calling for self-determination and full citizenship rights for the District of Columbia.

A resolution calling on the President to grant an unconditional release to Lolita Lebron, a Puerto Rican woman, and three other Puerto Rican nationalists, who have been imprisoned for more than two decades.

Resolutions expressing sympathy with the women of South Africa, proposing an end to U.S. trade with South Africa and withdrawing U.S. investments in South Africa; banning the circulation of South African gold coins.

Proposals on reproductive freedom:

Resolutions opposing the Hyde amendment; condemning practice of aborting female fetuses detected by amniocentesis; cutting off Federal funds and tax exempt status for hospitals refusing to perform abortions; requiring reporting of complications of abortion; providing Federal aid to pregnant women to help them keep their children; creating a Youth Bureau within HEW to combat teenage pregnancy; requiring IRS to investigate the Catholic Church because of antiabortion lobbying activities; opposing airline tariff on pregnant passengers.

Proposals on peace and foreign policy:

Resolutions opposing production of the neutron bomb, which would destroy people and preserve property; and a resolution emphasizing the ratification and implementation of the U.N. Covenant on Civil and Political Rights and the U.N. Covenant on Economic, Social, and Cultural Rights.

Proposals on employment and the economy:

Resolutions proposing boycott of J.P. Stevens and other large employers of women that are involved in strikes; requiring job applications to include information about volunteer work; including working class and poor women in all government decision-making, and including financial aid for the working poor in Federal and State guidelines; urging Federal aid to combat unemployment among black teenagers; supporting proposed Labor Department regulations to implement goals and timetables for women in construction; stating that taxes should not be based on marital status.

Proposals on the family:

Resolutions proposed providing more money for legal services for family law; creating National Commission on the American Family to review laws; asking conference to go on record as being pro-life, pro-family and pro-ERA; prohibiting consideration of financial status when determining child custody and assuring economic independence of all women.

Proposals on health and environment:

Resolutions proposing that mental health, alcohol and drug abuse services be included in health program; providing for health information, education and counseling; providing additional Federal funds for research on environmental health hazards; halting construction of nuclear power plants because of the hazards of radiation.

Proposals on language:

Resolutions proposing that in final report all references to states should include reference to territories and that the words "multicultural," "multilingual," and "ethnic" should be used in National Plan.

Miscellaneous proposals:

Among other resolutions submitted were proposals to: create an American Women's Museum; make the Women's Hall of Fame in Seneca Falls a national monument; support an end to hunger; recognize the role and contributions of Eleanor Roosevelt; include more southwestern Chicana women in the next planning committee for the second conference; permit private suits in Federal court for Title 9 violations; provide Federal funding for multi-purpose crisis centers for women in every city; add references to adult education; affirm the ownership rights of farm women as small business owners; direct the USDA extension service to cease advising against joint ownership of estates and change the tax laws to make joint ownership more advantageous to married couples; eliminate State and Federal estate and gift taxes on transfers of family-owned farms to heirs; hold a national conference on blacks and other minorities; express appreciation to members of the press covering the conference; require state legislatures to hold hearings on regional power; require the Federal Government to curtail spending; include the arts as an integral part of basic education; and end the tax exempt status of organizations that oppose equality.

Statements on Conference:

Resolution, accompanied by signatures of 171 delegates, opposing seating of Mississippi delegation because of its all-white composition; resolution defending Mississippi delegation; resolutions favoring holding of annual National Women's Conference; opposing holding of another conference; proposing that if any future conference is held every American should be invited and all viewpoints should be included; requiring IWY to make a cost estimate for each section of National Plan and to include a "minority report" in final conference report; proposing a commemorative stamp for the Conference.

"Minority Report"

A set of resolutions, described as a "minority report," was submitted by the chair of the Indiana delegation. The 10 resolutions supported a constitutional ban on abortion; opposed ERA; opposed federally controlled early child development programs; proposed legal protection for displaced homemakers in states with "no fault" divorce laws; opposed the IWY recommendations on international interdependence; proposed that all public education teach moral values, including honesty, acceptance of responsibility, respect for others, for parents and for those properly in authority, the importance of the work ethic and the existence of absolute values of right and wrong; proposed that the Federal Government withdraw from involvement in affairs of older persons which are better handled by family, churches, and local government; rejected the classification of women as "minority women" and said all Americans should be classified as first-class citizens and should continue their involvement, whatever their concerns, in all areas that will improve and affect their world and the home.

In addition, another "minority report," which was not formally submitted to the Resolutions Commission, was circulated among delegates and to the press. Its text is printed below.

RESOLUTIONS COMMITTEE:
Commissioner Ruth Clusen, chair
Commissioner Rita Elway
Commissioner Beverly Everett
Commissioner Gloria Steinem
Policy Coordinator Mim Kelber

"...TO ESTABLISH JUSTICE..." (Minority Report)

We declare this to be the official Minority Report of the National Women's Conference held in Houston, Texas on November 18-21, 1977.

We take this opportunity to speak for the majority of women, the homemakers and professional women of the United States who, by design of the International Women's Year national and State committees, are represented in Houston at the National Women's Conference by a minority of the delegates.

We represent women from all States and Territories, of varying races and ethnic backgrounds, lifestyles and circumstances, thus portraying a true cross-section of America.

We have met in concert because of the attempt by the National IWY Commission and the various State coordinating committees to stifle ideas and actions which are not aligned with the directives issued by the National IWY Commission.

From its inception this federally funded conference has deliberately excluded or given only token representation to the views of the traditional, family-oriented woman who has been virtually unrepresented on the National IWY Commission and the various State coordinating committees, as well as being totally omitted from the American delegation to the international meeting in Mexico City in 1975.

While claiming to represent all women, only about one-tenth of 1 percent of American women participated in the State conferences. While spending $5 million of the taxpayers' money, the planners of the IWY systematically eliminated any meaningful input from the viewpoint of the majority of Americans.

In spite of the aforementioned actions, women of common concerns have come together to develop this Call for Action, based upon logical, progressive, Judaeo-Christian principles which are in keeping with the principles upon which the United States of America was founded.

A Call for Action in this Nation from its women should include:

A limit on taxation and nonessential Government spending, which is contributing to the most discriminatory condition to all persons and especially to the housewife and elderly inflation;

A return to the primary function of the Federal Government: proper defense measures to assure peace for our children;

A return to the local level of government, which is most responsive to the needs of the people, the responsibility to care for the needy and to educate the children;

A call for legislation which is truly supportive of the family structure by insuring parents their full rights of caring for their children;

A righteous indignation and demand for cessation of child abuse, including the heinous and ever-increasing use of children for degenerate pornographic materials;

A rejection of the unisex "equality" that the so-called Equal Rights Amendment would bring about if ratified;

A demand that the sanctity of innocent life be safeguarded from conception to natural death.

Our American women should also call this Nation to its knees in repentance for its licentiousness committed in the name of freedom.

Finally, we believe that justice is the better portion of equality.

Therefore, "... to establish justice ... and to secure the blessings of liberty to ourselves and our posterity ...", we offer this Call for Action to the President, the Congress, and the people of these United States of America.

ARTS AND HUMANITIES

We find no evidence of invidious discrimination against women artists, actresses, musicians, or singers. Obviously, a painting or sculpture is gender free in its worth and as beheld by the viewer; a play which calls for a male lead cannot be portrayed by a woman any more than a man can sing a soprano lead in an opera. Artists in totalitarian countries are guaranteed "equality" in their treatment but are also under strict Government control, which clearly obstructs and prevents freedom of expression by these artists in their given fields.

We recommend that tax-supported libraries present an equal and balanced supply of books, films, and materials relating to studies of women which portray in a positive manner the traditional roles of wife, mother, and homemaker, instead of the predominance of material of the feminist viewpoint now found in the majority of libraries.

BATTERED WOMEN

We recognize the serious problem of the battered spouse and its detrimental effect upon the home. We recommend that local and State governments disseminate public information on the subject; further, that helpful programs and counseling be carried out locally which will allow the spouse and children to remain in their home with adequate protection from physical or mental abuse.

BUSINESS

The free enterprise system which has brought this Nation to economic prosperity can only function in a marketplace free of governmental controls and regulations. We feel it is time for women to stop seeking Federal solutions to personal problems.

CHILD ABUSE

We recommend adequate State and community funding be provided for protective services and specific training programs in prevention of neglect and abuse of children. We encourage the establishment of volunteer programs to assist appropriate agencies dealing with child abuse. Since we feel that a major cause of child abuse is the breakdown of the family, we call for local programs which would strengthen the family and home. We also recommend the establishment of a local family court system to promote family integrity. We encourage prompt adjudication in handling child abuse cases.

We recommend the establishment of effective central registries with the local divisions of family services to coordinate child and parental treatment among hospitals, doctors, and other concerned parties and agencies. A public awareness program should be conducted. Educational programs for parents and counseling treatment for child abusers should be made available. Punishment for those who inflict injury or cause death to a child should be administered promptly.

We abhor the increased use of children in pornographic materials. We strongly urge that strict Federal, State, and local laws be enacted which control the distribution of these pornographic materials. We urge prompt action and strong punishment for those convicted of offenses. We recognize that pornography is damaging not only to children and youth but to men and women as well.

CHILD CARE

Because federally controlled early childhood development programs empower the Government to choose the ideology by which young lives are molded, we oppose any move towards a Federal network of developmental day care centers. Child care should be the responsibility of the family first. Help should be given by local communities, churches, and businesses in developing better child care for those who find it necessary to avail themselves of such services. We favor State action to promote child care centers in the private sector with adequate protection for the safety and welfare of the child. Provision should be made for trained personnel. Where necessary, additional facilities for child care should be provided under the division of family services or through available local resources. We support aid in meeting child care costs, where necessary, made available through a division of family services when other assistance is unavailable.

CREDIT

We acknowledge the existence of adequate existing Federal laws governing credit opportunities for women and support enforcement by appropriate agencies of such laws.

We commend private lending institutions for seeking to inform women of their credit rights under the law. We discourage tax monies being spent to duplicate efforts in this area.

DISABLED

We recognize the special problems of the handicapped in their efforts to participate in the mainstream of American life. We applaud efforts within both the public and private sectors to provide full opportunity to the handicapped. We encourage service organizations, churches, and civic groups to increase their services for handicapped Americans.

EDUCATION

We fully support the ideal of equal educational opportunities for women but deplore any educational quotas, as they must, by their very existence, cause reverse discrimination. We believe that the most qualified students, regardless of sex, race, religion, creed, age, or national origin, should be admitted to tax-financed institutions of higher learning and graduate schools, including the fields of law, medicine, etc.

We believe that private institutions who receive no public funding should not be harassed by Government intervention and shall have the right to set their own admission and conduct standards.

We regret the ridiculous interpretation of "equal educational opportunity" which has resulted in sexually integrated physical education classes and teams in the public elementary and secondary schools. This has caused undue embarrassment and has even prevented, in many instances, full participation.

While we support the ideal of presenting to students all their occupational options we deplore the militant women liberationists' demands that an unrealistic picture of womanhood be painted by textbooks and curriculum through an elimination and downgrading of the role of homemaker. We recommend that young women be encouraged to train in the career of their choice, and that if they choose the career of wife and mother, they understand the value of that career to the strength of the Nation.

We recommend that school teachers, counselors, administrators, and school psychologists research studies which prove that sexually differentiated behavior is firmly rooted in the biological phenomenon of hormonal action on the fetal brain so they can understand the ultimate damage to the student that can result from unisex conformity and/or role reversal. (Dr. Rhoda L. Lorand of New York, clinical psychotherapist.)

We recommend the elimination of all Federal funding for a movement which claims that observable behavioral differences between sexes are the result of stereotyping and oppression.

We recommend that school materials portray male and female roles in a positive, realistic manner in order to encourage pride and dignity in the uniqueness and distinctiveness of males and females.

We recommend that appropriate courses about family life or sex education should be offered in elementary or secondary schools on an elective basis only. All films, books, and materials should be available for parental inspection prior to enrollment of a child in the course. We further recommend that the schools be prohibited from providing abortion referral services.

We would remind that education should be designed to attain the greatest intellectual development possible for such a child, emphasizing basic reading, computation, and communication skills, as well as a thorough understanding and respect for our republican form of government and the free enterprise economic system, which have resulted in the greatest freedom and highest standard of living in the world. We further desire that all public education encourage the following characteristics: honesty; acceptance of responsibility; respect for the individuality of others; respect for parents and those properly in authority; and the importance of the work ethic in achieving personal goals.

ELECTIVE AND APPOINTIVE OFFICE

We regret the false concept that there are "women's issues" which will be adequately understood and represented only by women. We believe that persons best qualified to represent the views of their constituents should hold public office, regardless of sex, race, creed, color, or national origin. Although we believe that political parties should encourage qualified women, as well as qualified men, to run for office, we reject the concept that women need preferential treatment in elective or appointive office. We recommend that qualifications for elective and appointive positions should be the consideration rather than the sex of the individual.

EMPLOYMENT

We support equal job opportunities, equal pay for equal work, and equal opportunity for advancement for qualified women. We do not support any type of quota system, as it discriminates against the more qualified in some instances and thus ultimately hurts the consumer.

We recognize that many existing laws and regulations give equal opportunity employment to all qualified persons, such as:

Equal Pay Act of 1963; Title 7 of the Civil Rights Act of 1974; Executive Order 11246, as amended by Executive Order 11375, Title 9 of the Education Amendments of 1972; Title 7 of the Public Service Act, as amended; Title 8 of the Public Service Act: Title 8 of the Civil Rights Act of 1968, as amended; Equal Credit Opportunity Act of 1974; Revenue Sharing (State and Local Assistance Act); and the 14th amendment (Equal Protection clause).

We believe that these laws should be fairly administered and enforced.

We believe that the majority of women who work outside their homes consider their families as their primary careers and are working because inflation has forced them into the labor market in order to keep pace with the wage-price spiral.

We therefore urge the Federal Government to cease its inflationary deficit spending, to substantially lower the debt-ceiling limit, and to lower taxes, thus giving American families more spendable income.

EQUAL RIGHTS AMENDMENT

We are unalterably opposed to any extension of the ratification period for ERA. If the amendment cannot be ratified within seven years, it obviously has no significant or worthwhile merit.

While we wholeheartedly favor equal pay, equal educational opportunities, and job opportunities for women, we cannot support this dangerous constitutional amendment.

It will do nothing to solve any of woman's real problems, such as inflation, rape, battering, pornography, etc. Instead, constitutional scholars and attorneys have warned us repeatedly that ERA can:

Remove the legal requirement that husbands support wives (Professor Paul Freund, Harvard);

Require the legalization of homosexual marriages and allow these couples to adopt children (Senator Sam Ervin);

Constitutionally mandate the "right" to kill unborn babies (Professor Charles Rice, Notre Dame);

Require the elimination of "separate but equal" team sports in public schools (Senator Sam Ervin);

Subject women to compulsory military service and combat duty on a par with men (J. Fred Buzhardt, General Counsel for the Department of Defense);

Remove from States the right to legislate in any of the affected areas, a precedent already established by the Katzenbach v. Morgan Supreme Court decision;

Be ultimately interpreted and judicially enforced by the U.S. Supreme Court (Professor Paul Freund, Harvard);

Remove from women engaged in physical labor the many protections provided by legislation and contracts (Justice Felix Frankfurter);

Forbid any religious body which has a tax-exempt status from refusing certain roles within their body to women or homosexuals (Representative Larry Vick, Texas);

and many other harmful effects.

Consequently, many individuals and organizations have gone on record against this amendment, including the Southern Baptist Convention, the National Council of Catholic Women, the Veterans of Foreign Wars, the Union of Orthodox Rabbis, the Lutheran Church (Missouri Synod), Farm Bureau (many States), Texas P.T.A., Federation of Women's Clubs (many States), Mormon Church, Church of Christ (many congregations), Right to be a Woman, Inc., Happiness of Womanhood, Family Preservation League, Union of Orthodox Jewish Congregations, National Women's Christian Temperance Union, Daughters of the American Revolution, Sons of the Confederate Veterans, Rabbinical Society of America, Pro America, Women for Constitutional Government, American Conservative Union, Young Americans for Freedom, Eagle Forum, Women for Responsible Legislation, American Legislative Exchange Council, Women in Industry, Inc., and hundreds of State and local organizations.

HEALTH

We oppose a national (Government) health program because it would be unbearably expensive and would eliminate freedom of choice. Further, national health care, as demonstrated by Great Britain and other countries, is inferior in quality of patient care and conducive to fraud on the part of both doctors and patients.

We believe that since an increasing number of women are entering the health care field, more and more women will be participating in governmental and private health care planning and policymaking bodies, so we see no need for governmental interference in this process.

We recommend that minority and low income students be encouraged to apply for admission to medical schools and public health services and be aided with scholarships, if qualified; we further recommend that quota systems be abolished in all fields, particularly in medical schools and public health services, since the best medical care for all persons will result from producing medical personnel from the best qualified applicants, based upon ability and aptitude, not race, creed, sex, religion, or national origin.

We oppose legalization or decriminalization of marijuana or other narcotics and favor stiff, mandatory penalties for the drug pushers.

HOMEMAKERS

We recognize that the homemaker has the major role in nurturing the family and influencing future generations and we deplore the fact that some are downgrading the role of homemaker instead of emphasizing the importance and total fulfillment realized by successful homemakers. We therefore emphasize in all possible ways the joys and rewards of being a homemaker and the vital necessity to our society to preserve the family unit and protect the woman who is the core of that unit by retaining laws which hold a man responsible for the welfare of his wife and children.

We believe that a homemaker's contribution is equal in importance and value to the contribution of the spouse who works outside the home, and the laws of our States and Nation should reflect this principle.

We reject any plan which would require husbands to pay additional social security taxes on their homemaker wives.

We urge that the 20-year minimum marriage requirement for a woman to receive social security under her husband's name be lowered to a more reasonable period. If divorce occurs prior to the minimum time established to assure the spouse will receive benefits, the court should compensate in another way for the lack of benefits.

We further recommend that women be encouraged to establish individual retirement funds rather than be wholly dependent upon social security; that in order to implement this, section 220 of the Internal Revenue Code be amended to allow nonworking spouses to contribute an amount to an IRA account equal to the amount contributed by the working spouse; further, that the contribution limits for participants in IRA accounts be raised.

We further urge that the integrity and stability of the social security system be assured by more fiscally responsible policies to eliminate inequities.

We deplore the "backlash" of the women's liberation movement which has resulted in the sometimes shameful treatment by the courts of women whose marriages have ended in divorce. We urge the courts to recognize that a man's ability to produce is related to his wife's efforts in the home and to return to the recognition of the wife's right to remain in the career of homemaker for her children even if her marriage is dissolved.

The concept of displaced homemakers is indeed one of concern. We urge churches, local governments, social services, and families to continue to develop programs which provide counseling, training, advice, and support for these women. We oppose expansion of the Federal bureaucracy as being inflationary and probably duplicative in this area.

We further urge that young women be encouraged to develop some marketable skills upon which they can depend later if needed, so that the cycle of the displaced homemaker can be broken in future generations.

INSURANCE

We recommend that the following improvements be made regarding insurance practices:

Coverage for medical expenses due to pregnancy under all comprehensive medical/hospital policies;

Newborn infants be eligible for coverage from birth;

Women with children born out of wedlock be as fully covered as others;

However, we do not recommend that using sex-based acturial and mortality tables for insurance rate computations be ceased, as this will prove more costly to women.

We fully recognize the importance of the father to even the newborn child. But we reject the concept of mandatory paternity leave as unrealistic and inflationary.

We do not believe that elective abortions should be covered by group health insurance, nor by tax-funded insurance programs such as Medicaid.

INTERNATIONAL AFFAIRS

☐ Women and Foreign Policy

We recognize that IWY's stated purpose of encouraging active interest in foreign policymaking is to lead more women to urge Government compliance with the World Plan of Action (*Department of State Bulletin*, 'The United Nations Conference of International Women's Year," page 242); and we further recognize that the World Plan of Action, adopted at Mexico City, June 1975, was not drafted by American women but rather by the United Nations Secretariat ("To Form a More Perfect Union," page 363), therefore is in no way representative of the thinking or wishes of the majority of American women.

We deplore that this World Plan of Action, among other untenable proposals, calls for the establishment of a New International Economic Order

to create "uniform" and balanced development of the international community to "insure a more equitable distribution of income among all sectors of the population," a system which could exist only under a totalitarian world government.

We believe that most citizens of the United States of America would not sanction such a World Plan of Action if presented to them forthrightly.

We therefore reject plans for International Interdependence and call upon the Congress to adopt a policy that only those individuals, regardless of sex, who are committed to the continued existence of the United States of America as a free and independent Nation under its Constitution be appointed to positions in foreign policymaking.

☐ United Nations Commission on the Status of Women and International Women's Decade

For the above-listed reasons, we reject the idea of further funding for or participation in the U.N. Commission on the Status of Women, or the U.S. International Women's Year Commission, or any conferences held in conjunction with them.

We specifically reject the World Plan of Action, including but not limited to the proposal to give up the American Canal in Panama.

Further, we deplore the deliberate and invidious discrimination against women who hold views contrary to the stated World Plan of Action and the National Plan of Action by virtually eliminating representation of their views during the planning and execution stages of the IWY Women's conferences, both at the national and State levels.

□ Women in Development
and International Education
and Communication

We recommend that the women of
the United States of America set an
example to women of other nations by
accepting our responsibilities as
women in our chosen roles as wives
and mothers, professional women
and politicians, giving them an example to emulate rather than trying by
and through the United Nations to impose our standards upon them.

□ Human Rights Treaties
and International Conventions
on Women

We recognize that treaties are the
supreme law of the land for the United
States of America and that all treaties
should be very carefully evaluated by
our U.S. Senate as to their possible
effect upon our citizens. We strongly
recommend that no treaties be ratified which might override the U.S. Bill
of Rights, such as the Genocide
Treaty.

We further recommend that no
more United Nations treaties be
ratified by the United States until and
unless the U.N. shows more real concern for the millions of human beings
living in totalitarian countries whose
basic human rights are violated daily
in countless ways through political,
religious, and other oppression.

□ Peace and Disarmament

Believing that a strong defense
posture is the only proven method of
controlled aggression against the
United States of America, we are
firmly in opposition to plans for disarmament, reduction in necessary military spending, and brainwashing of
school children to pacifist goals. As
women concerned for our family's
security and the security of yet unborn
generations, we urge a return by the
U.S. military to the undisputed position of number 1 in defense of our
liberties against aggressors.

MEDIA

While we recognize the need for
media coverage to fairly explore and
present all options for women, we do
not wish to see this done at the expense of the traditional, family-cen-
tered woman's lifestyle. We urge
media in general and interviewers in
particular to balance the predominantly feminist viewpoint shown today
by fairly and frequently interviewing
persons who hold traditional views.

We deplore secret and exclusive
contracts designed to promote only
one point of view, which have been
reached between feminist organizations and some segments of the
broadcast media.

We concur with the many authorities who are concerned about the
effect of television violence and sexual explicitness upon youthful minds
and actions. We urge parents to exercise their parental responsibilities in
selecting the types of programs they
allow their children to watch.
However, recognizing that a parent is
not at all times able to control television viewing by children, we further
recommend the boycotting of spon-
sors of television shows which are
sexually offensive or overly violent.

We urge the National Association of
Broadcasters and its member stations to further restrict programming
in the areas of sexually offensive and
violent content.

We particularly deplore the pornographic portrayal of women in a de-
meaning and insulting manner. We
urge strict community standards be
set which will control the distribution
of pornography.

We abhor the increased use of
children in pornographic materials.
We strongly urge that strict Federal,
State, and local laws be enacted
which control the distribution of these
pornographic materials. We urge
prompt action and strong punishment

for those convicted of offenses. We
recognize that pornography is
damaging not only to children and
youth, but to men and women as well.

MINORITY WOMEN

We recognize that women of all
religious, ethnic, cultural, and economic backgrounds have been a vital
force in the development of our Nation, our values, and our social structure. We reject the divisive techniques
of those who would exploit our
differences rather than build upon our
common goals. We accept all
Americans as first-class citizens and
urge that all women continue in their
involvement, whatever their concerns,
in all areas that will improve our country's way of life.

We encourage the continuation of
community services which aid minority groups in education, job skills
training, etc. We recommend that
minority groups have fair representation on the decisionmaking boards for
these services, thus enhancing rather
than destroying individual cultures.

OFFENDERS

We support reform of practices,
where needed, dealing with legal
counsel and referral services, improved health services for women in
institutions, and protection of women
prisoners from sexual abuse by other
inmates and correctional personnel.

We urge that corrections boards
provide improved educational and
vocational training in a variety of skills
for offenders. Programs should be included which develop within an offender a higher self-esteem. We urge
that law enforcement agencies,
courts, and correctional programs
give special attention to the needs of
children with mothers who are under
arrest, on trial, or in prison.

We reject the concept of sexually
integrated prison facilities for obvious
and proveable reasons of sexual
abuse. (Report on Sexual Activity at
Massachusetts Correctional Institu-

tion, Framingham, Massachusetts, June 1974, by State Representative Edward Coury.)

OLDER WOMEN

We urge State and local governments, public and private women's organizations, and social welfare groups to support efforts to provide social and health services that will enable elderly women to live with dignity and security.

We recommend that there be wide publicity on the positive roles of women over 50 with continuing education for women in their late middle years as well as for the elderly. Innovative curricula should include "preparation for retirement" and practical law and finances.

We further recommend that mandatory retirement should be phased out.

RAPE

We recommend that State and local governments revise their criminal codes dealing with rape and related offenses to provide for graduated degrees of the crime with graduated penalties depending on the amount of force or coercion occurring; to specify that the past sexual conduct of the victim can be introduced into evidence only after having been adjudicated relevant out of the presence of the jury and the public; to enlarge beyond traditional common law concepts the circumstances under which the act will be considered to have occurred without the victim's consent; and to require no more corroborative evidence than is required in the prosecution of any other type of violent assault.

We support the concept of the Rape Crisis centers being established by local governments and service organizations for the support of rape victims, with the confidentiality of their records being assured. Bilingual and bicultural information sources

should be made available where necessary.

We reject the concept of spouses as victims of rape, unless actually living apart but not yet legally divorced.

REPRODUCTIVE FREEDOM

We believe that no woman today should become pregnant against her wishes. However, with today's modern methods of contraception (even after rape), no woman should become pregnant unless she chooses to do so.

We realize that while a pregnancy may be unwanted, the child of that pregnancy is very much wanted by adoptive parents.

We believe that each human being from conception throughout the natural continuum of life has value and dignity before the law, and that the taking of innocent life is an anathema to our society.

We recommend that the Congress enact and the States ratify a mandatory human life amendment to the Constitution to protect all innocent persons, born and pre-born from conception.

We further recommend that no Federal or State tax money be used for abortion.

We support the right of all individuals and health care institutions to the protection of a "conscience clause" which would insure their right to refuse to perform or participate in abortions. We further recommend that no institution, private or public, be forced to offer abortion services against the wishes of its staff or trustees as a condition for receiving tax dollars.

We oppose allowing a minor girl to obtain an abortion without her parents' knowledge or consent. We further oppose a wife obtaining an abortion without the husband's knowledge and consent.

We strongly urge that all individuals and agencies undertaking to counsel

women on abortion must provide a detailed description of the stages of fetal development and the abortion technique to include the inherent medical risks and the potential for psychological damage.

We recommend that appropriate courses about family life or sex education should be offered in elementary or secondary schools on an elective basis only. All films, books, and materials should be available for parental inspection prior to enrollment of a child in the course. We further recommend that the schools be prohibited from providing abortion referral services.

We believe that the local school systems have enough financial burdens in trying to provide quality education without funding child care facilities for school-age parents.

RURAL WOMEN

We recognize and applaud the improved status of women in farming situations due to revised inheritance tax laws.

We further recognize that rural women are a minority group that works to supply the world with the necessities of life, such as food, fiber, health aids, medical research, and additional products. We have confidence in the ability of American agriculture to produce with efficiency, if allowed to function within the framework of a free market without Government restrictions or controls.

SEXUAL PREFERENCE

We oppose giving lesbians or homosexuals the privileges of adopting children, of teaching in schools, of acting as role models, or otherwise promoting their way of life.

We believe that the definition of a family should never be extended to in any way include homosexuals or biologically unrelated, unmarried couples or otherwise accord to them the dignity which properly belongs to husbands and wives.

STATISTICS

We believe that in order to cut the cost of Government and thus help reduce taxes and inflation, Federal statistical recordkeeping should be reduced rather than increased.

WELFARE

We cannot in any way support a socialistic policy such as a guaranteed income for all Americans. To further burden the hard-working American taxpayer to pay for such a scheme is unconscionable.

We support the concept of helping those who truly cannot help themselves but see churches and community services organizations, State and Local government, as more proper agencies than the Federal Government.

We urge training and guidance for individuals receiving welfare so that they can break the cycle and become productive citizens.

WOMEN'S DEPARTMENT

We strongly oppose the creation of a Cabinet-level Women's Department as unnecessary, inflationary, and creating more Government bureaucracy.

Signed,

State Senator Joan Gubbins, Indiana
Ann Patterson, Oklahoma
Frances Weidman, Alabama
State Senator Georgia Peterson, Utah
Carmie Richeson, Hawaii
Ruth Waite, Florida
Laurentia Allen, Massachusetts
Kay Regan, Washington
Betty Hanicke, Kansas
Vivian Adams, Illinois
State Representative Norma Russell, South Carolina
Eddie Myrtle Moore, Mississippi
Betty Babcock, Montana
Beverly Adams, Georgia

BLACK WOMEN'S PLAN OF ACTION
(See Minority Women Plank in National Plan)

PURPOSE

The entire world is focusing attention on women during these days of the International Women's Year (IWY) Conference. Women, as they are defining themselves, their needs, their problems, their aspirations, and their political and social challenges, are being assessed, explored, and, perhaps for the first time in the history of our planet, given the impact of a tremendous, unified consensus and through the Conference a vehicle for communicating to the world.

Within this impressive representation of women, one comparatively small segment richly deserves the special attention and scrutiny of the Conference. This small segment, black American women, has a long, harsh history of vital concern for civil liberties, and each generation of black American women has contributed mightily to the long struggle for the rights of women.

Since the social, political, and cultural background of black American women differs greatly from that of white women, and since, as a consequence, black American women view the world differently from white women, we present this position paper—not only as a representation of our views, to be recognized by the Conference and forgotten—but as a proposal that these views be considered and included in the total IWY program.

PERSPECTIVE

For more than a century American women have struggled against sexist denial of their rights as citizens. For almost 200 years black American women have struggled against a double deterrent to full citizenship—racist and sexist denial of their rights. The circumstance of being a double victim has cast black women into a role where they view prejudicial treatment, not from its cause, be it sexist or racist, as much as from its results—a violation of human rights. Thus the militancy of black women such as Sojourner Truth, Frances E. W. Harper, Sarah Remond, and Ida B. Wells Barnett was expressed from the context of human rights rather than from a limited focus on the rights of women or blacks.

Human rights has been the traditional political posture of black women leaders, from Harriet Tubman leading a band of black soldiers through South Carolina, burning plantations and freeing almost a thousand slaves, to a black Congresswoman of today, serving on a committee investigating equal employment opportunities.

Black women and white women have significantly different historical and cultural backgrounds and experiences, despite their common experience of oppression. Black women have endured a dual burden of racism and sexism. The entire range of assumptions, attitudes, stereotypes, and prejudices regarding women, the customs and arrangements affecting women which have served as obstacles to the full participation of women as equals with men, and the various processes of exclusion, rejection, and subjugation based upon race and color and built into the major aspects of the society have had the effect of maintaining special privileges and power for the benefit of the white majority. Further, these attitudes have reinforced each other. There have been occasions when the advantage and usefulness of racism to the fundamental working order of American society have interfered with the beneficial and positive alliance of minority and majority women in the United States. The particular manifestations of the unique dual burden, carried with remarkable strength, courage, and effectiveness by our forebears, have been disproportionately felt and are the source of continued double victimization. Additionally, common but also unique to the black female experience in the United States has been a history of necessary participation in the labor force which has had a particular impact upon relationships with one another and with black men. Generally, this involvement in the economic realm resulted in a sharp contrast between the social-economic relations of the majority female vis-a-vis the majority male and the black female vis-a-vis the black male. Because black women have a different past, a different present and, as a consequence of institutionalized racism, a different future from that of white women, it is doubtful that anyone in the United States can or should speak for them. Therefore, black women members of IWY assume the responsibility of their own interpretation of women's mission, believing that it is only on the basis of sound, historically correct analysis that women of the minority and majority in

the Nation may organize effectively around their specific experiences as women and press for not only women's rights, but more importantly, human rights.

UNIQUE NEEDS

Statistical evidence gives further evidence of the urgent need to consider human rights as a platform. Black women comprise 50 percent of the total population of black youth and 54 percent of the total population of adults. Historically, striving to maintain the integrity and dignity of their families, black women have carried heavy responsibilities as heads of households. Clearly, the fate of black Americans as a racial minority group and the development of black women in the United States are inextricably bound together. Just as clearly, inferior status as victims of oppression based upon race and sex impinges upon relations with males and other females. By examining primary indicators—employment, income, and education, the status of black women can be seen readily.

A review of the statistical evidence in the appendix shows that unemployment among blacks is twice as high as that of whites; black males and females have the highest rate of unemployment, the difference between the two sexes being negligible. In the labor market black women are in greater proportions than white women and for longer periods. A related significant fact is that black working mothers are more heavily represented than white mothers in the labor force (see table 5).

An important factor in the status of black females is concentration at the bottom rungs of the employment ladder (see table 6). Most begin participation at a low entry level and remain, with other minorities such as Native Americans and Hispanics, at the bottom. Females are concentrated in the service and clerical occupational categories. In addition to over-representation in service occupations,

black women are disproportionately represented both among those employed as private household workers and among those in non-union employment, thereby receiving fewer benefits from organized labor or social legislation. Scrutiny of wages earned by males and females reveals a disparity between the earnings of the two sexes.

Educational opportunity has long been perceived as not only a primary means to upward mobility and employment security but also the major focal point for both the removal of barriers to higher rungs of the occupational ladder and obstacles to increased social and/or professional capacities. Such opportunities for minorities generally and black females particularly have been limited historically by racism, sexism, institutional practices, and personal attitudes. Despite the attempt to close some educational gaps through affirmative action programs, the black female still suffers as a result of inadequate education and/or training in addition to sex and race barriers. Recent data indicate that the median school years completed by all black females were 10.9 as compared with 12.3 for white females. Moreover, college education statistics for the same period, show a major discrepancy between not only black and white females but also blacks and whites generally in regard to the completion of college: white males graduate at three times the rate of black females (see table 8). Furthermore, data from 1970-71 reveal that in the area of postbaccalaureate education, only 40 percent of all masters degrees are women's and only 14 percent of all Ph.D.'s have been earned by women.

CONCLUSION

An ethnocentric women's movement which minimizes, misconstrues, or demonstrates no serious regard for the interests and views of other disadvantaged groups and minorities sows the seeds of its own destruction, in the wake, eventually, of decreasing allies and mounting hostility. Most important, it will ultimately fail to achieve the crucial goal of the movement—recognition of all people regardless of sex, race, or creed on a basis of equality and human dignity and the improvement of the quality of life for all. Communication among women—across ethnic and racial lines—is the *sine qua non* of an effective women's movement and is necessary to militate against incorrect assessments of socioeconomic and political realities, ill-conceived analyses of women's issues, improper identification of enemies and allies, misdirection of energies and efforts, and inappropriate definitions of the women's liberation task.

As black women informed by our particular past experiences, we stress the danger of a distorted analysis which points to a lingering central conflict of the women's movement as one between women of the minority and the majority. The white male power structure has been adept, historically, at shifting arenas of competition, limiting opportunities, and assuming the power of definition in an effort to misrepresent divisions of greatest import in fundamental social change, such as that between advantaged white males as a group and all other groups in the society, who by comparison are significantly disadvantaged. Moreover, as black women informed by our past we must eschew a view of the women's struggle which takes as its basic assumption opposition to men, as distinguished from organizing around the principle of opposition to the white male power structure's perpetuation of exploitation, subjugation, inequality, and limited opportunities based upon sex or race. In this regard

TABLE 1[1]

1972 Civilian Labor Force & Unemployment in the Census Region by Color

	Total	Black & Other Race
Total	5.6	10.0
Northeast	6.3	9.4
North Central	5.0	12.0
South	4.8	9.1
West	7.1	11.2
Mid-Atlantic	6.1	8.9

TABLE 2

Unemployment Rates by Race & Sex

	Sex		
	Male	Female	Sex Differentials
Race			
White	4.3	5.6	−1.3
Black	10.0	9.5	.5
Race Differentials	−5.7	−3.9	

TABLE 3

Characteristics of Female-Headed Families, 1973

Female Head	White	Black
Percent of all families	9.6	34.6
Marital Status of Female Head		
Married, husband absent	19.0	36.2
Separated	14.6	32.6
Other	4.4	3.7
Widowed	41.0	28.1
Divorced	30.0	16.1
Single	10.0	19.5

[1]The assistance of Dr. Linda F. Williams with statistical data is gratefully acknowledged.

All statistics for this statement on the status of black women are taken from the United States Census Reports, *The Monthly Labor Review* (March, 1975) and the Bureau of Labor Statistics' *Special Labor Force Report* no. 175. The reader should note that the available data have been challenged by minorities with respect to reliability and there is a probability of understatement in regard to the life conditions of minority women which in fact may be more desperate than statistics indicate.

TABLE 4

Wife's Contribution to Family Income—Families With Husband and Wife Working by Race of Husband

	Mean Family Income	Earnings Average of Wife	Percent of Family Income
All White	$17,983	$4,483	24.9
All Black	$14,317	$4,645	32.4

TABLE 5

Working Mothers With Children Under 18 by Low Income Status and Race, 1973

	All Races Below Low-Income Level (%)	White Below Low-Income Level (%)	Blacks Below Low-Income Level (%)
All Women with Children	11.1	8.1	32.8
Female Headed Families	41.7	34.3	56.6

TABLE 6

Occupational Distributions of the 4 Race-Sex Groups, 1974

Occupation	White Males	Black Males	White Females	Black Females
Professional, Technical	14.5	9.4	15.4	11.7
Managers & Administrators	14.8	5.4	5.3	2.4
Sales Workers	6.4	2.8	7.4	7.7
Clerical	6.3	7.4	36.4	24.9
Craftsmen, Foremen	21.4	15.8	1.5	1.4
Operatives, except Transport	11.8	10.5	11.8	16.8
Transport Equipment Operatives	5.6	9.1	.5	.4
Laborers, except Farm	6.9	15.1	1.0	1.2
Farmers & Farm Managers	3.1	1.2	.3	—
Farm Laborers & Foremen	1.8	2.8	1.2	1.1
Service Workers, except Private Household	7.2	15.2	16.7	26.1
Private Household Workers	—	.1	2.5	11.3

one permanent issue of a vigilant, progressive women's movement must be, "who shall, in what manner, frame the issues to which women are to address themselves in a society whose majority is culturally conditioned to operate upon the basis of racist and sexist assumptions?"

Finally, in that the national IWY conference delegates have an advisory function with respect to the Federal Government and have not been invested with power to directly effect changes in the material conditions of women, it must be recognized as a vehicle for communication and political organization. With respect to this function, consciousness raising is the key, for it will be through correct, adroit analyses of societal realities, specific conditions of women, and the nature of the struggle that women can become a significant force for the eradication of oppression.

RECOMMENDATIONS

As black women we endorse the goal of eradicating racism and sexism from our society. We call for the united action of women in support of the improvement of the quality of life for all. In particular, the following concerns pertinent to the plight of black women are presented for support as part and parcel of those women's issues to be forwarded to the President and the Congress.

Education Recognizing the political, socioeconomic, and human costs of discriminatory education and educational opportunities limited by racism and sexism, we recommend that:

1. A concerted effort be made by the Federal Government and State governments via Federal funding to broaden educational opportunities for black women on an equitable basis.

2. Federal funds be made available to implement programs for (a) adult and continuing education; (b) extension curricula in rural areas; (c) literacy; and (d) alternative schools to meet the needs of black women aspiring to obtain basic skills or to resume their education.

3. Recognition be given to the problems and possible solutions to the plight of black female heads of households with respect to educational goals, and funding be allocated for training and education opportunities, financial aid, career counseling, child care, and other support services.

4. Efforts be launched to support scholarly research of black women subsequent to identification of such scholars.

5. Elimination of sex-role stereotyping in school systems be incorporated into training programs for educational administrators and decisionmakers and funding be made available for special programs.

Employment In response to the problems of unemployment and underutilization of black females as a resource in the labor force at all levels, policies and positions which either focus upon employment of women at the expense of black men or identify black women as threats to qualified non-minority females merely because the former fulfill minority and female affirmative action criteria must be exposed as fallacious and counterproductive. We recommend that:

1. Full employment and full utilization of black females at upper as well as entry levels of the labor force be implemented through enlargement of the job pool and nondiscriminatory consideration of black females for career advancement and upgrading.

2. Federal support of enforceable equal pay for work of equal value laws be intensified.

TABLE 7

Economic Status of Women: 1971

Major Occupational Group	Income	As percent of Men's Income (%)
Professional & Technical Workers	$8,346	69
Nonfarm Managers & Administrators	$7,312	56
Clerical Workers	$5,718	62
Sales Workers	$4,349	43
Operatives including Transport	$4,798	61
Service Workers, except Private Household	$4,280	60

TABLE 8

Years of School Completed by Race & Sex: 1974

| | College | | Median School |
	1-3 years	4 years or more	Years Completed
Total all races	11.9	13.3	12.3
White			
Male	12.9	17.7	12.4
Female	11.7	10.6	12.3
Black			
Male	8.6	5.7	10.5
Female	8.0	5.3	10.9

3. Recognition be made of the value of homemaking as well as of the inequities in employment as related to social security.
4. Opposition be stated to the downgrading of positions as a response to black and female workers' demands for equal treatment and protection of the wages for those whose jobs are downgraded.
5. Eradication of discriminatory social security practices be undertaken.
6. Recognition be made of employment inequities connected with service occupations and particularly as they relate to workers in private households.
7. Legislation which provides for alternative work patterns, flexible hours, part-time jobs and adequate child care facilities for black females who are working parents should be enacted.

Political Participation Believing that reform must be pressed through the political system, we recommend that:
1. Support be given to black women running for political office.
2. Black women on all levels of government work together on matters of mutual concern and that such efforts be supported by groups of black women within the constituencies of such officials.
3. Black women establish a viable network for exchange of information and action on issues affecting black women in particular and the black community in general. Also, that they vigorously pursue the advancement of the common interests of women through a network that crosses racial and ethnic lines.

Socially Progressive Services
With an uncompromising belief that our concern must be for the improvement of the quality of human life in order that full human development may be fostered in this society, we recommend that:
1. The Federal Government provide support for the development of programs for (a) adequate income maintenance and comprehensive care for the aged, the poor, and the dependent; (b) a viable national health care assistance system; (c) reliable and comprehensive child care services; (d) maternity benefits as part of a system of health or social insurance; and (e) extension of labor standards relevant to the health and welfare of workers now excluded.
2. The Federal Government and States make available by legislation and funding in conjunction with ability-to-pay schemata (a) public legal services and (b) hospital and mental institution care unencumbered by racist, sexist, or elitist institutional barriers.
3. Comprehensive rehabilitation programs for black female prisoners be developed and implemented in Federal, State, and local correctional facilities.

Statutory and Constitutional Law
We affirm rights basic to a free, humane society and recommend that the Federal Government be called on to use its full power to protect and support these human rights:

1. The right to equitable treatment under law to be construed as including (a) the eradication of discrimination based upon race, color, ethnicity, sex, or creed and support of ERA as part of this broad task, and (b) the full implementation of affirmative action programs as a means of remedying past deprivation of blacks victimized by a previous condition of servitude and/or quasi freedom.
2. The right to procedural due process, i.e., fair and impartial treatment by officials under law.
3. Rights of political expression—freedom of speech, press, assembly; freedom from surveillance, harassment and interception of private conversations; freedom to petition for redress of grievances.

DELEGATES TO IWY CONFERENCE AT HOUSTON

ALABAMA

DELEGATES
Elizabeth Ames
Kay Bakke
Ann Bedsole
Joanne Bloom
Mary Corley
Nancy Cox
Sandra Cox
Lois N. Crawford
Charlotte Davis
Natalie W. Dillard
Louise B. Edmonson
Vera Foster
Helen M. Given
Nancy Gonce
Helen B. McKnight
Janet L. McMillan
Neva Leger Moore
Marilyn Quarles
Catherine Reickenback
Sarah B. Robertson
Alice Robinson
Sara Sansom
Alice Smith
Frances Wideman

ALTERNATES
Patricia Edington
Janie Shores
Consuela Harper
Selena Andress
Lillian Andrews

ALASKA

DELEGATES
Nancy Anderson
Diane Carpenter
Shari Gross
Carolyn Jones
Dorothy Jones
Dove Kull
Cara Peters
Elaine Ramos
Dorcus Rock
Bessie Titus
Rosita Worl
Jane Yamashiro

ALTERNATES
Lynne Woods
Suzanne Iudicello
Michelle Jacobs
Linda Larsen
Sandra Hollinshead

ARIZONA

DELEGATES
Martha Ahearn
Juanita Georgia Alvarez
Maria Chavez
Mary Covington
Mary Crisp
Rosa Maria Diaz
Mary Douglas
Sue Dye
Shannon Garvin
Alison Marshall Hughes
Judy A. McCarthey
Carolyn Nakumura
Hilda Ortega
Vera Brown Starr
Jennifer Tom
Lorraine E. White
Mary Rose Wilcox
Mercy Valenzuela

ALTERNATES
Alice Bendheim
Jessie Sanchez
Becky Camacho
Consuelo Smith
Meridith Little

ARKANSAS

DELEGATES
Margaret L. Benton
Esther M. Boswell
Emily Sturtevant Burr
Marguerite A. Chapman
Cathyrn E. Hinshaw
Anne W. Jarrard
Diane Kincaid
Sister Mary Ann Knaebel
Jeane Lambie
Catherine B. Leapheart
Brownie Williams Ledbetter
Dr. Sara Murphy
Dr. Katherine S. Schneider
Lillie Mae Stevenson
Wanda June Tolfree
Leona A. Troxell
Barbara Weinstock
Pat Youngdahl

ALTERNATES
Barbara Taylor
Betty Miller
Ann Brewer
Ms. W. Payton Kolb
Robye Hall

CALIFORNIA

DELEGATES
Diane Abbitt
Angie Alarcon
Leatrice Alger-Goodwin
Irene Aparicio
Mary Arimoto
Jeane Bendorf
Bobbi Bennett
Alice Bibeau
Linda Bovet
Margaret Bradnum
Shirley Bronson
Yvonne Brathwaite Burke
Estelle Chacon
Anne Charles
Jeanne Cordova
Beatrice Cossey
Jean Crosby
Margaret Cruz
Josephine Daly
Grace Davis
Gwen Davis
Marguaritte Davis
Terry Decrescanzo
Gloria Muzquiz de Crouse
Jeri Delno
Patricia DiGorgio
Elva Donnel
Oreitha Eggleston
Donna Elder
Pat Ellison
Marguerite Ernstene
Lillene Fifield
Patsy Fulcher
Phillis Galisin
Rith Samberg Gelman
Ginger Gherardi
Flora Gilford
Frankie Jacobs Gillette
Lucy Gonzales
Rosie Gonzales
Viola Gonzales
Vivian Hall
Dina Igushi
Gloria Julagay
Helen Kawagoe
Ying Lee Kelley
Carmela Lacayo
Roxana Lightfoot
Mary B. Lindblom
Patricia Lopez
Phyllis Lyon
Beverly Fitch McCarthy
Rose Marie McDuff
Helen Magpali
Shelly Mandell
Del Martin
Kathy Martinez
Mary Maschal
Iris Feldman Mitgang
Lillian Mobley
Gloria Molina
Virginia Molina
Elba Montes
Aurelia Morris
Shirley Morris
Marilyn Murphy
Linda Myers
Helene Nemschoff
Priscilla Oaks
Suzanne Paizis
Jane Patterson
Carol Pendell
Nancy Lee Peterson
Joan Rich
Anne Rosen
Rina Rosenberg
Corinne Sanchez
Lydia Benavides San Fillippo
Margaret Sloan
Elizabeth Snyder
Geraldine F. Steinberg
Marjorie Stern
Hortencia Solis
Kogee Thomas
Yukie Tokuyama
Alice Travis
Mariko Tse
Dr. Dorothy M. Tucker
Marged Wakeley
Maxine Waters
Susanne Wilson
Margaret Wilkerson
Gloria Woody
Colleen Wong
Nelda Wyland
Bernice Zurbach

ALTERNATES
Patricia De los Santos
Fahari Jeffers-Msemaj
Alice Wright-Cottigim
Sally Martinez
R. L. Nowlin

278

COLORADO

DELEGATES
Margaret E. Ackerman
Janet Beardsley
Jeannie Cochran
Cleo M. Breeze
Juanita M. Dominquez
Susan Dorris
Genevieve N. Fiore
Mary Hoagland
Judy Hom
Jean Jackson
Cynthia Kent
Carol Lease
Marie Mendoza
Elizabeth Rave
Betty Salazar
Anna Marie Sandoval
Mary Bennett Sharf
Gwendolyn Thomas
Lenore Walker
Marcile Wood

ALTERNATES
Maria Pena
Marian Reardon
Linda Fowler
Lucille Cyphers
Marietta Benge

CONNECTICUT

DELEGATES
Audrey Beck
Kay Bergin
Maureen Brodoff
Shirley Bysiewicz
Becky Castro
Alice J. Chapman
Marione Cobb
Ann Crimmins
Ivor J. Echols
Betty Hudson
Julie Matthaei
Elsie M. O'Sullivan
Doris Roldan
Gloria Schaffer
Deanne Shapiro
Elizabeth Spalding
Vera Stecker
Joan Steffens
Suzanne Taylor
Dai Thompson
Patricia Wallace
Diana Woolis

ALTERNATES
Pearl Dowell
Mary Erlanger

Mary Ann Ettinger
Jacqueline Shaffer
Joan Weiss

DELAWARE

DELEGATES
Abi Atkinson
Jean Bowen
Mabel E. Cephas
Margaret Peg Draper
Vivian Houghton
Linda Hsu
Marilyn Hutmacher
Catherine Mancini
Jean A. Norwood
Roxanne Pitts
Helen Thomas
Lucille Ponatoski Toro

ALTERNATES
Patricia Chalfonte
Theresa Del Tufo
Gertrude Lowell
Emma Durazzo
Stephanie Twilley

DISTRICT OF COLUMBIA

DELEGATES
Mary Jo Binder
Charlotte Ann Bunch
Theresa Ann Clark
Alexa Perry Freeman
Helen H. Helfer
Etta M. Horn
Juanita Kennedy Morgan
Mary Spottswood Pou
Anne B. Turpeau
Barbara Lett Simmons
Ruth Anita Sykes
Paquita Vivo

ALTERNATES
Anita Shelton
Deborah Luxenberg
Rev. Imagene Stewart
Betty King
Ethel James Williams

FLORIDA

DELEGATES
Inez Almond
Marie Anderson
Susan B. Anthony
Donna M. Batelaan
Budd Bell
Rita Bornstein
Mollie Brilliant
Beverly Burnsed
Roseann Cacciola
Irene S. Caissie
Gwendolyn Cherry
Lee Drury De Cesare
Joan Cecilia Dekle
Jean Doyle
Eufaula Frazer
Julia Glocker
Dr. Freddie L. Groomes
Virginia C. Harlan
Dr. Maria C. Hernandez
Toni Jennings
Ellen Johnson
Ellen Kimmel
Winkie LeFils
Sallye B. Mathis
Marta McPherson Baez
Marie Mercer
Margaret L. Mosher
Katheryn Nelson
Emma Rembert
Barbara C. Roper
Edna Saffy
Maria Saiz
Yvonne Santa-Maria
Carole M. Sheahan
Mamie Shelby
Francena Thomas
Nancy S. Traver
Ruth Walte
Lori Wilson
Nancy Kelley Wittenberg

ALTERNATES
Deloras Knight
Beatrice B. Ettinger
Ruth Shack
Patricia Law Jones
Diana Campoamoa

GEORGIA

DELEGATES
Beverly Adams
Ella M. Alexander
Cynthia R. Banks
Rutha L. Bradley
Beverly A. Briscoe
Sandy B. Butterworth
Nemia M. Chai
Delores L. Crockett

Josefina A. Cross
Kathleen D. Crouch
Suzanne F. Donner
Eleanor R. Granum
Helen V. Head
Julia C. Hilburn
Odone B. Hill
Dorris D. Holmes
Vivian D. Hunt
Betsy R. Johnson
Martha D. Massey
Nannie L. McCormick
Lynthia Miller
Sandra Mullins
Vita R. Ostrander
Jeannette D. Perlinski
Stella J. Reeves
Eleanor L. Richardson
Tobiane Schwartz
Rosa S. Stanback
Lee Wysong

ALTERNATES
Cheryle T. Bryan
Kathryn Dunaway
Tony C. Posek
Martha O. Andrews
Margaret C. Briggs

HAWAII

DELEGATES
Delthia Akiu
Vicki Awa
Jayne Garside
Kathy Hoshiko
Dianne F. Kay
Verdetta Kekuaokalani
Cherlyn Kuohalogan
Barbara Louise Lundy
Julina Lung
Gerri Madden
Jo Ann K. Medeiros
Helen Priester
Carmie R. Richesin
Kapau Kaapu Sproat

ALTERNATES
Odette Villaneuva-King
Patricia K. Brandt
Colette Y. Machado
Wallette Garcia-Pellegri
Audrey Mertz
Margaret Ushijima

IDAHO

DELEGATES
Corlann Gee Bush
Jeanne Cassell
Alice Dieter
Norma Dobler
Alayne E. Hannaford
Betty Hoppe
Hope Kading
Ruth Pauly
Idaho J. Purce
Sue Reents
Ruth Marie Roelofs
Louise Shadduck
Marjorie H. Slotten
Anne Staton Voilleque

ALTERNATES
Jane Daly
M. Elena de la Garza-Hernande
Marjorie Titus
Joy Buersmeyer
Diane Davis

ILLINOIS

DELEGATES
Vivian M. Adams
Joanne H. Alter
Anne L. Austin
Willie Barrow
Nancy Berg
Peg Blaser
Arnita Boswell
Bonnie Bowlby
Mary C. Brennan
Mary Brown
Margaret Butler
Laura Canning
Susan Catania
Eugenia S. Chapman
Betty Christopher
Elizabeth Clarke
Mary Jean Collins
Anne Courtney
Margaret Cowden
Miriam Cruz
Anne Culhane
Clara Day
Darlene Degenhardt
Irma Diaz
Gladys A. Dickelman
Goudyloch Dyer
Ruth Edelman
Marie A. Fese
Kay Fors
Carol Frederick
Rosalie Glover
Violet F. Hamilton
Sheila Hart
Virginia Hayter

Jo Higgins
JoAnn R. Horowitz
Matilda Jakubowski
Marge Jindrich
Helen Louise Johnson
Roberta Johnson
Anita Kent
Marlene Kettley
Darlene Kemmerer
June Kuester
Anne Ladky
Mary Lawlor
Sara Lohr
Ruby Mabry
Judy Mack
Sylvia Margolies
Marge Markin
Barbara Merrill
Vera Meyer
Judy Mostovoy
Kathleen McCabe
Margaret McGeever
Rosemary Thomson

ALTERNATES
Patricia Bjelland
Johanna Miller
Colleen N. Cyrocki
Ann Belanger
Marilyn Risinger

INDIANA

DELEGATES
Elizabeth Abney
Peggy J. Bender
Alice B. Beutler
Jan Buechler
Ruth T. Cartwright
Mary C. Collins
Mattie M. Coney
Jan Conner
Beulah Coughenour
Karol DeVoe
Gertrude Dishmon
Anna Gilbert
Joan M. Gubbins
Jean H. Harvey
Jean O. Hill
Sandra Ann Houlihan
Mary E. Inderlied
Rolena J. Jackson
Gloria K. Lamper
Sita Keith Miller
Frances Opp Martin

Norine McClure
Michele McRae
Kathryn Nikou
Jean Patton
Evelyn Pitschke
Jacqueline Pyle
Joanne C. Reynolds
Lillian E. Steele
Vivian Voglund
Dorothy F. Wodraska
Frances Zink

ALTERNATES
Mary Reilly Hunt
Gloria Kaufman
Virginia Dill McCarty
Hazel M. Minnefield

IOWA

DELEGATES
Ellen Adelman
Margaret Anderson
Virginia Benware
Helen Blackburn
Roxanne Conlin
Mori Constantino
Minnette Doderer
Willie Stevenson Glanton
Eleanor Lampe
Jean Lloyd-Jones
Burtine Motley
Rebecca Motley
Felicia Mullin
Sister Irene Munoz
Kathleen O'Leary
Christine Pattee
Melvina Scott
Mary Louise Smith
Kappie Spencer
Nancy Sweetman
Betty Talkington
Dr. Annete Walters

ALTERNATES
Mic Denfield
Rose Granado
Beverly Smith
Elizabeth Starleaf
Adeline Wanatee

KANSAS

DELEGATES
Kay Camin
Sister Mary Agnes Drees
Rowena Gamble
Patricia Garland
Mary Ann Grelinger
Betty Hanicke

Janet S. Hoover
Gardella M. Hunt
Barbara Jeffries
Patricia D. Jones
Dominga R. Lopez
Helen Lee Mitchell
Wanda Sanborn
Linda Serrano
Patricia M. Storey
Nina Jean Strahm
Sylvia Turnis
Mary B. Umansky
Catherine M. Wahlmeier
Mary Westerman

ALTERNATES
Milicent S. Johnson
Peggy Melcum
Gloria J. O'Dell
Tonda Schinnerer

KENTUCKY

DELEGATES
Dr. Lilialyce Akers
Carolyn Bratt
Kizzie Cantrell
M. Diane Carlin
Dr. Necia Coker
Delores Delahanty
Pam Elam
Ellen B. Ewing
Lucy Freibert
Martha Grise
Allie Hixson
Nelle P. Horlander
Marie Humphries
Laura M. Jones
Pauline Jones
Heidi Margulis
JoEtta McCloud
Anita Nelam
Oteria O'Rear
Martha Pickering
Suzy Post
Doris Schneider
Mary Ann Tobin
Rebecca J. Westerfield

ALTERNATES
Mary Mullins
Mary Zriny
Vannie L. Taylor
Jean Severs
Emily C. Boone

LOUISIANA

DELEGATES
Dorothy Arceneaux
Barbara Bagneris
Mary Beasley
Lorna Bourg
Ruth Douglas Bradford
Fran Bussie
Clarence Marie Collier
Phyllis E. Covington
Pat Evans
Felicia Kahn
Dr. Judy Karst
Ann Knapp
Clay Latimer
Roberta Madden
Shirley Marvin
Corinne Maybuce
Ollie T. Osborne
Myrtle Pickering
Mildred Reese
Rupert Richardson
Annie Smart
Sibal Taylor
Karline Tierney
George Ethel Warren
Clara Mae Wells

ALTERNATES
Emily Hubbard
Evelyn K. Sisco
Sandra Thompson
Helen M. Barron
Shirley C. Temple

MAINE

DELEGATES
Cynthia Murray-Beliveau
Anne Hazelwood-Brady
Constance Depew
Paulette Dodge
Linda Dyer
Joann Fritsche
Claire Hussey
Vivian Massey
Kim Matthews
Kate McQueen
Merle Nelson
Lois Reckitt
Nan Stone
Sharon Renee Talbot

ALTERNATES
Ellen Weissman
Lillian O'Brian
Blaire McCracken
Janet Mills
Henrietta Page Crane

MARYLAND

DELEGATES
Deborah L. Benzil
Claire R. Bigelow
Amy T. Billingsley
Carol A. Bornee
Cleopatra Campbell
Shoshana S. Cardin
Lorraine Q. Cecil
Elvira J. Crocker
Linnea D. Dittmar
Cynthia Farquhar
Kathleen O'Ferrall Friedman
Barbara J. Gordon
Maxine Grissett
Betty K. Hamburger
Doris M. Johnson
Gloria T. Johnson
Sylvia H. Law
Sr. Mary E. McNamara
Pauline H. Menes
JoAnn M. Orlinsky
Kerstin B. Powell
Hedda S. Sachs
Bernice Sandler
Lorri D. Simmons
M. Emily Taylor
Ann W. Ventre

ALTERNATES
Daisy B. Fields
Kathleen M. Ryan
Diane R. Evans
Florence K. Bunja
Bertha C. Wise

MASSACHUSETTS

DELEGATES
Helen Allen
Laurentia Allen
Lee Blake
Rosalie Cooper
Martha Crowninshield
Diane Damelio
Joan Fiorino
Sally Garcia
Regina Healy
Wilma Scott Heide
Peg Ireland
Barbara Jocobskind
Carmenceita Jones
Muriel B. Knight

Linda Lachman
Lisa Leghorn
Marion London
Konstantine Lukes
Sally Lunt
Barbara Magovsky
Marcelle Mavidis
Isabel Melendez
Juanita Tosca de Melendez
Shelagh O'Donnell
Sharon M. Pollard
Anne del Prado
Alberta C. Settle
Barbara Sinnott
Barbara Smith
Katherine Triantafillo
Mary S. Vaz
Margo Volterra
Kari Wren
Harriette Zuckerman

ALTERNATES
Hedy Ferriera
Kathryn Di Francesco
Agnes Smith
Melinda Lust
Leslie S. Paul

MICHIGAN

DELEGATES
Mary Aikey
Sister Mary Aquinas
Victoria Barner
Laura Beckett
Lorraine Beebe
Ella Bragg
Patricia Hill Burnett
Suzanna Cadena
Ana Cardona
Rep. Barbara Rose Collins
Sara Costa
Rep. Daisey Elliott
Mary Ferrere
Mary Graves
Holly Greer
Grace Hampton
Phyllis Harrison
Octavia Hawkins
Georgia Johnson
Lorna Kahgegab
Jean King
Charleen Knight
Kari Lavalli
Beverley Leopold
Rae Levis
Ruth McNamee
Olivia Maynard
Helen Milliken
Shirley Monson
Linda Murakishi
Dorothy Newman
Shirley Oczus

Maria Luisa Patino
Connie Peabody
Carleen Pedrotti
Angeline Perry
Elly Peterson
Viola Peterson
Ranny Riecker
Judith Robinson
Ann Shafer
Patricia Cuza Silea
Odessa Smith
Nancy Stewart
Lillian Stoner
Audrey Thomason
Maria Velasquez
Delia Villegas Vorhauer

ALTERNATES
Bernice Zilly
Patricia Barbour
Florence Edelbrock
Marlene Elwell
Erma Henderson

MINNESOTA

DELEGATES
Jacqueline J. Bledsoe
Louise Bouta
Kathleen Bowman
Marianne Bruesehoff
Maria Callender
Loria Danage-Scott
Marquita Joan Finley C.S.J.
Judith Lambert Fisher
Sandra Fizer-Jones
Carol Flynn
Judie Fox
Sharon Day Garcia
Joan E. Guernsey
Valerie Lee Hess
Gloria Lyn Kumagai
Dr. Jewel G. Maher
Laurie Miller
Ann O'Laughlin
Mary Peek
Sharon Postma
Sue Rockne
Patricia Schamus
Peggy Specktor
Anne Thorsen Truax
Hattie Kauffman Wing
Kerry Woodward

ALTERNATES
Margaret Guthrie Smith
Jackie Richter
Julie R. Andrzejewski
Jeri Rasmussen
L. Elizabeth Moore

MISSISSIPPI

DELEGATES
Edna Alexander
Helen Boone
Dr. Curtis Caine
Dorothy Ellen Campbell
Pauline T. Earles
Patricia K. Fawcett
Mark A. Godbold
Dorothy Gunter
Shelton N. Hand
Dallas Wood Higgins
Mary Kerlee
Elizabeth (Liz) M. Mitchell
Eddie Myrtle Moore
Carolyn J. Morgan
Homer G. Morgan, Jr.
Jewel Vanera Morris
Pat Revell
Willie Latham Taylor
Norma Temple
William T. Temple

ALTERNATES
Evelyn Caine
Reid H. Smith
Jessie B. Mosley
Cora Norman
Janice Moor

MISSOURI

DELEGATES
Angie Bennett
Joan Brier
Shirley Clough
Mary Gale Doyle
Mae Duggan
Karen Dukewits
Frances Freck
Mary Gant
Joan Hart
Donna H. Hearne
Mary Fran Horgan
Peggy Keilholz
Adele Kelman
Patti Kemp
Delphone McLaughlin
Odile Mecker
Elaine Middendorf
Judith O'Connor
Ann O'Donnell
Frances Noonan

Eline Rodriquez
Jacqueline Schlef
Lucille Selsor
Clare Simon
Ann Slaughter
Louise Grant Smith
Mattie C. Smith
Mary Treis
Eleanor Wasson
Vi Wilson

ALTERNATES
Wilda R. Worley
Sue Shear
DeVerne Calloway
Frankie M. Freeman
Joan Krauskopf

MONTANA

DELEGATES
Ann M. Allen
Betty Lee Babcock
Peggy Christensen
Marilyn M. Degel
Leona J. Deisz
Delores Etchart
Marilyn Fernelius
Lois Halsey
Betty M. Johnson
Mildred Kantorowicz
Suzanne Pennypacker Morris
Sherrel E. Olsen
Bertha E. Weiloff
Joan E. Zormeir

ALTERNATES
Myrna Boyd Small Salmon
Naomi Powell
P. Lynette Little
Phyllis DeVore
Antoinette Fraser Rosell

NEBRASKA

DELEGATES
Ann Bower
Della R. Brauer
Naomi Brummond
Delores Bundy
Linda Dorcey
Judith Koester
Jeneta M. Dankert
Bernice Labedz
Lauby LaVaughn
Mary H. Ledbetter
Jane Martin
Rita Perez
Mary Alice Pratt
Velma Price
Pauline K. Reznicek
Barbara J. Zapotocky

ALTERNATES
Myrna McCulloch
Gladys Maciejewski
Marlene Parker
Diane J. Sarver
Mary Lou Streeter

NEVADA

DELEGATES
Kate Butler
Frankie Sue Del Papa
Renee Diamond
Ruby Duncan
Christina Everhart
Jean Ford
Senator Mary Gojack
Josephine Gonzales
Janet MacEachern
Blaine Rose
Assemblywoman Sue Wagner
Lois Whitney

ALTERNATES
Karen Hayes
Adelene Bartlett
Carrie Bagley
Janine Hansen
Patricia Little

NEW HAMPSHIRE

DELEGATES
Frances Abbot
Lynne S. Brandon
Anita Durel
Claire Goulette
Elizabeth S. Hager
Medora Hamilton
Ellen Hanley
Joan C. Lovering
Catherine P. McDowell
Anita Norman
Marilyn Patterson
Eva Sartwell
Sandra F. Smith
Eleanor M. VanderHaegen

ALTERNATES
Stephanie Merfeld-Gfroerer
Patti Blanchette
Susan Gladstone
Andrea Lee Savage
Shirley Ganem

NEW JERSEY

DELEGATES
Clara Allen
Fran Avallone
Valorie F. Coffee
Robbie L. Cagnina
Patricia Cherry
Alice Cohan
Sharon Cohen
Blanche Corbman
Lydia Cruz
Rosemary J. Dempsey
Katherine M. DiBenedetto
Evelyn S. Drum
Mae Massie Eberhardt
Constance Gilbert-Neiss
Lourdes Gonzalez
Carole A. Graves
Francine D. Harbour
Dolores M. Harris
Ming Hsu
Judith S. Knee
Carmela Lunt
Ruth Mandel
Ruth R. McClain
Myra Terry Meisner
Judy Murphy
Joan C. Neuwith
Priscilla Ransohoff
Lucy Rodrigues
Roberta Rossi
D. Joan Sampieri
Faith Schindler
Dorothy Dugger Schoenwald
Dorothy Riley
Theo Tamberlane
Eileen P. Thornton
Joanne Turner
Doreen Utman
Barbara Wickland
Betty Wilson
Delia Redondo

ALTERNATES
Ida Castro
Nancy Parratl Stultz
Alicia Smith
Constance Woodruff
Elizabeth Sadowski

NEW MEXICO

DELEGATES
Virginia Ahern
Cecilia Apodaca
Anne Bingaman
Ava Marie Bower
Vera Cushman
Agnes Dill
Patricia Luna
Elaine Mondragon
Charlie Morrissey
Juanita Hajera
Patricia Gallegos Rogers
Teresa M. Sanchez
Isabel Tellez
Frances Williams

ALTERNATES
Melissa Noland
Frances Jerry Eckert
Myrna J. Finke
Beverly Lucero
Bella R. McCabe

NEW YORK

DELEGATES
Cecile Ackmed
Cheryl Adams, Ph.D.
Francine Adelman
Kathy Allgood
Virginia Apuzzo
Sandra M. Bachety
Eleanor G. Bailey
Martha Baker
Carol Bellamy
Theresa D. Bergen
Catherine Bertini
Karen S. Burstein
Constance Cabell
Angela Cabrera
Mable Charles
Goldie Chu
Josephine M. Clark
Susan Cohen
Noreen Connell
Constance E. Cook
Eleanor Cooper
Adrienne Critchlow
Evelyn Cunningham
Diane Daniels
Karen DeCrow
Rita Dendariarena DiMartino
Kathy Doyle
Nancy C. Dubner
Marcia B. Dugan
Ruth Dunne
Sally Martino Fisher
Phyllis O. Flug
Jo Freeman

Meryl C. Friedman
Mary Goodhue
Shirley G. Gordon
Andrea Gruen
Ronni Haggarty
Pauline Haynes
Katherine Heaviside
Elaine Horowitz
Dianne Jackson
Shirley G. Jenkins
Arlyne Katz
Sandra Katz
Esther G. Kee
Lolita Kacson
Shawn Leach
Georgia McMurray
Rowena Chaiton Malamud
Bonnie Mandina
Annie B. Martin
Joyce E. Massey
Nettie Mayersohn
Olga Mendez
Frances Nathan
Mary Burke Nicholas
Christine Noschese
Dorothy Orr
Ursula C. Pinero
Loretta M. Piscatella
Clarice Pollock
Betty J. Powell
Alice Quinn
Ruth Ram
Carolyn Reed
Cleo Reid
Leta Richardson
Katherine Robinson
Helen Rodriguez
Lisa Rosillo
Dannie Rowell
Beulah Sanders
Susan Schwalb
Joan E. Short
Chaire Shulman
Barbara M. Sims
Lynda Spielman
Ferne Steckler
Annette Stoller
Anna Thompson
Opal Townson
Doris Turner
Mary Lou Welz
Ellen Willis
Dora Young
Lorraine Zimniewicz

ALTERNATES
Anne Troy Brown
Nina Bryce
Lynn Bugay
Margaret Prescod-Roberts
Eleanor Watrous

NORTH CAROLINA

DELEGATES
Yusufah Abdul-Rabb
Gail S. Bradley
Carol L. Brewington
Varie B. Brusso
Sylvia Crudup Cole
Miriam J. Dorsey
Jackie Frost
Carrie L. Graves
Tennala A. Gross
Jessie Highsmith Copeland
Della H. Jackson
Ruth B. Jones
Jackie D. Kaalund
Elizabeth D. Koontz
Lora Lavin
Lynn Heather Mack
Helen H. Mahlum
Anneliese Markus-Kennedy
Ruth Mary Meyer
Beverly R. Mitchell
Judith A. Parker
Barbara G. Ragland
La Verne Reid
Tibbie Roberts
Grace J. Rohrer
Miriam K. Slifkin
Amanda J. Smith
Sandra Thomas
Betty H. Wiser
Ruth Dial Woods
Sarah Workman
Danya Yon

ALTERNATES
Aggie Deese
Everline Mitchell
Sylvia T. deRosset
Rejeane B. LeFrancois
Molly L. Johnson

NORTH DAKOTA

DELEGATES
Alvina Alberts
Roberta Biel
Jane F. Bovard
Katherine K. Burgum
Aloha Eagles
Agnes Geelan
Juanita Helphrey
Pauline Howard
Corliss Mushik
Cynthia Phillips
Harriet Skye
Doris S. Wilke

ALTERNATES
Audrey Hiney
Joyce Schneider
Liz Maxwell

Alice K. Olson
Laurie Natwick

OHIO

DELEGATES
Judith Adamek
Constance Anders
Vera Blake
Jane Britt
Jane Campbell
Gloria Coles
Vittoria D'Amato
Barbara Desborough
Irma Donnellon
Mary Donovan
Dorothy Duke
Jane Eishen
Ernest Flores
Betty Ford
Susan Frampton
Nancy Gibson
Mary Gigandet
Eloise Granata
Mary Guarnieri
Nina Hatfield
Suanne Herman
Suzanne Hughes
Elinor Israel
Eva Janicek
Barbara Janis
Debra Kammerling
Ann Kitzmiller
Margaret Kling
Chestora Lee
Mildred Leithart
Constance Letta
Frances Lucas
Colista Malone
Norma Marcere
Lori Marinacci
Bette McClelland
Naomi McDaniel
Katherine McLandrich
Mary Miller
Lana Moresky
Meade O'Boyle
Fern Perin
Elizabeth Petree
Patricia Pichler
Geraldine Rinehart
Marsha Rinkus
Joanne Rose
Anne Saunier
Teresa Shofstahl
Dorothy Smith
Ida Staley
Stephanie Varga
Alice Ward
Barbara White
Mary White
Barbara Willke

ALTERNATES
Rosemary Beckman
Maureen Foster
Lois Leggat
Jane Leroux
Margaret Hartshorn

OKLAHOMA

DELEGATES
Joan L. Blankenship
Sue H. Bronaugh
Marie Cox
Margaret E. Edmiston
Dianne Edmondson
Mabel Faulkner
Beverly D. Findley
Grace Haigler
Maxine Hamon
Debbie Harrell
Mary Helm
Kay K. Hill
Ada R. Kerns
Phyllis W. Lauinger
Opal S. Lowry
Winnie Matthews
Glenda N. Matton
Martha I. May
Ann B. Patterson
Louise Ratcliff
Lennie P. Tolliver
M. Chris Wilson

ALTERNATES
Joan Hastings
Hannah Atkins
Ann Mulloy Ashmore
Fern Green
Janice P. Dreiling

OREGON

DELEGATES
Jane Cease
Rose Gangle
Phillipa Harrison
Margie Hendricksen
Cyndy Hilden
Charlene Holmes
Gretchen Kafoury
Jewel Lansing
Faith Mayhew
Gladys McCoy
Maria Parra
Berna Plummer
Robyn Remaklus
Mary Wendy Roberts
Jolene Sharp
Kim Skerritt
Guessippina Williams
Donna Zajonc

ALTERNATES
Jane Edwards
Linda Volz
Ann Stein
Jeanne Dost
Merri Souther

PENNSYLVANIA

DELEGATES
Barbara Abbott
Colleen Alexander
Ethel Allen
Rose Allen
Ethel Barnett
Yognidra Bhargava
Joan Biordi
Judy Block
Deborah Boyle
Geri Brown
Lorraine H. Brown
Nada Chandler
Augusta A. Clark
Jeanne K. C. Clark
Edwina Coder
Carol Coren
Elaine T. Esposito
Bosanka Evosevic
Alma S. Fox
Estelle Gould
Judy Hansen
Lillian P. Holliday
Ann W. Horner
Edith A. Huntsberger
Connie Hurley
Lorna S. Jaffee
Frankie Jeter
Marie R. Kenney
Nancy Kirk-Gormley
Jane H. Land
Lora Liss
Karen McCreesh
Barbara McDermott
Dagmar McGill

Phyllis Magerman
Julia Maietta
Sister Jacinta Mann
Maria Matalon
Jaleh Monsenin
Vicki Monream
Loretta Moore
Nancy M. Neuman
Vanessa Oruska
Audrey Peterson
Deirdre R. Pitt
Jeanette F. Reibman
Suzanna Rose
Molly Rush
Gloria Saskman-Reed
Pat Scarcelli
Elsa Puder Supplee
Gwen Visser
Grace Ware
Sylvia Waters
Nancy Weiland
Jane Wells-Schooley
Dixie White
Kay Whitlock
Joanne Fischer Wolf
Molly Yard

ALTERNATES
JoAnn Evans Gardner
Janet Schumann
Mary B. Kennedy
Elizabeth McCance
Elizabeth Bonczar

RHODE ISLAND

DELEGATES
Barbara B. Colt
Joan Cornell
Nancy L. Derrig
Marion H. Donnelly
Lesley Doonan
Janis Fisher
Patricia Houlihan
Beverly J. LaCorbiniere
Jean MacKenzie
Susan W. McCalmont
Helen Migliaccio
Joanne J. Rongo
Judie Schiedler
Gloria H. Spears

ALTERNATES
Helen E. Flynn
Rev. Irene R. Gooding
Joanne McOsker
Judith F. Ryder
Vera Vendettuoli

SOUTH CAROLINA

DELEGATES
Mary Ann Breakfield
Keller H. Bumgardner
Malissa Burnette
Pat Callair
Marianne W. Davis
Katherine Duffy
Carolyn E. Frederick
Louise Hill
Eunice D. Holland
Marguerite Howie
Diane A. Moseley
Elizabeth J. Patterson
Elaine Reed
Ellen Robertson
Irene Rudnick
Norma C. Russell
Nancy Sharkey
Modjeska Simkins
Joy Sovde
Candy Waites
Lucille S. Whipper
Janet N. Wedlock

ALTERNATES
Jeri S. Libner
Dorothy Franklin
Oliver Willis
Shirley Holcombe
George Ann Pennebaker

SOUTH DAKOTA

DELEGATES
Ruth Ann Alexander
Carol Anderson
Lee Burd
Lorraine Collins
Margaret Denton
Loila Hunking
Peg Lamont

Sandra LeBeau
Ina Litke
Doris Minner
Fayola Muchow
Mary Lynn Myers
Judith O'Brien
Jinny Tarver

ALTERNATES
Winifred Echelberger
Rith Karim
Florence Kranz
Ellen Dempsey
Victoria Reed

TENNESSEE

DELEGATES
Candace Adams
Betty J. Bishop
Daphne Marian Brady
Willie Pearl Butler
Kathryn I. Bowers
Carolyn Cowan
Lois DeBerry
Patricia Eames
Jo-Ann Edwards
Pat Erb
Verna M. Fausey
Judy Goans
Brenda M. Hunter
Betty Jean Jones
Shuchram Kamal
Marcia Kelley McCoy
Martha Ragland
Barbara Rawls
Mary S. Reed
Mary Sawyer
Betty Stubblefield
Lillian Ann Terrell
Sonia Walker
Becky Martin Weis
Leola Woody
Pam Wright

ALTERNATES
Barbara Lawing
Jane Eskind
Linda L. Miller
Paula F. Casey
Carol Lynn Yellin

TEXAS

DELEGATES
Betty Anderson

Linda "Pokey" Anderson
Owanah P. Anderson
Lupe Anguiano
Deane Armstrong
Cynthia Behon
Melva Becnel
Linda N. Briggs
Geraldine Brown
Penny Brown
Mary Castillo
Maria M. Cavazos
Marta Cotera
Eva C. Cuadra
Claire Cunningham
Dr. Hortense Dixon
Barbara Duke
Margie Flores
Sylvia R. Garcia
Ernestine V. Glossbrenner
Rita Gomez
Luz Gutierrez
Carol Hatfield
Naoma Hickie
Eddie Bernice Johnson
Ruth Kirby
Bonnie Lesley
Sharon Macha
Jane Macon
Minnie Maloy
Betty McKool
Dr. Mamie McKnight
Amalia Rodriguez-Mendoza
Elaine Opiela
Marie Oser
Betty Ann Peden
Dolores A. Puente
Irma Rangel
Barbara B. Reagen
Ann Richards
Janice Robinson
Irene Rodriguez
Estela Salinas
Teresa Saucedo
Dorothy Shandera
Loretta Jo Shaw
Martha E. Smiley
Sammye Stafford
Josephine H. Stewart
Claudia Stravato
Hermine Tobolowsky

Nikki Van Hightower
Patricia Vasquez
N. Carolyn Waddell
Sarah Weddington
Arthur Beatrice Williams
Penny Willrich
Janna Zumbrun

ALTERNATES
Mary C. Flinn
Ruby I. Gutierrez
Helen Wright
Millie Monte
Peggy Brandon

UTAH

DELEGATES
Belva Ashton
Dolores Bennett
Elaine Cannon
Margaret Cassum
Jennie Duran
Ruth H. Funk
Carol Garbett
Dixie Nelson
Stella H. Oaks
Jaynann Payne
Georgia Peterson
Lois Pickett
Belle Spafford
Naomi Udall

ALTERNATES
Dona Wayment
Florence Jacobsen
Gloria Firmage
Amy Valentine
Anne Leavitt

VERMONT

DELEGATES
Barbara Broadbent
Tine Calabro
Sister Elizabeth Candon
Faire Edwards
Rita Edwards
Karen Kent
Carol Marcy
Dr. Lenore W. McNeer
Joyce Slayton Mitchell
Phoebe Morse
Julie Peterson
Liz Yeats

ALTERNATES
Judy Barker
Judy Rosenstreich
Ann Sarcka

VIRGINIA

DELEGATES
Mollie Abraham
Bettie Baca-Fierro
Faye Benton
Martha D. Boyle
Agnes Braganza
Nancy Mowrey Brock
Kathryn Brooks
Ruth Harvey Charity
Martha Capps Chubb
Andrea Respess Clapp
Elizabeth A. Clark
Jean Marshall Clarke
Sylvia Clute
Flora Crater
Angella P. Current
Sandra Duckworth
Margery H. Edson
Madeline Ann Estabrook
Sarah Foster Furgeson
Audrey Dooling Ghizzoni
Maya Hasegaura
Fann Shirley Lee
Anne Lunde

Romayne Elizabeth Marschak
Vivian C. Mason
Jill Rinehart
Nora Anderson Squyres
Natalie Vaughan
Bessida Cauthorne White
Maude I. Woodyard

ALTERNATES
Carol Spenceley MacIntosh
Victoria H. Zevgolis
Hope Haley Montoni
Margo Kieley
Joann Pasquale DiCennare

WASHINGTON

DELEGATES
Lilly Aguilar
Lupe Alverez
Marion Ballantine
Patricia Benevidez
Linda Black
Kathy Boyle
Tina Cohen
Jackie Delahunt
Rita Duran
Delores Groce
Audrey Gruger
Dorothy Hollingsworth
Thelma Jackson
Elaine Latourell
Judith Lonnquist
Christine Marsten
Marianne Craft Norton
Michele Pailthorp
Kay Regan
Francis Scott
Elsie Schrader
Carrie Washburn
April West

ALTERNATES
Sharla Grover
Glenda Bowyer
Susan Roylance
Carla Robinson
Judy Quinton

WEST VIRGINIA

DELEGATES
Thais Blatnik
Bonnie Brown
Hazel Bond
Lois Christal
Mary Virginia De Roo
Sandra Fisher
Anise Floyd
Louis Kauffelt
Louise Leonard
Betsy McCreight
Ruthann McQuade
Linda Meckfessel
Margaret Cyrus Mills
Sally Richardson
Sharon Percy Rockefeller
Maxine Scarbro
Virginia Schoonover
Reba Thurmond

ALTERNATES
Nell C. Bailey
Jean Farley
Jacqueline Cook
Patricia Gunn
Barbara B. Midkiff

WISCONSIN

DELEGATES
Yolanda Ayubi
Norma Briggs
JoAnn Craft
Florence Dickinson
Mary Dodge
Joan Dramm
Dolores Greene
Sarah Harder
Ethel Himmel
Donna Jones
Edith Jones
Bea Kabler
Peggy Kenner
Susan Luecke
Midge Miller
Rose Mary Muller
Mary Lou Munts
Frances Oshkenaniew
Diana Philbrick
Vel Phillips
Juanita Renteria
Ellen O'Brien Saunders
Nancy Schooff
Marcia Schwartz
Mandy Stellman
Constance Threinen
Mary Turnquist
Barbara Ulichny

ALTERNATES
Arlys Gessner
Betty Reimer
Phyllis Kirk
Carmen Ramirez de Lewis
Katie Morrison

WYOMING

DELEGATES
Susan Bookout
June Boyle
Patricia Duncombe
Vida Haukaas
Alberta Johnson
Oralia Mercado
Helen F. Montez
Meredith E. Morrow
Nancy Peternal
Barbara Rufenacht
Laude Seidenberg
Thyra Thomson

ALTERNATES
Esther Eskens
Pauline Gonzales
Sally R. Vanderpoel
Lori Moberly
Barbara Northcutt

AMERICAN SAMOA

DELEGATES
Fa'au'uga Achica
Fialupe Aumoeualogo
Fiapa'ipa'i Fruean
Repeka Howland
Linette Hunter
Elisapeta Laolagi
Gretchen Makaiwi
Arieta Mulitauaopele
Pulu Peneueta
Vaoita Savali
Sa'eu Scanlan
Alauni Siatu'u

ALTERNATES
Jane Urhle
Tovea Tupa'i
Mua Lutu
Iloa Ripine
Arieta Vaima'ona

GUAM

DELEGATES
Katherine Aguon
Cecilia Bamba
Gregoria Baty
Joy Benson
Mary Elaine Cadigan
Karen Cruz
Clotilde Gould
Maria Leon Guerrero
Pilar Lujan
Nancy Sablan
Laura Souder
Priscilla Tuncap

ALTERNATES
Marilyn Abalos
Betty Bennett
Pilar Burgess
Juanita Charfauros
Gloria Mortera

PUERTO RICO

DELEGATES
Celeste Benitez
Maria Teresa Berio
Nancy Bosch
Ruth Fernandez
Myrna M. Fuentes
Leila Jimenez Lopez
Zayda Quinonez Perez
Isabel Pico
Emma de Hernandez Purcell
Angelita de Naveira Rieckehoff
Belen M. Serra
Luisa Maria Serrano

ALTERNATES
Carmen Jovet
Ivette Ramos
Isolina Ferre
Nilda Aponte-Rafaelle
Vickie Lou Aponte

DELEGATES
Magdalene Abraham
Anne E. Abramson
Delia Benjamin
Edith L. Bornn
Mavis Brady
Leona Bryant
Joycelyn Encarnacion
Mary Bastian Innis
Eudelta Joseph
Octavia Ross
Ruby Rouss
Elise Vialet

ALTERNATES
Oran Roebuck
Shirlee Haizlip
Enid Hodge
Laura Yergan
Leona Wheatley

TRUST TERRITORY

DELEGATES
Carmen Bigler
Neijon Rema Edwards
Elina Ekiek
Mary Berngun Figir
Agnes Helgenberger
Mina Irons
Katherine Kesolei
Gloria Litler
Senellie Phillip
Neime Salik
Elizabeth M. Sasakura
Yasko Selefis

ALTERNATES
Ines Ada
Karmerina Yamada

DELEGATES-AT-LARGE

ORGANIZATIONS:
Alpha Kappa Alpha,
Bernice Sumlin
Altrusa International, Inc.,
Etta Jane Butler
American Association of University
  Women,
Marjorie Bell Chambers
American Jewish Committee,
Ann Wolfe
American Association of University
  Professors,
Mary W. Gray
American Medical Women's Association,
Dr. Margaret Sullivan
American Newspaper Women's Club,
Lilian Levy

Another Mother for Peace,
Florence Ain
Association for Women in Science,
Judith A. Ramaley
Women's Center, University of Minnesota,
Joy Lynne Wetzel
American Women in Radio and TV,
Mary Elle Hunter
Association of Junior Leagues,
Joan E. Ruffier
B'Nai B'rith Women,
Betty Shapiro
Camp Fire Girls,
Marjorie P. Allen
Church Women United,
Rev. Mary Louise Rowand
Center for Concern,
Mary Burke
Coalition of Labor Union Women,
Olga Madar
Comision Femenil Mexicana Nacional,
Sandra Serrano Sewell
Daughters of Penelope,
Mary Manitzas
Federally Employed Women, Inc.,
Shirley N. Jones
Federation of Organizations for
  Professional Women,
Julia Lear
Future Homemakers of America,
Jeanine Bourgeois
General Federation of Women's Clubs,
Jerri Wagner
Girls Clubs of America,
Fannie Belle Burnett
Delta Sigma Theta,
Thelma Daley
Girl Friends,
Ruth Clement
Girl Scouts of the USA,
Nancy Porter
Hadassah,
Blanche W. Shukow
International Association for Personnel
  Women,
Antonia Weisgrau
Intercollegiate Association of Women
  Students,
Ann Gottberg
Leadership Conference of Women
  Religious,
Sister Jeanne Schweickert
League of Women Voters,
Ruth Hinerfeld
LINKS,
Pauline A. Ellison
Martha Movement,
Jinx Melia
Mexican American Women's Association,
Elisa Maria Sanchez
National Abortion Rights Action League,
Dr. Karen Mulhauser

National Association of Negro Business &
  Profe-sional Women's Clubs,
Mary E. Singletary
National Association for Women Deans,
  Administrators and Counselors,
Jane McCormick
National Association of Bank Women,
Ruth I. Smith
National Association of Colored Women's
  Clubs, Inc.,
Inez W. Tinsley
National Association of Commissions for
  Women,
Anita Miller
National Association for Girls and
  Women in Sports,
Carol Oglesby
National Association of Media Women,
Xerona C. Brady
National Association of Women Business
  Owners,
Juanita Weaver
National Association of Women Lawyers,
Mary Alice Duffy
National Association of Black Women
  Attorneys,
Wilhelmina Rolark
National Catholic Women's Union,
Mary Rose Geiger
National Committee Concerned with
  Asian Wives,
Mary Ann Kim
National Conference of Puerto Rican
  Women,
Gladys E. Rivera
National Congress of Neighborhood
  Women,
Laura P. Scanlon
National Council of Catholic Women,
Mary Helen Madden
National Council of Jewish Women,
Esther R. Landa
National Council of Negro Women,
Dorothy Height
National Council of Women of the USA,
Roberta Anschuetz
National Federation of Business &
  Professional Women's Clubs, Inc.,
Piilani Desha
National Federation of Democratic
  Women,
Judy Hardes
National Federation of Republican
  Women,
Patricia Hutar
National Federation of Temple
  Sisterhoods,
Millie Cowan
National Hook-Up of Black Women,
Theresa Faith Cummings
National Organization for Women,
Arlie C. Scott
National Secretaries Association,
Connie McCauley

National Women's Education Fund,
Willie Campbell
National Welfare Rights Organization,
Johnnie Tillmon
National Woman's Party,
Elizabeth Chittick
National Women's Trucking Association,
Jean Sawyer
National Women's Political Caucus,
Patricia Bailey
Overseas Education Fund of the League
  of Women,
Janeth Rosenblum
Pan American Liaison Committee of
  Women's Organizations,
Isabel C. Lee
Pilot Club International,
Jean Larson
Pioneer Women,
Charlotte Stein
National Committee Concerned with
  Asian Wives,
Mary Ann Kim
Organization of Chinese American
  Women,
Pauline W. Tsui
Quota International, Inc.,
Joyce R. Schafer
Rural America,
Harriet Barlow
St. Joan's International Alliance,
Frances McGillicuddy
Soroptimist International,
Dorothy V. Kissinger
Women in Communications,
Anne Hecker
Women in Community Service,
Mary Halleran
Women of the Church of God, Inc.,
Kay Shiveley
Women's Action Alliance
Madeline Lee
Women's Association for Defense,
Vlana Celewych
Women's Campaign Fund,
Ann Zill
Women's Equity Action League,
Jessie Baum
Society of Women Engineers,
Arminta J. Harness
Women's International League for Peace
  and Freedom,
Yvonne Logan
Women's Lobby,
Carol Burris
Women's Press, KNOW,
Jo-Ann Evans Gardner
Women Strike for Peace,
Mary Clarke

Young Women's Christian Association of
  the U.S,
Jean Childers
Zeta Phi Beta Sorority,
Janice G. Kissner
Zonta International,
Judge Mattie Belle Davis

INDIVIDUALS:
Margaret Adams
Rita Aherin
Alberta Alamada
Delores Alexander
Virginia Allan
Donna Allen
Marie Anastasi
Pamela Antisdel
Evelina Antonetty
Marguerite Archie
Julia Arri
Ann Attar
Mary Auburtin
Bernice Baer
Edythe Scott Bagley
Cynthia Baker
Peg Balazovick
Ernesta Ballard
Harriet S. Barlow
Etta Moten Barnett
Peggy Barnett
Polly Baca Barragan
Ellen Barrett
Selma Baxt
Ruth Begun
Lillian Benbow
Barbara Berger
Candice Bergen
Adrienne Beveridge
Clara Beyer
Barbara Bick
Barbara Blum
Deborah Bonanni
Corinne Bobbs
Gladys Boyd
Gene Boyer
Patricia Brandt
Antonio Brico
Brenda Brimmer
Mary Emma Britsow
Catherine Brotsis
Joan Brown
Martha Buddecke
Teri Buratti
Frannie Belle Burnett
Mary Burke
Avery Burson
Dolores Burton
Lorenia Butler
Fran Byrne
Josephine Caines
Kay Camp
Judy Carter
Virginia Carter

Ulana Celewyeh
Marie Ceselski
Dorinne Chancellar
Leona Chanin
Juanita Charfauros
Naomi Christensen
Arline Clark
Gay Cobb
Mary Coble
Denise Cocciolone
Catherine Conroy
Margaret Costanza
Sr. Carol Coston
Letty Cottin Pogrebin
Dorothy Cotton
Virginia Cowley
Lona Crandall
Barbara Crapster
Raquel Creitoff
Nancy Cross
Alberta E. Crowe
Diane Curry
Betty Davis
Clara Davis
Nancy Deane
Gracia Molina DePick
Patt Derian
Gretta Dewald
Ellen Gay Detlefsen
Sister Austin Doherty
Joan Draper
Jan Dreiling
Ellen Desselhuis
Hildred Drew
Evelyn Dubrow
Tara Duffy
Joan Dunlop
Veronica Dysart
Catherine East
Patricia Edington
Geraldine Eidson
Joan Engelke
Frances T. Farenthold
Lois Felder
Eunice Fiorito
Sr. Helen Flaherty
Kathleen Flake
Maria Angela Flores
Carolyn Forrest
Arvonne Fraser
Erika Freeman
Frankie Freeman
Betty Friedan
Patsy Fryman
Barbara Fultz
Jo-Ann Evans Gardner
Minnie Gaston
Kathleen Gentile
Ruth Bader Ginsburg
Elinor M. Glenn
Patricia Goldman
Sylvia Gonzalez
Joan Goodin
Martha Greenawalt

Eunice Guell
Elinor Guggenheimer
Natalie Gulbrandsen
Ruth Church Gupta
Mary Jeanette Hageman
Sandra Haggerty
Patricia S. Halpin
Ruth Mercer Hafer
Mary Hagemans
Sandra Haggerty
Lelia Hall
Bertha Hartry
Lillian Hatcher
Nancy Hawkins
Joanne Hayes
Ruth Haynes
Marilyn Heath
Dorothy Height
Lenore Henson
Ann Herbert
Diane Herrmann
Judith Heumann
Alice Heyman
Margaret Hickey
Bette Hillemeire
Madeline Hodrorf
Jeanne Holm
Karmen Hopkins
Suzanne Howard
Eunice Howe
Florence Howe
Cathy Howell
Sr. Alberta Huber
Shirley Hufstedler
Mary Elle Hunter
Mildred Jefferson
Nellie Stone Johnson
Sarah Johnson
Shirley Joseph
Nancy Douglas Joyner
Dorothy Jurney
Judith Just
Adeline Kahn
Inez Kaiser
Susan Kakesako
Deborah Kaplan
Karen Artero Kasperbauer
Rebe Kelle
Audrey Kelly
Marilyn Kent
Mary Keyserling
Karen Kester
Bobbie Greene Kilberg
Lillian Kimura
Edith S. Kjos
Dolores Klaich
Ruth Perlman Klebaner
Marjorie Knowles
Holly Knox
Ruth C. Kobell
Hesung Chun Koh
Odessa Komer
Florine Koole
Esther R. Landa

Kit Larson
Tonia Lasater
Linda Lee
Mildred Robbins Leet
Rejeanne B. LeFrancois
Pat Lehman
Carol Leimas
Rhoda Lerman
Judy Lerner
Anna M. Lewis
Marilyn M. Lewis
Sylvia Lewis
Judith Lichtman
Mary Littleton
Polly Logan
Barbara Love
LaVerne Love
Frances Lucas
Betty Lussier
Elaine Lytel
Maryann Mahaffey
Mildred Marcy
Anita Marcus
Shirley Marsh
Pauline Martinez
Sally Martinez
Natalie L. Mason
Billie Masters
Gloria Mattera
Frances McGillicuddy
Alice McKee
Jean McKee
Jane McMichael
Eloise McQuown
Daphne Meadows
Dorothy Meehan
Janice Mendenhall
Rayda Menendez
Ruth Meyers
Joyce Miller
Mary Miller
Maya Miller
Selma Joy Miller
Beatrice Milwe
Jessica Minor
Alix Susan Mitgang
Victoria Mangiardo
Carmen Monroe
Charlotte Montgomery
Jessie Mosley
Mary Munger
Toni Nathan
Catalina Navarro
Cynthia Navaretta
Margaret Neldrett
Mildred Nelson
Vivian Nelson
Constance Newman
Consuelo Nieto
Eleanor Holmes Norton
Carol Oglesby
Mary O'Halloran
Betty Smith Olivas
Ana Ortiz

Sue Panetta
Lynn Park
Brenda Parker
Norma Paulus
Anita Patterson
Marjorie Paxson
Ethel Payne
Katherine Peden
Ada Pena
Ana Maria Perera
Esther Peterson
Shirley Peterson
Theresa Pesl Plunkett
Luz Maria Prieto
Gail P. Quinn
Yolanda Quitman
Sally Millett Rau
Marguerite Rawalt
Dr. Nancy Reeves
Patricia Rengel
Ann Ridilla
Fran Rhome
Sylvia Roberts
Cammille Robinson
Jeanne Rosoff
Enid Roth
Nina Rothchild
Joan Ruffier
Mary Beth Salerno
Rickey Salisbury
Myrna Small Salmon
Edith Savage
Jennifer Lynn Sharkey
Cynthia Shaughnessy
Anita Bellamy Shelton
Dr. Victoria Shuck
Janet Sigford
Terri Singleton
Carol Silverthorn
Joy Simonson
Genevieve Sims
Rebecca Sue-Tomashevsky
Sandy Skorniak
Charlotte J. Smith
Deborah Smith
Ronni Smith
Ruth Smith
Jouise Smothers
Kay M. Shiveley
Olga Soliz
Olga Stawnychy
Karen Stroschein
Thelma L. Stovall
Mary Ellen Swanton
Amy Swerdlow
Janie Taylor
Lynette Taylor
Mamie Taylor
Tay Thomas
Johnnie Tillman
Mary Ellen Tisdale
Sheila Tobias
Rebecca Sive-Tomashevsky
Norma Tower

Jayne Townsend
Dorothy Tracy
Sr. Margaret Traxler
C. Delores Tucker
Eunice Turk
Silvia Unzueta
Lynn Van Dam
Edith Van Horn
Odette Villanueve-King
Theresa Villmain
Merlene Walker
Rosa Walker
Sarah H. Wallace
Mae Walterhouse
Frances Wapnick
Nan Waterman
Caroline Ware
Kappie Weber
Becky Weerem
Barbara Weinberg
Jean Westwood
Joy Wetzel
Ruth Weyand
Nancy Whistler
Dorothy White
Julia Wilder
Fay Williams
Joanne Williams
Edna Williamson
Nan Waterman
Veta Winick
Shirley Hill Witt
Marcia Wood
Unita B. Wright
June Zeitlin
Aviva Cantor Zuckoff

DISTINGUISHED WOMEN IN GOVERNMENT LECTURERS

"Briefings from the Top" was one of the programs featured at the Houston meeting. Women members of the Carter Administration and other prominent women took part in a continuous lecture series at the Albert Thomas Convention Center. Below is a list of the lecturers.

Barbara Blum
Deputy Administrator
U.S. Environmental Protection Agency

Sara Weddington
General Counsel
Department of Agriculture

Donna E. Shalala
Assistant Secretary for Policy
Development and Research
Department of Housing and Urban
Development

Cornelia G. Kennedy
U.S. District Judge
Eastern District of Michigan

Esther Peterson
Special Assistant to the President for
Consumer Affairs

Patsy T. Mink
Assistant Secretary for Bureau of
Oceans, International Environmental
and Scientific Affairs
Department of State

Jill Wine-Volner
General Counsel
Department of the Army

Margaret Costanza
Assistant to the President for the
Office of Public Liaison
White House

Alexis Herman
Director, Women's Bureau
Employment Standards
Administration
Department of Labor

Jane Lakes Frank
Deputy Secretary to the Cabinet
White House

Ruth Prokop
General Counsel
Department of Housing and Urban
Development

Shirley Hufstedler
U.S. Circuit Judge
9th Circuit

Arvonne Fraser
Coordinator, Office of Women in
Development
Agency for International Development

Barbara M. Watson
Assistant Secretary of State for
Consular Affairs
Department of State

Marife Hernandez
Chief of Protocol of the U.S. for New
York

Kristine Marcy
Federal Energy Regulatory
Commission

Esther Wunnicke
Federal Co-Chair
Federal Land Use Planning
Commission for Alaska

Patricia Wald
Assistant Attorney General
Department of Justice

Hazel Rollins
Acting Deputy
Economic Regulatory Administration
Department of Energy

Elsa A. Porter
Assistant Secretary for Administration
Department of Commerce

Patricia Albjerg Graham
Director, National Institute of
Education
Department of Health, Education and
Welfare

Eleanor Holmes Norton
Chair, Equal Employment Opportunity
Commission

Mary King
Deputy Director
ACTION

Virginia Dill McCarty
U.S. Attorney for the Southern District
of Indiana

Carol Tucker Foreman
Assistant Secretary of Agriculture for
Food and Consumer Services
Department of Agriculture

Mary F. Berry
Assistant Secretary for Education
Department of Health, Education and
Welfare

Carin A. Clauss
Solicitor of Labor
Department of Labor

Allie Latimer
General Counsel
General Services Administration

Irene Tinker
Assistant Director, Policy and
Planning
ACTION

Eileen Shanahan
Assistant Secretary for Public Affairs
Department of Health, Education and
Welfare

Barbara Babcock
Assistant Attorney General
Department of Justice

Linda Heller Kamm
General Counsel
Department of Transportation

Sarah T. Hughes
U.S. District Judge
Northern District of Texas

Elizabeth Bailey
Member, Civil Aeronautics Board

Margaret McKenna
Deputy Counsel to the President
White House

Pat A. Danner
Federal Co-chair
Ozarks Regional Commission

Beth Abramowitz
Assistant Director
Domestic Policy Staff
White House

Bernadine Denning
Director
Office of Revenue Sharing

Moderator:
Oceola S. Hall
Director, Federal Women's Program
National Aeronautics and Space
Administration

Assisted by:
Virginia Oldham
Acting Coordinator
Federal Women's Program
Veterans Administration

Joan Humphries
Federal Women's Coordinator
National Science Foundation

Moderator:
Doris Ross McCrosson
Director
Federal Women's Program
Government Printing Office

Assisted by:
Hattie L. Dorman
Supervisory Computer Systems
Analyst

Rose Thorman
Coordinator
Federal Women's Program
Bureau of Mines

Moderator:
Ledia E. Bernal-Tabor
Program Analyst
National Institute of Education

Assisted by:
Carol Sivright
Coordinator
Federal Women's Program
Region G,
Department of Health, Education and
Welfare

Ann Hudson
Claims Examiner Region 6
Office of Education

Room Coordinators:
Jeanne Randall
Deputy for Federal Women's Program
Department of Defense

Joy Bishop
Coordinator
Federal Women's Program
Department of Air Force

LIST OF OFFICIAL INTERNATIONAL VISITORS TO THE NATIONAL WOMEN'S CONFERENCE

Number Codes:
(1) Department of State-Sponsored International Visitors
(2) UNESCO International Media Workshop Participants
(3) Cuban Federation of Women
(4) African-American Labor Center Project
(5) German Marshall Fund Women and Work Program

Argentina:

Claudia Elena Van Loc (1)

Secretary-General, Institute of Social Development and Human Promotion

Australia:

Elizabeth Wood

Fulbright Scholar in U.S.

Austria:

Monika Fritz

Official Government Observer

Bangladesh:

Jahanara Imam (1)

Executive Member, Bangladesh National Women's Organization

Bolivia:

Elena Velasco de Urresti (1)

Mayor of Riberalta

Botswana:

Gagoitsiwe Sethokgo Sechele (1)

Training Office and Coordinator, Botswana Girl Guides Association

Brazil:

Lila Galvao de Figueiredo (1)

Founder of Brazilian Women's Society and member of Editorial Council of society's paper, Brazil Mulher

Nice Valadares (2)

Ph.D. candidate in communications, University of Texas, Austin

Canada:

Mary Donlevy

Teachers' Federation for Toronto

Louise Holmes

Commission on Status of Women

Audrey Shepherd

Commission on Status of Women

Chile:

Hilda del Carmen Ceballos (1)

Head, Women's Department, Railway Workers Federation of Chile

Colombia:

Mariella Carrillo Bedoya (1)

Regional Director, Colombian Institute of Family Welfare

Cuba:

Dora Carcan Araujo (3)

Cuban Federation of Women

Esther Veliz Diaz (3)

Cuban Federation of Women

Catalina Ribas Hermelo (3)

Cuban Federation of Women

Denmark:

Rosa Krotoschinsky (2)

Television critic and editor of Cultural Section of Sunday edition of Politiken

Dominican Republic:

Miriam Mendez de Pineyro (1)

National Congresswoman

Ecuador:

Elizabeth Coba (1)

Writer, Press & Public Relations Department, Office of the Comptroller General

Egypt:

Aziza Mohamed Abdel Halim Kararah (1)

Head, Department of English, Alexandria University; President, Egyptian Branch of International Federation of University Women.

Tomader Tawfik (2)

Director-General, Egyptian Television

Fiji:

Liebling Elizabeth Marlow (1)

Organizer of Women's United Action Movement

Anne Walker

Director, International Women's Tribune Center

Finland:

Helvi Sipila

Assistant Secretary General, United Nations

France:

Olga Baudelot (5)

French Ministry of Education

Michele Berthoz (5)

French Ministry of Education

Yasmine Zahran

Ghana:

Adelaide Asihence

African-American Labor Center Project

Kate Abbam (2)

Editor, *Ideal Woman*

Guatemala:

Hilda Weissemberg de Faeh (1)

President, Women's Civic Alliance

Guyana:

Yvonne Veronica Benn (1)

Coordinator for Linden District, People's National Congress

Haiti:

Rolande Chandler (1)

Professor of Spanish, School of Agriculture and Veterinary Medicine

Hedwige Kolbjornsen (1)

Director, Haitian Committee for Promotion of Handicrafts

Honduras:

Irma Acosta de Fortin

President, Central Council, National Party of Honduras

India:

Neera Akshyakumar Desai (1)

Head, Department of Sociology, S.N.D.T. College for Women

Ave Lawyer (2)

MA candidate, School of Journalism and Communications, University of Kentucky

Indonesia:

Siti Oetami Amin (1)

Chair, Surabay Branch, Indonesian Business and Professional Women's Association

Lily Rahayu Aribasah (1)

Secretary General, Business and Professional Women's Association

Iran:

Golrokh Yazdi (2)

Student at Stanford University, completing Masters degree in international communications

Israel:

Rivka Bar-Yosef

Status of Women Commission

Tamar Eldar (2)

Appointed Attache for Women's Affairs

Dr. Dina Goren (2)

On sabbatical leave in the United States

Jamaica:

Heather Hope Royes (2)

Cultural Affairs Office, Agency for Public Information, Jamaican Government

Gloria Scott

World Bank

Japan:

Tokiko Fukao (1)

Staff Writer, Women's Affairs Department, *Yomiuri Shimbun* daily newspaper

Kimoko Kubo

Journalist

Jordan:

In' Am Mufti (1)

Director, Women's Affairs Department, Ministry of Labour and Social Affairs

Kenya:

Lilly Bomet

African-American Labor Center Project

Korea:

Chija Kim Cheong (2)

Journalist; College of Education, Seoul National University

Lesotho:

H. M. Hlekane (1)

Social Worker, Ministry of Health

Libya:

Faridah Allaghi

Libyan representative on U.N. Status of Women Commission

Hosnia Markus

Office of Libyan delegation to U.N.

Mauritius:

Bigneswaree Seebaluck (1)

Junior Supervisor, Women's Association, Sugar Industry Labor Welfare Fund

Mexico:

Maria de los Angeles Ruvalcaba (1)

Jalisco State Deputy, Lawyer and Political Activist

Maria Elena Corona Villatoro

Editor, *La Imagen,* Sunday Supplement of *La Prensa*

Pilar Fernandez-Collado (2)

Assistant Editor at *La Colina*

Netherlands Antilles:

Beatriz Scoop (1)

Counselor in Organization and Human Resources Development

Nicaragua:

Gloria Ramirez de Ramirez (1)

Coordinator, Urban Program, Instituto de Promocion Humana

Yvonne Ortega de Castillo (1)

Director of Nursing, Ministry of Health

Panama:

Margarita Romero (1)

Secretary of Finance, Workers Union of Terminales Panama, S.A.

Paraguay:

Perla Matiauda de Cibils (1)

Chief, Planning and Programming Dept., Ministry of Education

Peru:

Maria Angela Sala Corbetto (1)

Editor *La Imagen,* Sunday Supplement of *La Prensa*

Philippines:

Trinidad Conchu de la Paz

Asia Foundation Project

Amelia Sinco-Guzman (2)

Public Relations Director

Seychelles:

Margarite Baptiste (4)

Treasurer, Seychelles Workers Education Committee

Sudan:

Thoraya Osman Saleh (1)

Assistant Secretary of Women's Affairs Committee

Fatima Ahmed Mahmoud (2)

Minister of Social Welfare

South Africa:

Virginia Thudiso Gcabashe (1)

President, Sibusiswe Clermont Child Care Association

Leonora Mbatha

United Methodist officer for the U.N.

Sweden:

Annika Baude

German Marshall Fund Project

Brigitta Wistrand

Chair, Fredrika Bremer-ForBundet

Switzerland:

Gret Haller

Swiss National Council of Women

Taiwan:

Cynthia Chen (2)

Correspondent for China Youth News Agency

Thailand:

Chandhanee Santaputra (1)

President, Women's Lawyers Association of Thailand

Trust Territory of the Pacific Islands:

Mary Bergnun Figir (1)

Mental Health Councellor, Yap Women's Association

United Kingdom:

Yvonne Tabbush

UNESCO

U.S.S.R.:

Nelya Ramazanova (1)

Editor, English Language edition of *Soviet Woman*

Venezuela:

Rosa Suarez de Brito (1)

Head, Social Service Dept., National Housing Institute

Adela Alonso

Consultant, International Women's Tribune Center

Togo:

Cheffi Meatchi (4)

Member of the Central Committee of the Office of Togo Women

Yugoslavia:

Neda Ostoic (1)

Psychologist; Chairperson, Radio and Television Zagreb Study Group for Communication Theory

Zambia:

Idah Simukwai (4)

Zambia Congress of Trade Unions Delegate to the United Nations

Mary Kazunga (1)

National General Secretary, Zambian YWCA

SKILLS CLINICS AND SUCCESS STORIES
Albert Thomas Convention Center
November 19-20, 1977

HOW TO INFLUENCE SCHOOLS by Clelia Steele and Lynda Weston. Ms. Steele is Associate Director and Ms. Weston is head of research at PEER (Project on Equal Education Rights). PEER is a Washington, D.C. based project of the NOW Legal Defense and Education Fund which monitors Federal enforcement of laws barring sex discrimination in education. This was a training session demonstrating the use of PEER's Title 9 Review Kit for people concerned with the fairness of the education being offered to children in their local schools.

HOW TO WORK EFFECTIVELY WITH YOUR POLITICAL PARTY by Betty King and Wilma Goldstein. Ms. King is a member of the Executive Committee of the Democratic State Committee of the District of Columbia and is Chair of its Standing Committee on Voter Education and Affirmative Action. Ms. Goldstein is Associate Director of the Campaign Division of the National Republican Congressional Committee. Both women are active in the National Women's Political Caucus. Discussion centered on why and how women should become involved with their political party and how party organizations can be used to promote women's issues and concerns.

THE MEDIA: MAKING THEM MORE RESPONSIVE AND RESPONSIBLE by Ellen Cohn, Janet Dewart, Alice Backes, Grace Nagata, and Belle O'Brien. Janet Dewart is Director of Specialized Audience Programs for the National Public Radio in Washington, D.C. Ellen Cohn is a writer, editor, and critic whose work has appeared in a wide variety of publications, including The *New York Times Magazine.* She has worked in radio and television as a writer/producer and is a former columnist for the *New York Daily News Magazine.* Ms. Backes is director of the Women's Division, American Federation of TV and Radio Artists. Ms. Nagata is vice-chair, National Latino Media Coalition. Ms. O'Brien works in Consumer Office of Federal Communications Commission. Media reform for the consumer, the employee, and the activist was the focus of discussion. Topics included programing and story content, portrayal of women and minorities, guidelines for fair treatment, and how to get your story covered.

COMMUNITY ORGANIZING by Caroline Sparks. Ms. Sparks is a member of Women's Action Collective, Columbus, Ohio. Basic concepts and techniques for organizing social change movements were reviewed. The strategy and tactics of selecting an issue and planning a campaign were analyzed.

LEGAL REMEDIES TO EMPLOYMENT DISCRIMINATION by Jill Goodman and Mayda Colon Tsaknis. Ms. Goodman is a staff member of the Women's Rights Project of the American Civil Liberties Union and the author of *The Rights of Women.* Ms. Tsaknis is a former trial attorney for the Equal Employment Opportunity Commission who is now in private practice. Existing laws barring employment discrimination, with a particular focus on pregnancy discrimination, were reviewed.

PARLIAMENTARY PROCEDURE FOR BEGINNERS by Elizabeth W. Brown. Ms. Brown is President of the Florida State Association of Parliamentarians and is currently the parliamentarian of the National Federation of Business and Professional Women's Clubs, Inc. Beginners were offered an introduction to the rules and procedures of parliamentary procedure.

ORGANIZING WORKING WOMEN by Lisa Portman. Ms. Portman is Assistant Director of the George Meany Center for Labor Studies in Silver Spring, Md. The Center is an adult education facility for full-time union officers and staff members. Ms. Portman examined some of the barriers that keep women from organizing; how to overcome those barriers; and the rewards and benefits gained through organization.

MOTHERS, INC., by Reida Lockwood, Laraine Benedikt, Linda Earnest, and Milly Douglas. These members of Mothers, Inc., of Austin, Texas, are all mothers who are concerned about the shared problems of mothers who work outside the home as well as those who do not. They discussed how they created a support system for mothers in Austin and how and why similar programs can be created elsewhere.

GETTING WOMEN APPOINTED TO STATE BOARDS AND COMMISSIONS by Anne Saucier. Ms. Saucier is the President of the Ohio Commission on the Status of Women and is an expert on sex discrimination in employment. Women's Ohio Volunteer Employment Network is establishing a network of women and organizations in Ohio to identify qualified women for public service and appointment to state boards and commissions. Ms. Saucier discussed the methods and skills used in this project and how similar networks can be established in other states.

GETTING YOUR POINT OF VIEW ACROSS by Jane O'Grady, Maria Portalatin, and Nancy Becker. Ms. O'Grady is a legislative representative for the AFL-CIO in Washington, D.C. Ms. Portalatin is a special representative of the United Federation of Teachers; President of the New York City central chapter of the Labor Council for Latin American Advancement (LCLA) and Vice-President of the national chapter of LCLA. Ms. Becker is President of her own consulting firm and is consultant for the Center for the American Woman in Politics, Rutgers University. Using the resources of the group, the focus was to learn and exchange information on organizing individuals and coalitions to achieve social change. They explored educational and organizational tools of communications among allied groups, with elected and appointed public officials, as well as with the larger community.

MYTHS ABOUT WOMEN by the Minority Women's Task Force of the Civil Service Commission's Inter-Agency Action Group. What are the myths about the Asian, Black, Indian, and Spanish woman that linger in our country? What are the cultural differences? What is fact and what is myth? These and other questions were answered through masked, costumed role play and audience participation.

COMMUNICATION STRATEGIES FOR CONTEMPORARY WOMEN by Dr. Janet Elsea. Dr. Elsea is Associate Professor of Communication and Theater at Arizona State University. She is also Director of the Communication Division at the University. The workshop focused on verbal and non-verbal skills women need to be effective communicators.

HOW TO RUN FOR OFFICE by Mary Beth Rogers and Jane Hickie. Ms. Rogers, who was Deputy Director of the 1976 Democratic Presidential campaign in Texas, owns a communications consulting firm and frequently conducts workshops in political campaign techniques. Ms. Hickie is administrative assistant to County Commissioner Ann Richards. She was county coordinator of the Farenthold for Governor campaign and is co-author of *Texas Women in Politics* and *Campaign Techniques for Women Candidates and Managers*. This session focused on the elements of planning a successful campaign at the local level. These principles of planning are also applicable to campaigns for statewide office. Material covered included targeting, analysis of candidate and district, campaign organization and staff support, media, polling, and strategies for direct voter contact.

HOW TO MARKET VOLUNTEER SKILLS AND EXPERIENCES by Marilyn Bryant. Ms. Bryant is a member of the Advisory Committee of the Governor's Office of Volunteer Services in Minnesota. She chaired "People Power," the first national conference on volunteerism which was held in 1974. This session updated and expanded traditional perceptions of volunteerism and recognized its relevance in meeting today's changing needs and expectations.

OPPORTUNITIES FOR WOMEN AS BUSINESS OWNERS by Patricia Cloherty and Barbara Dunn. Ms. Cloherty is Deputy Administrator and Ms. Dunn is Director of Women for the Small Business Administration (SBA). The SBA has pledged to assist women going into business as well as those engaged in entrepreneurial activity by informing them of SBA's services, and by providing them with such services where these contribute to creating a successful venture. Material covered included management skill, loans, and government procurement opportunities.

MARRIAGE, SEPARATION, AND DIVORCE by Roxanne Barton Conlin. Ms. Conlin is U.S. Attorney in the Southern District of Iowa and a former Assistant Attorney General of Iowa. She served as a consultant on the rights of the homemaker to the National Commission on the Observance of International Women's Year. Subjects discussed included marriage contracts, selecting a lawyer, strange laws that affect women and how to deal with them, the separated and divorced woman in transition, the value of the homemaker, and legislative reform.

STRATEGIES FOR ACADEMIC WOMEN ON THE MOVE by Dr. Cynthia Secor. Dr. Secor teaches women's studies at the University of Pennsylvania and is Director of the mid-Atlantic regional office of Higher Education Resource Services. This session focused on joining the decisionmakers, the new women's network, getting visibility on and off campus, using the professional association, organizing your campus, getting tenure, moving up in the administration.

COMPARABLE WORTH by Lynn Bruner and Helen Remick. Dr. Remick is the Director of Affirmative Action for Women at the University of Washington, Seattle. Ms. Bruner is a Supervisor of Compliance for the Equal Employment Opportunity Commission, Seattle, and a former member of the Washington State Women's Council. They presented an overview of the emerging area of comparable worth and explained how to apply comparable worth standards to a state civil service system and to a large university.

EMPLOYMENT OPPORTUNITIES FOR WOMEN IN THE SKILLED TRADES by Ann Emigh. Ms. Emigh is director and founder of Mechanica in Seattle, Washington. Mechanica is a referral service for women and assists them in entering apprenticeships and skilled trades. She discussed how to organize a skilled trades referral service for women and how to persuade government agencies to set goals for women on the workforce of government contractors.

BOSTON WOMEN'S HEALTH COLLECTIVE by Judy Norsegian and Norma Swenson. Ms. Norsegian and Ms. Swenson are members of the collective and co-authors of *Our Bodies, Ourselves*. The functions and methods of the collective were discussed as a model for women elsewhere who are interested in the self-help and health education movement. Current litigation on behalf of consumer health rights was reviewed. Current plans and activities of the National Women's Health Network were discussed.

SHELTER FOR BATTERED WOMEN by Rosemarie Reed, Judith Vandegriff and Jan Peterson. Ms. Reed is the Chair of the Board of Directors of the Center for the Elimination of Violence in the Family, Brooklyn, New York. Ms. Vandegriff is Legislative Aide to Congressman Newton Steers (R-MD). Ms. Peterson works for ACTION. Ms. Reed discussed the origins and functions of the Center, which received a $200,000 grant from New York State in order to create a refuge for battered women. The Center offers counseling, crisis intervention, hot line, medical and legal services, and training for advocates. Ms. Vandegriff discussed proposed and pending Federal and State legislation to assist victims of spouse abuse.

THE EAST LOS ANGELES RAPE HOT LINE by Diane Muniz. Ms. Muniz is the Director of the East Los Angeles Rape Hot Line, which offers the only bilingual (Spanish/English) hot line in Southern California. In addition, transportation and companion services are offered to rape victims. This rape crisis service is geared primarily toward the Spanish-speaking population in the area. Ms. Muniz discussed her project as a model for other communities.

WOMEN'S CRISIS CENTER (Ann Arbor, Michigan) by Jeanne Hunt. Ms. Hunt is coordinator of the Center, which began as a rape crisis center in 1972 and is now a multi-service drop-in and phone crisis counselling and referral service. Among its services are consciousness-raising groups, a computerized referral system listing all the services available in the area, a library, monthly newsletter, training for crisis counselors and workshop leaders, public education, a court deferred sentence program for women convicted of misdemeanors, and an HEW funded bibliography of audio-visual materials on rape.

DISPLACED HOMEMAKERS: TURNING SOCIAL INSECURITY INTO SELF-SUFFICIENCY by Laurie Shields. Ms. Shields ia a widow and a leader of the Alliance for Displaced Homemakers. She is also a national co-coordinator of the National Organization for Women's task force on older women. She reviewed efforts to obtain laws to recognize and assist the problems of displaced homemakers. The benefits and methods of organizing, rather than agonizing, were explored.

MINORITY WOMEN EMPLOYMENT PROGRAM by Alexis Herman. Ms. Herman is Director of the Women's Bureau of the U.S. Department of Labor. Ms. Herman was the national director of women's programs for the Minority Women Employment Program of the Recruitment and Training Program, Inc., of Atlanta, Georgia. The program helped minority women enter white collar positions in private industry and helped widen apprenticeship opportunities for women. The success of this program attracted national attention. Ms. Herman discussed this program as a model for consideration by women in other states.

IMPROVING THE STATUS OF WOMEN IN ART: SUCCESS STORIES AND STRATEGIES FOR GAINING RECOGNITION AND REWARDS. Moderator: Judith Brodsky, New Jersey artist, President, Women's Caucus for Art. Panelists: Miriam Schapiro, New York artist; June Wayne, California artist, founder of Tamarind Lithography; Howardena Pindell, artist, curator of New York Museum of Modern Art; Dorothy Hood, a Houston artist.

IMPROVING THE STATUS OF WOMEN IN ART: SUCCESS STORIES AND STRATEGIES FOR GAINING RECOGNITION AND REWARDS. Moderator: Elloise Schoeffler, Washington, D.C. Women's Art Center. Panelists: Arlene Raven, co-founder, Los Angeles Woman's Building; May Stevens, New York artist; Cynthia Navaretta, Chair Pro Tem of the Coalition of Women's Art Organizations; Jo Hanson, California artist.

WOMEN AND MUSIC. Moderator: Dr. Merle Montgomery, New York musician and composer, President, National Music Council. Panelists: Martha Moore Sykes, President, New York Opera Guild; Julis Smith, Denton, Texas, composer and pianist.

WOMEN IN THEATER, FILM, TELEVISION, AND RADIO. The panels on these arts were made possible through the help and cooperation of the National Endowment for the Arts and the Women's Caucus for Art.

CONSULTANTS FOR HOUSTON ORAL HISTORY PROJECT

Lydia Kleiner, Research Associate
Institute of Labor and Industrial
Relations
University of Michigan
Ann Arbor, Michigan 48104

Dr. Lyn Goldfarb, Director
Oral History Program
Institute of Labor and Industrial
Relations
University of Michigan
Ann Arbor, Michigan 48104

Dr. Alfredteen Harrison, Coordinator
of Historic Preservation
Jackson State University
Jackson, Mississippi 39217

Dr. Mollie Camp Davis, Chair
Department of History
Queens College
Charlotte, North Carolina 28274

Pamela Jacklin, Affirmative Action
Officer
Washington State University
Pullman, Washington 99163

Dr. Margaret Strobel, Director
Women's Studies, Department of
History
University of California
Los Angeles, California 90024

Dr. Athena Theodore, Professor of
Sociology
Simmons College
Boston, Massachusetts 02173

Dr. Adade Wheeler, Professor of
History
College of DuPage
Glen Ellyn, Illinois 60137

Dr. Ann J. Lane, Research Associate
Institute for Independent Study
Radcliffe College
Cambridge, Massachusetts 02138

Dr. Johny E. Mathews, Director
Oral History Office
University of Arkansas at L.R.
Little Rock, Arkansas

Dr. Jay Kleinberg, Assistant Professor
Department of History
University of Tennessee
Knoxville, Tennessee 37916

Constance L. Kite, Commissioner
Governor's Commission on the Status
of Women
Montpelier, Vermont 05602

Dr. Constance Ashton Myers,
Principal Investigator
NEH—IWY Oral History Project
Department of History
University of South Carolina
Aiken, South Carolina 29801

Dr. Charlotte M. Kinch, Oral History
Consultant
Santa Fe, New Mexico 87501

Dr. Marie Heyda, Associate Professor
Department of History
Aquinas College
Grand Rapids, Michigan 49506

Amelia Fry, Research Associate
Regional Oral History Office
The Bancroft Library, University of
Calif.
Berkeley, California 94720

Dr. Betty Miller Unterberger, Professor
of History
Texas A. and M. University
College Station, Texas 77843

Dr. Joan Hoff Wilson, Professor of
History
Arizona State University
Tempe, Arizona 85281

Kathy J. Carter, Social Case Worker
Division of Children's & Youth's
Services
Medical College of Georgia
Augusta, Georgia 30904

Laurel Shackelford, Staff Writer
The Louisville Times
Louisville, Kentucky 40202

Dr. Veronica Tiller, Professor of Native
American Studies
Department of History
University of Utah
Salt Lake City, Utah 84112

Dr. Marjorie Abrams, Personal &
Organizational Consultant
Miami, Florida 33145

Dr. June Hahner, Associate Professor
Latin American Studies
Department of History
State University of New York
Albany, N.Y. 12222

Dr. Jacqueline D. St. John, Associate
Professor
Department of History
The University of Nebraska at Omaha
Omaha, Nebraska 68101

Dr. Jeanne Marie Col, Assistant
Professor
Graduate School of Public Affairs
State University of New York
Albany, New York 12222

Rachael E. Myers, News Staff
Reporter
WIS Radio
Columbia, S.C. 29210

Dr. Elaine M. Paul, Academic Advisor
Comprehensive Manpower Program
Aiken Technical College
Aiken, S.C. 29801

LIST OF HOUSTON EXHIBITORS NATIONAL WOMEN'S CONFERENCE

STATES

Alaska
American Samoa
Arkansas
Arizona
California
Colorado
Connecticut
District of Columbia
Florida
Georgia
Guam
Hawaii
Idaho
Illinois
Indiana
Iowa
Kansas
Kentucky
Louisiana
Maine
Maryland
Massachusetts
Michigan
Minnesota
Missouri
Nevada
New Hampshire
New Jersey
New Mexico
New York
North Carolina
Ohio
Oregon
Pennsylvania
Puerto Rico
Tennessee
South Carolina
Texas
Trust Territories
Utah
Vermont
Virginia
Washington
Wisconsin
Wyoming

OTHER EXHIBITORS

A.I.D., Women in Development
Alcohol, Drug Abuse, and Mental
 Health Administration, DHEW
Amalgamated Clothing and Textile
 Workers Union
American Association of University
 Women
American Civil Liberties Union
American Federation of Government
 Employees
AFL-CIO
American Federation of State, County,
 and Municipal Employees
American Nurses' Association
Americans for Democratic Action
American Women's Museum
Armadillo Mountain
Association of Libertarian Feminists
Atomic Industrial Forum
Bisexual Center
B'nai B'rith Women, Inc.
Books America
Bridges Book Center
California Sisters
Carolyn's Creations
Catalyst
Catholics for a Free Choice
Chicana Caucus — National Women's
 Political Caucus
Coalition of Labor Union Women
Comision Femenil Mexicana Nacional
Committee for Artistic and Intellectual
 Freedom in Iran
Community Services Administration
Craft Collection
Daughters Publishing Company, Inc.
Deep Within
Defending Women's Rights
Dinner Party Project
Eagle Forum
Eastern Airlines-sponsored Travel
 Information
Emphasis
Encyclopaedia Britannica, Inc.
Equal Employment Opportunity
 Commission
Equitable Life Assurance
ERAmerica, Inc.
Feminist Forge
Feminist Horizons
Feminist Press
Ferne Sales and Manufacturing
 Company
Florine, Inc.
Food and Drug Administration
The Freewoman

Full Partnership
Fund for the Improvement of Post-
 secondary Education (FIPSE)
 (DHEW)
Funky Slogans
Giovanni's Room
Girl Scouts of the U.S.A.
G. Randle Services
Health Resources Administration
Hogie Wyckoff
Houston Area Feminist Federal Credit
 Union
Houston Breakthrough
Houston Right to Life
Indian Health Services
International Làdies' Garment
 Workers' Union
International Organization of Women
 Executives
IWY Support Coalitions
KNOW
Kraal Gallery
Labyris
Leadership Conference of National
 Jewish Women's Organizations
League of Women Voters
LULAC National Education Service
 Centers, Inc.
Meredith-O'Reilly
Metro Media Ltd.
Missouri Right-to-Life
Mood Indigo
Motherroot Publication
NASA
National Abortion Rights Action
 League
National Advisory Council on
 Women's Educational Program
 (DHEW)
National Association of Social
 Workers
National Association of Women
 Business Owners
National Association of Women
 Lawyers
National Board YWCA of the USA
National Chamber of Commerce for
 Women
NCDC
National Commission on Working
 Women
National Congress of Neighborhood
 Women
National Council of Catholic Women
National Council of Jewish Women

National Council of Women of the U.S., Inc.
National Council on Alcoholism
National Gay Task Force
National Organization for Women
National Organization for Women, Dallas
National Paraplegic Foundation
National Woman's Party
National Women's Health Network
National Women's Political Caucus Network
New Directions for Women
National Retired Teachers Association and American Association of Retired Persons
Outdoor Women
Overseas Development Council
Overseas Education Fund of the League of Women Voters
Pioneer Women
Planned Parenthood Federation of America
Pleiades
Puerto Rican Women, Cuban Women, Mexican Women
Quixote Center
Quest, A Feminist Quarterly, Inc.
Religious Coalition for Abortion Rights
Safari
Seral's Emporium
SherArt Images, Inc.
Select Imports
Simplicity Pattern Company
Sisters Sol Screens
Smithsonian Institution
Socialist Workers Party
Soroptimist International of the Americas, Inc.
Sports Etc., Inc.
Tape Services Unlimited
Texas Southern University
Texas Women's Political Caucus
TODAY Publications & News Service
Treasures from the Sea
UAW International Union
Unitarian Universalist Women's Federation
United Nations Association of the United States of America, Inc.
U.S. Bureau of the Census
U.S. Civil Service Commission
U.S. Commission on Civil Rights
U.S. Customs Service
U.S. Environmental Protection Agency
U.S. Government Printing Office
U.S. Department of Labor
U.S. Postal Service

U.S. Small Business Administration
U.S. Treasury, Office of Revenue Sharing
Utah Women's Association
Wages for Housework
Wolfworks
WomanMade Products
Womansplace
Womantours
Womanyes
Women Against Violence Against Women
Women of Achievement
Women in Community Service, Inc.
Women Strike for Peace
Women Today
Women's Action Alliance
Women's Campaign Fund
Women's Caucus for Art
Women's Hall of Fame
Women's Equity Action League Fund
Women's International Bowling Congress
Women's International League for Peace and Freedom
Women's Sports Foundation
Women's Success Teams, Inc.
YWCA Madras India, NAVAJEEVAN: "A New Life"
Zonta

PUBLICATIONS OF THE NATIONAL COMMISSION ON THE OBSERVANCE OF INTERNATIONAL WOMEN'S YEAR

"... To Form A More Perfect Union ..." Justice for American Women (IWY report). Released July 1976. A 382-page report containing 115 recommendations designed to end the barriers to women's equality. Copies are available from the Superintendent of Documents, U.S. Government Printing Office, Washington, D.C. 20402, Price: $5.20.

The Legal Status of Homemakers in (name of State). Released on a state-by-state basis. A series of 51 booklets describing the legal status of homemakers in marriage, widowhood, and divorce in each of the States and the District of Columbia. Available from the Superintendent of Documents, U.S. Government Printing Office 20402. Price: $1.25.

Media Guidelines. Leaflet (L-1). Released July 1976. Ten guidelines on the image and employment of women in the mass media. Also includes a "Checklist for the Portrayal of Women in Entertainment Programming and Advertising."

How To Move Women Into Appointive Office. Leaflet. Released May 1976. Suggestions for groups and individuals on increasing the number of women in public office.

Chronology of the Women's Movement in the U.S. 1961-75. Released spring 1976.

Chart on the Federal Laws and Regulations Prohibiting Sex Discrimination. A detailed chart which describes who is covered and who enforces these laws and how to file sex discrimination complaints.

The Creative Woman. Released January 1977. A report on the IWY recommendation relating to the arts and humanities. Available from the Superintendent of Documents, U.S. Government Printing Office. Stock number 040-000-00368-1. Price: 90¢ plus 10¢ postage.

American Women Today and Tomorrow. Released March 1977. A report by the Market Opinion Research Survey conducted for the IWY Commission on the status of women in the United States.

WORKSHOP GUIDELINES

Stock Numbers
Order From
Superintendent of Documents
U.S. Government Printing Office
Washington, D.C. 20402
$1.25 each

W-1	Improving the Status of Women in the Arts and Humanities	052-003-00480-1
W-2	Child Care	052-003-00476-3
W-3	Credit	052-003-00485-2
W-4	Education	052-003-00477-1
W-5	Employment	052-003-00489-5
W-6	Equal Rights Amendment	052-003-00484-4
W-7	Female Offenders	052-003-00487-9
W-8	Health	052-003-00488-7
W-9	International Interdependence	052-003-00479-8
W-10	Legal Status of Homemakers	052-003-00492-5
W-11	Strategies for Change	052-003-00494-1
W-12	Media	052-003-00491-7
W-13	Older Women	052-003-00490-9
W-14	Sexual Preference	052-003-00493-3
W-15	Rape	052-003-00478-0
W-16	Teenage Pregnancy	052-003-00482-8
W-17	Wife Abuse	052-003-00486-1
W-18	Women in Elective and Appointive Office	052-003-00481-0
W-19	Insurance	052-003-00483-6

OUR SPECIAL THANKS...

We would like to thank the following friends of the National Women's Conference:

Paul Boesch
Alma Butler
Marion E. Coleman
Century Development
The Charter Company
Coca Cola Co.
Mr. & Mrs. Carl Detering
C. Pharr Duson, Jr.
Congressman Bob Eckhardt
E. L. Feldhousen
Muriel Folloder
Congressman Bob Gammage
Gladys Heldman
Lt. Governor Bill Hobby and Diana Hobby
Mayor Fred Hofheinz
Hudson on Memorial
Mr. & Mrs. Patrick Keegan
Ray King
Lincoln-Mercury
M. David Lowe
Jerry Lowery
Mary Ann Loweth
Dorothy Moates
Sister Mary Henrietta Murphy, CCVI
Gayle Pierce
Patricia Poyma
President's Council on Physical Fitness & Sports
Robert Sakowitz
Mona Sanchez
Senator John Tower
Earl Vandiver
American Institute of Cooperation
Borden Foundation

Bureau of Educational and Cultural Affairs, Department of State
Civil Service Commission
Colgate-Palmolive
Cooper Union
Department of Agriculture
Department of Health, Education & Welfare
Department of Justice
Department of State-Printing, Distribution, and Visual Services
Department of Transportation
Department of Treasury
National Endowment for Arts
Environmental Protection Agency
Equal Employment Opportunity Commission
Equinax Theatre
Federal Women's Program Coordinators
Gannett Foundation
General Services Administration-Houston Area
House of Coleman
Hyatt Regency Hotel, Houston
International Paper Company
Lighthouse for the Blind, Houston
M.D. Anderson Foundation
National Aeronautics & Space Administration

National Association of Girls and Women in Sports
N.C. Council of Women's Organizations
President's Council on Physical Fitness
Renaissance Gallery
Office of Revenue Sharing
Barbara Price, Women in Production
Radio Information Center for the Blind, Philadelphia
Road Runners of America
Steve Ross, Warner Communications
Seneca Falls Hall of Fame
Seneca Falls Hall of Fame
Seneca Falls Historical Society
Ntozake Shange
Richard Simonson
Simpson College
Smithsonian Institute, Division of Political History
Soroptimist International of the Americas
Southwest Personnel Services
St. Joseph's Hospital
The German Marshall Fund of the United States
United Nations Association of Houston
U.N. We Believe
U.S. Catholic Conference
U.S. Commission on Civil Rights
United States Information Agency
Wells College
Women's Basketball Association
Women Sports Magazine
Women Today, Myra and Lester Barrer
Virginia Farm Bureau

Judy Tallwing and E.R.A McCarthey

E.R.A. McCarthey finalized the design of this book and brought it out. Her mother Judy was a delegate whose fascinating story of strength and determination can be read on vintage pages numbered 119 and 150. Judy brought E.R.A. into the world as soon as she returned to Arizona from the conference, at which she overcame her labor pains. Judy then brought baby E.R.A. to the White House in March 1978, when this report was delivered to the President. Diana photographed them and also Gloria, holding E.R.A. As the decades went by, Gloria and Diana corresponded, as about Diana's efforts to lobby for a US postage stamp series devoted to the women leaders of the 1970's that she photographed. They also reminisced and wondered about Baby E.R. A. Meeting Judy again, meeting E.R.A. again, meeting Sylvia, Peggy and Michele - the three final torch bearers - in person and several times, are delights I am honored to share with you, as you share the delights of meaningful meetings, in thought and with each other.

Gloria Steinem

Dear Diana,
Thank you so much for the photograph with Era — the youngest participant at Houston! I wonder what she's doing as a grown-up? I did indeed sign and send in the form you sent for the citizens' Stamp Committee — hope it helps —

with good wishes,
Gloria Steinem

NEW YORK NY 100

03 MAR 2007 PM 12 L

Tribute to Clara Jackson McLaughlin "Sunrise October 22,1939   Sunset October 3,2021"

Clara and daughter Rinetta at the FNWC by Diana Mara Henry

"I did not have to go to any history book to search for a trailblazing Woman Hero as I had my hero raising my brother and I right in front of me...Forever my best friend and dear mother."
-Rinetta McLaughlin Fefie

Highlights of tributes to the life of Clara Jackson McLaughlin in the in the Special Issue of the *Florida Star* and the *Georgia Star*, two of Clara McLaughlin's publications: "starting her journalism career which in high school by writing producing and distributing the school's first student newsletter...graduating from the historic all-black Lincoln High School, attended Hampton Institute where she majored in music ....Joined the US Navy as a Woman Accepted for Volunteer Emergency Service (WAVE) working as a yeoman and organist in the Navy Chapel....following her military service, attended Howard University , serving as Co-editor-in Chief and then Editor-in-Chief of the school's yearbook...became the first HBCU to win the "All American Award" for a student publication....Ms. McLaughlin was a published author penning her first book for black parents on childcare titled *Black Parents' Handbook A Guide to Healthy Pregnancy, Birth and Child Care* (1976).... the first African American female in the United States to become founder, major owner, and CEO of a network in 1979 (KLMG-TV, CBS affiliated)....host of a weekly radio talk show, "IMPACT," focusing on African American issues, media participant on "Week in Review" on Jacksonville's PBS television affiliate..." Just a few glimpses of such a life!

A note on connections from Diana Mara Henry: I hope all who read this reprint will appreciate that the photographs and words in this Official Report are not just two-dimensional. They did not begin on the page or in Houston and they did not end there. They are a minute part of the weave of connections of the thousands of other participants, amongst themselves, over decades, miles, and with all those whose lives connected with them. In this way, you too, the reader, are part of the story and part of us. We may not always know how meaningful our meetings have been to one another; but somewhere, even now, someone is remembering us and bringing the impressions formed and lessons learned into their world, which circles back to us. Thank you for being part of the story. "To democratize history....to include as many voices as possible.... to provide diversity not just in terms of what's included in historical narratives but also who gets to contribute, who gets to shape those narratives...."
- Larisa Klebe, Program Manager, the Jewish Women's Archive.

Women so influential to the movement and to the conference, who hold a place in our hearts.

Bettye Lane was a photographer whose ardent presence and dedication to recording the causes of social justice for women began in 1960 and lasted till her death in 2012. Collections of her photographs are housed at Duke University Libraries and at the Schlesinger Library, among other archives. These photographs by Diana Mara Henry show her celebrating with Jean O'Leary at Houston and photographing at the Judy Chicago exhibit at the Sarah Institute in NYC.

Lee Novick was the coordinator for the magnificent national conference that is the subject of this book. She appears on pages 134 and 135, deserving far more. Lee helped organize Jewish groups to attend the 1963 Civil Rights March on Washington and became chief aide to Bella Abzug on Bella's arrival in Congress in 1970. During much of the 1980s she taught at U C Berkeley's graduate school of public policy. She is now Rabbi Leah Novick, following her ordination in 1987. Seen in this photograph by Diana Mara Henry, she is leading a tour backstage for IWY Commissioners before the conference opening.

Nikki R. Van Hightower
Author of *That Woman: The Making of a Texas Feminist*
Women's Advocate for the City of Houston in 1977

Iconic tee shirt logo by Valerie Pettis
Photo courtesy Nikki Van Hightower

INDEX

Made in the USA
Monee, IL
05 March 2025

13142026R00177